Doing Rhetorical History

STUDIES IN RHETORIC AND COMMUNICATION
Series Editors:
E. Culpepper Clark
Raymie E. McKerrow
David Zarefsky

Edited by Kathleen J. Turner

Doing Rhetorical History
Concepts and Cases

The University of Alabama Press   Tuscaloosa and London

Copyright © 1998
The University of Alabama Press
Tuscaloosa, Alabama 35487-0380
All rights reserved
Manufactured in the United States of America
∞
The paper on which this book is printed meets the minimum requirements of
American National Standard for Information Science-Permanence of Paper for
Printed Library Materials, ANSI Z39.48-1984

Library of Congress Cataloging-in-Publication Data

Doing rhetorical history : concepts and cases / Kathleen J. Turner,
editor.
    p.   cm. — (Studies in rhetoric and communication)
    Includes bibliographical references (p.   ) and index.
    ISBN 0–8173–0925–X (paper meets minimum requirements)
    1. United States—Historiography. 2. United States—Politics and
government—Case studies. 3. Communication in politics—United
States—History—Case studies. 4. Rhetoric—Social aspects—United
States—History—Case studies. 5. Rhetoric—Political aspects—United
States—History—Case studies. 6. Speeches, addresses, etc.,
American—History and criticism—Case studies. I. Turner, Kathleen J.,
1952–   II. Series.
    E175 .D65 1998
    973′.07′2—ddc21
                                                98–19754

British Library Cataloguing-in-Publication data available

In memory of
Marie Hochmuth Nichols
and
Robert G. Gunderson:
We honor their legacies
even as we transform them.

Contents

Part II: Doing Rhetorical History: Case Studies

Acknowledgments

This volume is the culmination of the hard work and dedication of many scholars over many years. Its genesis may be traced to a panel on "The Rewards and Challenges of Research in Archives" at the Western States Communication Association convention in Phoenix in February of 1991. The panelists and the respondent arrived, eager to share their insights—but because the session had been scheduled for the final slot of the final day of the convention, no one else showed up. Undaunted, the participants retired to the bar for an animated discussion, from whence grew a Speech Communication Association seminar in November of 1992, the Greenspun Conference on Rhetorical History in March of 1995, and ultimately this volume.

Sadly, not all of the many individuals involved in this process are represented in this volume. Although versions of several of the essays contained herein first found public voice at the Greenspun conference, this is not a publication of proceedings. Thus our first salute is to our colleagues who joined with us at various points of the project to make significant contributions but could not be included here.

Another round of huzzahs belongs to Richard J. Jensen and the Greenspun School of Communication at the University of Nevada-Las Vegas for hosting the Greenspun Conference on Rhetorical History, "Rhetoric, History, and Critical Interpretation: The Recovery of the Historical-Critical Praxis." Without Greenspun's sponsorship the conference would not have been possible; without Dick's tireless logistical planning and organizational prowess the conference would not have been the delightful gathering of colleagues in a relaxed environment that it was.

A third set of kudos belongs to The University of Alabama Press for having the faith and fortitude to bring this volume to print. We are all grateful to the two anonymous readers who gave the project its initial thumbs-up; to E. Culpepper Clark, David Zarefsky, and Raymie McKerrow, who are the series editors (with a special nod of thanks to the latter from the volume editor, who relied on his advice at several key points in the project); and particularly to Curtis Clark, who has proven to be a helpful, cheerful, efficient, and wonderfully laid-back editor at The University of Alabama Press.

From the technologically challenged volume editor, who regards computers as a combination of glorified typewriters and evil spirits, comes deep gratitude to James A. Mackin at Tulane, who tamed the mighty beast to provide one integrated, publisher-ready computerized version with a minimum of fuss and a maximum of quiet support.

The introductory chapter is based in part on "Rhetorical History as Social Construction," a paper delivered at the Southern States Communication Association convention in Tampa, Florida, in April of 1991.

Some material from chapter two was adapted from E. Culpepper Clark, "Argument and Historical Analysis," in *Advances in Argumentation Theory and Research*, ed. J. Robert Cox and Charles A. Willard (Carbondale: Southern Illinois Press, 1982), 298–317; and from Raymie McKerrow, "Perspectives on History and Argument," in *Proceedings of the Second International Conference on Argumentation*, ed. Frans H. van Eemeren, Rob Grootendorst, J. Anthony Blair, and Charles A. Willard (Amsterdam, The Netherlands: International Society of the Study of Argumentation, 1991), 5–12; the material is used with permission.

Steven R. Goldzwig thanks the Bradley Institute for Democracy and Public Values and the College of Communication Scholarship and Creative Activities Committee at Marquette University for their assistance in funding the research represented by chapter eight. He is also indebted to the professional archival staff at the Truman Library.

Bruce Gronbeck thanks the University of Iowa's Project on Rhetoric of Inquiry for support for his project represented in chapter three and for a space to think it through. POROI's administrator, Kate Neckerman, was especially helpful.

Travel funds for Carol Jablonski's 1993 visit to the Dorothy Day–Catholic Worker Collection at Marquette University on which chapter ten is based were provided as a Faculty Development grant by the

College of Arts and Sciences, University of South Florida. She is grateful for the assistance of Phil Runkel during her two visits as well as during subsequent contacts. She is also grateful to W. Kevin Cawley at the University of Notre Dame Archives for his assistance during her search there for materials related to Day's acceptance of the Laetare Medal.

Timothy Jenkins thanks Dr. James R. Andrews for his patient direction of the thesis from which his chapter is drawn, and Dr. J. Michael Hogan and Dr. J. Jeffrey Auer for their keen insights as members of the committee.

Some material in chapter nine was drawn from Gregory A. Olson's book, *Mansfield and Vietnam: A Study in Rhetorical Adaptation* (East Lansing: Michigan State University Press, 1995).

Finally, each and every one of us thanks the spouses, significant others, children, friends, pets, and associates who have lived through this process with us. May this be the beginning of a grand rhetorical history!

Doing Rhetorical History

Introduction

Rhetorical History as Social Construction

The Challenge and the Promise

Kathleen J. Turner

When I was on the faculty at the University of Notre Dame, now president but then associate provost Monk Molloy asked me what it was like to be a female professor at Our Lady's University. I responded that it was a lot like studying the humanities at Purdue, site of my graduate studies, where engineering, agriculture, and technology are still engraved on the institutional psyche even if removed from the university shield: a few people are openly antagonistic toward you, but most just don't quite understand what you're doing there. As I regard the role of rhetorical history in the field, I at times have a sense of, as Yogi Berra would say, "déjà vu all over again."

From one perspective, rhetorical history should have a most honored status. After all, the current field of communication derived from the historical study of rhetoric. The embodiment of this tradition may be found not only in the early issues of the *Quarterly Journal of Speech* but also in such publications as the classic three-volume publication of *History and Criticism of American Public Address*.[1] In the final quarter of the twentieth century, however, as the press toward theoretical conceptions has driven analysis, as a host of "isms" has defined criticism, and as the "publish or perish" ethic has accelerated the research track, the predominance of the field has moved away from historical perspectives. Faculty members on dissertation committees reject with great disdain work they regard as "*mere* history"; editors of our journals assert that "there is little news in [a] 'see, the method works' or [a] 'gosh, the library has materials' approach"; colleagues proclaim, "tell me what your details mean in . . . the language of theory—or leave me alone."[2]

Perhaps part of the problem rests with the ways in which rhetorical history has been conceptualized. Even the classic articulations of the strengths of historical studies—by, for example, Baskerville, Gronbeck, and Bryant—have talked about history as descriptive rather than evaluative, as a preliminary step for criticism, as a service to the field and to historians rather than valuable analytical scholarship that stands on its own.[3] Such conceptions delineate a constrained role for rhetorical history as drudge work for the good stuff, as lowly handmaiden to the important poobahs of the field and the academy.

history as viewed as preliminary

Yet many scholars in the field continue to find benefits in rhetorical history beyond these. I contend that we need a far broader conception and far deeper appreciation of the roles of rhetorical history. Both as methodology and as perspective, rhetorical history offers insights that are central to the study of communication and unavailable through other approaches. Historical research provides an understanding of rhetoric as a process rather than as simply a product; it creates an appreciation of both the commonalities among and the distinctiveness of rhetorical situations and responses; it tests theory and complements criticism while standing as a distinct and valid approach in and of itself. This volume bears witness to the depth and breadth of insights proffered by rhetorical history.

By way of introduction to these essays I propose viewing rhetorical history as social construction. The ambiguity of the phrase is intentional, for it contains two related but distinct meanings. Rhetorical history as social construction includes both 1) the ways in which rhetorical processes have constructed social reality at particular times and in particular contexts and 2) the nature of the study of history as an essentially rhetorical process.[4]

Rhetorical Processes in Historical Contexts

If we truly believe (as I do) that "rhetorical studies are properly concerned with the process by which symbols and systems of symbols have influence upon beliefs, values, attitudes, and action,"[5] then historical research is an essential part of rhetorical studies. Broadly speaking, *whereas rhetorical criticism seeks to understand the message in context, rhetorical history seeks to understand the context through messages that reflect and construct that context.* To understand how those symbols and systems of symbols may have "suasory potential and persuasive effect,"[6] we need both rhetorical criticism's

2 / Kathleen J. Turner

message-centered focus and rhetorical history's contextual construction. Note that I am defining rhetorical history not as a temporal juncture but as a research approach: one can take a historical approach to the rhetoric of Madeleine Albright just as one can take a critical approach to the rhetoric of Sojourner Truth, and the field needs to do both.

Consider, for example, Greg Olson's fine study of Senator Mike Mansfield's role in American foreign policy regarding Southeast Asia from his earliest, fleeting encounters with the region through his support of Premier Diem of South Vietnam to his final, pivotal opposition to American involvement in the conflict.[7] The historical perspective enables Olson to examine Mansfield's careful, systematic accretion and presentation of knowledge about Indochina, which led to an ability to influence U.S. foreign policy in Asia and a high measure of respect on Capitol Hill, in the White House, from the media, and around the world. It also allows Olson to trace the evolution of Mansfield's position across decades, from active supporter to quiet critic to outspoken opponent of American policies regarding Vietnam. Drawing from archival holdings ranging from Mansfield's own papers to the collections of three presidents to the Senate Historical Office, the primary resources enable Olson to delineate not only the nuances of Mansfield's rhetorical adaptations but also the disparities during the 1960s and early 1970s between his expressions of public support for American actions and his increasingly vigorous private dissent with presidents, administration officials, and congressional colleagues. Olson could have provided a critically rather than historically oriented study, with a careful delineation of the rhetorical strategies employed by Mansfield in, say, his proposals of four amendments on Indochina in 1971—and I'm sure I would have learned from that, too. Yet how enriching is his (re)construction of the evolution of positions and arguments across half a century, detailing Mansfield's rhetorical journey as it shaped and was shaped by the rhetorical forces he marshaled and encountered. To characterize Olson's work as merely a descriptive preamble to criticism is to ignore the strength and quality of the contribution he has made to our understanding of rhetorical processes. His chapter in this volume further develops one aspect of that project to show how Mansfield's credibility proved the "deciding factor" in the Eisenhower administration's approach to Diem.

The distinctive rhetorical knowledge gained through historical perspectives is also demonstrated by Moya Ball's examination of the decision-making processes undertaken by the Kennedy and Johnson administrations concerning the escalation of the Vietnam War.[8] By investigating the language used by the presidents and their key advisors as well as the patterns of interaction among them, Ball identifies the relationships between the rhetorical views of the world embedded in their exchanges and the decisions they made based on those symbolic conceptions. The historical approach allows Ball to explain how the perspectives of the Kennedy administration set the stage for the expectations and approaches of the Johnson administration and how the determination of American policy evolved between 1961 and 1965. Using archival resources, she reveals how critical decisions about American involvement in a crucial conflict developed within the dynamics of the group processes, including the preponderance of sports metaphors, the scramble for positions of influence and status, and the surprising roles of each president. The fruits of Ball's labors inform her contribution in chapter four of this volume as she examines the theoretical implications of rhetorical history, using the significance of her findings to challenge Janis's conception of "groupthink."

The work of Olson and Ball demonstrates the rich potential of rhetorical history for producing rhetorical knowledge. Far from engendering a kind of quaint antiquarianism,[9] the melding of historical and rhetorical methodologies can contribute to an understanding of the complex latitudinal and longitudinal processes of social influence. As David Zarefsky notes in chapter one, single messages are rarely instrumental in and of themselves; rhetorical history can trace symbolic social constructions. (Re)creating a sense of how Lyndon Johnson fought the dual wars of Vietnam and the press, for example, required an exploration of the myriad interpersonal, public, and mediated messages confronting the president and the ways in which, for instance, charges of capricious travel plans affected Johnson's rhetorical strategies as well as the media's coverage.[10] Rhetorical history offers us the opportunity to see rhetoric as a perpetual and dynamic process of social construction, maintenance, and change rather than as an isolated, static product.

Moreover, rhetorical history can contribute to historical knowledge. Here I am not thinking primarily of, as Baskerville put it, "the ways in which historians of public address may be of assistance to the general historian" by "record[ing] accurately and artistically the history of our art as it relates to more general history."[11] Rather, I am suggesting that the rhetorical perspective can contribute particular insights to an understanding of history. To begin with, a rhetorical view of the world means that we ask questions different from but related to those of our colleagues in the humanities and social sciences. As historian Harold Woodman observed of my work on Johnson, I asked questions that historians would not think to ask, and those distinctive questions resulted in findings that historians value. Historians might focus on policy making and implementation, on relations between the White House and the Capitol, maybe even on media coverage or public opinion polls—but they generally would not think to ask how Lyndon Johnson's relationship with the press influenced his handling of Vietnam. As Zarefsky notes in chapter one, "by studying important historical events from a rhetorical perspective, one can see significant aspects about them that other perspectives miss"; thus he makes "an argument not only for the place of historical studies within rhetoric but also for the contribution of rhetorical studies in the larger scholarly enterprise."

The rhetorical perspective affects not only the questions we ask of history, but also what we consider to be "evidence" and how we interrogate that evidence. Open any standard text in historiography—for example, Barzun and Graff—and the first virtue of the historian will be defined as "accuracy."[12] Yet as rhetorical scholars weaned on the realm of the contentious we are accustomed to examining what Bryant called the fictions we live by as well as those we live under.[13] Whether LBJ was Darth Vader or the Caped Crusader, for example, is not so much an issue of accuracy as one of what Karlyn Kohrs Campbell calls "social truths"—truths that may conflict but that are perfectly valid for each of those who hold them.[14] Certain stories of Lyndon Johnson's political maneuverings may be apocryphal, such as the account of his grabbing Frank Church by the lapels after the senator from Idaho spoke against his Vietnam policy and telling him to just try getting money for a dam out of Walter Lippmann instead of the president next time. Similarly, the valued figure types for women as featured in comic strips across a century have changed more drastically, more frequently, and in different ways than the actual bodies of the American female. In each case, however, accuracy is only one rather minor and elusive consideration; the power of such stories and images as symbolic constructions of reality for their publics is precisely the stuff of the rhetorical historian.[15]

This rhetorical perspective may be particularly valuable to historical research at a time of significant changes within the field of history itself. As David Potter observed, many historians still lament the loss of the comforting certitude and determinism that has implicitly undergirded political history (a.k.a. "battle-and-king" history or "drum and trumpet" history).[16] In its stead historians face the greater uncertainties posed by social and cultural history, which "tends to emphasize underlying given factors and intractable components in the life of a people, leaving the reader"—and, I would suggest, often the historian—"with a sense of being in the grip of blind and uncontrollable forces." Moreover, Potter avers that "historians are, in fact, ill-equipped to deal with the fears, the anxieties, the frustrations, the aggressive impulses of a society."[17] Ah, but the fears, the anxieties, the frustrations, the aggressive impulses of a society are the very stuff of rhetorical studies! Seeing the rhetorical process as the central epistemic function by which societies constitute themselves repositions rhetorical historians from "overspecialized outsiders" looking in on the field of history[18] to essential participants in the construction of history—if we accept the challenge.

Essays in this volume demonstrate the promise of accepting that challenge. Consider how six in particular deliver insights. To illustrate the advantages of a constitutive approach to rhetorical processes, James Jasinski focuses in chapter five on the anxieties of a new nation about the conceptualizations and ramifications of sovereignty as played out in *The Federalist Papers*. Jasinski explores how the constitutional issues concerning the scope of government were constituted, both literally and figuratively, through revisiting as well as reconceptualizing certain British assumptions about the political system. By investigating how Hamilton and Madison created arguments about such issues as a standing army, Jasinski illustrates how the "specific discursive strategies and textual dynamics" of the campaign to ratify the American Constitution served to "shape and reshape the contours of political concepts and ideas" such as sovereignty. Jasinski's analysis contributes to historical as well as rhetorical knowledge, demonstrating that a constitutive approach to rhetorical processes provides powerful insights into the political and historical changes in the early life of the nation.

The issue of sovereignty echoes in James Andrews's comparison in chapter six of the issues and tensions leading up to the inaugural addresses of Abraham Lincoln and Jefferson Davis. Andrews uses published letters, documents, papers, memoranda, diaries, and speeches to explore what led these two new presidents to grapple rhetorically with sovereignty and the attendant issue of legitimacy, drawing differently from their argumentational heritage in the process. By casting these two statements as culminating points of enduring and intermingling debates over "the defining characteristics of the American nation," Andrews in turn suggests how these competing conceptions set the stage for the bloody conflict that followed. The differing rhetorical constructions drew from what might be called the "pool of conventional wisdom"[19] in quite different ways to frame the Union and the Confederacy within distinctly different social truths.

Those competing social truths may also be seen in the research of Timothy C. Jenkins, represented in chapter seven, as he follows the rhetorical estrangement of Missourians in the wake of Fort

Sumter and President Lincoln's call for state militia to aid the Union. Through newspaper editorials, letters, memoirs, and proclamations, Jenkins traces the state's growing anger against the North as well as the increasing realization of its ties to the South. Against that broader background he then examines how C. F. Jackson, the governor of Missouri, negotiated that increasing estrangement through both rhetorical and military action. Jenkins demonstrates that the attitudes of the state and its leadership evolved in response to various statements and events, as the "aggressive impulses of a society" were reigned in, redirected, and then encouraged over time.

Fears and anxieties constitute the focal point of Steven R. Goldzwig's inquiry in chapter eight into the Truman administration's desegregation of the armed services. Searching through the files at the Truman Library, Goldzwig found not only the president's public and private statements about desegregation but also a bevy of memoranda, reports, and other documents. Thus he discovered how the president and his Fahy Committee sought to convince recalcitrant military leaders that integration was not only necessary but beneficial to the armed services. As Goldzwig notes, both Truman and his committee members tied equality of treatment in the military to the credibility of the United States's public claims of democratic principles and practices, and they viewed charges of bigotry and prejudice as powerful weapons against national security in the cold war. In contrast, high-ranking members of the Army in particular regarded desegregation as weakening their military mission, even as they argued that the armed services already provided opportunities for minorities unequaled elsewhere in American society. As Goldzwig notes, symbolic processes are essential in the creation and understanding of history: "It makes a difference who gives advice, who takes the advice, who ignores it, and why." His essay shows that the difference is important to both historians and rhetoricians.

Fears of a different sort mark Carol Jablonski's analysis in chapter ten, as she examines the implications of the letter Dorothy Day wrote but did not send to decline an award from the University of Notre Dame. Jablonski places this missive in the context of Day's Catholic Worker movement, with its goals of pacifism and social justice, following Day's rhetorical journey from being a young witness to the destruction of the San Francisco earthquake to being the reluctant recipient of a premier Catholic university's highest honor. Using this historical understanding Jablonski contends that this activist leader resisted the assimilation and elevation connoted by the acceptance of honors—but could not find a way to resist Father Hesburgh's exhortations on behalf of the Laetare Medal. Thus the evidence of correspondence that can only be found in the archives provides crucial insight into the rhetorical negotiation of social movement leadership.

The rhetorical leadership of social movements also serves as the key focus for Hammerback and Jensen's essay in chapter eleven. They employ the rhetorical heritage of Mexican Americans, the plan as a rhetorical form of particular historical significance to those of Mexican descent, and Cesar Chavez's rhetorical persona to explain the significance of Chavez's "Letter from Delano" to the growers' association, and the inappropriateness of the growers' public response. Their assessment casts the exchange as a conflict between significantly different rhetorical as well as cultural backgrounds.

As these essays suggest, then, rhetorical history as social construction may be viewed first as the study of rhetorical processes in historical contexts, a study making a distinct contribution to both rhetorical and historical knowledge. Whether tracing the evolution of a state's dissatisfaction with the national government or examining how an administration brought about desegregation almost a century later, these scholars contribute to historical, critical, and theoretical knowledge about both rhetoric and history. Through rhetorical history, we can understand how rhetoric has enabled, enacted, empowered, and constrained the central concerns of history: human action and reaction.

The Rhetorical Nature of Historical Research

This notion that the process of history is essentially rhetorical provides a natural transition to my second point: that the study of history is essentially rhetorical as well. Rhetorical history is a social construction not only in the sense that rhetorical processes constitute historical processes but also in the sense that historical study constructs reality for the society in which and for which it is produced. Such a view counters the popular conception of history as a mirror of the past that is reported by objective historians. As Gunderson suggests with characteristic incisiveness, "those who claim to be objective usually have deceived themselves; or perhaps they may be simply insensitive."[20] Human beings are not objects but subjects; thus we can only be subjective. In place of the passive, inanimate, utterly unselfconscious and unselective mirror are individuals working within their societal context to create stories about the past. In so doing historians inevitably bring their own perspectives to their work, and as Arthur Schlesinger Jr. notes, perspective "is not a state of reality; it is a state of mind."[21]

The notion that "history is a construct" created by human beings embraces Carl Becker's concept that "history is the self-consciousness of humanity," what Barzun and Graff have termed "one of the ways in which we think."[22] As stories about humanity, history consists of symbols created by people about people, places, and events. It is the very capacity that we possess as symbol-making beings that enables us to create the languages that cross the boundaries of time and space in order to recreate those significant images that constitute "history." To point to Zarefsky's analysis in the next chapter, analyzing the rhetorical dimensions of history is compelling "not because rhetoric is somehow ancillary to history but because it is central to it." Bruce Gronbeck's delineations of the rhetoric of history underscore the value of understanding history as a discursive practice.[23] In their essay on the rhetorical construction of history, E. Culpepper Clark and Raymie McKerrow push the point even further to argue, "just as a rhetor uses argument and style to call into existence a 'people' who never 'are' in a permanent sense, the historian uses evidential rules and argumentation to recreate a past that never 'was' in a true and complete sense, at least for those who lived it." All three essays suggest the fundamental, profound, and integral connections between rhetoric and history.

This construction of a culture's self-consciousness occurs within the rhetorical confines of the society in which and for which the history is produced. As E. H. Carr suggested, history is "an unending dialogue between the present and the past," serving both society's functional need to come to an understanding of itself through its past and its poetic need to imagine the lives and experiences of generations gone by.[24] In the process, to quote Sartre, "the historian is himself [sic] historical; that is to say that he historicizes himself in illuminating history by his projects and those of his society."[25] Not surprisingly, the histories produced by ancient Greek and Roman societies emphasized preparation for the political and military life central to those cultures, and the current popularity of social and cultural history reflects our sense that the diversity and complexity of (contemporary) life must somehow be accounted for. In his fine analyses of the rhetorical dimensions of historical arguments, Ronald H. Carpenter has pointed out that, for instance, Frederick Jackson Turner's frontier thesis garnered a phenomenally positive public reaction because the American public of the 1890s and beyond wanted and needed to believe that they possessed frontier attributes even in the face of the stresses and strains of an urban, industrialized society.[26] In each case the histories serve the society's particular yens for particular kinds of historical knowledge and self-knowledge. Carpenter's analysis suggests the power of what Gronbeck in his chapter terms "the rhetoric of collective memory," the socially constructed, collectivized discourse that shapes and reshapes history as myth and exhortation for the present.

Moreover, the dialogue between past and present constructs the past as "a well of conclusions from which we draw in order to act."[27] In his chapter Zarefsky observes that "historians not only argue *about* history; they also argue *from* it." Historians are joined in this debate by politicians and the public, as Gronbeck notes herein in his discussion of arguments from the past. History is not simply an ongoing conversation but an "argument without end,"[28] an ongoing polemic by which societies are constituted. Indeed, that argument may end only "when the issues as well as the people are dead."[29] Think of how many times during the Persian Gulf conflict and debates over American involvement in the Bosnian-Croatian crisis we heard the phrase "the lessons of history." Of course, the difficulty is, which lessons from what history are we to learn? "The lessons of Vietnam," for example, came up time and again in Senate debates, editorial cartoons, and barroom discussions, but that phrase occurred equally in arguments that we should not get involved as in arguments that we must get involved. The continual rewriting of the history of Vietnam indicates the extent to which historical writings are a process of coming to grips with the present by reconceptualizing the past, as these rhetorical uses of history suggest.[30] "If poetry is the little myth we make," posits Robert Penn Warren, then "history is the big myth we live, and in our living, constantly remake." Orwell's aphorism from *1984* phrases the point rather more bluntly: "Who controls the past controls the future; who controls the present controls the past."[31]

Our social construction of the past, then, is guided by and contained in the symbols and systems of symbols that give currency to our attitudes, values, beliefs, and actions. Historical research makes sense within the context of that framework. Consider, then, the popular metaphor: doing history is like putting together pieces of a jigsaw puzzle. Yet that jigsaw puzzle is of a distinctive kind in at least three ways. First, historians cannot look at the picture on the box top, for there is none. They are guided—at once only, and fully—by the conceptions of their time and of themselves.[32] Historians do employ generalizations, "particularly generalizations about the different ways in which human beings react to different kinds of situations"; but given the way that historians cherish the particularities of their research they are reluctant to acknowledge that in place of the explicit pictures on the box tops are the implicit pictures in their heads.[33] "All history," in Marwick's characterization, "is interpretation,"[34] the result of conceptualizations within the leveling and sharpening of societal values.

Second, the "jigsaw puzzle" of history does not come with a clear and complete set of 500 pieces to be used in specific ways. It is as if pieces from numerous jigsaw puzzles were tossed in together, requiring one to wade through a sea of possibilities. Who indeed cannot appreciate Mary Stewart's retrospection: "If I had read more widely I should never have completed this book. More: if I had even known how much there was to read, I would never have dared to start to write at all."[35] Stewart's comment substantiates Gunderson's observation that "historical research can encourage a certain humility."[36] Spicing up this hunt through the often superabundance of options—especially for more contemporary research topics—is the fact that some of the most vital pieces for the particular puzzle under construction are invariably missing completely. For example, as I have noted elsewhere, despite the hundreds of linear feet of documents in presidential libraries, presidents are rarely directly present; rather, they are like the father in Strindberg's *Miss Julie:* "offstage and unseen, but constantly the focal point."[37] The sheer volume of materials may encourage "a fox-terrier school of scholarship, in which every scrap of information is important."[38] As a result, the art of historical research resembles a fractured St. Francis's prayer: it requires the strength to discard extraneous materials, the serenity and perceptiveness to fill in the gaps, and the wisdom to know the difference.

A third peculiar characteristic of historical jigsaw puzzles is that the pieces are not discrete, unchanging units. They are rather more like amoebas, changing shape and significance depending on the context in which they are placed. Carl Becker addresses this amorphous nature of historical "units" when he asserts that

historical facts are after all not material substances which, like bricks or scantlings, possess definite shape and clear, persistent outline. . . . A brick retains its form and pressure wherever placed; but the form and substance of historical facts, having a negotiable existence only in literary discourse, vary with the words employed to convey them. . . . It is thus not the undiscriminated fact, but the perceiving mind of the historian that speaks: the special meaning which the facts are made to convey emerges from the substance-form which the historian employs to recreate imaginatively a series of events not present to perception.[39]

Unlike the pieces of a jigsaw puzzle, the shapes of which are constant and discrete, the components of history are not simply variable but are called into existence in the process of constructing the history.

Becker dismisses the notion that history can be "just the facts, ma'am": "Left to themselves, the facts do not speak; left to themselves they do not exist, not really."[40] Clark and McKerrow extend this line of analysis when they argue that "historians often call into being a past that could never have known itself, at least in terms the present seeks to know it."

Thus, whereas jigsaw pieces exist apart from the puzzle to which they belong, historical facts rely on the narratives in which they are used to make sense—indeed, to call them into being. "Evidence" may be a better term than "fact," with the latter's persistent connotations of Truth and Certainty. To borrow Barzun and Graff's vivid phrase, facts "come dripping with ideas."[41] In contrast to the discrete connotations of the term *fact*, something cannot be evidence unless it is evidence *of* something; as Collingwood asserts, "nothing is evidence except in relation to some definite question."[42] The process of doing history, then, is fundamentally a process of selection and production. Accordingly, McKerrow notes, historians "do not so much consign meaning to events as they constitute it."[43]

These concepts of the creation of meaning through historical scholarship are much with me as I work to construct a rhetorical history of images of women in comic strips across a century. I am conscious, for example, of selecting and molding various pieces of a massive, moving historical jigsaw puzzle as I try to identify connections and disparities between the depictions on the funnies pages and (for instance) the advertisements, movies, fashions, etiquette columns, employment patterns, and economic factors surrounding them in the socio-rhetorical landscape of each era. I set *Winnie Winkle the Breadwinner* and *Tillie the Toiler* of the twenties amidst a profusion of flappers, flivvers, phonographs, finery, and phones, whereas the original *Brenda Starr* resonates with the images of the forties, from Rita Hayworth to World War II. Yet even as I look to *Harper's Bazaar* and *My Man Godfrey* for clues with which to contextualize the comic strip portrayals, I also know that when I myself pick up a *Cosmopolitan* or watch *Working Girl*, I am "simultaneously infuriated and seduced"[44] by the images of what the modern woman is supposed to be like. Moreover, I am aware that, as Clark and McKerrow, as well as Carl Becker, would suggest, I am not only selecting and molding but also in the process fundamentally creating a historical perspective even as I write. Thus the construction of my rhetorical history entails healthy measures of speculation, bemusement, and caution.

That rhetorical history also has required the construction of a kind of methodological jigsaw—pulling together concepts from the sociology of beauty, the cultural history of technology, the socioeconomic roles of women, and the analysis of art history in order to (re)create an understanding of depictions of young females in leading roles in newspaper comic strips. To borrow Warren Susman's characterization, "the writing of cultural history has always meant a search for a new form, a new language, a new perspective: theme and variation, a fugue-like principle of over-all organization, perhaps repeating but also discovering new notes to describe and probe."[45] The concept of a collage of communication messages that I have developed—the overlapping, contextualizing patterns we create from the myriad of messages we receive—is one result of that search for "a new form, a new language, a new perspective."[46]

I confess that it is not always a comfortable process as I turn my end-of-the-twentieth-century analytical lenses on early-twentieth-century messages—and on the messages of my youth and my adulthood, often combining feminist despair with guilty pleasure. Although a belief in the centrality of rhetorical processes in historical contexts urges me onward, a sense of the rhetorical nature of historical research gives me pause. Thus I confront the clash of the Greek maxims: Know thyself—but remember that knowledge is tragedy.

And thus we return to the point that the study of history is a rhetorical construction providing a view of reality for its society. That history deals with particularistic topics in a time-bound manner makes it none the less global in its implications; as Potter points out, "a microcosm is just as cosmic as a macrocosm."[47] In constructing a sense of reality for the society in which it is produced, the study of history is an essentially rhetorical process.

Doing Rhetorical History:
The Challenge and the Promise

In his essay for this volume, the self-described optimist David Zarefsky puzzles over what he terms a "strange defensiveness" among those conducting rhetorical histories. Although he diplomatically avoids using my name, the identity of the "conference organizer" is clear. I planned the 1995 Greenspun conference on "Rhetoric, History, and Critical Interpretation: The Recovery of the Historical-Critical Praxis," and it did indeed grow out of not only a faith in rhetorical history but also a measure of frustration over its current status. The heritage of the field clearly includes historical studies, and rhetorical histories are still published; yet both the present and the future are hobbled by what are at the least misconceptions about rhetorical history and what from some quarters constitutes a distinct sneer—witness the thesis directors, the editors, the colleagues cited at the outset of this introduction.

And yet I am not comfortable concluding that I, and those like me, therefore fall into the category of "pessimist." I am energized by the power and perceptiveness of rhetorical histories as represented in this collection; and I am confident that increasing numbers of scholars within and outside of communication will realize the significant insights to be gained through rhetorical history, both as methodology and as perspective. In fact, I choose to regard the differences of opinion even among the authors of these essays as a sign that, using the yardstick cited earlier, neither the people nor the issues are dead.

The discussions were certainly lively at the Greenspun conference that inspired this volume, where many of those differences were in evidence. "Age," for example, served not only as a chronological framework and as a fantasy theme among the participants, as befits scholars dedicated to history, but also as a division. Those older and more established in the field tended to believe that history and criticism are part of the same enterprise and thus nearly inseparable, that rhetorical history thrives, that publishing opportunities abound, that little need be done to improve the status of historical scholarship. Zarefsky, for example, argued that "for the most part, the distinctions among history, criticism, and theory in rhetorical studies are unnecessary and without foundation." Those younger in the field, on the other hand, regarded rhetorical history as a distinctive pursuit, perceived that that pursuit is not sufficiently valued by the field, despaired of getting their work published, worried about the effect of limited outlets on their professional futures—and, in one case, had just been denied tenure because his exquisitely researched, well-written rhetorical history had taken so long to produce. Even Zarefsky's optimistic assertion that "any scholar is free to study anything" is constrained by his observation that "when it comes time to publish the results of the research . . . it is a different matter." As Carpenter points out in his concluding essay, one of the many tolls exacted by the "publish or perish" ethic in higher education is the exceptionally high cost of investing the time necessary for painstaking archival research and historical writing. Scholars are free to study whatever they like, but without publication they lack not only an audience but also employment.

As might be expected, the disputations include the labels one uses to describe oneself and one's research. Carpenter, for example, describes himself as a "rhetorical critic," whereas many of us value him as a preeminent rhetorical historian.[48] As for myself, I have chosen the self-descriptor "rhetorical analyst" intentionally, for I use history, criticism, and theory in my scholarship—generally in combination but usually in that order. I believe that distinctions may be usefully drawn without resorting to caricatures. At the same time, by doing so I am neither denying nor denigrating history's connections to criticism and theory; on the contrary, I celebrate them. I just wish the sense of collaboration and cooperation were more broadly shared. When, for example, has an essay been rejected by a reviewer demanding, "Where's the historical news for rhetorical studies in this study?" or "Tell me what your findings mean in the language of history"? Yet as Moya Ball contends in chapter four, "when we deny history, we deny ourselves."

Such denials cost our field and those with which we are affiliated. Look at how each of the insights of rhetorical history delineated at the outset of this chapter can be seen in the essays that follow. First, historical research provides an understanding of rhetoric as a process rather than simply as a product: witness, for example, Jenkins's tracing of the process of rhetorical estrangement in both Missouri newspapers and the gubernatorial office at the beginning of the Civil War, Jablonski's exploration of a Catholic activist's struggle to figure out how to decline an honor in a way that would uphold her lifelong beliefs but still not offend, and Olson's delineation of Mansfield's creation of his own credibility on Southeast Asia and its subsequent effects on the conduct of foreign policy. Second, historical research creates an appreciation of both the commonalities among and the distinctiveness of rhetorical situations and responses: note the theme and variation of the rhetorical negotiation of tension, for instance, in the struggles of dueling chief executives to establish rhetorical legitimacy and define sovereignty, as outlined by Andrews; in the efforts to win compliance if not hearts and minds in the integrated reconstitution of the Army, as recreated by Goldzwig; and in the clash of cultural heritages in the publicly exchanged correspondence of Chavez and the growers' league, as profiled by Hammerback and Jensen. Third, historical research tests theory and complements criticism while standing as a distinct and valid approach in and of itself, as demonstrated by Ball's analysis that challenges the concept of "groupthink" and Jasinski's delineation of the advantages of a constitutive rather than instrumentalist framework for rhetorical analysis.

Fine as these studies and their companion essays are, they but limn the contributions to be made by rhetorical history. The conceptualizations and methodologies of rhetorical history will only increase in significance during the burgeoning "Communication Age" as we seek to cope with our present and prepare for our future by better understanding our past. Yet as one observer mused, "History is one of the few resources Americans haven't fully exploited."[49] May rhetorical scholars help remedy the situation!

Part I

Conceptualizing the Interconnections
of Rhetoric and History

1

Four Senses of Rhetorical History

David Zarefsky

A strange defensiveness attends discussions of rhetorical history. It is evident even in the call for the conference that gave birth to the essays in this volume. The conference organizer noted that "the predominance of the field has moved away from historical perspectives" and that reviewers and dissertation directors may "reject with great disdain work they regard as 'mere history.'" A similar defensiveness resonates through Baskerville's query of two decades ago: "Must we all be 'rhetorical critics'?"[1] It sometimes seems as though historical studies are doubly beleaguered. Temporally they are challenged by the discipline's growing concern for the contemporary. Methodologically they are vulnerable to the press for the critical or the theoretical.

Defensiveness seems strange, however, because the communication discipline has always embraced pluralism in its approaches, because it is not hard to argue that historical studies yield knowledge and insight, and because even a casual inspection of journals and books will suggest that good historical scholarship in rhetoric does get published and that it attracts a healthy audience. Far from struggling to establish itself, historical scholarship appears to be alive and well. We might legitimately ask, "What do we have to be so defensive about?"

Probing this anomaly is the purpose of this essay. The heart of our problem is sloppiness in the professional discourse, and perhaps in the thought, of rhetorical historians. We do very well at drawing distinctions that do not matter, and yet we fail to be precise about those that do. We take for granted the motives that impel our own inquiry, as if they also should impel editors to publish and colleagues to read what we write. As a result, we engage in a pseudocontroversy largely via stereotypes. In the course of examining these claims, I will—as my title suggests—delineate four different senses of the term "rhetorical history" and discuss the sorts of scholarship that fit naturally under each.

Distinctions That Do Not Matter

The first step is to clear away some unneeded apparatus. For the most part the distinctions among history, criticism, and theory in rhetorical studies are unnecessary and without foundation.

The history/criticism distinction can be addressed first. For many years, *the* method for scholarship in rhetoric was the "historical-critical" method. The Brigance and Hochmuth volumes, for instance, bore the title *A History and Criticism of American Public Address*.[2] These volumes and others inspired a generation of scholarship that was quite similar. It was biographical, it focused on the public oration, and it sought to determine effectiveness by empirical measures. But then a reaction set in. In retrospect, these early studies were seen as weak. By applying a predetermined template to one speaker after another, they yielded little valuable insight except that virtually anything could be made to fit the mold. For this reason they were denigrated as "cookie cutter" studies. And they were what historical scholarship was. Moreover, they seemed antiquarian at a time when the turmoil of the late 1960s focused attention on the present. How, after all, could formulaic studies of dead orators speak to the great crises of the day?

To distinguish their work from studies like these, scholars took apart the combined term "historical-critical" and emphasized that they were critics, not historians. This was the basis of the distinction against which Baskerville complained in 1977. To sustain the distinction it was necessary to imagine a caricature of at least one of the terms. History, it was sometimes said, dealt with facts and chronicle, criticism with interpretation and judgment. Yet only a little reflection is needed to see the error in this thinking. The historian cannot recount *all* of "what happened," and the historian's view of "what happened" is influenced by his or her own perspective. Facts do not speak; they must be spoken for. Historical scholarship is an interaction between the scholar and the historical record. Necessarily, then, it is interpretive. Regarding the selection of some historical materials and not others, it is well to remember Burke's dictum that a reflection of reality is also a selection and a deflection.[3] Regarding the interaction of the scholar and the record, we need only recall that this is why it is possible—even necessary—to revisit the historical record and develop "new" histories as our own frame of reference changes.

Granted that historians make judgments, are these judgments critical? In theory they don't have to be. But making choices and selections at random and without reflection surely does not produce strong scholarship in this or any other discipline. To equate historical scholarship with *bad* historical scholarship is an obvious mistake. Good historical scholarship is also critical.

Baskerville recognized all this, yet he maintained that "to insist that an historian must be 'critical' is not the same as asking that he [*sic*] become a critic."[4] To sustain *this* side of the distinction requires a caricature of criticism, just as the other side required a caricature of history. Critics of discourse are not like judges in a beauty contest, awarding ratings of "6.5" or "8" based on intuition. Proclaiming an object good or bad on the basis of impulse rather than reason is bad criticism, just as unconscious selection of details is bad history. Good criticism, like good history, is reflective; it offers reasons to sustain judgments.

And those reasons involve, to a greater or lesser degree, historical considerations, since rhetoric is concerned, as Aristotle said, with the available means of persuasion *in a given case*. It is a field that cannot be reduced to a closed system, beginning as it does by denying that there are universally applicable principles. When Wichelns wrote that rhetorical criticism was not concerned with permanence or beauty but with effect,[5] he was not urging us to focus on empirical measurements of the effect of a speech. Rather, he was directing our attention to the fact that rhetoric is situational. Its assessment must be made somehow in the context of that situation. Admittedly, situations are not "given" and there is much room for argument about what the situation is. Such argument, too, is a source of productive criticism.

History and criticism are not identical, but they are overlapping circles. And rhetorical history is done in the area of overlap. This still is not to say that it is all alike. Any rhetorical act is an interaction between text and context, and one can imagine a continuum of scholarship that gives greater emphasis to one or the other. There is a difference, for example, between Michael Leff's work on Lincoln's "House Divided" speech and my own.[6] Leff has produced a masterful account of the rhetorical movement within the text and has given less attention to the speech as a historical event. I have focused more on why Lincoln needed to distinguish sharply between himself and Douglas and why the speech became an albatross for Lincoln during the ensuing senate campaign. These studies differ, to be sure. But to call Leff a critic and me a historian would be to make a useless distinction that would trivialize both of our studies. Leff's work is powerfully informed by historical understanding of the strength of conspiracy arguments and "machine" metaphors during the 1850s, and mine is powerfully informed by critical awareness of how Lincoln took familiar materials and arranged them in new ways for telling impact.

The concern of the late 1960s and early 1970s over whether to call oneself a historian or a critic gradually abated. To the pessimist it abated because criticism pushed history to the sidelines of the discipline where it has remained ever since. To the optimist (and I am one) it abated because historical scholarship became more sophisticated. It strove for and often achieved a higher level of quality that, because it involved critical judgment, made the distinction superfluous.

This possibly dead issue, the relationship between history and criticism, has been exhumed because it illustrates a style of thought and discourse that contributes to a feeling of defensiveness—making distinctions that are not necessary, and doing so by invoking caricature or stereotype to describe that from which one seeks to distinguish one's own work. These same tendencies reappear in a more recent dispute about the relationship between history and theory.

Readers of the *Western Journal of Communication* know that James Darsey, echoing Baskerville's question, took on a ten-year-old essay by Roderick P. Hart and asked, "Must we all be rhetorical theorists?"[7] Darsey objected to the view, which he attributed to Hart, that historical studies in rhetoric were justified primarily or exclusively by their contribution to rhetorical theory and that the study of historical particulars was of little value in itself. Precisely this claim has been made by some scholars—for example, by Bowers, who suggested that the function of criticism (and he probably would include history) is "pre-scientific,"[8] that the critic's intuitive and idiosyncratic insights might yield useful hypotheses that, if tested scientifically, might then produce reliable knowledge about communication. It is not necessary to embrace Bowers's fondness for the scientific method to follow his claim that theoretical knowledge is about generalizations, not particulars. Nor is it necessary to take Hart as a foil in order to appreciate Darsey's complaint. Anyone who ever received a rejection letter saying that his or her pet project made no contribution to rhetorical theory can empathize.

But once again scholars may have rushed to make a distinction—or to allow one to be made against them—without thinking carefully about what "theory" means here. It should be clear at the outset that any scholar is free to study anything. No reason or justification is needed, save for intellectual curiosity. When it comes time to publish the results of research, however—to share them with others—it is a different matter. At this point the scholar is making claims on the time and attention of others: of editors who are asked to allocate scarce pages to this project rather than another, and of readers who cannot possibly keep up with everything and need reasons to attend to one study rather than another. The reasons I have for doing my study may be very different from the reasons I offer that it should interest you, just as for our colleagues in the social sciences there is a difference between the logic of discovery and the logic of justification. But I am obliged to explain why my study should interest you. This is the famous "so what?" question: Why should you care?

Sometimes, caught up in his or her own research, a scholar may resent having to answer this question. Surely something that is self-evidently fascinating to me will be to you as well. So one answers the question perfunctorily and then wonders why editors reject his or her work. Or one might resort to the most hackneyed answer of all: that our study should be published because nothing like it has been published before. As I always explain to graduate students who try this argument, the premise permits more than one inference. It may be that nothing has been published because the topic has not been shown worthy of publication, in which case the question comes right back: Why is *this* study worthy of publication? How does it answer the "so what?" question?

A slight derivative of this refrain is the claim that a study should be published because it pushes the envelope, expanding the boundaries of discourse. So much ink has been spilled over canonical works, the argument goes, that it is time to turn our attention to something different. Even though people should study what they want, this is a very weak justification for publishing "canon-stretching" work. First, the premise is false. Surprisingly little attention has been given by rhetorical scholars to the canon, even to such speeches as Webster's Reply to Hayne, Lincoln's First Inaugural, or Martin Luther King Jr.'s "I Have a Dream." Even more important, this claim only returns to the original "so what?" question: Why should an editor or reader care whether we enlarge our understanding of the canon? The answer must be that doing so achieves some larger purpose, and *that*—rather than some sense of liberation for its own sake—is the reason to publish the study in the first place.

This larger purpose, this answer to the "so what?" question, is what is sought by the expectation that historical scholarship make a contribution to theory. What it takes to answer the question will depend on where one chooses to publish and what audience one chooses

Scholarship
as
Burke's
conversation

to engage. Scholarship enacts Kenneth Burke's endless conversation that began long before we arrived and continues long after we are gone.[9] This is true not only for the mythical "community of scholars" but for particular scholarly communities as well. To be judged *relevant*, what we say must fit in to the context of that conversation. To be judged *important*, it must somehow influence the conversation so that its subsequent path is different from what it might have been otherwise.

A personal example may be useful here. Recently I published an article in the *Journal of the Abraham Lincoln Association*.[10] My subject was Lincoln's implicit theory of persuasion, my project to unpack the statement that "public sentiment is everything," which he made in the Ottawa debate with Stephen A. Douglas in 1858. Readers of this journal could be presumed to be interested in Lincoln, so I did not need to defend studying him. Rather, my answer to the "so what?" question was that the study helped to resolve a paradox: How could Lincoln oppose slavery so strongly in principle yet support only modest, incremental, or infeasible remedies? My contribution to theory was to a theory of Lincoln's life and motivation. I hope that I offered a strong alternative to the views that Lincoln was either insincere or hypocritical.

Now suppose that I had sought to publish the study in the *Journal of American History*. Because of Lincoln's obvious historical significance, I might not have needed lengthy justification for studying him. But this journal has a broader mission. What does my study of Lincoln contribute to the larger issue of how to understand the political crisis of the 1850s and the coming of the Civil War? And what in turn does *that* contribute to how we understand American constitutionalism or the place of race in American society? I will make a contribution to theory if I show how my study helps to answer those questions.

Finally, suppose that I try to publish this study in the *Quarterly Journal of Speech*. Here what defines the scholarly community is not an interest in Lincoln, or even in history, but an interest in understanding human communication. This time the editor and readers will rightly ask such questions as what does the study tell us about rhetorical invention? about public moral argument in times of crisis? about how public figures address multiple audiences simultaneously? The study will contribute to theory insofar as it suggests answers to these questions or makes a difference to the conversation about them. When we are called to contribute to "rhetorical theory," I believe we are being asked nothing more or less than to say something that addresses such questions as these. Rhetorical theory, after all, is not a body of covering-law statements but rather of predictive generalizations and explanation-sketches induced from experience. It is not asking too much that the results of historical scholarship contribute to this theoretical enterprise nor that the rhetorical historian should be called upon to make a case for the contribution rather than assuming it to be self-evident.

Does it follow, then, that studies of *individual cases* (the primary work of the historian) are suspect because they do not yield *general* knowledge? Not necessarily. Hart is right to remind us that study of atypical, exceptionally memorable cases of public discourse may not inform our understanding of the ordinary and the mundane. Moreover, computer technology and quantitative methods—now employed routinely in most fields of historical scholarship—do permit us to generalize about large and otherwise insignificant bodies of ordinary discourse rather than relying exclusively on accumulation of examples. All that is to the good. Individual cases, however, also contribute to theory. They suggest models, norms, or exemplars; they offer perspective by incongruity on the ordinary cases; they yield insights that may apply by analogy either to ordinary cases or to other extraordinary cases; and they sometimes yield a "theory of the case": a better understanding of an unusual situation important in its own right.

What has been suggested so far is that historical scholars allow themselves to be put on the defensive by making useless distinctions and accepting the baggage that goes along with them. Distinguishing between history and criticism by suggesting that historical studies are only chronicles of facts puts historical studies in a one-down position, and undertaking studies on that basis produces bad scholarship that justifies the charge. Accepting a distinction between history and theory that makes historical scholarship noninterpretive and self-contained will lead naturally to complaints that "mere history" contributes only to satisfying the scholar's narcissistic urges, and producing scholarship that fails to engage the "so what?" question will give legitimacy to that complaint.

Distinctions That Do Matter

But scholarly errors are not only of commission. Just as many scholars are too ready to make distinctions that do not matter, they are reluctant to be precise enough about those that do. There is perhaps no better example than the key term, "rhetorical history." Twenty years ago Gronbeck confidently defined "rhetorical history" as "the study of the historical effects of rhetorical discourse."[11] Although some of his distinctions between history and criticism remain tenable, Gronbeck probably would now find this crisp definition somewhat more problematic. I know that I do.

For one thing, the definition may identify a research area that is basically a null set. Few indeed are the times when any single rhetorical discourse can be shown to have specific historical effects. Important as it is to the rhetorical scholar, such discourse is usually not that powerful apart from the entire social constellation of which it is a part. Public-opinion polls and similar audience measures are both flawed and evanescent, and there is little evidence to establish that public discourse has historical effects—as Professor George Edwards trenchantly made clear in a recent essay.[12]

rhetoric does not act alone, historically

Even more important, Gronbeck's 1975 definition is a reductionist view of what rhetorical historians do. Few would be comfortable thinking of public discourse as an independent variable interjected into a situation or of their work as identifying or measuring dependent variables that are linked to it. Scholars sometimes muddy the issue by writing up work in causal language even when that is not what they mean. More often, what we really are doing is supplying a context or frame of reference that enables us to understand historical events differently.

There are (at least) four different kinds of inquiry embraced by the term "rhetorical history." These distinctions are useful not for boundary drawing but for understanding the richness of our field (and, perhaps, for being less defensive about it). Although they are distinct, they clearly cross-fertilize. And recognizing the distinctions may enable us to answer the "so what?" question better. I refer to these four senses as follows: the history of rhetoric, the rhetoric of history, historical studies of rhetorical practice, and rhetorical studies of historical events.

Probably the least problematic of these divisions is the history of rhetoric—the development, from classical times to the present, of principles of effective discourse. There is little question that this effort—which might be considered a branch of the history of ideas—is important, because it traces the development of our theories and concepts, some of which (such as *kairos* or decorum, *ethos* or enthymemes) go back to the classics and some of which (such as presumptions, identification, terministic screens, and hegemony) are of more recent origin. Examining the development of rhetoric in the context of the eras and societies in which it evolved is of obvious importance to understanding the current state of our knowledge and our discipline. And, just because it *is* "our" knowledge and "our" discipline, it seems obvious that rhetorical scholars should undertake this work. (Even as I make this statement, I can't help observing that several graduate programs in the discipline have not kept a strong anchor in Greek and Roman rhetoric or in the development of rhetoric from those days to this.)

The "so what?" question, though, applies even to this branch of inquiry. It is not hard to imagine antiquarian projects that seemingly contribute little to theory: the discovery of an unknown but unimportant treatise, the identification of national rhetorical traditions without arguing for the importance of the differences among them, or the unearthing of a previously unidentified figure or trope. But we also can appreciate the theoretical contributions of such synthetic works as George Kennedy's study of the evolution of rhetoric under Greek, Roman, Christian, and secular leadership or of Wilbur Samuel Howell's contextualization of rhetoric within the intellectual traditions of seventeenth and eighteenth century England.[13] And the "so what?" question is addressed in less-sweeping works as well.

Recently, Edward Schiappa has offered a new reading of Protagorean fragments based on the assumption that the idea of rhetoric did not develop until about one hundred years later than commonly supposed.[14] He answers the "so what?" question not by arguing that Protagoras is self-evidently an important historical figure so that any study of his fragments is valuable, but rather by claiming that understanding the Sophists in a different way casts a different light on the origins and purposes of the discipline, the charges Plato brought against rhetoric, and the dialectical tension between rhetoric and philosophy. The dialogue in which he, John Poulakos, and others have participated raises the interesting issue of whether what some have called a postmodern rhetoric is really a return to the premodern system of the Sophists.[15]

For another example, Michael Leff has focused on the Ciceronian concepts of prudence and decorum.[16] His answers to the "so what?" question have related these traditional rhetorical virtues to the concept of civic humanism, to republicanism, to debates over the founding of the United States government, to the Whig tradition in American politics, and to the current concern about the erosion of the public sphere. The point in citing these examples is not to suggest that the history of rhetoric must be made more "relevant" in any narrow sense of the term. Not all issues engaged by the history of rhetoric are "hot button" issues of the moment. Rather, the point is that even studies *of* theory are called upon to make a contribution *to* theory that in some way transcends the particular case under study and participates in a larger scholarly conversation.

The second division identified above is the rhetoric of history. It had developed from the rejection of an earlier belief, identified with von Ranke, that historians somehow could reproduce the past on its own terms. Now, most historians regard historical discourse as emerging from an interaction between the historian and the record. So, Megill and McCloskey write, "the rhetoric of history is concerned with the tropes, arguments, and other devices of language used to write history and to persuade audiences."[17] And this study is undertaken not because rhetoric is somehow ancillary to history but because it is central to it. What Megill and McCloskey describe as "the metaphor of going to the solid facts and looking at them" is a powerful but mythical description of what historians do. Accordingly, the rhetoric of history studies the inventional and presentational practices of historians as a specialized discourse community, much as the rhetoric of science and the rhetoric of law do with respect to those specialized communities. This branch of inquiry is partly a study of how historians talk and write *about* history. I offered a brief example of such a study in an essay about how historians in different time periods have attributed causality for the American Civil War.[18] Much fuller treatments of the rhetoric of history can be found outside the rhetoric discipline, with names such as J. H. Hexter, Hayden White, Hans Kellner, and Nancy Struever coming to mind.[19]

Historians not only argue *about* history; they also argue *from* it, using historical premises to justify current actions and beliefs. This too is a rhetoric of history, which Depoe has labeled ideological. In his recent book-length study,[20] he examines how Arthur M. Schlesinger Jr. argued from the premise that there are predictable tides in American politics to the conclusion in support of liberal programs during the 1950s and 1960s and to the prediction of a coming liberal resurgence that has been seen on the horizon almost since the election of Richard Nixon. Nor are professional historians the only figures who engage in argument from history. Analogical reasoning from history has a powerful influence on policy makers, as Richard Neustadt and Ernest May demonstrated in their study, *Thinking in Time*.[21] And, in general, a culture develops a collective memory— a storehouse of common knowledge and belief about history that forms the premises for arguments and appeals.[22] Examples include the belief in American exceptionalism, the belief that Franklin D. Roosevelt launched both the modern presidency and the welfare state, the belief that the cold war could not be won if there were "another Munich," and the belief for twenty years that we should not contemplate "another Vietnam." Whether academic or popular, these examples all illustrate another important distinction in rhetorical history, one to which the discipline has not paid enough attention.

The "so what?" test for research in this area is to ask what such research contributes to a more general understanding of how history is used. We are far from knowing much about how collective memory is formed and modified or about how professional historians conduct discourse differently from amateurs. (The recent intense controversy over National History Standards may shed light on the latter question.) What is not needed, however, is to justify studies of the rhetoric of history on the imperialistic basis that history, like anything else, can be rendered rhetorical. Such imperialism is a reaction to the tendency of others to marginalize rhetorical studies, but trying to take over the world advances neither credibility nor scholarship.

These first two senses of rhetorical history probably are not what most of us envisioned by the term, although I do believe they are important subsets of it. The third and fourth senses, however, are the intellectual progeny of what used to be regarded as the "history of public address." That term has come under some question, both because the objects of study are broader than "public address" and because scholars often are not studying the history of public address itself but instead are using public address as a window to study the history of something else.

The third sense of rhetorical history, then, is the historical study of rhetorical events. There are several ways in which to proceed. Rhetorical discourse could be studied as a force in history. Notwithstanding the earlier qualifiers, it is—but less because it produces tangible effects than because it alters an ongoing social conversation. Franklin Roosevelt's First Inaugural Address and Lyndon Johnson's Voting Rights Act message are examples that come to mind.

Or rhetorical discourse could be studied as an index or mirror of history. This was the approach urged by Ernest Wrage, who found in public discourse a repository of history's intellectual substance revealing how ideas were affected by the process of sharing them with others.[23] Or historical study could be undertaken of key arguments or even terms, as Condit and Lucaites have done with their account of the evolution of public understanding of the term "equality."[24] Or more microscopic studies of the inventional history of particular discourses could be undertaken. I found it useful, for example, to discover that Lyndon Johnson's eloquent warning to the South about civil rights, delivered during a speech in New Orleans in 1964, was entirely *ad-lib,* or that the origin of Abraham Lincoln's famous "Freeport Question" was in a letter he received from *Chicago Press and Tribune* editor Joseph Medill.[25] Or patterns can be found in groups of discourses that suggest a rhetorical trajectory, as Leland Griffin found in the writings of Lee Harvey Oswald and as several scholars have found in the justifications for escalation during the war in Vietnam.[26]

Of all the branches of rhetorical history, this one has undergone the most change compared to the literature of one or two generations ago. Gone is the assumption that a single all-purpose method will work.

Gone is faith that one can assess causality with the flimsiest of empirical evidence. Increased is the need for sophistication in historical methods, especially in finding, interpreting, and assessing primary sources rather than relying on the judgments of others. Increased is the expectation that research will result in book-length studies. And, along with that, increased is the expectation that scholarship will be accessible to, and pass muster with, scholars in many other disciplines as well as our own. These considerations particularly require subverting the faulty distinctions between history and criticism, history and theory, that can result simply in the production of bad work. They require that the "so what?" question be addressed on several levels. How does historical scholarship enhance our understanding of the rhetorical event? And how does that further larger purposes, not just for one's discipline but for the scholarly community in general?

My final sense of rhetorical history, the study of historical events from a rhetorical perspective, is the most elusive but possibly also the most rewarding. It begins with the assumption that the rhetorical historian has the same subject matter as any other historian: "human life in all its totality and multiplicity."[27] What distinguishes the rhetorical historian is not subject matter but perspective. The economic historian might view human conduct from the perspective of the market, the political historian from the mobilization of interest and power, the intellectual historian from the standpoint of the evolution of ideas, and the rhetorical historian from the perspective of how messages are created and used by people to influence and relate to one another.

In this sense of rhetorical history, the historian views history as a series of rhetorical problems, situations that call for public persuasion to advance a cause or overcome an impasse. The focus of the study would be on how, and how well, people invented and deployed messages in response to the situation. Hogan's recent exploration of the nuclear freeze campaign offers a rhetorical history of the freeze movement.[28] Windt's study of protest rhetoric of the 1960s interprets that period as the frustration of traditional genres of discourse and the creation of alternatives.[29] My own work on the War on Poverty tried to interpret the social policies of the 1960s, as well as their perceived failure, as responses to rhetorical situations,[30] and a recent book review essay in the *Quarterly Journal of Speech* hints at the potential for studying the coming of the Civil War as the story of the collapse of a discourse community.[31]

Studies of this type are potentially valuable because they may offer a powerful answer to the "so what?" question. By studying important historical events from a rhetorical perspective, one can see significant aspects about those events that other perspectives miss. If that is so, then there is an argument not only for the place of historical studies within rhetoric but also for the contribution of rhetorical studies in the larger scholarly enterprise. Of course, this is a *potential* contribution. The proof comes in the insight offered by individual studies.

That last point is a fitting commentary on all four of these senses of rhetorical history. The purpose of mapping them is not to suggest boundaries or compartments but to open possibilities for productive inquiry. Realizing the (at least) four-dimensional nature of rhetorical history, we begin better to appreciate the contributions it can make to rhetoric, to history, to the communication discipline in particular, and to the state of knowledge and insight more generally. Doing this work, and doing it well, should provide the evidence that can dispel defensiveness by distinguishing between "mere history" and good history.

Some, however, may still raise two more questions. Why do historical scholarship at all? And why do it in rhetoric programs and communication departments?

There is an extensive literature on the importance of historical scholarship. In brief, historical study aids in understanding the present by placing it in the context of the past. It counters a common presentist assumption that what happened had to happen—and it does so by directing attention to the roads not taken. And in an era concerned with cultural pluralism, history like the arts is valuable as an enlargement of human experience—as Bernard Bailyn recently put it, "a way of getting out of the boundaries of one's own life and culture and of seeing more of what human experience has been."[32]

But why should rhetoricians do history, especially when there is also a history department? There is real irony in the disciplinary purity implied in this question. Rhetoric and communication, often marginalized in the academy, have thrived in part because of their obvious connections to many other disciplines. As the walls separating disciplines are bridged, if not leveled, communication stands poised to offer a success story of truly multidisciplinary study. This is not the time to cannibalize ourselves by arguing that important parts of what we do are really the province of other disciplines. That is a slippery slope that will not stop with historical studies. Peter Ramus tried that 400 years ago and we have been living with the results since.

Having said that, though, there are indeed reasons that rhetoricians *especially* should study history. Their efforts will help to articulate the rhetorical climate of an age: how people defined the situation, what led them to seek to justify themselves or to persuade others, what storehouse of social knowledge they drew upon for their premises, what themes and styles they produced in their messages, how their processes of identification and confrontation succeeded or failed. It is precisely the commitment and training in rhetoric that sensitizes one to these dimensions of the rhetorical experience.

Rather than being defensive, scholars have good reason for optimism. Rhetorical history is a vibrant, multidimensional field. Good work is being done; it is even being published and recognized! As we do more, and as we do it better, we will achieve the goal of "the recovery of the historical-critical praxis."

2

The Rhetorical Construction of History

E. Culpepper Clark and Raymie E. McKerrow

"The whole idea of objective historical reality is naive."
—E. L. Doctorow

"The proposition that history is another form of fiction is almost as old as history itself." —M.-R. Trouillot[1]

Scholars of rhetoric have long been interested in the processes by which historians establish their claims. As an inherent outcome of that process, "revisionism" is proof of history's socially constructed meaning and its fluidity. Because history emerges from the world of ordinary language and its meanings are so observably negotiated, rhetoricians especially are interested in its lordly dominance of discourse. When invoked, its power is willingly conceded. If history does not in fact stand apart from its agents (historians and their communities) as an independent reality, people think it does and that is its currency. Even after scholarly reflection, the emperor still looks regal, despite transparent claims that he has no clothes.

Thus talk of history as fiction is conceptually interesting if empirically wide of the ontological mark. The phenomenon is made all the more intriguing when one considers the most influential twentieth-century accounts of U.S. history. High on that list, if not topping it, would be *Gone with the Wind*, followed closely by *Roots*, both works of fiction, although *Roots* did parade for a time under the rubric "faction" as if that were a distinction that made a difference. It is our position that history's grip is ontological, not in any *essentialist* way, or even as *weltanschauung*, but rather from an argumentative perspective. The way the discourse is constructed establishes its ontology. Because history is chronological, it is presumed to be causal even when flagrantly *post hoc ergo propter hoc*. Because its sense-making is also anthropological, it reveals similarities between past and present that are inherently parallel cases and, as a result, compelling. What follows is an elaboration of this view of history as argumentative discourse. In elaborating, we ask questions that deliberately separate history from its conventional reality in order better to understand its ontology and thereby its rhetorical force.

The epigrams about history and fiction that open this essay suggest such a separation, as well as two "truisms" about rhetoric's relationship to history—that *expressed* history is rhetoric and that, as a rhetorical construction, history is allied, albeit tenuously, with the fictive arts. If as Becker says, and we believe, "history is the memory of things said and done," then history emerges from the ephemera of recollection and establishes some order to memory.[2] It becomes not only what is remembered but how it is remembered. This obvious relevance of rhetoric to history has occupied the attention of numerous scholars, with renewed emphasis since Hayden White's *Metahistory* outlined the impact of tropological choice on the telling of history. Our purpose is not to review the positions taken by others but rather to establish the ontic relationship between rhetoric and history.

The more obvious relationships between rhetoric and history have been articulated variously as "the rhetoric *of* history," "rhetoric *and* history," and "rhetoric *as* history." Those who examine "the rhetoric *of* history" do so with the conviction that narrative form generally and stylistic choices specifically affect the content of historical knowledge. Historians, in this view, are active performers, employing rhetorical devices in the presentation of their views. More important, their stylistic choices *influence the constitution of the historical event itself* and in so doing affect its meaning. As Hayden White argues, the four major tropes—metaphor, metonymy, synecdoche, and irony—prefigure the manner in which history becomes knowledge, which is but another way of establishing the ontic relationship because these tropes are inherent to expression.[3] Although this perspective is an important one, and one we shall return to, its weakness lies in fostering a perception that rhetoric can be divorced from history, thereby making history the plaything of style and presentation.

The second perspective, "rhetoric *and* history," moves us in the direction of Michael Calvin McGee's observation that rhetoric is a "*force in history.*"[4] From this position, rhetoric moves from style or method to its role in the construction of social reality. The sense in which rhetoric participates in the construction of reality is readily understood. From rhetorical touchstones such as the Gettysburg Address to ideographs like equality, rhetoric is both intentional and instrumental in shaping history. But it is the third relationship, that of "rhetoric *as* history," that alters the focus to the ontological relationship between the past and its expression, that is, a narrative construction of memory.

History is the ultimate parallel case, a connection between past and present for the purpose of evaluating existing conditions and charting courses. It is, therefore, by its very nature an *argument*—a selective remembering to validate thought and action. Preachers, pundits, and politicians are chief among its panderers. ("History tells us," *they* say, and of course, it tells us what *they* want it to say: "Any nation that taxes its citizens more than a third of their wealth is one with the Roman Empire," or is it "Nineveh and Tyre," well, some such.) Nor are professional historians immune from constructing a usable past. As much as they appreciate and demonstrate differences between now and then (for it is the study of differences over time that makes history, chronologically speaking, history), they ultimately succumb to making the past usable, that is, with the emphasis, anthropologically speaking, on similarity or how history relates to present assumptions and knowledge about labor and capital and organization, which is, argumentatively speaking, a parallel case, the most seductive if most tenuous form of argument.

History and Fiction: The False Analogy

The purpose of history is to explain the present by connecting it to the past. It is used to confirm, justify, and occasionally modify behavior, but even as criticism, its ultimate aim is to affirm both collective identity and self-worth. In this respect, history is a "restorative art."[5] It seeks to make whole the fragmentation of our lives. This therapeutic effect is a universal motive and inclines all people to their personal and collective histories. That striving, through whatever medium and method employed, is an ontology. Whether synchronic or diachronic and whether expressed in the quasi scientism of empiricism or the more apparent relativism of literary narrative, history is inescapably a rhetorical re-presentation of the self or a community.[6]

Presentism does not make history as slippery as a barrel of eels. White himself demonstrates that a rhetorical conception of history does not open it to the excesses of relativism. History can be distinguished clearly from fiction:

As long as history was subordinated to rhetoric, the historical *field* itself (i.e., the past or the historical process) had to be viewed as a *chaos* that made no sense at all or one that could be made to bear as many senses as wit and rhetorical talent could impose upon it. Accordingly, the disciplining of historical thinking that had to be undertaken, if history considered as a kind of *knowledge* was to be established as arbitrator of the realism of contending political programs, each attended by its own philosophy of history, had to consist first of all in its de-rhetoricization.[7]

In the received view, fiction deals with imaginary happenings, whereas history deals with real events. Thus, in the naive sense of turn-of-the-century positivists, historians were passive transmitters of past accounts; they played a role similar to griots in Africa or ministers who merely "stand in" for God: the Word unaffected by the messenger. White provided the partial corrective by observing that "in point of fact, the narratives produced by historians lend themselves to analysis in terms of their rhetorical topoi."[8] In contrasting White's view of rhetoric as tropological to a broader perspective, and one that is classically grounded, Nancy Struever notes that "the discipline of history is argument." History not only considers "essentially contested concepts" but is itself "an essential contest."[9] Allen Megill and Donald McCloskey concur: "A work of history . . . does not derive chiefly from solitary illumination in the archives. . . . Histories can be read as orations."[10]

The claim that historians are rhetors in their own right buttresses the first of the three relationships (rhetoric of history) articulated earlier but does not go far enough to support the claim that history is itself a rhetorical construction, if not a fiction. Kenneth Burke's observation that the selection of a reality is simultaneously a deflection and a rejection applies as well to history as it does to criticism.[11] What gets "left out" in a historical reconstruction, however precise the methods used in deriving the data on which interpretation rests, influences the final creation. In a reworking of a prior claim, we propose that history "exists, in a material sense, in and through the language that constitutes it."[12]

Beyond being constituted in language, history is simultaneously a real and an invented account of what "happened." Its "realness" is assured in part through the process of investigation into events that are undeniable in their occurrence. The Holocaust happened. Atomic bombs were dropped on Hiroshima and Nagasaki. Clinton did win reelection to a second term as president. The archival landscape is littered with diaries, letters, and other documentary expressions of intent. These expressions constitute "facts" that, although they must be explained, are beyond reinvention. As Michel-Rolph Trouillot notes, "nowhere is history infinitely susceptible to invention."[13] But even in its facts, perhaps particularly in its facts, history is tendentious. How many people were martyred in the American South during the civil rights movement, beginning with the murder of Emmett Till on August 28, 1955, and ending thirteen years later with the assassination of Martin Luther King Jr. on April 4, 1968? If one answers forty, the most probable count, a hot debate will ensue. "Even if the count is validated by those sympathetic to the movement (Southern Poverty Law Center), it includes only the known dead," one might argue. "But even if the unknown are factored, the number still pales compared to those who died beyond Mason and Dixon's line in the three summers of urban rioting that began with Watts in Los Angeles and ended in Detroit, where forty-one alone died in that city's summer of discontent," another might say. And so on until partisans of the record negotiate a meaning to it all—or not.

But history's "realness" owes more to its ontological status than its method. History is something the past and present both insist upon. Its creation, as T. S. Eliot would have it, is "eternally present." Its god is the simultaneously forward- and backward-looking Janus. Each generation, each individual (unless pathological) strives to be remembered and remembered well. Diaries, records, and artifacts beg a favorable reading. History's actors require only that they be seen as well intentioned, interesting, and wise, perhaps even famous. The present has its own interest in reassembling the past. How were my forebears like me? How did their strivings resemble mine? What in their accomplishments confirm my sense of direction? These and a host of other questions help to determine the parallels between now and then and what those parallels portend for the future.

Viewed another way, history is a gigantic conversation between past and present. The participants in this conversation, aided by historians, griots, or one's favorite aunt *qua* culture-bearer, decide what is true or real.[14] They know the difference between fiction and history and have no difficulty in distinguishing. That the participants may be right or wrong as to facts and interpretations has nothing to do with the "realness" of their endeavor and what that endeavor is about. Being "right or wrong" is about history. It is not a question they would put to fiction, except in the "stranger-than-fiction" sense, which remains a license they would give a writer of fiction but would withhold from the historian. Put yet another way, fiction writers often (though not always) strain for verisimilitude. Historians must.

Although history in the vernacular is assumed to be "out there," an external reality, its inventional nature is also assumed in the same way people know *not* to believe the newspaper even as they believe it. To use Jean Howard's notion, history is always *partial* and *interested*—*partial* in the sense that it remains incomplete with respect to the reality it presumes to depict and *interested* in the sense that it is an interpretive rendering of the evidence.[15] The historian constructs an argument through the process of selection. Process is key in regarding history as a rhetorical construction: history is not the object of understanding but rather its process. To *objectify* history, to attempt a comprehension of the whole complex chain of causation or even to assume that such a comprehension is the ideal that governs the practice, is an impossibility that—were it attainable—would quickly void history of any meaning. As Claude Lévi-Strauss notes, "history is . . . never history, but history for. It is partial in the sense of being biased even when it claims not to be, for it inevitably remains partial—that is incomplete—this is itself a form of partiality."[16] The partiality of selection goes to perspectives as well as to facts. For example, one cannot write the history of slavery from all its perspectives—master, abolitionist, slave. One must instead argue for one or some combination but never from all. To argue that all perspectives have equal claim to the rectitude of historical evolution would be, in Lévi-Strauss's scheme, to rob American slavery of any meaning whatsoever, for American slavery "as commonly conceived" would never have taken place.

But do partiality and interest lead inexorably to fiction? The old line that fiction is about invention of scenes whereas history is about the collection and remembrance of past facts is, as we have seen, not tenable. Some novelists have made much of the intersection of fiction and history, claiming that their work operates from a historical base but takes liberty to create not "what happened" but "how what happened affected the soul of a nation or community." However, this blurring of lines between the two "disciplines" misses the point.[17] Although novelists may write fiction that captures the *soul* of a community in a manner not available to the historian, and although we may in turn read fiction to gain a better understanding of the past, this is not the same as suggesting that what the historian produces, constrained by claimants to the historical record, is also a rhetorical fiction. As Trouillot suggests, "the line between history and fiction is not independent, but contingent on situation . . . [and is] expressed concretely through the historically situated evaluation of specific narratives."[18] What is determined to be true (and false) of the soul of a community is not a product of an independently observed past; rather it is an integration of the past and present with respect to what is important, what counts, to those constructing the history for their own moment in time.

What fundamentally separates the historian from the novelist is the historian's determination to authenticate the record, to satisfy the audience that, in fact, what is said to have happened did indeed happen. White is correct in suggesting that the process is not random but based on rules of evidence.[19] But what White neglects to note is that the rules are not read into the record from the outside but are themselves rhetorically constructed conventions that have been given community sanction. Although sanctioned history may be obdurate and perdurable, there is nothing immutable about it. Apart from community assent or collective memory, it does not exist in an independent reality drawn on by the historian for the purpose of assuring a re-presentation (although, as noted earlier, that is its common conception and perforce its persuasion). Just as a rhetor uses argument and style to call into existence a "people" who never "are" in a permanent sense, the historian uses evidential rules and argumentation to recreate a past that never "was" in a true and complete sense, at least for those who lived it.[20]

In fact, historians often call into being a past that could never have known itself, at least in terms the present seeks to know it. It is one thing to select evidence from a diary in which an author has intentionally set forth conditions for its interpretation. It is quite another to assemble information and to ask questions of that evidence that go beyond the ken of those whose experience the history records. Bernard Bailyn provides an apt illustration in commenting on the difference between what he terms "manifest" and "latent" history. He notes that prior generations of historians studied evidence made manifest through the intentional act of writing letters, diaries, newspapers, and their like.[21] Historians today are less content to "find" manifest evidence and more intent on "discovering" evidence that has until recently been latent in such data pools as census questionnaires or slave-market records. They even put slaves and masters on the couch to explore psychological questions that would never have occurred to the original actors. By appropriating the methodologies of the social sciences in the process of discovery, historians assume even more the role of *rhetorical agents* as they invent ways to reconstruct history and thereby to argue its meaning.

History is thus incapable of being de-rhetoricized, for to do so is to strip history of its inventional nature. It is equally incapable of being seen in other than argumentative terms.

History and/as Rhetorical Argument

The acceptance of history as argumentative is Hobbesian: it sees the connection in terms similar to Richard Weaver's notion that rhetoric translates truth into prudentially palatable terms. As Gigliola Rossini notes, "to a rhetorical knowledge Hobbes opposed 'authentic' knowledge which was built upon a proper use of language provided by definitions of the meaning of words and of their order within speech."[22] In his analysis of Rankean historiography, Jörn Rüsen (1990) shows how the relationship has been carried forward: "Rhetoric is the use of language for strategic purposes, whereas scientific historiography uses language to articulate the results of empirical research. To put it simply: truth instead of tricks."[23] For Ranke, convincing argument followed method and thereby avoided fiction. Where history had been aimed at an audience, Ranke provided a history aimed at an empirically established truth. From this perspective, argumentative as well as literary forms were subordinate aids in the transmission of truth; they had no real role in its construction. The truth of history was external, approachable through sound method. In essence, if the historian had done the research task well, the rest followed as a matter of practice (much like Whately's advice to the rhetor on delivery: think about the subject first, presentation second).

A more contemporary example of the separation of history and argument is presented through the work of the *Annales* historians. In commenting on Braudel, Stuart Clark observes that "the principle that reality presupposes meaning remains for Braudel a critical weapon. He is not interested in applying it to those users of language (in its wider sense) whom we call historical agents. Their meanings are not regarded as being implicated in what is to count as reality for them. . . . Braudel's own realism therefore consists in a desire to show how the world *was* in times past, irrespective of how it was seen by those who lived in it."[24] Arguments are conditioned by the structures of social practices and not by the actions of persons. The assumption that people were aware of their own history as they lived it is not a critical factor. Thus history is to be found in indices that exist quite apart from the social construction of history that arises through contemporary discourse. The unintended, even the unimaginable, becomes as important if not more salient than the intended utterances and strivings of a time.

This disjunction may explain why Le Roy Ladurie, Braudel's successor, accepts the controversial conclusions in Robert Fogel and Stanley Engerman's study of slavery, rooted as they were in indices not apparent to those who constructed their lives within the peculiar institution. Fogel and Engerman's *Time on the Cross* paralleled the methods of the *Annales* historians in grounding historical claims in evidence pertinent to latter-day social scientists. As Ladurie argues:

The authors have demonstrated that slavery in North America was an extremely profitable system; that it was by no means moribund, regardless of what has been said, in the years preceding the Civil War. . . . The black slaves in the south were very efficient workers, often skilled, and able to tackle urban as well as rural tasks. They led a normal family life, which was not, in the great majority of cases, interrupted by individuals being sold away.[25]

But even Ladurie cannot suspend judgment. Perhaps in expiation for the structuralist conclusion, he declares the South's human relations to be "odiously backward" (although undoubtedly profitable to some) and cautions that "by carrying out this potentially dangerous demonstration, Fogel and Engerman did not intend to justify or rehabilitate in any sense the horrors of slavery."[26] If history were not inherently rhetorical in the sense of providing one reality at the expense of other possibilities, Ladurie's moral outrage would be unnecessary. By focusing on economics, Fogel and Engerman, as well as Ladurie, overlook other possible meanings/realities. In a commonsense reaction to Fogel and Engerman's work, J. H. Plumb expressed the limitations of cliometrics: "Historians ought to be sufficiently well trained to beware of books which fly in the face of human reality, no matter how festooned with arithmetic."[27]

Are there other possibilities, even given the data Fogel and Engerman provide? In fact, had Fogel and Engerman drawn different conclusions from the data, their rebuke would have been less severe, as the data supported inferences far more critical of the institution of slavery than they were willing to draw. For example, the authors acknowledge a psychological dimension to slavery not addressed in their method and yet proceed to reach conclusions that demand psychological answers. This can best be seen in returning to the conclusion (Fogel and Engerman's seventh of ten such conclusions) Ladurie referred to above: "The belief that slave-breeding, sexual exploitation, and promiscuity destroyed the black family is a myth. The family was the basic unit of social organization under slavery. It was to the economic interest of the planters to encourage the stability of the slave families and most of them did so. Most slave sales were either of whole families or of individuals who were at an age when it would have been normal for them to have left the family."[28] This is perhaps a startling conclusion until one realizes, first, that few historians have denied the importance of family in slavery—indeed the very importance of family is what transformed any threat to its well-being into an unconscionable act—and, second, that the master class need destroy but one family to prove their right and power to accomplish such destruction and to induce the terrible prospect among all slaves. The statistical improbability of a nightmare does not lessen its grip the morning after.

Thus Fogel and Engerman flew in the face of a human reality expressed in a historical tradition. They got at the tangible, cognitive levels of the South's peculiar institution but lost the intangibles that gave the institution meaning, meaning that was fully debated and articulated at the moments of interest to Fogel and Engerman. They did not conform to the sense-making imperatives that move from out of the past to shape the present and from out of the present to shape the past. In Ladurie's case, the presumption that a slave's life is "normal" is a value judgment that contaminates the very "purity" of the statistical methodology used to calculate economic conditions. In the process of doing history, and in commenting on its "object," Fogel and Engerman, as well as Ladurie, allowed a method for objectifying history to substitute for the mediating function of rhetorical argument.

History need not function separate from the argument that contains it. As Thomas Farrell suggests, "arguments develop their meaning in history."[29] The import of this relationship is that history and argument are inextricably linked. One cannot argue in the present without a sense of history being implicated in the "meaning" of the argument. Similarly, one cannot formulate a history without simultaneously creating an argument that a particular interpretation is merited.

There is, however, a special sense in which historical argument functions. It should be clear by now that the warrant in historical argument is not the kind of connector one finds in tightly conceived relationships between types of arguments and positions or in formal rules of inference. Although a particular argument form may be used by a philosophical perspective or by a "field," the perceived relationship is one of convenience rather than necessity. In particular, Weaver's claim that one can identify a person's politics by the argument form selected is "not only vague, but also wrong."[30] The form of argument selected, as in the case of a tropological argument, will have significant effects on the kind of reality depicted. In turn, the selection of social themes or oppositions will call to mind one argument form rather than another as "best suited" for the process of laying out one's thought. For example, Bruce Gronbeck illustrates that "synechdochal argument is the perfect way for a Namierite to argue, because its focus upon the part-whole relationship is reflected in Namier's focus in the individual-institution relation in society."[31]

Nor does the warrant function in a protological fashion. As White observes, "not logic, then; and not 'free poetry'" underwrites the argument process because "neither can serve as the organon or fashioning principle of historical discourse." But rather a combination of the historian's "'experience' and the 'sense of reality'" acts as the warranting principle.[32] The warrant in this instance is not content free, not simply an inferential rule of connection. Its content is the (ommon fund of human experience. The appeal is to the common sense of experience, and it occurs at that point wherein the historian becomes so suffused in the data or signs of thought as to make the historical action sufficiently intelligible. If the historian cannot rethink the given action in Robin G. Collingwood's sense (as apparently Fogel and Engerman could not), no explanation serves as ground for further inquiry. If the historian can link thought to action in an argument that is coherent on its face, there is no need for further explanation. The action to be explained is individuated and specific, and it must be approached from the inside (the thought content of the action), not from the outside (some universal principle of generalization that validates the interpretation as "real" for all time).

Common sense as historical warrant

Rex Martin links two passages in Collingwood's earlier work, *The Idea of History*, to explain this critical notion:

"For history, the object to be discovered is not the mere event, but the thought expressed in it. To discover that thought is already to understand it [i.e., the event]. After the historian has ascertained the facts, there is no further process of inquiring into their causes. When he [*sic*] knows what happened, he already knows why it happened" [IH, 214]. The exact meaning of this passage has been widely disputed but when it is read in conjunction with another, less cited passage, Collingwood's point becomes . . . unmistakable. "There is no such thing as the supposed further stage of . . . scientific history which discovers their causes or laws or in general explains them, because an historical fact once genuinely ascertained, grasped by the historian's re-enactment of the agent's thought in his mind, is already explained" [IH, 176–177].[33]

Thus, what takes place in the historian's mind—linking thought to action, making sense of the historical record in light of present understanding—is critical to the process of constructing history. But the question remains of how the historian communicates this understanding to the common reader.

As Jacques Barzun observes, "[the reader's] understanding, his [*sic*] sense that something has been explained, derives entirely from what William James called the 'sentiment of rationality,' the impression that familiar and unfamiliar elements have been put into intelligible relation by someone who gives tokens of trustworthiness. That is intelligible to him which he finds sufficiently congruent with experience (direct or vicarious) to make him accept the neighboring strangeness and integrate it into a new imaginative experience."[34] The mode of arguing that is most adept at displaying this "imaginative experience" through rhetorical topoi is that of *narratio*, literally, the recitation of "facts" drawn from the historian's understanding of the past. It is through narrative, with its attendant stylistic devices drawn from rhetoric, that the coherence between thought and action is established. It is through narrative that data are patterned to yield claims that make sense in terms of experience. As Trouillot suggests, "what history is changes with time and place or, better said, history reveals itself only through the production of specific narratives. What matters most are the process and conditions of production of such narratives."[35]

As narratives are produced, the method for establishing the narrative will always yield a certain ambiguity. Nothing is ever decided once and for all. History, once written, is not immune to time. Consequently, the language of the historian is closer to that of the raconteur than to the social scientist. Knowing what to leave out and how to pattern a story is the only way to create that sense of "constructed reality" to be read by another as "a history" of our past. This does not mean that historians cannot make use of empirical data or that they need not rigorously investigate the historical record. Rather, it is to suggest that, ultimately, the rhetorical voice is of a different register—it is tuned to a different sense of rhythm and timing than is that of the social scientist. Both history and social science use each other in their respective realms; they are, as Barzun points out, "preliminary to each other."[36]

Doing Rhetorical History

The relationship we have advanced focuses on the role of argument and narrative in the construction of history. What this relationship implies is perhaps shown best in contrast to an "objective" sense of history: "The idea of thought or philosophy as edification and rhetoric is attractive, but ultimately it cannot advance the human quest for improving the quality of personal and social life. That requires knowledge of the real natural and social contexts of action and consciousness, knowledge that is ultimately persuasive because it allows scientific interventions from non-scientific motives."[37] As Edgar Doctorow's observation at the outset of this essay indicates, the perspective we have taken directly opposes a view of history as the depiction of an objective, scientifically assured reality. Within the context of the ontic relationship we have sought to establish, rhetorical history may be articulated in a sense that recognizes the role of language in the construction of history, as well as in a sense that positions one to use history as an impetus to social change.

But recognizing the role of language is not in itself sufficient to create the kind of rhetorical history we are advocating. That there has been a "linguistic turn" in the doing of history is not in doubt. In this turn, the focus is on the centrality of language in the "reading of texts" and in the writing of history.[38] In Dominick Lacapra's words, "a different understanding of intellectual history as a history of texts may permit a more cogent formulation of problems broached by established approaches and a more mutually informative interchange with the type of social history that relates discourse and institutions."[39] What is intended, as noted by Carole Blair and Mary Kahl, is history conceived as a conversation with the past.[40]

The focus on language in this narrow "textual" sense is evident in historical studies of conceptual change.[41] Although amenable to a conception of history as rhetorical/argumentative, these studies do not go as far as critical rhetorical theory in underscoring the sense in which language constitutes reality in the present and provides an avenue for the critique of freedom. Strictly speaking, conceptual historians do not focus directly on "argument" per se; rather, the relationship must be read into their analyses. This tendency can be seen in Quentin Skinner's observation that one must gain a sense of what "the writer may have meant by arguing in the precise way he [sic] argued."[42] Although an understanding of historical argument is presupposed in this context, it nonetheless remains at the level of what Richard Rorty terms "historical reconstruction."[43] It does not extend beyond this sense to one in which the argument constitutes a given reality or alters a preexisting one. The conceptual historian's sense of historiography sees language as having a function but resists the notion that argument can go beyond explanation to critique. As a further example, Terence Ball suggests that "the task of a critical conceptual historian is to chart changes in the concepts constituting the discourses of political agents living and dead."[44] Ball's project considers language to be an objective property of reality; the analysis proceeds on the assumption that language will give access to "what really happened" as the changes in key concepts altered the options available to agents of change. This narrow sense of historical construction can only be seen as rhetorical by accident rather than by design.

On the other hand, doing rhetorical history as we envision the process can be exemplified in the following statement: "Key to this way of thinking about the rhetorical tradition, then, is the conception of discourse as an instrument of power—a conception that makes possible an investigation of the ways in which language, used in the service of power, forms human subjectivity. . . . The historian is always called upon to discern how rhetoric shaped or was shaped by concrete sociopolitical relations and, thereby, to determine rhetoric's complicity with dominating groups."[45] Discourse does not simply

limitations of conceptual histories

express positions of political actors but is *force* in its own right. Rhetorical argument functions, in this context, to promote or displace power relations within and among people.

Conclusion

Through rhetoric, history is created anew in the process of each revision. Our understanding of the past depends on the historian's selection of a mediated reality and the further mediation of that reality through a narrative that bespeaks its "presence" in our own time. The argument that is presented via the narrative is always partial and interested, never complete or indifferent. In this context, history is best understood as the process of understanding, never its object. Its method is the recitation of data provided by actors interested in the historical record. It is that interest of actors that establishes the ontic relationship between rhetoric and its construction of history as a narrative told—only to be retold anew in a future that year by year recedes before us.

3

The Rhetorics of the Past

History, Argument, and Collective Memory

Bruce E. Gronbeck

Within the western tradition of rhetorical speculation, history writing as a discursive practice became problematized in the eighteenth century. Especially in the British rhetorical tradition, in the lectures on rhetoric offered by Adam Smith, Joseph Priestley, and Hugh Blair, analysis of the rhetorical dimensions of narrative discourse focused on the writing of history.[1] Although these theorists thought that accurate description of the past was the central mission of historians, Adam Smith, as the first British rhetorician to write extensively about history, recognized that some historians practiced what he called an "oratorical method"; he found that both classical and contemporaneous historians used discussions of consequences and implications of actions in the past to deliver moral and political lessons to their audiences. So Thucydides was said to have written the history of the Peloponnesian War so that "posterity may learn how to produce the like events or shun others."[2] The social visions and moral uplift of Herodotus, Tacitus, and Livy also impressed Smith (Lec. 19, 101–6 passim). Likewise, Hugh Blair, recognizing that "Truth, Impartiality, Fidelity, and Accuracy, are the fundamental qualities of an Historian," nonetheless considered that "wisdom is the great end of History. It is designed to supply the want of experience. . . . Its object is, to enlarge our views of the human character, and to give full exercise to our judgment on human affairs."[3]

I will not chart the twists and turns in the rhetorical history of history from this point. Others have done that far better than I can.[4]

I mean to suggest only that the rhetorical study of history as something more than reports of the past has occupied the attention of significant theorists for a quarter of a millennium. The rhetoric of history writing has been developed into a thriving specialty, especially since the demise or at least serious illness of scientific history.[5]

More particularly, my purpose here is to compare various relationships between rhetoric and the past. Rather than merely extend the eighteenth-century rhetorical theorists' discussion of the rhetoric of history writing, I want us to open our vision somewhat wider to examine two other sorts of relationships between rhetoric and the past: the rhetorical use of the past in the construction especially of political arguments and the rhetorical evocation of the past, in particular, of what is now talked about as collective memory. Thus, I wish to discuss rhetoric and history, argument, and collective memory. Before proceeding with that task, I first should review some background assumptions that will frame our thinking about the past and its relationships to rhetoric, history, and memory. Then we can contrast three sorts of historically relevant types of discourse and conclude with some ideas for future studies that I think will enrich rhetorical thought.

The Past, Memory, History, and Rhetoric. This essay is predicated on the following assumptions:

1. *The past is inaccessible and even unknowable.* If we take the past to comprise all that has happened to everyone at every time and every place before now, the past is inaccessible. We have no access to the past as such, only to documentary, iconic, and recollected traces of those happenings. Human activity is ephemeral; it can be remembered but not relived. It also is unknowable. To be sure, you can "know" what you yourself can remember of events and even can read or see what others think they have experienced or remembered, but such knowledge is always partial, usually self-centered and even self-interested, and subject to the vagaries of surviving documentation. Thus, when Julius Caesar accidently burned the great library of Alexandria, we were deprived of information key to the reconstruction of the intellectual life of the Mediterranean from a formative period of Western civilization. Great segments of the past became inaccessible and unknowable, as were all those aspects of the Euro-African past never recorded at all.

2. *History is a discursive practice, a discourse about the past.* History is not to be confused with the past, for history is a collection of stories and arguments about some set of events from before.[6] The reason that Adam Smith and other eighteenth-century rhetoricians began to write about history was that they understood that history is talking about, rather than merely chronicling, the past.

48 / Bruce E. Gronbeck

3. *History is a bivocal discursive practice, one that is both narrative and argumentative in voice and social understanding.* Most history is an argumentatively formed narrative—simultaneously a story and an interpretive or realistic argument about the past. Being both argument and narrative gives history what J. H. Hexter called the *he he !* rank and file problem: how can a dual-genred discourse be composed and evaluated? The answer is as a rhetorical undertaking.[7]

4. *The professionalization of history has created gaps between academic historians' and public readers' versions of the past.* Michael Janas recounts the growing professionalization of historians across the nineteenth and twentieth centuries.[8] As academic historians—like the rest of the professoriate—gradually defined their intellectual enterprises in increasingly arcane and specialized ways, usually in terms of schools of history (political, economic, social history) and in terms of method (documentary, testimonial, oral, and self-reflexive methods), they began to produce a discourse composed primarily for other academicians. Popular histories—the books your mother and mine ordered from the book club or checked out of the local library—have come to have almost no connection whatsoever with academic histories.[9] Academic and popular histories represent clearly separable discursive practices.

5. *The past, moreover, is more than merely of historical interest; its importance to social, political, moral, and economic analyses of problems and their presumed alleviation is undeniable.* That is, the past is not the possession of historians, for they occupy but one demographic category of human being with claims to understand and possess portions of the past. Just as the past should not be confused with history, so should the past be understood broadly as a resource for human beings of many different stripes and many different purposes. The past ought to be thought of as prologue for varied social dramas: political deliberation over future action, economic controversy over what indicators of supply affect what indexes of demand, myths of origin that ground the religious dogma and the collective identity of a people, and repository of the neuroses and psychoses that affect us individually and collectively. Even Freudian psychotherapy is founded on reconstructing the past. The past is in eminent domain, a set of life experiences open to everyone with an ax to grind or a Gordian knot to cut. The past may not be knowable or accessible, but it is pragmatically utile.[10]

6. *And, therefore, multiple rhetorics of the past have been practiced by various groups of advocates.* The past can be endlessly argued over and argued with. It can itself be a battleground or it can be raided, rebuilt, and perverted for any number of human purposes. In the form of traditions, the past appears to make direct demands on

our hearts and minds; yet those same traditions can be sites of struggle for contemporary social-political supremacy, as when the citizens of Georgia fight over the symbolic meanings attached to the Confederate battle flag and its place in Georgia's state flag of today.[11]

That last assumption brings us to the topic at hand. I wish to offer for contemplation three rhetorics of the past. *Rhetoric* will be understood with Donald Bryant as "the rationale of the informative and suasory in discourse,"[12] which is to say the underlying, self-interested purposes for which public discourses are constructed, purposes focused on controlling and structuring information and the valuative mindsets that form the bases of others' thoughts and actions. For this essay, rhetoric is to be envisioned, therefore, as a rationale of—that is, a justification for and an account of—the ways particular kinds of public discourse are built by one group of human beings to influence the beliefs, attitudes, values, and behaviors of other groups. More particularly, three rationales for ways the past is mined, shaped, and used to persuade audiences to alter their understandings of and activity in their life-worlds are examined in this essay.

Those three rationales for persuasive discourses working with and through the past can be called rhetorics of history, argument, and collective memory.

The Rhetoric of History

Rhetoricians, especially, have attempted for some time to understand what kind of discursive practice historians engage in. That practice, as noted, is simultaneously narrative and argumentative, concerned with what Spengler identified as *nacheinanderung* (one-after-anotherness) and *nebeneinanderung* (relationships between simultaneous events).[13]

The rhetorical problem central to historical discourse, I would suggest, is the search for ways to bridge historical narratives and interpretive arguments. Can the story being told from traces of the past be made to seem like a transparent look at the past? Can historical discourse be so constructed that its arguments, its interpretations of that past, appear to flow naturally from its story? That sense of naturalization, for Hayden White, is created through the rhetorical construction of context. Says White: "The informing presupposition of contextualism is that events can be explained by being set within the 'context' of their occurrence. Why they occurred as they did is explained by the revelation of the specific relationships they bore to other events occurring in the circumambiant historical space. . . . The Contextualist insists that 'what happened' in the field can be accounted for by the specification of the functional interrelationships existing among the agents and agencies occupying the field at a given time."[14]

How are such contexts constructed? Let me review two of the many rhetorical techniques that are regularly employed by historians:

Bracketing. A key opening move for any historian involves framing the period that is about to be interpreted, for such framing sets out the domain of the writer—the bracketed segments of time and space that will be turned into historical discourse.[15] Let me offer some examples from histories of eighteenth-century England. The great nineteenth-century historian, William E. H. Lecky (1839–1903), for example, set his overall brackets at 1688–89, the period of the Glorious Revolution that drove the Stuarts off the throne, and at 1832, the year of the First Reform Bill that redistributed some parliamentary seats to give cities more representation. He then divided that era into two parts, 1688–89 to 1760, which he assigned to the ascendency of the Whigs, and 1760 to 1832, which he thought was contextualized by the Tory ascendency. Never mind that the Tory party had disintegrated; Lecky knew who the Tories were. This splitting of the frame in his eight-volume history of England (1925) allowed Lecky to construct a narrative about progressive democratization in the first half of the century, about frustrated democracy under George III, and about the triumph of middle-class democracy in the 1832 Reform Bill. The temporal brackets he set worked well to emphasize popular party politics and to project a moral sense of frustrated then triumphant democratic consciousness.[16]

Lecky was a historian who believed that the world had never "seen a better Constitution than England enjoyed between the Reform Bill of 1832 and the Reform Bill of 1867."[17] During that third of a century, he saw Great Britain governed with power in the hands of the upper middle class, "not the class most susceptible to new ideas or most prone to great enterprises, but [one] distinguished beyond all others for its political independence, its caution, its solid practical intelligence, its steady industry, its high moral average."[18] His history of eighteenth-century England, therefore, was framed so as to provide maximum evidence for that judgment.

Causal connections between context and events. A second rhetorical art needed by historians is the ability to make a particular context seem necessary and sufficient to account for the events from the past under scrutiny.[19] So, for example, one can do a political, an economic, a social, or even a rhetorical history of the American Revolution.[20] The political history would focus on the rise of a Yankee political mentality, putting emphasis on both the disintegration of party politics in England after the Seven Years' War and the popular-political force of the Stamp Act, the Townshend Duties, the Quartering Act, and the like. Such a history would almost have to deal with the re-conceptualization of politics that was required to rationalize and legitimate revolutionary political acts. An economic history likely would begin with the Sugar and Molasses Acts, passed by Great Britain as revenue bills but interpreted in the colonies as interference with trade; review the growing independence of the colonies in terms of trade, manufacturing, and fiscal policies; and even depict the course of the war as being strongly affected by the British gentry's refusal to grant the increasing internal taxes needed to pursue a distant and expensive conflict. A social history would document the change in collective identity, as has Richard Bushman's history of the shift from Puritan to Yankee self-conceptions in Connecticut.[21] A rhetorical history of the war would focus, of course, on the narrative and argumentative discourses that reframed the American vision and motivated a people to risk all in the name of independence.

The point here is that a <u>particular context is both a way of looking</u> <u>and a mechanism for coherence</u>. As Kellner notes, "[Historical] narrative exists to make continuous what is discontinuous; it covers the gaps in time, in action, in documentation, even when it points to them."[22] Key to narrativization is the casting of a context that frames the historical enterprise generally and seemingly identifies and organizes a series of past events so that they can be narrativized, that is, bound together into a story. In turn, the events so organized become, often transparently, evidence that can reinforce the utility of the context itself as a way to understand and account for human affairs; social histories, especially, in that they are contraposed to traditional perspectives, often use our interest in their subject matter as evidence for the importance of such studies. Thus Marxist historian E. P. Thompson argues that eighteenth-century English society must be approached as a paternal rather than a political entity, as a site of a hegemonic relationship he calls a "paternalism-deference equilibrium,"[23] because it shows us the actual mechanisms rather than merely the structure of political power. By the end of that essay—and certainly in his earlier book—Thompson urges that social politics rather than institutional politics are at the center of English history. He argues that the power of his perspective is seen in the lives of

the poor stockinger, the Luddite cropper, the "obsolete" hand-loom weaver, the "utopian" artisan, and even the deluded follower of Joanna Southcott. . . . Their crafts and traditions may have been dying. Their hostility to the new industrialism may have been backwardlooking. Their communitarian ideals may have been fantasies. Their insurrectionary conspiracies may have been foolhardy. But they lived through these times of acute social disturbance, and we did not. . . . In some of the lost causes of the people of the Industrial Revolution we may discover insights into social evils which we have yet to cure.[24]

Thus Thompson uses the minibiographies that constitute much of his book, *The Making of the English Working Class*, as testament to the utility of social history generally.[25]

As well, of course, the events of the past, once positioned in a narrative, can be used to argue outside the narrative itself as evidence for some social or moral lesson. Thompson said as much in the last sentence of the above excerpt. In addition, in volume five of his history of eighteenth-century England, Lecky stops for four pages to examine the "qualities of mind and character which in modern societies have proved most successful in political life."[26] Indeed, Lecky constantly generalizes and intellectualizes the events of eighteenth-century British politics, rehearsing abstract philosophical positions, moral codes, oratorical flourishes, expressions of legal doctrines, and even literary culture that influenced the course of the past and, as well, serve as social-political-legal lessons for other times. The temptation to be a historicist—a person who believes in the cycles or regular rhythms in human experience through time—is strong; the fantasy of being able to recycle others' lives as guides to our own sociodramas has many adherents in most societies.

We will go no further with this idea for now because it becomes the point at which the discourses of professional historians impinge upon the discourses of social decision makers and reformers, whose use of the past will occupy us shortly. So, consider where we are conceptually. We have examined rhetorical techniques essential to the historian's discursive activity. Yet, framing and establishing causal connections between contexts and events are but two pieces of rhetorical artillery in the armory of the historian. Other weapons are there: a variety of argumentative forms,[27] multiple ways to test evidence, stylistic devices that caulk the fissures in narrative and argumentative structures, and even battles over the credibility of historians themselves.[28] More remains to be done to outline the strategic dimensions of the rhetoric of history.

Consider one last characteristic of the rhetoric of history: *it is a constructionist activity* in the strong sense of that term. In history, the past is constructed into narratives and arguments about the significance of those narratives. Especially in the book-length history, there is often a feeling even that a "Great Story," a unified and totalizing story about the "Great Past" understood as all worth knowing from that past, has been related.[29] Among popular histories, certainly

William Shirer's *The Rise and Fall of the Third Reich* is such a work; a presidential biography such as McCullough's treatment of Truman promises to be such a work as well.[30]

These works are thoroughly constructionist in their force in that a vision or understanding of the past is built in such a way as to suggest the completeness and adequacy of the project. Creating a sense of thoroughness and satiation, plenitude and satisfaction, is the product of a constructionist rhetoric.

Arguments From the Past

A second kind of rhetoric of the past does more than construct a history. It depends explicitly on the appropriation of the past for presentist purposes. Such a rhetoric of the past is seen in the legal use of precedents to guide judicial decision making, a mother's admonition to her child not to climb too high in a tree because of what happened the last time the child did, Freudian psychoanalytic histories that are used to guide therapy,[31] and legislative debates that turn on discussions of the founding fathers or a rehearsal of earlier legislation. In each of these cases, the past is not being reconstructed around the truth conditions that propel the professional historian's culling of the past for significant information;[32] rather, the past is used explicitly for guidance of present-day concerns or problems.

I have already published a paper on this subject in the 1991 Alta proceedings,[33] so I will do less with concrete examples. There I argued that public deliberations often appropriate the past in two ways. One form is the genetic argument, the argument that runs some concept, idea, pattern of activity, or valuative commitment to an originary moment in time and place. That originary moment then can be posited as a beginning, with the present time and the decision some individual or group faces as a significant point in a story that reaches from that origin until now.

To take a simple example, it makes a great deal of difference whether Americans posit the seventeenth-century British religious dissenters or the eighteenth-century revolutionary colonists as originary models. Is the essence of Americanism to be found in the political theocracy of the Puritans, where individual initiative, unquestioned commitment to values entailing particular personal and social responsibilities, and localist cultural standards dominate the social system? Or is Americanism rather grounded on the revolutionary principles, the Yankee mentality, where liberty is understood in both individual and collective contexts, equality is coequal with liberty as a central value, commerce is understood in terms of exchanges or transactions where both parties gain value, and collective civic rather than religious principles reign supreme? America's present-day conservative and liberal visions are, in many of their manifestations, based on these competing originary moments.

More specifically, genetic arguments from the past seem to work in two ways: either (1) an advocate can rely on our general belief in progressivism to argue that action today will advance some aspect of life along a course we can see stretching from the past to the present to the future, or (2) a rhetor can return to the originary moment of some part of civic life to essentialize it, asking for a recommitment to a presumably primal but presently ignored value or mindset. Martin Luther King Jr.'s "I Have a Dream" speech of 1963 captures the progressivist version of the argument nicely. King structured the speech around a movement from 1863's Emancipation Proclamation to the 1963 March on Washington into a dream of a future of racial harmony, civic equality, and universal brotherhood.[34] James Hanson's analysis of the *Communist Manifesto* suggests that Marx and Engels offered a genetic argument of the second sort when they posited an edenic state, one existing prior to feudal class divisions and industrialized capitalism, when collective ownership centered social relations. The moral imperative of the communist movement, in this view, is then a return to earlier values and structures—much more a rebirth than a radical revolution.[35]

The other form of argument from the past that appears regularly in social-political controversy is the analogical argument. As Mandelbaum notes, "Explanations that rest on subsuming a particular case under previously familiar types of cases are to be found in all aspects of life," including public deliberation.[36] Meteorologists use historical data to build laws associating climatological causes with climatological effects; children are reminded how angry father gets when they scream too loudly before supper; and the grayest beard on the Senate Agriculture Committee inevitably will tell a story about a past change in agricultural policy that produced an ugly outcome, thus seeking to suppress a change in policy today.[37]

The idea of analogical argument references a whole family of arguments that assert important similar or dissimilar relationships between two or more persons, places, things, or events in order to support a disputable proposition. What have been called arguments from parallel case[38] and arguments from reciprocity[39] also fall into this family of rhetorical weapons. David Zarefsky's analysis of similarities between the nineteenth-century slavery debate and the twentieth-century abortion debate illustrates the analogical argument from the past. The similarities in situation, motivation, ideological orientations, and projected outcomes between discussion of the Dred Scott decision and the controversy focusing on the nullification of *Roe v. Wade* show the persuasiveness of arguments from the past to guide present-day controversy.[40]

In this second kind of rhetoric of the past, therefore, the past is not so much constructed—though of course it really is—as it is appropriated, made into something useful for today, into a tool to solve some problem or block some proposal. The past can be hammered into stories that promise glory or shame, ease or difficulty, glorification or eternal damnation as we relive it again today.[41] Historian A. L. Rowse has suggested that "there is no one rhythm or plot in history; but there are rhythms, plots, patterns, even repetitions. So that it is possible to make generalizations and to draw lessons."[42] It is that historicist understanding of the unfolding of collective life that makes genetic and analogical arguments from the past so compelling in human affairs.

The Rhetoric of Collective Memory

We come, finally, to a third kind of rhetoric from the past—the rhetoric of collective memory. This sort of rhetoric is quite similar to the arguments from the past just discussed; the rhetoric of collective memory also works by building symbolic bridges between today and yesterday. The difference is that the primary movement is not from the past to the present but the other way around. A society's collective memory is regularly reshaped by today's interpreters so as to make it more useful in the present.

The concept of "collective memory" resists easy delineation. A collective memory belongs not to an individual or the presumably continuous record constructed in histories but rather to a family, group, or larger social unit that attaches special meanings to particular events from the past. It often comprises moral stories—social and political myths, fables, fairy tales, and what Aristotle called reminiscences, that is, special events imbued with socially charged significance.[43] Social memory is a collectivized discourse; it is the construction of no single rhetor, but, as Lévi-Strauss remarked about myth, it is built by everyone who recounts a socially advisory or constraining story about the past.[44] It is less argumentatively than exhortatively formed; the moral of the story is its *raison d'etre*. The collective memory is recalled, seemingly, so as to let the past guide the present, but it can do so only when the past itself is remade. In the words of the author of the first book on collective memory, Maurice Halbwachs: "If, as we believe, collective memory is essentially a reconstruction of the past, if it adapts the image of ancient facts to the beliefs and spiritual needs of the present, then a knowledge of the origin of these facts must be secondary, if not altogether useless, for the reality of the past is no longer *in* the past."[45]

About the same time, George Herbert Mead observed that "a person has to bring up a certain portion of the past to determine what his [*sic*] present is, and in the same way the community wants to bring up the past so it can state the present situation and bring out what the actual issues themselves are."[46] In a somewhat more cynical mood, Mead also noted that "The past which we construct from the standpoint of the new problem of today is based upon continuities which we discover in that which has arisen, and it serves us until the rising novelty of tomorrow necessitates a new history."[47]

Rhetorically, what we are discussing is a species of epideictic, of commemorative discourse. In commemorative discourse the past is not simply constructed or appropriated, as in the other rhetorics of the past, though of course construction and appropriation are in fact occurring. Additionally, in such discourse the past is evoked. Some present need or concern is examined by calling up a past, shaping it into a useful memory that an audience can find relevant to the present. The past thus can guide the present, but the present also is reconfiguring the past; therefore, through evocation of collective memories, past and present live in constant dialogue, even in a hermeneutic circle where neither can be comprehended without the other.

Robert Penn Warren noted that "to be an American is not . . . a matter of blood; it is a matter of an idea—and history is the image of that idea."[48] That notion is nowhere better illustrated than in Michael Kammen's visionary *Mystic Chords of Memory: The Transformation of Tradition in American Culture.* Kammen divides an American history wherein collective memory becomes important and disputable into four periods: pre-1870, 1870 to 1915, 1915 to 1945, and 1945 to 1990. He then examines the struggles over memory between those who saw the past as important vs. those who repudiated its burdens; between the rise of a modernist vision wherein immigrants and others had to accommodate themselves to a civic religion and national culture vs. the counter of localist or regional traditions that resisted the homogenizing effects of nationalized collective memory; and between active contestants attempting to remake the collective memory, as in the 1960s, vs. reconciliators who often induced amnesia and thus silenced voices from the past. The rhetoricity of these processes Kammen suggests with these words: "Public memory, which contains a slowly shifting configuration of traditions, is ideologically important because it shapes a nation's ethos and sense of identity. That explains, at least in part, why memory is always selective and is so often contested."[49]

Kammen's project is monumental. A more focused study of the operation of collective memory is Schwartz, Zerubavel, and Barnett's examination of the curious recovery of the story of Masada with the rise of Zionism in the early twentieth century. As the Palestinian Jews were taking root following the post–World War I Balfour Declaration, the Zionist community faced a series of frustrations: immigration quotas, anti-Semitism, Arab resistance, broken families, and a hostile land. The dialectic of hope and despair, excitement and nostalgia, optimism and disillusions is captured in Yitzhak Lamdan's 1927 poem, "Masada." Rather than retelling the story of the battle of Masada, in which a remnant of Jewish resistance in A.D. 73 turned to suicide rather than surrender to Titus's Roman army, Lamdan's poem is a rumination that considers the present in terms of the past. An early canto affirms the confidence Masada gives the settlers:

> Then the dance of Masada is heard in the ears of the world!
> A chant for the dance of the solution: "let the 'no' to Fate dare!"
> Bolster the leg, strengthen the knee, round and round increasingly!
> Ascend, chain of the dance! Never again shall Masada fall!

A later canto documents the suicides that were common among despondent settlers in Palestine:

> Dumbly do my steps lead me to the wall, dumbly as all steps
>   in which fear of the future is moulded . . .
> High, high is the wall of Masada, therefore does the ravine that
>   crouches at its feet go deep . . .
> And should this voice have cheated me—then would I cast myself from the heights of the wall into the ravine that there be
>   no record of the remnant, and nothing remain![50]

In Lamdan's poem "Masada," Schwartz, Zerubavel, and Barnett suggest, we find an allegorical relationship between the inhabitants of the ancient mountain fortress and twentieth-century Palestine. I would go further: in the poem, Masada and the Jewish settlements are merged, each read and understood through the other. The mixture of defiant hope and bleak despair that characterized both the historical reconstruction of Masada and the exercise in carving out a new nation allowed Masada to be understood through the settlements and the settlements to be epitomized by the recounting of triumphant suicide.

The rhetoric of collective memory, therefore, as I noted earlier, is a special kind of commemoration—an evoking of a past to frame a present but also to conform that past to the present. It is a discourse of absolute identification—an interpenetration of then and now wherein the hermeneutic circle spins in exceedingly small rotations.

Some Final Thoughts

In writing her innovative *The Art of Memory* in 1966, Frances Yates found the subject "curiously neglected."[51] She would never open a similar book in the same way today. Stirring the idea of memory into the mix of a classic trio of terms—rhetoric, argument, and history—has enriched the study of discursive constructions of past and present in exciting ways. Fred Reynolds's new anthology on rhetorical memory testifies to the subject's currency.[52]

The three rhetorics of the past each work with and through memory in different ways. The historian constructs the past; the disputant appropriates it; and the commemorator evokes it. All three rhetorics discursively bridge past and present, though via different rhetorical techniques. Historians set brackets and articulate causal connections between contexts and events in order to naturalize or make coherent the stories and interpretations they are offering. Disputants seek out genetic and analogical arguments that give the past a measure of control over the present and future. And commemorators evoke a past so as to let the present shape it into a memory capable of being annealed with now, thereby accounting for the life-world and collapsing old and new identities.

These comments should be taken as preliminary thoughts, for much more work needs to be done, especially on historically based political argumentation and on collective memory as a site of rhetorical struggle. More work like that done by Janas needs to proceed within the rhetorical community.[53] We have only begun to open the varied rhetorical relationships between past and present social and political situations. Only after many more studies of situated rhetorics of history will we be able to theorize those rhetorics with confidence.

The rhetoric of collective memory provides especially exciting new ground for scholarship. The few studies out there—not only Janas's dissertation but also John Nerone's article on professional history and social memory, Robbie Cox's work on memory in Marcuse's writings, and Michael Billig's essay on collective memory, ideology, and British royalty—show great promise.[54] Rhetoricians have an excellent opportunity to contribute to a burgeoning literature coming from historians, sociologists, and literary critics. I hope we pick up the challenge.

The Popular Memory Group of Birmingham's Centre for Contemporary Cultural Studies employs the term "popular memory" to reference "the power and pervasiveness of historical representations, their connections with dominant institutions and the part they play in winning consent and building alliances in the processes of formal politics."[55] The past is, thus, quite naturally a site of rhetorical struggle, often for political control, over those representations. Controlling discourses about the past may not guarantee political control of the present, but such discourses are nonetheless powerful weapons of sociopolitical organization. One need not bring up only Adolf Hitler, though he was a master manipulator of the past. We can look to our own time, to Richard Nixon's construction of a history of Vietnam in his November 1969 speech on the war, Ronald Reagan's grounding of American civic values in John Winthrop's 1630 speech on "the city on the hill," George Bush's 1992 convention film that positioned him in the pantheon of great American presidents, and Bill Clinton's 1992 acceptance speech, built around a new covenant that worked desperately hard to evoke the sanctity of Israel's old covenant with Jahweh. Owning some important pieces of the past is always good for present purposes.

The rhetorics of history, argument, and collective memory in one way or another all run on the dialogue between tradition and progress that will ever be a central engine of America. As Kammen notes, "The party of hope and the party of memory will continue to jostle each other for position."[56] It is for the rhetorician to discover and make public the rules of that game.

4

Theoretical Implications of Doing Rhetorical History

Groupthink, Foreign Policy Making, and Vietnam

Moya Ann Ball

Commenting on the early romance North Americans had with the automobile, E. B. White wrote that they "rode in a state of cheerful catalepsy."[1] That is, automobile enthusiasts had moved so swiftly through so many exciting developments that there was a suspension of sensation in which they lost contact with their environment. At times, I detect a similar cheerful cataleptic state in the speech communication discipline in which scholars become so caught up with the excitement surrounding new methodological models that they are willing to suspend their contact with what may be the more enduring but, perhaps, more pedestrian methods of inquiry such as rhetorical history.

Take Gronbeck, for instance, who, in making the distinction between rhetorical history and rhetorical criticism, labeled the former an "exercise" in historical writing and the latter "a critical venture" that is "interesting and insightful."[2] His assumption, made over two decades ago, appears to be that doing rhetorical history is a descriptive endeavor that is not evaluative, not insightful, and not theoretically important. More recently, Hart accused scholars involved in public address research of producing "a historical recounting" in which "theory construction is offered no ride at all."[3] Those of us who practice rhetorical history may have shared Medhurst's experience of having a paper returned to him by a reviewer with the comment that, although he had chosen to examine a politically and historically important speech, his work did not have a "shred of newsworthy theoretical commentary."[4] Some of my work on Vietnam decision making received the reviewer's comment, "you are writing history, not rhetoric."

The purpose of this essay, therefore, is to attempt to answer some of the aforementioned criticism by exploring the theoretical implications of doing rhetorical history. To that end I argue that rhetoric and history, by virtue of their nature, must necessarily nourish each other. Further, using examples from research on Vietnam decision making, I demonstrate that doing rhetorical history has important theoretical implications and serves an epistemic function as well.

Rhetoric and History

That rhetoric and history are intertwined is an ancient idea. Isocrates asserts that "there is no institution devised by men which the power of speech has not helped us to establish."[5] Hochmuth Nichols traces the importance of history to orators such as Pericles and Cicero, suggesting that the influence of rhetoric on history is equally apparent.[6] Arendt writes that "history as a category of human existence is older than the written word," and then she adds, "but the transformation of single events and occurrences into history was essentially the same imitator of action in words which was later emphasized in Greek tragedy."[7] Arendt's "imitator of action" is rooted in the Greek word, "mimesis," which is strongly related to the role of rhetoric.[8] In this role, rhetoric re-presents the world, and events in the world, in a language that, in effect, remakes reality. In the late seventeenth and early eighteenth centuries, Vico, then chair of rhetoric at the University of Naples and later dubbed the "father of modern history,"[9] underlined the idea that language was the key to history. According to Vico, "the structures of communication . . . become the documents upon which historical community rests."[10] For Vico, history is constituted through communication. Thus, when we deny history, we deny ourselves.

Rhetoric, then, is an historical product as well as an historical process.[11] It is part of an ongoing historical conversation that is rooted in the past, has meaning in the present, and has implications for the future. Doing rhetorical history is double-edged: it is a rhetorical perspective for investigating historical happenings, and it is a recognition that historical happenings come about most often because of and through rhetorical discourse. A rhetorical perspective brings back the human focus in historical research, and the historical record places rhetorical discourse in context.

The preceding discussion implies that trying to separate rhetoric and history may be a moot undertaking. I do not want to suggest, though, that rhetoric and history are parasites, each living at the other's expense. Rhetoric and history do nourish each other; however, there is a difference between doing rhetoric and doing history. A rhetorical perspective allows us to ask "different questions than those posed by history."[12] A rhetorical perspective prods us to ask what persuasive discourse means within its historical context. At this juncture researchers must begin to consider the theoretical implications of their work. As Benson claims, "to squelch history and criticism would be to impoverish theory, which must be not only a rival but also a colleague of history and criticism."[13] Indeed, the root word of "history" is connected to *histor*, meaning "to judge." As rhetorical historians, we make informed judgments about the communication of the past, intertwining rhetoric, history, and criticism in the process. As we begin to make meaning out of discourses in historical contexts, we step closer also to the theoretical implications of rhetorical history. As Nerone points out, histories present the past in story form, and "theory is a big story that can be used to give more meaning to a lot of little stories."[14]

In the remaining sections of this essay I intend to use examples from research on Vietnam decision making to demonstrate the theoretical implications of doing rhetorical history. Certainly, there is a grand tradition in speech communication of doing the kind of rhetorical history that produces sensitive insights leading to significant theorizing.[15] This essay, then, attempts to continue in that tradition.

Decision Making as a Rhetorical Act

My research of the John F. Kennedy and Lyndon B. Johnson administrations was guided by the general question, "Why didn't Presidents Kennedy, Johnson, and their key advisors seize opportunities for peace?" Put another way, "Why and how were decisions made to escalate the Vietnam War?" Many books have been written in which scholars examined subjects such as the historical roots, the military strategies, the effects, and the decisions of the Vietnam War.[16] Scholars, though, who paused at all to examine White House decision making, were more interested in external constraints on the decision making—in events in the world that stimulated certain decisional responses. In most cases, the communication of the decision makers was only peripheral to the events. In contrast, I was interested in the internal constraints on the decision-making process, including the communication patterns, rhetorical strategies, and interpretations of events shared by the presidents and their advisors. I assumed, therefore, that communication was the central force in the decision-making process.

After examining thousands of pages of documents, memoranda, cables, letters, and group transcripts collected from the Kennedy and Johnson Presidential Libraries, I confirmed that high-level policy making, carried out over a long period of time, is a rhetorical activity.[17] Thus, rhetorical activity occurs not only in the public address of presidents and other spokespersons but also in the more private communication of policy-making groups.[18] As in public address such communication is intentional; the decision makers take sides, and rhetorical strategies are used to garner support; the communication has past as well as future implications; it is problem solving; and identifiable patterns can be discovered in the language used.

There are other reasons, though, for examining decision making from a rhetorical perspective. When decision making is difficult and is carried out over a long period of time, the decision makers are sometimes driven to choose outside the boundaries of rules and inside themselves. It is here that the role of values, attitudes, and beliefs comes into play. It is here that the rhetorical perspective is most useful. The language surrounding such values, attitudes, and beliefs is often poetic, metaphorical, and filled with narratives, myths, and fantasy themes that require an art of deciphering. Rhetoric is that art.

Another reason for using a rhetorical perspective in decision-making research is that there is a dialectical tension between permanence and change in policy making. It is out of this tension that rhetoric is generated. Rhetoric is the arbitrator in the dialectic, mediating between permanence and change as well as thought and action. A rhetorical perspective is an imperative in trying to understand such tension.

Having argued for a rhetorical perspective in decision-making research, let me now turn to my Vietnam work. The following examples demonstrate that doing rhetorical history can generate theoretical as well as historical knowledge.

Groupthink and Cohesiveness

In a germinal and imaginative work, social psychologist Irving Janis used a case study method to examine several historical groups and, subsequently, to verify his hypothesis that groups that are highly cohesive become victims of what he labels "groupthink."[19] Janis explored disastrous decisions such as those made in the Kennedy administration's "Bay of Pigs" fiasco and in the Johnson administration's Vietnam deliberations. He identified high group cohesiveness as being the prime condition for groupthink: "The more amiability and esprit de corps among the members of a policy-making in-group, the greater is the danger that independent critical thinking will be replaced by groupthink."[20] I must stress that Janis's symptoms of groupthink, such as stereotyping the enemy, illusions of invulnerability, and a belief in the group's inherent morality, make good sense. My problem is with his major assumption that a high level of cohesiveness is the prime condition for groupthink.

Although Janis concedes that some level of cohesiveness may generate a tolerance for disagreement that is to be welcomed in decision making, he consistently maintains that cohesiveness leads to defective decision making.[21] The difficulty with this premise is that neither the Kennedy nor the Johnson groups could be described as cohesive.

First of all, my research suggests that a communication climate of conflict and confusion dominated the Kennedy foreign policy–making group.[22] There was conflict between individuals, between departments, and between different factions such as the newer Kennedy appointees and the older bureaucrats. Had such conflict been reserved for substantive policy issues only, the result may have been better decisions; however, it often revolved around clashes over procedure and struggles for personal status and stronger group roles. For instance, I discovered that an internal guerrilla warfare was waged within the corridors of the White House. This internal conflict reflected a dominant fantasy type—that life is a war to be fought at home as well as abroad.[23] Accordingly, people inside as well as outside the administration were labeled as either heroes or villains.

Even those at the center of the decision-making circle did not escape conflict over territory and status. The CIA director, John McCone, and the secretary of defense, Robert S. McNamara, tended to clash;[24] President Kennedy did not like Paul Nitze, a key member of the Department of Defense;[25] Maxwell Taylor, chair of the Joint Chiefs of Staff, disdained Roger Hilsman of the State Department;[26] and Hilsman and McNamara clashed.[27] Even though Dean Rusk was secretary of state, he always seemed to be outside the center of the decision-making activities. In an oral history interview, Robert Kennedy maintained that the president had planned to get rid of Rusk before the 1964 election.[28] In short, this was not a cohesive group. Because these decision makers shared a group fantasy type of "loyalty to the president," the argument can be made that they were bonded to the president but not to each other. In some respects there was a form of adhesion present but not cohesion. There is a difference.

When Lyndon Johnson became president, he actively campaigned to retain most of John F. Kennedy's key advisors. In this way, although there were some rhetorical modifications to their communication,[29] much of the original rhetorical pattern remained. President Johnson and his advisors developed a norm of presenting a unanimous front to outsiders, but underneath there was pushing and shoving between members, in-house spying, and political in-fighting between the White House staff and the Departments of Defense and State. As in the Kennedy administration, the conflict seemed to be of a more personal nature, relating to individual differences, power struggles, and departmental competition. In particular, the "awesome foursome," as President Johnson, McNamara, Rusk, and National Security Advisor McGeorge Bundy were called, were not cohesive. For instance, in March 1964 there were rumors of trouble between Bundy's staff and the State Department that were directly related to Bundy's lack of trust in Rusk's leadership.[30] Bundy's lack of trust in other key advisors was exhibited also in the way he operated an informal network of "spies" set up in other departments. For example, Klein, situated in the Department of Defense, routinely supplied Bundy with information about McNamara.[31]

Neither the Kennedy nor the Johnson decision-making groups could therefore be called cohesive in the sense that Janis uses the term. This discovery not only calls into question the central assumption of Janis's theory, but it lays some doubts on social scientific studies that have since relied on the relationship of cohesiveness to groupthink.[32] This discovery speaks clearly, also, to the way in which rhetorical history generates theoretical knowledge.

Rational versus Nonrational Models of Decision Making

Graham Allison, using the Cuban Missile Crisis and the Kennedy group as his foci, argues that decisions in foreign affairs cannot be explained by a rational action model of decision making.[33] On the other hand, Robert Newman, rejecting Allison's model of "bargaining games," suggests that argument or rationality determined President Kennedy's decisions and not "politicking."[34] By doing rhetorical history, I discovered that foreign policy making is a great deal more complex than any analysis that distinguishes between the rational and the nonrational would indicate.

The decision making of the Kennedy and Johnson groups integrated politicking, emotions, rationality, and sagas in a complex and dynamic search for a solution. Their politicking revealed itself in their communication climate of conflict, in their sharing of group fantasy themes in which life was a war, and in their use of a persistent sports metaphor in which war was a game that could be won or lost but never negotiated. Such emotions as pride, fear, anger, and hostility surfaced in shared themes in which the United States had to prove it was not a "paper tiger" and in which the country had to restore its lost prestige.[35] These decision makers surrounded themselves with the symbols of a cold war rhetorical vision in which its weapons were words.[36] In the Kennedy administration such a vision was transformed with the rhetoric of the New Frontier, which included themes of youth, action, guerrilla warfare, Jungle Jim, and Green Berets. Ironically, in this new rhetoric talk and words were seen as passive, and passivity was constantly associated with the "older" Eisenhower administration.[37]

For both the Kennedy and the Johnson groups, North Vietnam became the lightning rod for all that was wrong with the world, and Ho Chi Minh and his followers were painted verbally as lawless villains.[38] Both administrations proposed to fight North Vietnam and communism with the tools of a technocratic meritocracy. Consequently, in a revealing blend of their emotions and cognitions, they seemed to "celebrate their rationality." They made numerous trips to Vietnam, searching for empirical evidence to back up their plans; they laid the groundwork of contingency planning; they used the arithmetic of guerrilla warfare as a litmus test for measuring an as-yet-undeclared war's progress; they used statistics as weapons to counter the attacks of opposing opinions; and, especially in the Johnson administration, they embraced a classical problem-solving process.[39]

These decision makers, then, were passionately rational men who gathered facts and evidence, sorting them through the "terministic screen" of their rhetorical vision or their shared social reality.[40] Doing rhetorical history, therefore, leads me to suggest the need for a model of decision making that incorporates both the rational and traditionally nonrational elements of decision making. Policy making over long periods of time involves cognitions, emotions, and will in a complex convergence. In some respects Kuhn refers to this process when he writes in *The Essential Tension* about ways in which convergent and divergent thinking may occur simultaneously in group work.[41] Then he asks how these different modes can be reconciled in problem solving. My research indicates that the sharing of dramatic communication such as that found in Bormann's Symbolic Convergence Theory—the sharing of sagas, metaphors, and other figurative language as found in specific rhetorical strategies—provides a link between convergent and divergent thinking, between cognitions and emotions. In policy making cognitions and emotions act in concert.

The link between cognitions and emotions may be subjectively experienced. Approaching decision making as a rhetorical act accounts for that subjectivity. Subsequently, I think that more decision-making research needs to ask and answer questions regarding the tensions and reconciliations of cognitive/emotive and discursive/nondiscursive language. More decision-making research needs to adopt a rhetorical perspective.

The Epistemic Function of Rhetorical History

As demonstrated in the preceding discussion, my findings about the decision-making activities of the Kennedy and Johnson administrations differ, sometimes in substantive ways, from the conclusions of Janis, Allison, and Newman, who took social-psychological, political, and communication perspectives respectively. Certainly, some discrepancies in the findings may be attributed to differences in perspective, but the traditional role of historical research cannot be overlooked. Some of those differences are because those researchers did not have access to declassified archival resources at the Kennedy and Johnson Libraries. For the most part Janis, Allison, and Newman relied on secondary sources and accounts rather than the rich primary materials available today. Even though historians have tended to make greater use of archival resources than have speech communication scholars, archivists at both the Kennedy and Johnson Libraries maintain that their libraries are grossly underused.[42] Archival collections, however, contain a wealth of resources for communication scholars who are willing to combine their perspectives with the meticulous data-gathering techniques of historical researchers. Indeed, it seems to me, that when a communication researcher begins to depend on archival sources for his or her interpretations, the real business of analysis begins in that, instead of relying on the authority of secondary accounts, we are left with primary sources that demand our making statements of our own, that demand we become active rhetorical analysts.

The differences between my findings and those of Janis, Allison, and Newman can be accounted for partially by differences in method as well as access to and use of primary sources, but what about differences in findings between those works in which scholars have done extensive archival research? A case in point is the difference between my research results and those of Larry Berman, who did extensive work on Lyndon Johnson's role in the Vietnam War. Like many other scholars, Berman initially places the blame for the Vietnam War squarely on the shoulders of Lyndon B. Johnson.[43] He suggests that

President Johnson orchestrated the war with the roles of advisors being only incidental to the decision-making process. Saying that he has allowed the primary documents to "speak for themselves," he describes Johnson's plan, making few references to the group process or to communication.

Taking a rhetorical perspective, I found evidence that suggests that, until the *overt* decisions to send in ground forces to South Vietnam were expressed in July 1965, Johnson, rather than planning the tragedy, seemed to persistently stall on further action. Indeed, he seemed to be led by his advisors more than he led them. In previous work I suggest that the Johnson group's communication, much of which was rhetorical in nature, prevented them from applying brakes to the Vietnam War's policy-making wheels. A distinct communication culture that had been established in the Kennedy administration and reinforced in the Johnson White House could point them in no direction other than intervention. As Kenneth Burke might have said, their communication was more than the motivation behind the action; it was the action itself.[44]

My research, therefore, yields a different kind of knowledge from that of Berman's. My assertions also conflict strongly with those made by John M. Newman, whose book, *JFK and Vietnam*, became the basis for Oliver Stone's movie *JFK*.[45] Stone rests his movie on the hypothesis that President Kennedy was assassinated by a government conspiracy mainly because he had let it be known that he was planning to withdraw U.S. support from Vietnam. No one can know what Kennedy would have done had he lived. To date, though, I have found no evidence that Kennedy was seriously considering withdrawal from Vietnam.[46]

John Newman bases some of his ideas on the evidence that President Kennedy had told Senators Morse and Mansfield that he would withdraw by 1965. I discovered, however, that initially the threat of withdrawal had been used to frighten Diem, the prime minister of South Vietnam, into cooperating with the Kennedy administration's plans for further action.[47] This rhetorical strategy was used also to pacify potential dissenters. Examining group transcripts, I discovered that President Kennedy had been upset with McNamara for talking about the option of withdrawal, and McNamara replied that he had talked about withdrawal only "in order to meet the view of Senator Fulbright and others that we are bogged down in Vietnam for ever."[48]

Other group meetings in October 1963 revolved around whether to pursue a coup against Diem. Actually, the president and his advisors had discussed the need to get rid of Diem as early as July 1961.[49] By June 1963 Diem and his brother Nhu's oppressive actions had become a political embarrassment. Additionally, Diem had stalled on further American involvement in South Vietnam, and there were rumors that he and his brother were "flirting" with the idea of negotiating with North Vietnam.[50] This, then, was a prime opportunity for the United States to withdraw from Vietnam without any apparent loss of prestige. Instead, the coup was actively encouraged, the only fear being that if the coup were unsuccessful the war effort would be slowed down.[51] This was not the talk of a group about to withdraw from Vietnam.

Implications

I have tried to demonstrate that doing rhetorical history generates theoretical as well as historical knowledge. Using a rhetorical perspective to examine a key historical event generated new knowledge about that event.[52] The generation of this new knowledge can be explained partially by access to more declassified sources. Another explanation has to do with the use of those sources, with the use of the evidence. Unlike Berman I do not think that sources can ever speak for themselves. As Collingwood, the noted historian, suggests, evidence is only evidence when it is interpreted.[53] Thus, differences in findings have a lot to do with differences in critical interpretations. My bias here is that rhetorical and communication scholars are trained to be sensitive to the subtleties of language and that a rhetorical perspective allows an insight into discourse that may not be so apparent in other disciplines. So, for instance, after having concluded as far back as 1988 that President Kennedy had been involved in decisions about Vietnam, I was interested to hear historians and political scientists say at a 1993 conference that they were becoming more interested in the Kennedy administration's influence on the Vietnam decisions of the Johnson administration.[54] I heard such scholars as Berman and Gibbons vehemently disagree with John Newman's assertion that the Johnson administration represented a reversal in the Kennedy Vietnam policy. It is true that my work on Vietnam and foreign policy making has not produced any brave new theory as yet; it has generated fresh insights, though, that may prove to be theoretically and historically rich.

Doing rhetorical history has confirmed for me that rhetoric "stands in a historically fluctuating relationship with other disciplines," and, as Barthes continues, rhetoric "must always be read in the structural interplay with its neighbours—it is the play of the system which is historically significant."[55] Some of those neighbors in my research included political science, social psychology, and history.

Doing rhetorical history suggests to me also that it may be a form of what Glaser and Strauss have termed "Grounded Theory."[56] Grounded theory is the process by which researchers discover theory from the basic data collected. Such theory is inductively derived from the study of the phenomenon it represents. Grounded theory, therefore, has much in common with the case study method. Case studies cannot attain prediction and control, but they can provide explanations of relationships and an understanding of the meanings that actors ascribe to their behaviors. Explanation and understanding are the building blocks of theory, particularly when the research findings are incorporated into the broader domain of comparative analysis.

Rhetorical history as Grounded Theory

My final argument, therefore, is that we need to be doing more rhetorical history so that we have enough data to provide the basis for multiple comparative analyses and, hence, significant theorizing. In 1977 Hawes pointed out that other disciplines have spent years making observations, describing observations, and systematically interpreting those observations.[57] He goes on to suggest that the problem with the communication field has been that there was insufficient description and interpretation prior to the search for covering laws. Twenty years have past since Hawes's comments, and during that time I think the communication discipline has made tremendous strides in its data gathering and theorizing. Still, there always will be more work to do and many more archives to use. The work of collecting primary sources is endless, and usually any knowledge or theory generated at any given time is an "interim report." That is, as more collections are opened, and as more documents are declassified, rhetorical history is written anew. This predisposition to change is what makes scholarship an exciting adventure. It is this uncertainty that dictates that we need to be doing more, not less, rhetorical history. Janik and Toulmin contend that "those who are ignorant of the context of ideas are . . . destined to misunderstand them."[58] Doing rhetorical history enlightens our understanding and grounds our theory in a real and historical world.

5

A Constitutive Framework for Rhetorical Historiography

Toward an Understanding of the Discursive (Re)constitution of "Constitution" in *The Federalist Papers*

James Jasinski

Introduction

Starting with Wrage's 1947 essay on public address and intellectual history and continuing through McGee's 1980 study of "ideographs," rhetorical scholars have exhibited a keen interest in political concepts or "ideas." Unfortunately, the relationship between concepts and ideas and historically situated rhetorical practice (the "text") has not received careful attention in our scholarship. In Wrage's original formulation, the text is a "repository of themes and their elaborations from which we may gain insight into the life of an era as well as into the mind of a man [*sic*]." As Gaonkar has observed, in Wrage's perspective the text "is not a central locus of concern. . . . Wrage does not appear to be interested in the mode of articulation and textualization of the struggle of ideas manifested in" the text. Thirty-three years later McGee makes ideographs the building blocks of rhetorical practice, yet the text remains largely the same inert repository that it was for Wrage. The text remains, as it was for Wrage and his students, "transparent"; "there is no trick," McGee writes, "in gleaning from public documents the entire vocabulary of ideographs that define a particular collectivity." McGee's interest in studying the popular "usages" of ideographs, like Wrage's attempt to access the "popular mind" through "fugitive literature," avoids the question of conceptual or ideational textualization. Despite Wrage's provocative quest to study the "refractions, modifications, or substitutions" effected

[margin handwritten note: is treated as transparent]

through rhetorical practice, rhetorical scholars have, until recently, deferred the question of what happens *to* ideas *in* practice.[1]

As language has become the lingua franca of the humanities, intellectual historians have begun to devote significant attention to the rhetorical features of public discourse. At the same time, rhetorical scholars, drawing inspiration from the historical tradition of rhetorical theory as well as related work in other disciplines, have also begun to feature the text prominently in critical and public address scholarship. One common feature that unites various forms of historiographic inquiry (including rhetorical, intellectual, and literary) is renewed reflection into the nature of discursive influence. From Wichelns to Wrage to Bitzer and beyond, rhetorical scholars in the speech communication discipline have operated within an instrumentalist framework with respect to discursive influence. This framework, as Gaonkar notes, evinces a "delimited notion of the power of rhetoric."[2] The instrumentalist framework focuses attention on a relatively narrow sense of historical context, usually encourages critics to assess textual influence on the immediate audience, and attempts to assess the advocate's attempt at solving a particular problem or exigence. Within the instrumentalist framework, the force of a situated utterance is exhausted within the confines of the immediate situation. Critical and historical inquiry remains captive to the advocate's purpose and the exigence and constraints of the situation. Conceptual reflection on the category of influence raises the issue, in Gaonkar's words, of "the extent to which rhetoric can shape and reshape our perception of political and historical reality."[3] An emergent trend in rhetorical scholarship, and humanities inquiry generally, privileges what I term a constitutive framework for assessing discursive influence. A constitutive approach to rhetorical history takes up Wrage's challenge to study the refractions and modifications of political concepts and ideas, in other words their (re)constitution, as they unfold in textual practice.

The aim of the present project is to sketch a constitutive approach to rhetorical historiography. The next section of the essay outlines the broad parameters of this approach by identifying four essential constitutive dimensions of discursive practice. One of these dimensions, linguistic and conceptual constitution, is further developed in the latter half of the essay. The discussion in this portion of the essay proceeds by using the project of "conceptual history" as a vehicle for identifying the common concerns linking the rhetorical and intellectual historian. Despite their avowed objective, intellectual historians and political theorists operating within the conceptual history tradition frequently defer the text in their effort to describe and explain the processes and mechanisms of conceptual change.

Extending Gaonkar's insight that rhetorical critics "might deepen our sense of the dynamic relationship between public address and its ideological background . . . by attending to the integrity of the text as a field of discursive action,"[4] I suggest that a constitutive approach to rhetorical history operating in the dimension of conceptual (re)constitution explores the ways specific discursive strategies and textual dynamics shape and reshape the contours of political concepts and ideas. The final section of the essay illustrates this claim through an extended case study that explores the (re)constitution of "constitution" in *The Federalist Papers*.

A Constitutive Approach to Rhetorical Historiography

A constitutive, as opposed to an instrumental, orientation to rhetorical influence is an often unnoticed but embedded element of the tradition of rhetorical thought. Beiner locates an instrumental/constitutive tension in Aristotle's *Rhetoric*.[5] Drawing on the work of George Kennedy, Leff identifies "a basic and persistent distinction embedded in the classical tradition" between two "senses" of persuasion, intentional and extensional, that roughly correspond to an instrumental and constitutive orientation to influence.[6] A constitutive "turn" in rhetorical historiography is, then, both a return to a neglected aspect of the rhetorical tradition and an encounter with a broader "constructivist" or structurational agenda in the humanities and social sciences. This broader agenda rejects the once traditional view that language is principally a medium of representation. A constructivist or constitutive orientation to discursive influence focuses on the imbrication of the performative and representational capacities of language. Linguistic or discursive practices create what they describe as they simultaneously describe what they create.[7] Louis Montrose summarizes this position: "Representations of the world in . . . discourse are engaged in constructing the world, in shaping the modalities of social reality, and in accommodating their writers, performers, readers, and audiences to multiple and shifting subject positions within the world they both constitute and inhabit."[8]

The constitutive dimension of discursive influence can be specified further by modifying Leff's intentional and extensional distinction. Intentionally, texts exhibit constitutive potential through the invitations inscribed in various discursive forms (tropes, arguments, etc.). Extensionally, texts exhibit constitutive force through the cultural circulation and discursive articulation of their textual forms in ways that enable and constrain subsequent practice. Texts invite their audience to experience the world in certain ways via concrete textual forms; audiences, in turn, appropriate, articulate, circulate, and/or subvert these textual forms in ways that release and transform their potential constitutive energy.[9] Conceptualizations of constitutive potential and force do not entail, as critics of the linguistic turn in history, for example, charge, a form of linguistic determinism. Wayne Booth, one of a large number of contemporary scholars exploring the constitutive capacity of discursive action, suggests that the opposition between autonomy and determinism is a false dichotomy. Discursive influence is the condition of human existence; "influences," Booth writes, are "the very source of my being." It is, he continues, "futile" to curse one's "fate as an essentially conditioned creature."[10] Discursive constitution specifies the way textual practices structure or establish conditions of possibility, enabling *and* constraining subsequent thought and action in ways similar to the operation of rules in a game.[11]

In contemporary rhetorical studies explicit reflection on the constitutive potential and constitutive force of discursive practice has emphasized the formation of subjectivity and collective identity, but these effects do not circumscribe the range of rhetorical influence.[12] There are (at least) four constitutive dimensions that merit the attention of rhetorical critics and historians. In addition to self-constitution and the formation of subjectivity or subject positions, discourse functions to organize and structure an individual's or a culture's experience of time and space, the norms of political culture and the experience of communal existence (including collective identity), and the linguistic resources of the culture (including, in particular, the stock of fundamental political concepts that shape the culture's understanding of political existence). These dimensions can be distinguished analytically but interact in rhetorical practice and in critical reflection upon public practice.[13] A systematic explication of these dimensions is beyond the scope of the present project; what follows is a brief overview of some of the relevant scholarship that elucidates these dimensions.

Social theorist Anthony Giddens thematizes notions of human agency and practical consciousness in his structurational approach to social analysis. In so doing Giddens highlights the relationship between text production and human subjectivity: "To study the production of the text is at the same time in a definite sense to study the production of its author. The author is not simply 'subject' and the text 'object'; the 'author' helps constitute him- or herself through the text, via the process of production of that text."[14] Stephen Greenblatt, in his study of "self-fashioning" in renaissance textual practice, echoes these assumptions about the relationship between discursive action and the formation of subjectivity. In this study Greenblatt identifies a process that looms large in contemporary social theory and criticism. Individual and/or group self-constitution is enabled by various strategies of "othering" that secure a privileged identity for an individual or group at the expense of specified others. The constitution of these "others" (e.g., ethnic or racial minorities, women, individuals from a different socioeconomic position) constrains their possibilities as it enables the self-identity of those who control or dominate the culture's discursive forms.[15] This dialectic is illustrated in Carroll Smith-Rosenberg's study of the constitution of a "new American subject" during the founding period. Smith-Rosenberg traces the emergence of a "privileged middle ground" where the American subject—"republican citizen, American national, and middle-class actor"—resided, ironically enabled by those excluded "negative others": "the white middle-class woman, the American Indian warrior, and the enslaved African American."[16] The dialectic between self and other functions as a central element in this dimension of discursive constitution.

Individuals, communities, and cultures exist in time and space. But time and space are not merely empirical givens; rather, as many contemporary theorists, critics, and historians observe, they are experiential potentialities shaped by discursive and cultural practice.[17] Temporal experience is, at least in most Western cultures, structured in terms of past, present, and future. But each of these general experiential structures, along with the experience of temporal flow, admit multiple constructions. For example, the past can be experienced as remote, irrelevant, inaccessible, or mysterious, a resource for inspiration and guidance, a pattern waiting to be replicated, a problem to be solved or a burden to be accepted or rejected. The present can be experienced as a continuation of the past or a departure from it; it can be marked by urgency, characterized via reference to its developmental pace (ranging from a sense of gradualism to uncontrolled acceleration) or its texture (present time as part of an unfolding process or as a discrete event). The future can be experienced as an obligation, an imposition, or a promise and can be anticipated somewhere along a continuum ranging from hopeful optimism to pessimistic dread. These variable experiences of time are shaped and reshaped through textual practice. For example, Cox's study of King's "I Have a Dream" speech, and Hariman's rejoinder, thematize the constitution of temporal experience in and through King's performance. Cox emphasizes the metaphoric critique of gradualism and the effort to construct a sense of urgency whereas Hariman calls our attention to King's unstable political position that led, he suggests, to the subtle reconstitution of gradualism.[18] Although their readings focus on different temporal effects, Cox and Hariman both illustrate the constitutive potential of textual practice with respect to temporal experience.

Spatial experience lacks the general cultural coordinates or categories that help shape our experience of time. But the (re)constitution of spatial experience is, nonetheless, equally pervasive. Perspective, a critical component in human perception, can be manipulated in ways that modify (by enabling and constraining) spatial experience. Texts have the capacity to position their audience in different ways, in some cases moving them "closer" to an object or bringing the object into the "presence" of the audience and in other instances moving them further "away" from an object.[19] These instances of increasing or decreasing distance can alter and reshape human interaction and relationships (e.g., "intimate" political biographies contribute to the restructuring of political space). Discursive action contributes to other forms of spatial reconstitution. Stephen Kern, for example, notes the reconstruction of traditional spatial categories such as "between the sacred and the profane space of religion."[20] Of paramount importance to rhetorical scholars is the ongoing discursive negotiation of the spatial categories "public" and "private." Spaces considered as essentially "private" a generation or two ago (most especially the "home") have been reconfigured as the result of a plethora of discursive forces (e.g., legal, feminist, bureaucratic, and children's advocates).

Political theorist Bruce James Smith opines that "the preservation of public life is among the most difficult of human projects."[21] Public life, political culture, and community all gesture towards the practices and institutions that make collective life and a common identity possible. Since the time of Machiavelli, according to the account provided by Pocock, political communities in the Western world have been confronted with their own temporal finitude, with the possibility of their demise.[22] Communities, and the political cultures that sustain them, face the ongoing challenge of preservation or, in David Carr's terms, "self-maintenance"; communities invariably are engaged in the ongoing project of reconstitution.[23] Communal reconstitution can take a variety of discursive forms and rely on different textual practices as specific questions of social and political authority, power, bonds of affiliation, meaning, value, and institutional practice are confronted and negotiated.[24] A history of American public discourse is, then, in part the reconstruction and analysis of specific moments wherein an American community, and its constituent sub-communities, confronted threats to its existence (internal as well as external) and engaged in its own reconstitution.

The linguistic turn that has reshaped humanities scholarship over the last few decades maintains, in Murray Edelman's terms, that

[margin note: communities continually reconstitute themselves via discourse]

"language is the key creator of the social worlds people experience."[25] A <u>constitutive approach to rhetorical historiography must also recognize that language itself is (re)constituted</u> through performance. Giddens points out, for example, that "every instance of the use of language is a potential modification of that language at the same time as it acts to reproduce it."[26] The idioms of public life (e.g., liberalism, conservatism, free market capitalism, pro-choice or pro-life) and the specific concepts that organize, link, and separate these idioms are continually reconstituted through quotidian interaction as well as more nuanced textual practices. Charting such alterations in "usages" is a central aspect of a constitutive rhetorical history.[27]

The analysis of linguistic and conceptual change raises important conceptual questions about the nature of constitutive analysis. Giddens argues that "the reproduction of language, . . . as condition and result of the production of speech acts and other forms of communication, *is not a motivated phenomenon.*" Giddens quickly qualifies his position to a degree (maintaining a few sentences later that "reproduction is not *generally* a motivating force among . . . language-speakers"),[28] but the overall thrust of the argument remains consistent: linguistic and conceptual reconstitution is largely epiphenomenal and not the result of intentional discursive action. It seems clear that constitutive influence (along all four dimensions) is frequently epiphenomenal. In these cases the challenge to the rhetorical historian is to trace the slow transformation of subjectivity, temporal and/or spatial experience, sense of community and political culture, and/or language as they are articulated and rearticulated in discursive action. But it seems equally clear that rhetorical action embodies a purposive element that should be taken into account in analysis. The challenge posed by Giddens's position is how to reintroduce intentionality into constitutive inquiry in a way that does not completely collapse the distinction between instrumental and constitutive inquiry. Part of the answer to this challenge lies in the distinction posited earlier between intentional potential and extensional force; an author or speaker may desire to alter the meaning of concepts or reshape an idiom, but such a desire may not be shared by audiences that circulate and rearticulate the linguistic changes. The audience's actions in this case actualize the constitutive potential of the text, thereby generating extensional force, without their necessarily sharing in the intentions of the author or speaker. More generally, the point that needs emphasis is that intentions are not necessarily excluded in constitutive inquiry. The difference, in my mind, between the instrumental tradition and the emergent constitutive approach is that in the former, intentions typically function as an organizing framework for analysis, whereas in the latter they are decentered and refracted.[29] That is, rather than organizing the elements of text with respect to the intentions of an author or speaker, constitutive inquiry focuses on the inevitable multiplicity of intentions that inhabit a text and tries to chart the interaction between, and the influence of, these often disparate motivational forces.[30]

In addition to the problem of intentionality, conceptualizing constitutive influence as essentially epiphenomenal problematizes the role of textual action in the process of change. On the subject of linguistic transformations, Richard Rorty maintains that the process of change is not a matter of choice or decision; it merely happens as a by-product of continuous linguistic redescriptions of the world. So, for example, Rorty writes that Europeans "gradually lost the habit of using certain words and gradually acquired the habit of using others." Changes of this sort are the result of new ways of describing the world; for Rorty, "intellectual history," and by extension rhetorical history, is essentially the "history of metaphor."[31] As important as metaphors can be in terms of all four dimensions of constitutive influence, the rhetorical historian's ability to *account* for change is severely diminished by Rorty's version of linguistic reconstitution. By focusing on large paradigm shifts as a paradigmatic instance of change, Rorty essentially abandons locally grounded textual practice as a source of innovation and an object of critical and historiographic reconstruction. A concrete example can help illustrate the problem. In his discussion of the transformation of the concept of sovereignty during the American revolutionary period, Bernard Bailyn notes that

the arguments the colonists put forward against Parliament's claims to the right to exercise sovereign power in America were efforts to express in logical form, to state in the language of constitutional theory, the truth of the world they knew. They were at first, necessarily, fumbling and unsure efforts, for there were no arguments—there was no vocabulary—to resort to: the ideas, the terminology, had to be invented. How was this to be done? What arguments, what words, could be used to elevate to the status of constitutional principle the division of authority that had for so long existed and which the colonists associated with the freedom they had enjoyed?[32]

In a way, Bailyn's approach to the issue of conceptual change is vastly different from Rorty's. Bailyn emphasizes argument, Rorty metaphor; Bailyn explores grounded textual practices (Otis, Dickinson, etc.), whereas Rorty's approach tends to abandon the particular. But, in the end, Bailyn cannot accomplish the task he sets for himself: he cannot explain *how* the American colonists "invented" a new language. His account is not fundamentally different from Rorty's and can be recast into Rorty's terminology: the colonists gradually lost the habit of using certain words and gradually acquired the habit of using others. Bailyn documents this shift in great detail, but his documentation does not probe beyond the surface manifestation of terms into the textual action that enabled the conceptual transformation.[33]

Explaining conceptual change through attention to textual dynamics is a central feature of the conceptual history interdisciplinary movement. Indebted to the German tradition of *Begriffsgeschichte* as well as to the pioneering work in historical language analysis by intellectual historians J. G. A. Pocock and Quentin Skinner, conceptual history offers "a political theory of conceptual change." In the next section of the essay, I explore the work of one representative conceptual historian in order to uncover the movement's analytic and explanatory strategies. The purpose of this review is to illustrate how a constitutive rhetorical history of conceptual change is a necessary corollary to a political theory of conceptual change.

Analysis and Explanation in Conceptual History

James Farr outlines the political theory of conceptual change in two key essays.[34] Reacting to the limited or constricted sense of language present in a good deal of historical analysis, Farr develops a distinction that parallels the emerging instrumental/constitutive division in contemporary rhetorical studies. Farr argues that "the discussion of language can and should be recast in order to accent what we might call its *activating* and *constituting* dimensions" (emphasis in original). The activating or instrumental dimension is preoccupied, Farr suggests, by the linguistic activities of "describing or referring." Although these activities must not be ignored, an exclusive focus is problematic in that "such a purely descriptive view of language and meaning fails to capture the political and rhetorical activity that language makes possible." Using the Declaration of Independence as an example, Farr itemizes the complex of actions that the text performs—declaring, warning, inspiring, and unifying—constituting, in essence, "one people." A constitutive understanding of language appreciates the reciprocity between "the political constitution of language and the linguistic constitution of politics."[35] Discursive action constitutes the concepts that shape a social world so as to enable and constrain subsequent thought and action. A particular idiom enables advocates to conceptualize events in a particular way, as, for example, a "conspiracy," while simultaneously constraining alternative conceptualizations. The conceptual historian describes how discourse functions to establish such conditions of possibility or how textual forms enable and constrain beliefs and practices. In this way conceptual change is linked to discursive action and political innovation.

The central problem for Farr and many conceptual historians is explaining the process of change. How does discursive action change or modify concepts and thereby introduce new conditions of possibility? "Conceptual change," Farr writes, "might be understood as one rather striking imaginative outcome of the process of political actors attempting to solve the problems they encounter as they try to understand and change the world around them." The negotiation of problems is ongoing because "problems never rest," but the discursive process itself generates problems as advocates "may discover *new* problems or *reconceptualize* old ones" along the way. Conceptual change in these cases does appear, however, to be epiphenomenal. Although pragmatic problems are not unimportant to the process of conceptual change, Farr focuses on "a special class of problems": contradictions. "Whereas 'problem' covers an enormous range of solvable difficulties or removable obstacles which a belief system might face," Farr notes that "a contradiction implies manifestly *inconsistent* beliefs *within* a system. . . . Hence contradictions imply more than mere conflicts, and they are logically (and perhaps psychologically) less easily shelved than are many other kinds of problems."[36]

Given the subversive potential of contradictions, Farr suggests that the dual processes of "contradiction and criticism" function as the primary discursive "mechanism" for generating conceptual change. As Farr explains: "conceptual change may be understood as one imaginative consequence of political actors, in concert or in conflict, criticizing and attempting to resolve the contradictions that they discover or generate in the complex web of their beliefs, actions, and practices." "Contradictions," Farr maintains, "are rarely found. . . . Rather, [they] emerge in the extended implications or unintended consequences of two or more beliefs within a belief system; or they emerge in the confrontation between beliefs and certain actions or practices . . . or they emerge in the fault lines between two belief systems that are competing for the allegiance of those who struggle to hold them simultaneously; and so on and so on." Emergence is not inevitable; criticism functions to "bring these contradictions to the surface—that is, to the level of reflection and articulation." The point of exposing contradictions is to negotiate or resolve them; in that process "changes in belief or action or practice" occur. All contradictions are "historically contingent." This means that efforts to expose, criticize, and resolve them will always be uneven. Farr draws on a famous passage from Walt Whitman to help illustrate the fact that in numerous cases individuals "live with contradictions." The key issue, Farr reminds the reader, is that "contradictions figure, at best, as need, not necessity; as determinant, not determinism." The value of this account, this "political theory," of conceptual change "resides, not in generality as such, but in the *historical understanding* that it makes possible, indeed demands and underwrites."[37]

The critical issue that needs attention is what degree of historical understanding the conceptual history movement and the twin concepts of contradiction and criticism make possible. Farr maintains that "conceptual histories must *explain* the emergence and transformation of concepts as outcomes of actors using them for political purposes." Such explanations are possible by turning to the textual "site" and "reconstruct[ing] . . . a concept within an imposing edifice of meaning . . . [or] uncovering layers of meaning amidst pamphlet warfare or the manipulative rhetoric of partisan speechmaking."[38] But Farr's metaphor of the textual "site" resides in the same metaphoric terrain as Wrage's text-as-"repository." Criticism and contradiction occur within the textual site or reside in the textual repository, but neither metaphor provides the resources for engaging how criticism and contradiction are manifested in the text. If one is interested, as Farr maintains he is, in uncovering the *mechanisms* of conceptual change, then examining the contents of the site are insufficient. Attention needs to be devoted to the integrity of the text as a field of discursive action, to the specific textual or discursive forms that do the work of criticism and the negotiation of contradiction.[39] Such an effort would make possible a richer historical understanding of the way practical situated discourse functions as a force of conceptual change. A few brief examples, prior to the extended illustration, can help make this point.

Consider first the issue of criticism and its role in exposing contradictions. Farr writes that "contradictions emerge in the extended implications" of belief systems. As a question of textual action, how are belief systems "extended"? What inventional resources can an advocate employ in order to reveal the potential contradictory implication of a belief system? Perelman and Olbrechts-Tyteca provide an illuminating discussion of these resources in their description of techniques for presenting theses as incompatible. One such technique they label an "extension of the field of application." Using Bentham as an example, they show how it is possible for an advocate to "bring out [an] incompatibility . . . [by] extend[ing] the argument's field of application." Consider this passage from an editorial essay on gun control and gun violence: "Flawed though their logic may be, they [gun advocates] believe their only protection against an armed criminal is a gun. Carry that argument to the extreme, and everyone who goes to McDonald's would be armed, along with all plastic surgeons, all small urban children, anyone who might be anywhere an unhinged gunowner with a gripe might show up." As Perelman and Olbrechts-Tyteca suggest, the essayist works to "extend the field" of the pro-gun position in order to reveal its "flawed logic," its contradiction, so that conceptual change becomes possible.[40]

Consider a second case. Farr draws on Whitman to illustrate the fact that contradictions will not always be resolved; at times they are simply endured. But are there particular textual forms that aid in the management or dissolution of contradiction? One such form may be the oxymoron.[41] Farr glimpses this possibility in a brief comment on how, in late-eighteenth-century America, the expression " 'commercial republic' no longer sounded like an oxymoron."[42] But Farr does not seem to acknowledge the cognitive or constitutive potential of the oxymoronic form as a mechanism for managing contradiction. The tension or incompatibility between commerce and republican virtue may have been managed through the invention and deployment of the oxymoron. Again, greater attention to the text as a dynamic field of action may enrich the explication of mechanisms of conceptual change. The next section of the essay offers a more detailed illustration of this proposition.

(Re)constituting Constitution

The conceptual evolution of the concept "constitution" is exceedingly complex.[43] For many scholars, the essence of constitutionalism is found in the various efforts of historical agents to limit sovereign power or prerogative. Understood in this way, the process "constitutionalism" and the product "constitution" have always been beset by a seemingly irreconcilable conceptual tension or contradiction. On the one hand, what we might call the tradition of constitutional discourse maintained that sovereignty must be limited to be legitimate and fulfill its essential function of protecting individual rights. On the other hand, embedded in this tradition is the contrary idea that in every society a sovereign power exists that is supreme, absolute, and incapable of limitation. In premodern political theory this tension was latent. McIlwain observes the struggle in the thirteenth-century writings of Henry de Bracton, who maintained that the sovereign power of the monarch could be limited and absolute at the same time. This observation led McIlwain to wonder: "Was Bracton, then, an absolutist or a constitutionalist, or was he just a blockhead?"[44] The tension grew explicit in the British constitutional struggles of the seventeenth century and continued into the eighteenth-century dispute between Great Britain and her American colonies. Early modern political writers like Filmer and Hobbes maintained that the idea of limiting sovereignty is a contradiction. In *Leviathan* Hobbes wrote "that the Soveraign [sic] power, whether placed in One Man, as in Monarchy, or in one Assembly of men, as in Popular, and Aristocratical Common-wealths, is as great, as possibly men can be imagined to make it. And though of so unlimited a Power, men may fancy many evill [sic] consequences, yet the consequences of the want of it, which is perpetuall warre [sic] of every man against his neighbour, are much worse."[45] Gough concludes that for Filmer and Hobbes sovereignty was "an absolute power, not subject to any law"; within any polity there existed "some power which neither will or ought to be bounded."[46] As Graham Maddox notes, modern "constitutionalism was a specific response to the problems of sovereignty."[47]

One of the many dilemmas facing writers in the constitutional tradition was specifying the institutional mechanism(s) for limiting sovereign power. In English Whig political discourse, for example, the idea of a fundamental law limiting the sovereign was, according to Gordon Wood, "enforceable only by the people's right of revolution, a final sanction that dissolved the contract of government, leaving people free to do as they would in the future."[48] The conceptual and political history of constitutionalism involved a search for alternative means for limiting sovereign power, something beyond revolutionary insurrection. Among the conceptual innovations noted in the relevant scholarship are (a) a refinement of the distinction between ordinary law and statute and the idea of fundamental law and (b) the belief that fundamental law, to be legitimate and effective as a limit on sovereign power, must be inscribed in written documents. As James Madison notes, with perhaps a touch of hyperbole, in *Federalist* #53: "The important distinction so well understood in America between a Constitution established by the people and unalterable by the government, and a law established by the government and alterable by the government, seems to have been little understood and less observed in any other country."[49]

The American experiment with written fundamental law emerges as the political and constitutional solution to the problem of sovereignty.[50] But the precise way in which the written Constitution functions to limit sovereign power remains a matter of some dispute. What might be called a Jeffersonian tradition of American constitutionalism maintains that the Constitution works to limit power by specifying or enumerating specific powers that may be exercised by the federal government and establishing equally specific injunctions on fedcral power; the Constitution stipulates what the federal government is authorized to do and what it is prohibited from doing. Limits are clearly inscribed in the text, making the literal language of the text paramount, and are enforced by the courts or, in one strand of this tradition, by the interposition of the states.[51] An examination of key argument structures in the *Federalist* essays problematizes this Jeffersonian account. By probing these argumentative structures an alternative account of the nature and process of limiting sovereign power can be reconstructed so that we can grasp important nuances in the development, or constitution, of American constitutionalism.

The attempt to limit sovereign power through express injunctions or prohibitions (imposed on the sovereign as well as agreed to by the sovereign) is a crucial component in the development of the constitutional tradition in western Europe and the United States. In essay #78 Alexander Hamilton appears to agree that injunctions and prohibitions constitute the essence of constitutionalism: "By a limited Constitution, I understand one which contains certain specified exceptions to the legislative authority; such, for instance, as that it shall pass no bills of attainder, no *ex post facto* laws, and the like. Limitations of this kind can be preserved in practice no other way than through the medium of courts of justice, whose duty it must be to declare all acts contrary to the manifest tenor of the Constitution void" (466). In this passage we find the key elements of the American constitutional tradition: a written document that is fundamental, restraints on power, and the enforcement mechanism of judicial review. Yet a careful reading of the essays as a whole reveals considerable ambivalence to the idea of absolute prohibitions as an effective and appropriate limit on federal power.

"Publius's" antagonism toward prohibitions and other "fixed rules" is understandable, in part, given the nation's situation in 1787. Unlike British efforts at constitutional reform throughout the seventeenth century that sought to curb the excesses, first, of the crown and, then, of a sovereign Parliament, the principal problem of the new nation in the eyes of nationalists like Hamilton and Madison is the lack of sufficient power or "energy" in the federal government. Their animosity toward continuing injunctions accumulates in the text. For the most part, "Publius" grudgingly accepts the relatively small number of explicit prohibitions written into the Constitution (generally those that ensure individual liberty) while arguing strenuously against various Antifederalist proposals to, for example, prohibit standing armies during periods of peace or limit the federal government to external (e.g., import duties) as opposed to internal (e.g., direct taxes) sources of revenue.

Hamilton initiates the assault on explicit prohibitions in essay #23. The specific topic of the essay is national defense, but it appears in the larger context of a discussion of the need for an energetic national government. In this number, Hamilton argues that because circumstances cannot be fixed or limited, it is impossible to limit the powers of the government to provide for the common defense through absolute prohibitions (153–54; see also #34, 207). As Hamilton writes in #26: "The idea of restricting the legislative authority in the means of providing for the national defense is one of those refinements which owe their origin to a zeal for liberty more ardent than enlightened" (168). Repeatedly, Hamilton rejects the feasibility of absolute prohibitions against federal power (e.g., #30, 188; #31, 193).[52]

Hamilton's second major argument against explicit prohibitions focuses on the interpretive disputes that they will most likely generate. Reviewing the language used by Antifederalists in advocating a prohibition on standing armies, Hamilton contends that it will "introduce an extensive latitude of construction" that, ultimately, "would afford ample room for eluding the force of the provision" (165). In the end, Hamilton writes, "public necessities" will always triumph over "parchment provisions." He continues: "Wise politicians will be cautious about fettering the government with restrictions that cannot be observed, because they know that every breach of the fundamental laws, though dictated by necessity, impairs that sacred reverence which ought to be maintained in the breast of rulers towards the constitution of a country, and forms a precedent for other breaches where the plea of necessity does not exist at all, or is less urgent" (167). Two observations about Hamilton's discussion are pertinent. First, in these essays he effects an at least potential reversal of the emerging tradition by revealing that explicit prohibitions and injunctions, one of the staple features of early modern constitutionalism, are ineffective and quite possibly dangerous to the project of constitutional government. Second, although promoting a "sacred reverence" for the constitutional text, Hamilton's discussion reveals an underlying anxiety about the status of the text that, as we will see, reverberates in the essays.

"Publius" confronts the challenge of limiting government by adumbrating a distinction between a government limited from certain activities and one that is limited to certain activities. "Publius" accepts a modest range of traditional prohibitions but urges his readers to resist "fettering" the government (helping to set in motion a hermeneutic tradition whose traces are evident in judicial rulings on gays in the military). The rejection of limitations from certain activities leaves open the possibility of limiting government to certain activities; this understanding of the force of the Constitution, that it limits government to specified enumerated powers, is at the center of the Jeffersonian tradition. But "Publius" undercuts this understanding of the practical force of the Constitution. Madison, in a strategy Wills labels "exhaustive division," argues in #44 that the powers of the federal government cannot, in fact, be enumerated.[53] This impossibility renders the "necessary and proper" clause, a provision that looms large in Antifederal opposition, a necessity. By rejecting enumerated powers and questioning the viability of strict constitutional prohibitions, "Publius's" argument, as David Epstein writes, "suggests the imprudence not only of the restrictions the Antifederalists propose, but also the Constitution's own project: a government of enumerated powers."[54] At the beginning of essay #26, Hamilton acknowledges that the traditional dilemma of reconciling the contradiction or incompatibility between sovereignty and limitations, public power and private rights "is the great source of the inconveniences we experience, and if we are not cautious to avoid a repetition of the error in our future attempts to rectify and ameliorate our system we may travel from one chimerical project to another; we may try change after change; but we shall never be likely to make any material change for the better" (168). Innovative change and a reconciliation of the dilemma of sovereignty and limitations is possible, "Publius" suggests, if the Constitution and constitutional order are understood in a particular way. Two argumentational structures are crucial in shaping this understanding. First, "Publius" introduces a second-order distinction that further reformulates the idea of limits. Specifically, "Publius" distinguishes between limits based on enumerated powers and limits derived from enumerated objects. Second, "Publius" reinforces the possibility of (real) limits on power through a dissociative structure that relegates "parchment" or merely theoretical limitations to the realm of appearances while locating a variety of structural restrictions that, if understood and allowed to operate, will effectively limit power.[55] Let me try to explain the way these argumentative structures work to constitute new possibilities for constitutional government.

In number #14 Madison begins a subtle reconstruction of the idea of limited Constitution: "In the first place it is to be remembered that the federal government is not charged with the whole power of making and administering laws. Its jurisdiction is limited to certain enumerated objects" (102). The distinction is implicit because Madison does not expressly contrast enumerated powers and objects. But the idea of enumerated objects is repeated in a number of essays (#23, 155; #25, 163; #27, 177; #39, 245; #41, 263), giving it a presence in the text that invites a comparison with the idea of enumerated powers. This implicit distinction allows "Publius" to negotiate the traditional dilemma of sovereignty (how to limit the sovereign power) as well as the interpretive problem posed by article 1, section 8 of the

Constitution (where grants of authority are made to the federal government). As Goodwin notes, argumentative distinctions tend to assume a basic "yes, but" structure. The distinction formulated allows "Publius" to acknowledge (the "yes") that the Constitution does enumerate specific powers *but* this specification is more properly understood within the context of articulating the objects or "ends" of federal action. Madison opens #41 by chiding Antifederalists for their "method" of analyzing the proposed Constitution. Their arguments "against the extensive powers of the government . . . have very little considered how far these powers were necessary means of attaining a necessary end" (255). By isolating and then emphasizing individual powers rather than the end or object of federal action, Antifederalists "dwell on . . . inconveniences" and ignore the broader and more important question of how "to advance the public happiness" (255–56). The shift in focus from powers to objects or ends also allows "Publius" to negotiate the dilemma of sovereignty by granting (the "yes") the traditional view that sovereign power is absolute (the position taken by Great Britain during its political dispute with the colonies and later rearticulated by some Antifederalists) *but* denying that this problem is insuperable.[56] "Publius" seems to suggest that the Constitution republicanizes and federalizes the essentially premodern notion that the sovereign is supreme within its appropriate sphere.[57] The objects or ends articulated in the Constitution create a sphere of action within which federal power is sovereign while nevertheless constraining federal authority.

The problem of sovereignty in the new nation is more complicated, however, because of the ascendency of the doctrine of popular sovereignty.[58] In America sovereignty was believed to reside ultimately in the people and not in government. So the broader problem that a constitutional order must address is how the people's sovereignty can be limited. As we will see more fully in a moment, "Publius" did not believe that written fundamental law by itself was sufficient. In the final analysis, popular sovereignty cannot be limited; the people always retain their traditional and fundamental right of revolution and ability to alter the government (for example, #28, 180). If sovereignty could not be absolutely limited, it could be discursively and politically restructured in a way that allowed for a satisfactory negotiation of the problem. As Goodwin suggests, distinctions inevitably divide the conceptual field under consideration. In the case of popular sovereignty, "Publius's" distinction between powers and objects leads to the position that, although it may ultimately be incapable of limitation, sovereignty can be divided; different objects can be assigned to the different governmental branches and levels that structure the constitutional order in such a way that popular sovereignty is assured even as it is limited.[59] A recurring dissociation argument vividly illustrates the importance of structure to "Publius's" vision of constitutionalism.

"Publius's" reconceptualization of the idea of limits is further refined in the essays through a dissociative strategy that divides parchment, paper, or merely theoretical limitations of power from more effective alternatives. Through the dissociative process, "Publius" relegates the first form of limitation to the realm of "appearances," thereby reconstituting their status as a limit; they are, in effect, only apparent limits that are practically inadequate.[60] Evidence of this strategy appears in a number of the *Federalist* essays. In #20, for example, the reputation of the "celebrated Belgic confederacy" is challenged because its "practice" did not conform to "parchment" (135; cf. the theory/practice dissociation in #18, 123). As noted above, in #25 Hamilton maintains that "parchment provisions" are incapable of restraining government when "public necessit[ies]" are involved (167). In #48 Madison notes that however important "discriminating, . . . in theory, the several classes of power" may be, the real "task is to provide some practical security for each [branch of government], against the invasion of the others." "Will it be sufficient," Madison inquires, "to mark, with precision, the boundaries of these departments in the constitution of the government, and to trust to these parchment barriers against the encroaching spirit of power?" (308). Madison's "conclusion . . . is that a mere demarcation on parchment of the constitutional limits of the several departments is not a sufficient guard against those encroachments which lead to a tyrannical concentration of all the powers of government in the same hands" (313). In #61 Hamilton claims that a mere written "declaration" regarding electoral qualifications "would certainly have been harmless. . . . But it would, in fact, have afforded little or no additional security against the danger apprehended" (372). Or, again, in #73 Hamilton discusses "the insufficiency of a mere parchment delineation of the boundaries" between the departments of government (442).

The relegation of parchment provisions to the realm of appearances demonstrates "Publius's" reservations about the efficacy of the written word and further illustrates the linguistic anxiety of the era.[61] As Madison's lengthy digression on language in #37 reveals, leading thinkers of the founding period recognized but remained apprehensive about the linguistic and discursive basis of politics. And this apprehension shapes "Publius's" understanding of a written Constitution. Although Madison can write in #53 about "constitutional security" being guaranteed "by the authority of a paramount Constitution" (332), the numerous observations about parchment provisions problematize this assertion and suggest that a written text, by itself, cannot control power. As Hamilton notes in #29, "render[ing] an army unnecessary will be a more certain method of preventing its existence than a thousand prohibitions on paper" (183). "Real" limits, not mere written appearances, are necessary and "Publius" tries to demonstrate how the proposed Constitution will foster a constitutional order that makes "real" limits a live possibility.

Gordon Wood suggests that the colonists' experience with Great Britain established that "Parliament could not be restrained from violating the fundamental principles and rights embedded in the ancient common law and the constitution by the inner workings of the institutions of government." The inadequacy of existing institutions meant that "somehow these principles and rights must be protected and guaranteed by lifting them out of government."[62] A written, fixed Constitution became the commonly accepted way to "lift" and "protect" the fundamental principles of the polity. But "Publius's" skepticism about the efficacy of written prohibitions and protections points to a revalorization of the "inner workings of government." According to Epstein, "*The Federalist* insists that any real protection against abuse [of power] is to be found not in any limitation of the government's powers but in the government's *structure*, in how it is 'modeled.'" He continues: "More generally, *The Federalist* defends a 'structure' of government which limits government by the interaction of men's [sic] natural passions."[63] "Publius's" emphasis on structure, documented by Epstein, is strategically effective in the context of the ratification debates in its potential to shift the focus of debate away from individual powers and their likelihood of usurpation or abuse (a central facet in Antifederalist discourse) and on to the issue of systemic organization (e.g., #23, 156; #31, 196). In addition, structure functions as or constitutes the realm of the real in "Publius's" dissociative argument. For "Publius," the proposed Constitution provides the structure for a constitutional order that, when embodied by live human agents, will effectively limit power. This position is advanced in numerous passages in the essays. Perhaps the most famous example is Madison's account of ambition counteracting ambition in #51 (322–23). Another example can be found in Hamilton's discussion of the "real" method to protect against the dangers of a standing army. A third example is in Hamilton's seemingly paradoxical argument in #25 that it is safer to entrust military power in a potentially untrustworthy national government than it would be to place that power in the supposedly more trustworthy state governments. As Hamilton explains, "As far as an army may be considered as a dangerous weapon of power, it had better be in those hands of which the people are most likely to be jealous than in those of which they are least likely to be jealous. For it is a truth, which the experience of the ages has attested, that the people are commonly in danger when the means of injuring their rights are in the possession of those of whom they entertain the least suspicion" (164). By placing the military power in the hands of the national government, the Constitution helps structure an order that channels the people's apparently natural suspicion toward those who hold the power. Much like the logic embedded in the saying "keep your friends close but your enemies closer," Hamilton maintains that the people will be safe, and power effectively limited, not through parchment provisions but a constitutional order that checks power through the natural suspicions of the people.

Conclusion

This essay has tried to work on two levels. In the first portion of the essay, the focus was conceptual. In that portion I advanced an idea of constitutive rhetorical historiography as a supplement to the dominant instrumentalist tradition in rhetorical scholarship. Constitutive rhetorical historiography does not abandon the instrumental perspective but rather attempts to fold the instrumental moment of discursive action into the larger process of social and cultural (re)constitution. Four dimensions of discursive (re)constitution were identified: subjectivity and identity, temporal and spatial experience, community and political culture, and language and political concepts. The value of this historiographic perspective can only be judged in terms of its contribution to our understanding of the role of discursive action in history. The latter portion of the essay moved to the practical or substantive level of historical understanding and sought to illustrate the constitutive framework via a case study of the conceptual (re)constitution of the concept of "constitution" in *The Federalist Papers*. The analysis of the strategies of distinction and dissociation in the *Federalist* essays raised two key issues.

First, the analysis contributes to ongoing inquiry into the relationship between British and American constitutionalism. It confirms the position held by some scholars (e.g., Katz) that despite important differences (a written text, the lack of final legislative sovereignty) there remains a deep affinity between British and American constitutionalism.[64] "Publius's" emphasis on the structure of the constitutional order partially (re)constituted the British system's faith in the "inner workings of the institutions of government" (a faith, I might point out, that appears completely absent in late-twentieth-century American politics). Second, the analysis illustrates a peculiar ambivalence on the part of Hamilton and Madison toward the written text. The *Federalist* essays seem to celebrate while also problematizing the written constitution. The constitutive significance of this double gesture, inscribed most clearly in "Publius's" dissociative strategy, merits continued inquiry. At a minimum "Publius's" ambivalence acknowledges and helps perpetuate the traditional tension between law and politics, a tension that continues to enable and constrain the possibilities of constitutionalism in America.

Part II

Doing Rhetorical History:
Case Studies

6

Oaths Registered in Heaven

Rhetorical and Historical Legitimacy in the Inaugural Addresses of Jefferson Davis and Abraham Lincoln

James R. Andrews

Rhetoric in the Creation of Nationalism

In October 1862, after almost eighteen months of fighting, the American Civil War showed no signs of ending—and certainly not of forcing the reunion of the North and South. The seeming success of the Confederacy prompted the British Chancellor of the Exchequer, William Gladstone, to observe (prematurely as it turned out) in a highly controversial speech that "We may have our own opinions about slavery; we may be for or against the South; but there is no doubt that Jefferson Davis and other leaders of the South have made an army; they are making, it appears, a navy; and they have made more than either, they have made a nation."[1]

As historians and other students of nationalism clearly recognize, however, a specified territory formed into a political unit does not necessarily become a "nation." A "nation," much as a "class," does not spring full blown from a divine head; it does not automatically grow from a prescribed set of circumstances. The problem of Confederate nationalism, for example, has evoked a spectrum of interpretations from Civil War scholars. Recently, in an excellent study of the ideological contradictions and paradoxes on which Southern nationalism was founded—and on which it ultimately foundered—Drew Gilpin Faust emphasized that nationalism "is not a substance available to a people in a certain premeasured amount; it is rather a dynamic of ideas and social realities that can, under the proper circumstances, unite and legitimate a people in what they regard as reasoned public action."[2] Faust reviews the varied interpretations of Confederate nationalism, often as it relates to the issue of why the Confederacy lost the war intermingled with the nature of the antebellum South, and argues for a closer investigation of Confederate ideology. She suggests that a dynamic view of nationalism directs attention "to the social groups seeking to establish their own corporate ideals and purposes as the essence of group self-definition" and maintains that because "ideas are social actions, albeit symbolic ones . . . they must be treated in this way as facts, analogous to any other historical data."[3]

Noted Civil War historian Carl Degler has observed that "nationalism . . . is not a commodity or a thing, it is created"; it may be seen "as a process, in the course of which flesh and blood leaders and followers creatively mold and integrate ideas, events, and power to bring a nation into being."[4] Ideas interact with events that surround them, with the people who formulate and deal with ideas, and with those who generate and react to the power that influences events; all this forms the mix that both leaders and listeners must confront and/or conquer in the quest for identity. There is, in short, a rich and tangled context that mingles with text and within which the text must be interpreted.

There surely are few scholars left who view rhetoric as it is sometimes popularly imagined and journalistically depicted, that is, as "mere rhetoric," a window dressing that ornaments reality or a mask that obscures it. On the contrary, regarding rhetoric as distinct from reality is the *opposite* of a basic assumption made here. Rhetoric—the substance of messages, the means whereby those messages are shaped and conveyed, the underlying assumptions on which those messages are built, and the root values and ideals that those messages depict—is an essential force in shaping our understanding of social reality. That is to say, how events and ideas are talked about gives meaning to events and ideas. Those documents most revered in nineteenth-century America—the Declaration of Independence and the Constitution—themselves the product of antecedent thought, were generally seen by citizens of the republic as seminal. From them were derived vague, but highly charged, symbolic political/social precepts and virtues to which there was almost universal adherence but which required interpretation. The Declaration asserted that "all men are created equal" and labeled unalienable and God-given the rights to life, liberty, and the pursuit of happiness. To protect such rights, the Declaration proclaimed, governments were instituted and derived their power from the people who were governed; when governments failed in their mission, the people had the right to overthrow those governments. Over a decade later the Constitutional Convention produced a document that, according to its preamble, was intended to make the union of states more perfect. It professed to aim at insuring justice, tranquility, and protection from enemies; it sought to promote the general welfare and to secure liberty. In spite of a rancorous debate over its ratification, the Constitution, when adopted, was transformed into the wellspring of political virtue.

So, everyone believed in liberty and popular sovereignty, in union and justice; but everyone certainly did not share the same meaning when these words were used to censure or praise, to urge change or protect the status quo. Everyone most assuredly did not agree on who "We, the people of the United States"—for whom the framers of the Constitution professed to speak—really were or through what instruments and institutions the people acted and spoke, any more than everyone agreed on how and to whom the Declaration's phrase "all men are created equal" applied. As David Zarefsky and Victoria Gallagher have argued, the Constitution's ambiguity made its meaning and application a source of public argument whereas, paradoxically, its veneration made it a "sacred text" to which verbal combatants appealed as an authority. What Zarefsky and Gallagher describe as the strategy of the defeated Antifederalists might be applied in a general sense to all those engaged in public argument who sought to find support in fundamental texts: "Rather than *fight* it, better to *capture* it and read their own interests into it, using its ambiguous language to identify it with their own point of view."[5]

The making of a unified American "nation" was, of course, a complex process. A web of related, contested ideas emerged, through argument shaped by events and tempered by power, from the smoke of battle, ideas refined and defined a bit more sharply by the victors. Throughout the antebellum period, different groups competed to impose their own meaning on root values as the quintessential definition of what was fundamentally "American." A close examination of symbolic social action embedded in the language of political discourse—that is to say, careful investigation of American rhetoric as embodied in significant historical texts—may, indeed, go a long way toward reconstructing the essential qualities and underlying tensions that compete for hegemony in forming a national identity. The aim here is, through a case study, to uncover significant clues as to *how* the *process* of determining who Americans thought they were and what they were becoming played out within its own context.

Rhetoric, viewed as persuasive discourse, can be examined as a strategy employed to channel the process; rhetoric, viewed as revelation, can be studied in order to uncover the powerful formulative forces moving beneath the surface. That is to say, the public articulation of ideas can be overtly persuasive as the speaker or writer attempts to win others to her or his view or to reinforce mutually shared values or goals. At the same time public messages can covertly communicate a myriad of unspoken forces—assumptions, values, perspectives—that shape public perceptions of and reactions to events. Public discourse provides a rich source for discovering the evolving nature of the underpinnings of the idea of a "nation" and for displaying the ways in which the elements in an emerging "nationalism" are manipulated, in Faust's phrase, to "unite and legitimate a people."[6] In other words, we may discern in public messages an ideology that affectively, effectively, and reflectively energizes the idea of an American nation. In this study I want to illustrate the way in which the values in tension might be identified and analyzed in rhetorical texts by a comparative critical investigation of Lincoln's First Inaugural Address and Jefferson Davis's Inaugural Address.

Two Presidents

In early 1861, as the crisis deepened, William T. Sherman met with friends in Louisiana before heading North. In a farewell meeting with Sherman, Mrs. Braxton Bragg, wife of the future Confederate General, fretted over her husband's chances of obtaining a suitable commission. "You know that my husband is not a favorite with the new President," she remarked. When Sherman responded that he wasn't aware that Colonel Bragg knew Mr. Lincoln, Mrs. Bragg answered "quite pointedly" that she "didn't mean *your* President, but *our* President."[7]

The Braggs' president had been installed in office only days before. On Saturday afternoon, February 10, 1861, Lee Daniel was at work in the Vicksburg telegraph office when a telegram of great importance, addressed to Jefferson Davis, arrived. Recognizing the urgency of the message, Daniel consulted Davis's friend James Roach, and soon a messenger was galloping south toward Davis's plantation, Brierfield, with the news that the Mississippian had just been unanimously elected president of the Provisional Government of the Confederate States of America. Davis, who had anticipated a military commission in the new confederacy, was taken aback. Standing with Mrs. Davis in the rose garden, the new president alarmed his wife as he studied the telegram in his hands. He "looked so grieved that I feared some evil had befallen our family," Verna Davis reported later. After "a painful silence," Davis told her of his election "as a man might speak of a sentence of death."[8]

Although he fought hard for political office, Davis always maintained his adherence to the republican principle that "the office seeks the man." Such was surely true in this case; he had not sought to lead the new confederation, and Davis saw clearly that the path lying before him and before the seceded South would be a rugged one. Never one to shirk his duty, however, Jefferson Davis obeyed the summons and left on the difficult journey to Montgomery on February 11. And a hard journey it was; the provisional president began it by barely catching up with the riverboat that was to carry him to Vicksburg. From then on, as he wrote to Verna, he was "in a crowd of people and events." From Vicksburg he moved on to Jackson and then endured a two-day trip by rail to Atlanta, sleeping in his clothes and stopping about twenty times to make speeches "in response to the calls from the crowds." Along the circuitous route—Davis himself had observed that it was easier to get to Montgomery from Washington, D.C., than it was to get there from Jackson, Mississippi—bonfires lit his way and cannons boomed in salute. West and south through Georgia and Alabama, Davis's special car crawled toward Montgomery, reaching the provisional capital late in the evening of February 16.[9]

On the same day that Jefferson Davis began the arduous trip to Montgomery, Abraham Lincoln, president-elect of the United States, bid "an affectionate farewell" to his friends in Springfield and set out for Washington. His trip, too, was tiring—and longer; it took Lincoln until February 23 to reach his capital. Unlike Davis, Lincoln had been anticipating the trip for months. Since his election in November, Lincoln partially filled the long hiatus wrestling with patronage problems, but more than the spoils of political victory occupied the president-elect. It was everywhere apparent that the heated atmosphere was developing into the ultimate political crisis in the country's brief history. Lincoln's very election to office horrified and angered the South. Most Southern spokespeople and most of the Southern press refused to acknowledge any distinction between the president-elect and the hated radical abolitionists. In the weeks before the election lurid descriptions of the effects of a Republican victory filled the pages of the Southern press. The implacably secessionist *Charleston Mercury* told its readers that Hannibal Hamlin, the Republican vice presidential candidate who would, if elected, preside over the Senate, was chosen largely because he was a mulatto; the black abolitionist Frederick Douglass was said to be in line for a seat in the cabinet. A Republican victory, the *Mercury* reflected darkly, presaged "a total annihilation of all self government or liberty in the South." The rabid disunionist paper did predict, however, that were the South to control its own destiny—separated from the Republican-dominated North—it would "bound forward in a career of prosperity and power, unsurpassed in the history of nations." Thus it was that ardent secessionists, such as Edmund Ruffin, actually welcomed Lincoln's election as a certain prelude to dissolution of the union. As he traveled through North Carolina on his way to Charleston on November 7, 1860, Ruffin heard that New York would go for Lincoln and thus secure the presidency for the Republican candidate: "It is good news for me," he recorded in his diary.[10]

Most, however, were unsure of what would actually happen. One ramification that became clear in the weeks that followed was that the other states of the Deep South would emulate South Carolina in seceding from the union and answer her call for a convention to establish a new confederation. Within a few months seven states left the union and sent their delegates to Montgomery to effect a new government. President Buchanan's convictions illustrated the atmosphere of stalemate and indecision that enveloped the country: the outgoing chief executive held that secession was unconstitutional but at the same time disavowed the right of the federal government to coerce the defiant states. The ineffectual Buchanan might be referred to contemptuously by U. S. Grant as "the present granny of an executive," but few did know what was to be done in the maddeningly uncertain future.[11]

The tangle of emotions and prognostications was bewilderingly contradictory. In both sections the possibility and/or desirability of war was contested. The fire-eaters, anxious to seize the opportunities Lincoln's election afforded them, deprecated the notion that secession meant war, brushing aside fearful arguments against leaving the union. Robert Barnwell Rhett was reported to have claimed that he would eat all the bodies of those slain in a war and the former South Carolina senator James Chestnut Jr. said he would drink all the blood spilled, so sure were they—or so sure did they profess to be—that secession would not be violently contested by the North. As Georgia prepared for a state convention, secessionists stumped the state assuring voters that secession would not lead to war. In the North, moderates like the outgoing governor of Massachusetts, Nathaniel Banks, insisted that war was not imminent and expressed the hope that "the lapse of time alone, will heal all dissensions." Indiana's new governor, Henry S. Lane, likewise a moderate, urged conciliation and suggested that his state would "cheerfully and promptly" extend "all their just rights as equals under the Constitution" to sister states of the South. Even as Southern members departed, delivering valedictories tinged with sadness, or with menace, or with contempt, both houses of Congress desperately established committees charged with finding a peaceful way out of the approaching conflict. And, summoned by Virginia, delegates from twenty-one states gathered in Washington for a peace convention dedicated to finding a compromise adequate to hold the union together.[12]

On either side there were those who thought the other would not put up much of a fight. A joke current in the South was that if you should meet a Yankee with a gun leveled at you, all you need do was to pull out your pocket book and ask the Yankee how much he wanted for the gun: "right there the fight would end." Speaking to a Republican crowd in Milwaukee a few days after Lincoln's election, Carl Schurz pointed out that Southern leaders—concocting the "most preposterous apprehensions" for Southern safety, "indulging in extravagant designs," "plotting treason," and "preparing to exhaust the financial resources of their states"—would lead to their own ruin. Once Southerners realized the disastrous economic consequences of their actions and once they apprehended that the North, "conscious of their strength and righteous intentions," would not be bullied, the "dangers and difficulties" facing the Southern states would be apparent, and the people would renounce the "politicians who have compromised themselves" by counseling secession. Years later, U. S. Grant described the discussions in Galena, Illinois, following the election of Abraham Lincoln. Sitting in Grant's little store, locals speculated on whether the South would really carry out its threats to break up the Union. "It was generally believed there would be a flurry" and "that some of the extreme Southern States would go so far as to pass ordinances of secession," Grant wrote. "But the common impression was that this step was so plainly suicidal for the South, that the movement would not spread over much of the territory and would not last long."[13]

Immediately following the presidential election, Edmund Ruffin commented in his diary on those Northerners who seemed to share the sentiments of Grant and his friends. He observed that "the northern people . . . are not yet startled from their delusion. . . . They continue to believe that there is no danger of southern people resisting northern outrages & now established domination, & they ascribe all demonstrations to the contrary as mere bluster & boasting." Immersed in the heady atmosphere of Charleston, watching as the South Carolina legislature passed the secession ordinance and inaugurated "the revolution of 1860," Ruffin certainly absorbed much of the blustering oratory. Bands played and politicians made speeches, the likes of Congressman Keitt roundly denouncing the "accursed union" to the cheers of large crowds. The fire-eating Ruffin, however, accurately discerned the determination beneath what Northerners perceived as Southern braggadocio. Ruffin himself was to be honored by induction into the Palmetto Guards and, on the morning of April 12, 1861, was afforded the privilege of firing the sixty-four-pound Columbaid that hurled the first shell into the walls of Fort Sumter.[14]

Indeed, the hopes of moderates, the partisan expressions of sectional confidence, and the convictions that neither side would fight were more than countered by bellicose expostulations of radicals and by countervailing fears from all quarters. The belligerent Texan, Louis Wigfall, taunted Northerners from the floor of the Senate. After the *Star of the West*, sent by the federal government to supply Fort Sumter, was turned back at Charleston Harbor, Wigfall sneered, "Your flag has been insulted; redress it, if you dare. You have submitted to it for two months, you will submit to it for ever." For their part, Republican radicals called for the punishment of traitors and the passage of a force bill. Abolitionists who, according to Southern opinion, were the allies of Lincoln and his Republican party, in reality held contradictory opinions concerning the new president; many agreed with Wendell Phillips, however, that the best result of sectional conflict would, indeed, be separation from the morally tainted South. "The Union," Garrison wrote to Lynda Mott in January of 1861, "is surely going to pieces! 'Glory to God! Amen!'"[15]

Hopes and fears clutched and collided; cries and alarms disturbed or exhilarated; the oppressively heated atmosphere became unbearable as the storm approached. Repeatedly Lincoln was urged to make conciliatory statements that, presumably, would calm Southern fears. He resisted doing so, asserting that he had "already done this many—many times," and anyone who really wanted to know his position could read it.

After November 6 the president-elect held steadfast to his resolution to withhold all public comment until he could speak with the authority of office. While he waited in public silence, Lincoln vigorously instructed his supporters privately not to acquiesce in any proposals that jeopardized fundamental Republican principles. Lincoln was quite prepared to assure the South that his government would enforce the fugitive slave laws. Of more serious concern to Lincoln were the compromises being discussed in Congress and at the Peace Convention; he worried that these proposals, if accepted, would undermine his determination to hold absolutely firm "on the question of *extending* slavery." In words ultimately to be voiced in the Inaugural Address, Lincoln assured Alexander Stephens of Georgia that a Republican administration would not interfere directly or indirectly with slavery within the states: "The South would be in no more danger in this respect than it was in the days of Washington," Lincoln told the future vice president of the Confederacy. He nevertheless recognized that "You think slavery is *right* and ought to be extended; while we think it is *wrong* and ought to be restricted."[16]

Finally, after three months of waiting, the long, exhausting trip to Washington began. The presidential train, bedecked with American flags, chugged from Springfield to Indianapolis, across Ohio, into upstate New York, down to New York City, through New Jersey into Philadelphia, and finally to Harrisburg. Lincoln was persuaded of the possibility of a plot to assassinate him as he changed trains in Baltimore and reluctantly agreed to slip quietly into Washington via a night train. In the early hours of Sunday morning, February 23, the weary president-elect arrived in his capital.

Lincoln's progress through the North was marked by his repeated protestations that he "would make no long speeches." Obviously, his Inaugural Address would set out Lincoln's policy, and he had no intention of upstaging himself. As he explained on several occasions, he did not think it wise "to speak in detail of the course I shall deem it best to pursue. It is proper that I should avail myself of all the information and all the time at my command, in order that when the time arrives in which I must speak officially, I shall be able to take the ground which I deem the best and safest, and from which I may have no occasion to swerve." Furthermore, Lincoln's policy of "eloquent silence" was designed to navigate among the dangerous shoals of conflicting opinion not only in the country generally but in his own Republican party.[17]

Lincoln's short responses to official welcomes and enthusiastic calls from the crowds did, however, occasionally allow glimpses into his thoughts. He told an audience in Indianapolis that it was the business of the people to answer the question, "Shall the Union and shall the liberties of this country be preserved to the last generation?" And he expressed doubt that enforcing the laws and holding government property could be called "coercion" or "invasion," a statement threatening to conservative business interests, too tepid for radicals, and unnerving to Southern unionists and border state supporters.[18]

The speeches that followed on the tour tended to be less provocative but did offer hints of Lincoln's intentions. The citizens of Cleveland were warned that "if we do not now join to save the good old ship of the Union this voyage nobody will have a chance to pilot her on another voyage." In Syracuse Lincoln prayed for "the perpetuity of those institutions under which we have so long lived and prospered," and the New Jersey state senate was told that the future president was "exceedingly anxious that this Union, the Constitution, and the liberties of the people shall be perpetuated in accordance with the original idea for which that struggle [the Revolution] was made."[19] The president-elect thus seemed committed to the preservation of the Union, although he was not specific as to the course he would take. He asserted that none would do more to preserve peace than he and assured his listeners that "the Government will not use force unless force is used against it," but he also allowed that "it may be necessary to put the foot down firmly."[20] Americans, confused and contentious, faced the future uneasily. In the midst of what Sherman called the "warm discussions about politics" that were going on throughout the country, Americans—now apparently disunited into two countries—went about the business of inaugurating their two presidents.[21]

Abraham Lincoln, sixteenth president of the United States of America, and Jefferson Davis, provisional president of the Confederate States of America, both faced monumental challenges in addressing the varied audiences that would attend to their first words as chief executives. Both, of course, recognized the extreme gravity of the situation and both had immediate political concerns that shaped their rhetorical strategies. In fact, Jefferson Davis and Abraham Lincoln had very similar tasks: each had to convince the other side of its own resolve, and each had to solicit the support of wavering states.

Within this network of restraints the two presidential antagonists struggled. Understanding the tactical moves each made in order to promote strategic aims also uncovers the root of the clash: the struggle to control the answer to the question of what made an American government legitimate. That struggle revolved around conflicting interpretive claims regarding the meaning and application of basic tenets of an American political system judged against the purity of historical lineage.

The two addresses illustrate the conflicting views of the foundations upon which an American nation should be constructed, views that were, in varying ways, resolved or reconciled through the Civil War and its attendant rhetoric. Two themes generate the principal points of clash in the contest between these rhetorical antagonists: _political genealogy_ and _sovereignty_. These themes are not, of course, unique to Lincoln and Davis; on the contrary, they are the result of evolutionary argument stretching back to the early years of the Republic. Nor are they entirely separate; they are strands that contestants wished to weave into different patterns to compose an "American" tapestry. Let us briefly consider each of these themes before turning to the texts.

Political genealogy. By 1825 John Quincy Adams could begin to talk of the Constitution as "the work of our forefathers," and Martin

Van Buren, a dozen years later, acknowledged upon taking the presidential office that "unlike all who have preceded me, the Revolution that gave us existence as one people was achieved at the period of my birth."[22] As the century progressed the immediacy of the country's founding documents and the vivacity of the founders themselves receded. Nevertheless, the views of the founders and the interpretations of the documents they had made were not diminished in significance.

It was important for contending parties to establish themselves as the legitimate descendants of the venerated authors of independence and inventors of American constitutional government. When Webster challenged Hayne over the "Carolina" doctrine in their famous 1830 debate, for example, he sought to refute Hayne's assertion that nullification was but the doctrine of 1798 as embodied in the Kentucky Resolutions. After the debate both nullifiers and nationalists solicited support from James Madison for their contrary opinions because both wished to invest their interpretations of the famous resolutions with the power of legitimacy that the father of the Constitution could bestow. Madison's eventual qualified public endorsement of Webster's interpretation, however, failed to quash Calhoun's nullification doctrine as espoused by Hayne.[23]

Thirty years later the battle over who could best claim the inheritance of the founders still raged. This is apparent, for example, in Abraham Lincoln's speech at the Cooper Union Institute, wherein he adopted as "a text for this discourse" a line from a speech by his old adversary: agreeing with Senator Douglas's assertion that "Our fathers, when they framed the government under which we live, understood this question just as well, and even better, than we do now," Lincoln took extraordinary pains to trace the actions of the founding fathers, "the thirty-nine" framers of the Constitution, to prove that "in their understanding . . . [nothing] in the Constitution . . . forbade Congress to prohibit slavery in the federal territory."[24]

The struggle for legitimacy was not exclusively—or perhaps even primarily—an innocent and sincere search for the "true" meaning of the founders; rather, it was an important means of lending credence to a particular position and strengthening the rationalization of that position. All sides contesting for their own group's control of the American ethos claimed for themselves the genealogical sanction due to authentic descendants. The dispute over legitimacy had powerful implications: the true heirs of the "sacred texts" would, in a sense, "own" them and command their meaning. Just as significantly, the controversy centered on who would control time: those who could successfully capture the "true" meaning of the past were endowed with the power to discriminate between legitimate and fraudulent policies and thus to project the historically faithful course for the future.

Sovereignty. From the debate over the ratification of the Constitution until the Civil War itself, the issue of the powers and rights of the states versus those of the general government was exceedingly thorny. At the outset, before the Constitution's fate was determined and before the document's apotheosis, the likes of James Wilson were declaring that the new government was "not a government founded upon compact; it is founded upon the power of the people. They express in their name and their authority, '*We the People do ordain and establish.*'" Before the Pennsylvania Ratifying Convention Wilson argued emphatically that such language was "not an unmeaning flourish." Rather, "the expressions declare, in a practical manner, the principle of this constitution. It is ordained and established by the people themselves."[25] Indeed, it was decidedly not an unmeaning flourish for Patrick Henry, either. Henry demanded to know "what right had they to say, *We, the People.* . . . Who authorized them to speak the language of *We, the People,* instead of *We, the States?*" In urging his fellow Virginians to reject the Constitution, Henry thundered, "The people gave them no power to use their name."[26]

Ratification, of course, did not begin to define categorically the relationship between the states and the federal government any more than it did the more subtle and deeper questions of who "the people" were, who spoke for them, and what relation they bore to their government. The Virginia and Kentucky Resolves spawned by the Alien and Sedition Acts, the Nullification doctrine growing out of the debates over the tariff, the irreconcilable division over the right of Congress to regulate slavery in the territories exacerbated by the vast acquisition of land after the defeat of Mexico, Calhoun's exposition of "concurrent majority," and Douglas's plan for "squatter sovereignty" were all examples of theoretical justifications or practical resolutions produced by the clash over how the notion of government of the people would and should work out. On the eve of the Civil War, following over a half century of self-congratulation and of prideful pointing to the American example set for the world, there was really no consensus on the meaning of democracy and republicanism.

These fundamental themes, political genealogy and sovereignty, mingle in interesting ways in the two inaugurals. In a certain microcosmic sense they represent the constitutional/legal fault lines along which the rhetoric of nationhood traveled. Close examination of these addresses yields interpretive contrasts from which may be projected the differences that had to be surmounted—by both rhetorical and coercive means—before the union could be recast as a nation.

Two Inaugurals: Point, Counterpoint

In examining the ways in which the defining characteristics of an American nation, as represented in these interwoven themes, were rhetorically negotiated in each address, let us consider the addresses of Davis and Lincoln contrapuntally.[27]
Introduced by Howell Cobb of Georgia, Davis stood between the impressive columns flanking the entrance to the Alabama state-house and began an address whose opening would have been difficult to distinguish from the exordia—or, at times, perorations—of past inaugural addresses of presidents of the United States. Davis adhered to the convention wherein presidents declared their unworthiness, expressed their gratitude, maintained the fiction of a disinterested election, and called on the sustaining force of the people and their representatives. In this, Davis followed the examples of Thomas Jefferson, James Madison, Andrew Jackson, and Franklin Pierce, and implied the formal aspect of legitimacy by adherence to generic features of an inaugural address. Furthermore, in Davis's words "Called to the difficult and responsible station of Chief Executive"(46) is embedded the traditional, familiar content and mode of address, a view of American political ideals and practices that is especially interesting when contrasted with Lincoln. Davis is "called." Washington, Jefferson, Madison, Monroe, John Quincy Adams were all "called" by their "country" or the "voice of their country" or some unnamed higher power—by implication the "people." The "call" takes on its sacred connotations—the voice of the people is the voice of God. As one is "called" to ministry, so one is "called" to public office.
Davis consistently expressed his belief in the republican maxim that the office sought the man—not the other way around. Although self-deprecating allusions and the fiction that one did not seek the office were consistent features of antebellum inaugurals, a subtle shift in language had been occurring over time that signaled the shift from republican elitism to more popular democracy. Andrew Jackson did not allude to a call in his 1829 inaugural; rather, Old Hickory had been "appointed to perform [his duties] by the choice of a free people" (55). His second inaugural uses the word "call" but in a different sense: "The will of the American people, expressed through their unsolicited suffrages, calls me before you to pass through the solemnities preparatory [to taking office]" (58). Polk, in 1845, was "chosen by

the free and voluntary suffrages of my countrymen," and Zachary Taylor declared himself "elected by the American people" (89; 99). "Appointed," "chosen," or "elected" by the people are terms with a much less vague—and much more political and democratic—ring to them than the more spiritual, less procedural "called."

The foundation of the "office-seeks-the-person" belief—and what it implies in terms of the exercise of the popular will—lies in earlier notions of republicanism. Briefly put, the classical republicanism that dominated the thinking of the Enlightenment and influenced the founders equated political virtue with disinterested public leadership. That is, one was disinterested if one could subordinate one's own interests to the public interest. To do so one had to be independent. It is clear that the notion of the "sovereignty of the people" did not entail the direct participation of all the people; such action would have been impractical (although it did exist in the practices of some town meetings) as well as imprudent. Those who could be independent were those who had both the leisure and the financial resources to put the public good ahead of personal gain—as, for example, the large plantation owners of the South were thought to be.

This notion of republicanism provided support for the political elitism that prevailed in the eighteenth and early nineteenth century. (One need look no further than the electoral college for a concrete example of how this elite republicanism plays out.) Who was it, after all, who "called" Jefferson Davis to his presidency? It was the delegates sent to Montgomery by the legislatures of the states that had seceded from the union.[28] These delegates established a provisional government, and Davis was its provisional president. There was no expectation, however, that provisional meant temporary. (Indeed, in November Davis was elected to the presidency without opposition.) Although Davis did, in the second sentence of the second paragraph, look "forward to the speedy establishment of a permanent government to take the place of this" and acknowledged that it would have greater "moral and physical power," there is no indication that such power would flow from a more popular election. In fact, the bulk of the speech is predicated on the assertion that the people of the South had spoken (46).

And what of Lincoln? His legitimating opening is parsimonious in the extreme. "In compliance with a custom as old as Government itself," he proceeds to take the oath "prescribed by the Constitution of the United States" (119). This opening is, however, a strong assertion of legitimacy. His compliance is directly linked to "Government itself," stretching back to the first inaugural, and sanctified by the touchstone of legitimacy, the Constitution: he is the direct descendant of Washington and the founders. Later in the text Lincoln returned to his place in the succession of legitimate leadership. The new president reminded the nation that it was "seventy-two years since the first inauguration of a President under our National Constitution." He placed himself in direct line with the "fifteen greatly distinguished citizens" who had administered the executive branch of government and recalled "this scope of precedent" with which he entered "the same task for the brief constitutional term of four years" (121).

In both speeches, of course, efforts to establish legitimacy appear throughout the text, interlaced with interpretations of sovereignty. Jefferson Davis cast his appeals in the tones of a moral and political rectitude that asked only for the right to proceed peacefully along the path of independence, enlisting both the Declaration and the Constitution to justify the new Confederacy.

The formation of the Confederacy illustrated the "American idea that governments rest upon the consent of the governed" (46). What followed this contention was something of a pastiche, as Davis culled from the sacred texts phrases meant to sustain his argument that secession was but the animation of the right of the people, embodied in the states, "to resume the authority delegated for the purposes of government." Repeating the words of the Declaration, Davis reminded all that "it is the right of the people to alter or abolish governments whenever they become destructive of the ends for which they were established." If the declared purpose of the "compact of Union," as stipulated in the Constitution, was "to establish justice, insure domestic tranquillity, provide for the common defense, promote the general welfare, and secure the blessing of liberty to ourselves and our posterity," then, Davis maintained, the states who had entered the compact had the right to dissolve it when "the ends for which it [the union] was established" were "perverted." (Lincoln, in contrast, contended that the Union was older than the Constitution, emphasizing the one clause in the preamble that Davis omitted in his recitation of the Constitution's purposes: "to form a more perfect Union.") The process, as Davis described it in a telescoped version of a historic argument, was simply "a right which the Declaration of Independence of 1776 had defined to be inalienable"; the states, "as sovereigns, were the final judges" of when and how to exercise that right (47).

The right asserted in the Declaration, however, did not quite fit the Southern argument that had been long developing. Thirty years before, Webster had acknowledged that "there may be extreme cases in which the people, in any mode of assembling, may resist usurpation, and relieve themselves from a tyrannical government" and affirmed that "no one will deny this." This "right of revolution," however, was not what Southerners wished to rely on, as Hayne admitted when he agreed with Webster that he did not contend "for the mere right of revolution, but for the right of constitutional resistance" by the states.[29] The "Carolina doctrine" of interposition stopped short of secession but was the antecedent interpretation prerequisite to Davis's proclamation that the action of sovereign States in forming a Confederacy was legally warranted. Only by accepting such a premise could one embrace the notion proffered that it was "by abuse of language that their act has been denominated a revolution" (47). The heritage claimed by Davis could not be to the right of revolution—that is, to the right to *overthrow* the government proclaimed in 1776 and established in 1789—but, rather, to the *return* to that government's true principles. Indeed, the states comprising the Confederacy had "labored to preserve the Government of our fathers in its spirit" (47), and it was this new country whose leaders had written "a Constitution differing only from that of our fathers in so far as it is explanatory of their well-known intent" (48). Although the confederated states "changed the constituent parts," they had not changed "the system of our Government." Indeed, the Constitution of the Confederacy, according to Davis, was "the Constitution of our fathers" revised only in a way that "reveals its true meaning" (49–50). Davis's prayer was that "the God of our fathers" would "guide and protect us in our efforts to perpetuate the principles which, by his blessing, they were able to vindicate" and "establish and transmit to their posterity" (50).

Davis and his compatriots in the Deep South were obviously to be seen as the fathers' posterity, the legal heirs of the Revolution and the direct progeny of the Constitution's makers. Their legitimacy was based on the sovereignty of the states and the rights of the states to act in the name of the people. The "government created by the compact ceased to exist" as a result of "a peaceful appeal to the ballot-box," Davis claimed. For their part, Northerners found it hard to imagine the Confederacy as the fruit of electoral victory. The avidly pro-Lincoln *New York Evening Post,* for example, compared Lincoln, "the constitutionally elected President of twenty-five millions of free people, [who] represents not only the principle of order in general, but the noblest constitution of government that ever the wisdom of man devised," with Davis, "the chosen officer of a packed convention of disaffected traitors and schemers."[30] The elitist republican conception of the people—citizens first of their states and represented by their states, acting only through the political leadership dominant in their states—controlled the political imagination of the South and particularly of the ruling class. In sharp contrast was Lincoln's perception of legitimate descent embodied in and animated by a distinctly more democratic spirit.

Lincoln's brief opening was followed by an unusually brisk confrontation of immediate realities. (Only Franklin Roosevelt's First Inaugural matches the tone and conveys the determination to face the obvious, preoccupying crisis.) Lincoln would not talk of matters that were of "no special anxiety or excitement." He went immediately to Southern apprehensions that "their property and their peace and their personal security are to be endangered." To counter such fears, Lincoln referred to the many public speeches he had made and reiterated—by quoting from one speech—that he had "no purpose, directly or indirectly, to interfere with the institution of slavery in the States where it exists. I believe I have no lawful right to do so, and I have no inclination to do so" (119). Lincoln went on to cite the Republican platform, to insist that no section was "in any wise endangered by the incoming Administration," and to pledge adherence to uphold the fugitive slave law as deriving from what is "plainly written in the Constitution" (120). Furthermore, the president-elect called upon all, in both "official and private station," to follow his own resolve "to conform to and abide by all those acts which stand unrepealed" (121).

Certainly it was inevitable that secessionists, who would brook no compromise that would take their states back into union with the North, would hear in the Inaugural "the clank of metal," as George Templeton Strong admiringly put it, and understand the implications for armed conflict that were conveyed in Lincoln's words.[31] But these words would come later in the address. This opening pledge not to interfere with Southern institutions may have been meant to allay fears of Southern Unionists or to settle the qualms of border-state politicians; it may have been a statement to establish "for the record" the peaceful intentions of Lincoln and the Republican party. Be that as it may, this section of the Inaugural, by stressing the strict adherence to the legal strictures imposed by the Constitution and pledging to enforce even laws odious to the Republican conscience, enhanced the legitimacy of Lincoln's claim that the new Republican administration had inherited the mantle of the Constitution makers. Moreover, Lincoln moved from his efforts to assure all who would listen that his administration would follow Constitutional law and his admonition for all others to follow such an example to the argument that "in contemplation of universal law and of the Constitution the Union of these States is perpetual." Developing this argument from fundamental law to the Articles of Association in 1774 to the Declaration and finally to the Constitution itself, Lincoln forged the links that associated his constitutionalism with America's past and led him to conclude that it was his duty in the future to "take care, as the

Constitution expressly enjoins upon me, that the laws of the Union be faithfully executed in all the States" (122). As heir to the past he controlled the future.

The other major legitimizing force, indeed the principal one, was the extent to which the respective presidents spoke for the "people." Davis, of course, saw the states as the bulwark of the people's rights and the vehicles through which the people's will could be carried out. He claimed "an abiding faith in the virtue and patriotism of the people" (46), but they were, for him, a "people united in heart, where one purpose of high resolve animates and actuates the whole" (50).

Lincoln, of course, thought it plain that "the central idea of secession is the essence of anarchy" because it taught the lesson that when minorities refused to acquiesce in decisions of the majority, they could always secede in an endless downward spiral toward chaos (123). Lincoln's inaugural was imbued with a democratic ethos that defined the people broadly and construed their powers as grounded in majority rule. Lincoln's assertion that he was enjoined to support the laws in all the states was followed by the direct assertion that he meant to do so, *unless*—this being the only exception, this the only preventative to action to preserve the Union—"unless my rightful masters, the American people, shall withhold the requisite means or in some authoritative manner direct the contrary" (122).

It was at this juncture in his address that Lincoln made a critical rhetorical move. He conceded that, if there be "persons in one section or another who seek to destroy the Union at all events and are glad of any pretext to do it," it would be useless to try to convince them: "I need address no word to them" (122). His subsequent effort to demonstrate that hazarding "so desperate a step" would be but to fly from imagined ills to "certain ills" (122–23) is buttressed by attempts to prove that no unconstitutional actions had been taken against the South and by a recitation of issues in contention, issues that "the Constitution does not expressly" resolve (123). For Lincoln, there was only one way to resolve them: "If the minority will not acquiesce, the majority must, or the Government must cease. . . . The rule of a permanent arrangement, is wholly impossible" (123).

Lincoln readily admitted that if the minority were deprived of its "clearly written constitutional right" by the "mere force of numbers," then, "in a moral point of view," revolution would be justified (123). Of course, in Lincoln's opinion no such right had been violated, whereas Davis asserted that the South, "through many years of controversy," had "vainly endeavored . . . to obtain respect for the rights to which we were entitled" (48). And while Davis considered it an "abuse of language" to call the establishment of the Confederacy a revolution, Lincoln held to the constitutional position that whenever the people "shall grow weary of the existing Government, they can exercise their *constitutional* right of amending it or their *revolutionary* right to dismember or overthrow it" (125). For Lincoln there was no middle ground, no concurrent majorities, no right of secession, no dissolution of the compact by ordinances or resolves—the majority rules or the minority claims the right of revolution. The South had eschewed the constitutional route and was skittish in claiming a right of revolution that would have severed its direct links with America's political forebears. For his part, Lincoln demonstrated to his own satisfaction that the inherent right of revolution was not warranted in this case. Accordingly, there was left no legitimate basis for a Southern Confederacy: Lincoln and his administration represented the only legal, Constitutional government. As the instrument of the majority, the federal government became, for Lincoln, the instrument of the people.

Thus did both Lincoln and Davis strive to capture the high constitutional, legal ground that would define the constituency of each as the legitimate heirs to the Revolutionary heritage and as authentic interpreters of the founders. Embedded within this struggle were the conflicting notions of the people, informed by republican elitism on the one hand and majoritarian democracy on the other.

As a counterpoint to establishing their genealogical roots and locating the nexus of sovereignty—that is to establishing "right"—was the steely avowal of potential "might." Both Lincoln and Davis saw the need to assure the other of the steadfastness of his resolve; both had to balance professions of peaceful intent against signs of weakness.

Firmly describing separateness as a fait accompli was, of course, strategically important to Davis and those who chose him, especially those secessionists who feared a slide back into union. The suspicions harbored by Howell Cobb, Robert Barnwell Rhett, and others had to be allayed; it was "necessary that it should at once be *known*" that secession was irrevocable and that there was "to be no reconstruction," Louis Wigfall opined in commenting favorably on Davis's address the day after it was given. In this Davis had satisfied the uneasy.[32] Independence, he declared, had been "asserted," leaving no doubt as to his intention to "maintain" it. Such firmness was a tactical move designed not only to convince fire-eaters of Davis's unyielding stance but also to stiffen the backbone of waverers, to force the border states into a clear choice of confederacies to which to belong, and to dampen the ardor of Northerners who were sure that Southern bravado would crumble in the face of Northern determination. And, clearly, it was to alert the joyous, jostling Montgomery throng that "thorns innumerable" were likely to be encountered.

"An appeal to arms" could, Davis believed, well be forced on the South and every military and naval precaution would be taken; the times were "perilous" (48–50).

"I trust this will not be regarded as a menace," Lincoln said, "but only as the declared purpose of the Union that it *will* constitutionally defend and maintain itself" (122). Speaking to crowds on his way to the inauguration—even as Davis himself was assuming his office—Lincoln had given strong hints, as in his speech to the New Jersey senate, that "it may be necessary to put the foot down firmly." The Inaugural stressed the president's determination to "hold, occupy, and possess the property and places belonging to the Government and to collect the duties and imposts," while offering the guarantee that "there will be no invasion, no using of force against or among the people anywhere" (122). Even so, Lincoln's penultimate paragraph could have left no doubt that the new administration would not coexist with the new Confederacy: "In *your* hands, my dissatisfied fellow-countrymen, and not in *mine,* is the momentous issue of civil war" (126). Because Jefferson Davis had proclaimed that the "position we have assumed among the nations of the earth" and the "career of independence" into which the Confederacy had entered was to be "inflexibly pursued," there could be little room for doubt that the eruption so deprecated would come (46).

The South, Davis made clear, viewed their "late associates" as capable of a "lust of dominion" that could cloud their judgment and inflame their ambition, and he feared that the Northern states were quite capable of bringing on untold suffering through their "folly and wickedness" (48, 49). Lincoln, on the other hand, averred that "we are not enemies but friends." His oft-quoted peroration, despite its plea to avert a break in the already strained "bonds of affection," and despite its appeal to the "better angels of our nature" (126), could hardly have been expected to mute the clank of metal.

It is worth noting what both addresses failed to say. Neither Davis nor Lincoln faced the fundamental American value that was a virtual fault line along which the most serious ideological fissure traveled. No meaning of a basic American value was more contested in the antebellum period than was the meaning of "liberty." "Liberty" was a word "the world has never had a good definition of," Abraham Lincoln told the crowd come to hear the president open the Maryland Sanitary Fair in 1864, and "the American people [were] . . . much in want of one." The *meaning* of liberty, of course, was very much at the heart of the great fraternal conflict foremost in Lincoln's mind. That concern, however, lay in the future. The inaugurals pay scant attention to liberty. Davis did make allusions. He justified withdrawal from the Union on the basis of the perversion of the purposes for which it had been formed, including securing the blessings of liberty (47). Only in his impassioned peroration does Davis again even mention "liberty." It is clear, however, that liberty was one of the primary values for which the South would fight: the "people united in heart" would not deign to weigh the sacrifices they may be called on to make against "honor and right and liberty and equality" (50). Lincoln uses the word "liberty" only once and that in reference to the "safeguards of liberty" that would prevent the injustice inherent in a free person being surrendered as a slave (120).

By 1861 the ideological argument over liberty and its relationship to union had hardened. Webster's "Liberty and Union, One and Inseparable" had found acceptance as a basic truth in the North, whereas Calhoun's famous toast, thrown in the teeth of Andrew Jackson, both established the primacy of liberty over union and defined liberty as a function of the rights of states: "The Union, next to our liberty most dear. May we all remember that it can only be preserved by respecting the rights of the states and by distributing equally the benefits and the burdens of the Union."[33] Of course, like many other issues related to defining an American nation, the liberty debate involved not only the meaning of the term "liberty" but also the question of who was the protector of the people's liberty. Davis, in his inaugural, quite obviously equated liberty with Southern independence, with the rights of the states to act as sovereign entities. It was in this sense that Southerners would continue to contend that the war was a struggle for their liberties. But the real confounding variable in the liberty debate was the slavery issue. Lincoln's reference in the Sanitary Fair speech makes clear that the anomaly of fighting *for liberty* and to *preserve slavery* was recognized by many beyond the confines of dedicated abolitionists.

In the spring of 1861, however, neither side wished to confront head-on the ideological implications of slavery. Davis clearly hoped to attract foreign support for the fledgling country, particularly from Great Britain. He was at pains to point out that in cotton production "the commercial world has an interest scarcely less than ours." Efforts by the Union government to thwart trade would be "a course of conduct . . . as unjust toward us as it would be detrimental to manufacturing and commercial interests abroad" (48). Great Britain, the most potent and recognized force in the interdiction of the slave trade with its widely acknowledged antipathy to slavery and penchant for abolitionism, would hardly find a war on behalf of the rights of slaveholders appealing.[34] On the other hand, the struggle for liberty and independence against oppressive, bullying powers brought out in the British the kind of romantic sympathy epitomized in Lord Byron's martyrdom in Greece and the righteous indignation expressed in

Gladstone's fulminations against Neapolitan tyranny. Implying a connection between independence and liberty and arguing for legitimacy were sufficient for Davis to appeal to Europe, to potential adherents from the border states, and to consumers at home in the Deep South.

Lincoln seemed bent on avoiding the moral intensities that might evolve from the merest whiff of abolitionism and thus their divisive effects. As Thomas Wentworth Higginson observed of the Antislavery Society, "The *moral* position of this Society is the highest and noblest possible; but their practical position does not take hold of the mind of the country."[35] As the inaugural illustrates, it was "going in for the union" that Lincoln saw as his constitutional duty, the legitimate role of the national government, and the only grounds both politically defensible and inclusively persuasive. Lincoln's monumental understatement—"One section of our country believes slavery is *right* and ought to be extended, while the other believes it is *wrong* and ought not to be extended. This is the only substantial dispute" (124)—seems grandly ironic in the light of hindsight and even more so when the words of Lincoln's *second* inaugural are recalled: "The slaves constituted a peculiar and powerful interest. All knew that this interest was somehow the cause of the war" (127). But in March of 1861 few outside the still unpopular abolitionist ranks were willing to recognize slavery as a fundamental cause. Certainly Lincoln preferred to put his case forward on unionist principles, which is to say national principles that affirmed the direct descent of his administration from the founding ancestors, that privileged constitutional law, and that assumed the primacy of the people speaking through the central government.

Conclusion

A careful reading of both inaugurals displays the competing assertions of legitimacy and uncovers the contrasting assumptions of popular sovereignty that underpinned the mutually exclusive claims. The inaugurals might best be understood as the culminating statements in the long rhetorical battle leading up to the outbreak of military hostilities. They represent a crisis that had to be passed in order to establish an "American" nationalism. The speeches are obviously persuasive in the sense that each speaker hoped, by establishing the essential rectitude of his position, to reinforce his own followers and attract allies. As unionist and disunionist speaking to each other, however, the addresses exhibit a firmness that approaches belligerence, an inflexibility that presages war. Indeed, the two inaugurals may be seen as the last justificatory statements of the two combatants, their final efforts to absolve themselves of responsibility for fratricide, and the microcosmic embodiment of two ideational missiles that careened through the early years of the country's history. These ideas of legitimacy and sovereignty—and the contrasting perceptions of liberty—could not but collide. With the collision of ideas came the collision of flesh and steel, and from the blood and from the rhetoric of the Civil War emerged a new configuration: finally a new American "nation."

7

Borderland Denouement

Missourians and the Rhetorical Inauguration of the "Unholy Crusade," Spring 1861

Timothy C. Jenkins

"The middle of March is now upon us," a struggling St. Louis lawyer wrote his parents in the turbulent spring of 1861. "Business has not improved much since I last wrote—but the affairs of our country look to be in a more hopeful condition under our new Administration. . . . It is a fixed fact that Missouri will not leave the Union," the young Republican promised, his spirits buoyed by the final days of the recently adjourned Missouri State Convention. The convention, which could have passed an ordinance of immediate secession, balked at the prospect, hearing "nothing but Union speeches" in its concluding sessions. "One thing . . . is settled," editor R. H. Miller informed his readers: "Unless a greater revolution takes place" than the recent movement to proclaim "that Missouri is opposed to secession, *very much so*," and "anything like a [federal] military despotism," the state's course in the crisis of national unity seemed fixed. "The people of Missouri . . . require a peaceable and just settlement of all our national difficulties," Miller announced; "They will remain *true to the Union*, as long as the Union remains *true to them*."[1]

Yet many Missourians were bitterly disappointed with the resolutions passed by the state convention. "The Convention has been guilty of falsehood and deceit," proclaimed George G. Vest, leader of the "States' Rights" caucus in the Missouri House of Representatives. "It says that there is no cause for separation. If this be so, why call a Convention? . . . I appeal to the people of Missouri to maintain their rights," he urged; "I defy the Convention. They are political cheats, jugglers, and charlatans, who foisted themselves upon the people by ditties and music and striped flags." Extreme as his position seemed, Vest spoke for an increasingly disenchanted and restive constituency. Governor Claiborne Fox Jackson of Missouri had become one of their numbers in recent weeks, as had Sterling Price, former governor and state convention president. Conservatives in the state were at a loss to explain their restlessness. "It seems we are to have renewed turbulence, agitation and conflict," lamented editor William F. Switzler, puzzled by the wake of the state convention. "Men [sic] among us are strangely frenzied . . . [and] restless," he wrote; they "are determined something shall turn up." The optimism—or delusion—of February and the early days of March had, as one contemporary explained it, given way to creeping disillusion and "the conclusion that war was inevitable." Convinced that "a collision would sooner or later take place between the Federal Government and the South, and that Missouri would have to take part in the conflict," new converts rallied around Governor Jackson in his effort to unite the state behind the people of the South.[2]

The purpose of this essay is to illustrate how Missourians rallied to the side of the South and how the ferment of latent disillusionment transformed into open disaffection and alienation. The notion of *rhetorical estrangement* undergirds this essay, suggesting that as discontented collectives face limited deliberative options and deteriorating relations with other collectives, the rhetorical discourse of opinion leaders assumes a distinctive character, one calling attention to and emphasizing diverging political opinions and collective values. This characteristic of radicalizing collectives functions, ultimately, as a means of preparing for the emergence of revolutionary activity.[3] Toward illustrating the features of rhetorical estrangement, I will first explore how President Abraham Lincoln's call for militia forces in the wake of Fort Sumter created a far-reaching wave of discontent in Missouri. Following this I will detail the subsequent activities of Governor C. F. Jackson and explore how the state's deteriorating relationship with the federal government was reflected in Jackson's "special session" address to the Missouri General Assembly.

Calls to Arms

An uneasy period of relative inactivity descended on Missouri in the weeks following the state convention. "At present there is no adequate cause to impel Missouri to dissolve her connection with the Federal Union," the delegates of the convention had proclaimed in March, "but on the contrary she will labor for such an adjustment of existing troubles as will secure the peace as well as the rights and equality of all the States." Although the citizen-representatives of the convention demurred on the matter of secession, they had issued a sternly worded denunciation of "coercion"—the use of the military to enforce federal law—of the seceded states, endorsed the finely crafted series of federal pacification measures known as the "Crittenden compromises," and expressed general sympathy and amity toward Missouri's Southern sisters.[4]

At best, the Missouri State Convention's final resolutions constituted a mixed message; they were neither hot nor cold but rather a lukewarm response directed at the North and South alike. Some, like the hopeful editor of the *Liberty Tribune*, claimed to hear the "clear voice" of the convention proclaiming "that the honest, unsophisticated yeomanry of this State stand inflexibly opposed to all sectionalism, useless agitation, demagogues, and disunion; and that they strongly prefer amity to civil strife." Other opinion leaders even found genuine reason to celebrate, touting the resolutions as "the promise of a brighter day." Missouri "has rebuked Disunion more sternly than any of the other Border States," a Republican editor in St. Joseph announced, and now "a more healthy public attitude is pervading the State." Many editors, however, saw neither clarity nor victory from the convention, only continued uncertainty and ongoing reason for caution. "Missouri will in no event now to be foreseen, short of war by the federal government, go out of the Union," the editors of a St. Louis paper maintained, "but may do so if force is used." Should a reconstruction of the Union prove impossible, they ventured, Missouri would "favor measures for a peaceable separation" of the Southern states—assuming the new administration in Washington City would accept one. "Much depends upon the future course of Lincoln," the editors of the *Bolivar Courier* agreed; his actions would decide "whether our national difficulties will be settled."[5]

Missourians waited anxiously for the enunciation of the Lincoln administration's policy toward the seceded states. After a few weeks of palpable uncertainty, editors and citizens alike discerned the portents of impending trouble. "A short time [ago], the administration seemed to indicate that it had made up its mind to let the Israelites go free, and not pursue them into the Red Sea," the *St. Louis Herald* allegorized, and a "peaceable separation of the seceded States from the rest of the Union" appeared possible. But now "things have a greatly less pacific look than they had. . . . Coercion is perhaps not *determined on*," the editors granted, "but there are signs that the administration are strongly *inclined* to use it. The preparations for war are unmistakable." Such gloomy news confirmed the nagging fears of a sectional collision held by many Missourians. "We have hard times here still, with a prospect of still harder times and more than that, a prospect of 'Civil War,'" reported one St. Louis correspondent. "Rumors of war are rife" from all quarters of the nation, he continued, "and when it does come we will have warm times in St. Louis," because "everybody has taken sides either for or against us." "We of the Border Slave State[s] will suffer most from Civil strife," the writer closed, "but I can't now see how it can be otherwise."[6]

Many Missourians shared in this gloomy assessment, either viewing war as inevitable or perceiving themselves as powerless to prevent it. Anxiety kept state residents on edge, apprehensive of every report boding ill. Editors in the state did their best to sort fact from rumor and even attempted at times to blunt the impact of especially ominous incoming news. By mid-April, however, that was becoming an increasingly difficult task. "The news by telegraph this morning looks like we are on the eve of hostilities in the Gulf States," a Liberty, Missouri, editor reported on April 12: "We trust the news may prove untrue, and that this nation may yet be spared the horrors of civil war." That same day, the exasperated editor of the *Richmond North-West Conservator* gave in to his dismay. "The telegraph has again got to work, and numerous articles and dispatches seem to be the order of the day," he observed. "Every paper comes freighted with war news—and if we were to believe everything we see and read, we would conclude that the whole country would soon be in a blaze of war, and that ruin and destruction was upon us." "We don't believe there will be much fighting," he tried to assure his readers, "for we don't think Lincoln is 'much military.' In this, however, we may be disappointed."[7]

Unfortunately, events in the South conspired to "disappoint" these optimistic Missouri editors. In faraway Charleston, South Carolina, on April 12, Confederate batteries began bombarding Fort Sumter at the sleepy hour of 4:30 A.M. The Civil War had begun.[8]

Editors in Missouri wasted little time in commenting on the commencement of hostilities. "If war shall ensue" from the Sumter affair, the editor of the *St. Joseph Gazette* argued, "it will grow directly out of the refusal of the government at Washington to recognize the government at Montgomery, in the withdrawal of U.S. troops from the soil of the Confederate States." Other editors soundly castigated President Lincoln for the ominous turn of affairs. "If the news be true," conservative editor Robert H. Miller ventured, "we are forced to the conclusion that the Lincoln administration has been playing a game of double-dealing and bare-faced treachery worthy of the days of the guillotine. . . . They have been holding out peaceful intentions knowing at the time they were deceiving and betraying their Southern brethren," he continued: "Give us anything but cowardly treachery." In St. Louis, the moderate *Missouri Republican*—ironically, a Democratic organ founded in the days of Thomas Jefferson's "Democratic-Republicans"—agreed, charging Lincoln with "hoodwinking the people by professions of a desire to secure the peace of the country" while privately planning "hostile operations against the seceding States." Now the people of the United States "have in prospect a long civil war, in which one assurance can be given," its editors averred, "that no matter what may be the expenditure of life and money, the seceding States never can be conquered. A more unrighteous and unpopular war was never inaugurated. And we look to the people of the free States . . . now, on the instant, to put forth their solemn protest against the prosecution of this unnatural war." As for the response of Missouri, "Let us await events," they urged; "Mr. LINCOLN will learn, when it is too late, that it is easier to inaugurate a war than to make it popular, or find for it defenders among the mass of the American people."[9]

If many Missourians had thought they might avoid the conflict, however, they were about to discover that they were sadly mistaken. On April 15, 1861, President Lincoln responded to the attack on Fort Sumter with a general proclamation that would force them to take sides. According to Lincoln, the execution of federal "laws" had been "obstructed" in the seven seceded Southern states "by combinations too powerful to be suppressed by the ordinary course of judicial proceedings or by the powers vested in the marshals by law." So as to reverse these conditions the president called upon the remaining states of the Union to supply seventy-five thousand militia men "to suppress said combinations and to cause the laws to be duly executed" in the seceded states. The War Department quickly followed with specific, telegraphic instructions to the governors of the remaining states; Missouri's expected quota totaled 3,123 men and officers.[10]

On the evening of April 15, Governor Jackson informed the press that he had received notice from the War Department "making a requisition on him for four regiments of men." Apparently distrustful of such a momentous telegram, the governor declined further comment and announced he would not "answer the request of the President, for volunteers, until he receive[d] the request officially" through the mails. While Jackson waited, anticipating the worst, Missouri's editors rushed to reply in their own colorful fashion. Perhaps the most vociferous of these replies issued from the normally staid *St. Louis Missouri Republican:*

The people of Missouri desire above all things to see the Union re-established, and harmony and good feelings restored between the two sections, but if Mr. LINCOLN has been told that Missouri would place men under his charge to whoop South Carolina or Louisiana, or any other State, back into the Union, they have abused his confidence most shockingly. The people of Missouri will do their own thinking and their own fighting, whenever that is necessary to be done, but they are not going to become parties in a war against their own countrymen on no better pretexts than those furnished by Mr. LINCOLN. . . . We need not wait for the answer of the Governor of Missouri to this demand upon the State for her quota of troops. *The people are ready to respond now, that they will not contribute one regiment nor one company for any such purpose.* They will not make war upon the South. . . . They have, in every possible way, declared their hostility to *coercion* in any form.

Other segments of the Missouri press concurred. "The Northern States will have to furnish the men almost exclusively" to fill the president's requisitions, Francis M. Taylor of the *Randolph Citizen* predicted. "Requisitions are made, it is true, on the border slave States, but they will be treated with the contempt and execration they so richly deserve," contended Taylor. "This call for troops will tend to alienate the affections of the people of the border slave states from the Union, and turn them Southward," he warned. "They can now see unmistakably what is expected of them by the Black Republican Administration, and that is, to take up arms to shed the blood of their Southern Brethren. . . . Rather than do that," Taylor concluded, "we KNOW they will choose secession. If fight we MUST, we prefer to fight the Black Republicans."[11]

While the Missouri press simmered over the call for troops, the governors of the Middle South and border states began contemplating their responses. Even as governors from the Northern states responded with enthusiasm and zeal, chief executives in the remaining slave states recoiled in undisguised scorn and open disbelief. One of the first to reply was Governor Beriah Magoffin of Kentucky, who bluntly refused the president's request for troops on the same day the orders issued from Washington. "In answer I say emphatically," Magoffin replied, "Kentucky will furnish no troops for the wicked purpose of subduing her sister Southern States." Governor John W. Ellis of North Carolina, professing doubt as to the genuineness of the requisition, sounded a similar note of disdain. "I regard the levy of troops made by the Administration for the purpose of subjugating the States of the South as in violation of the Constitution and a gross usurpation of power," Governor Ellis exclaimed; "I can be no party to this wicked violation of the laws of the country and to this war upon the liberties of a free people." An equally dubious John Letcher, governor of Virginia, followed the lead of Ellis and Magoffin the next day. "Your object is to subjugate the Southern States, and a requisition made upon me for such an object . . . will not be complied with," Governor Letcher bristled. "You have chosen to inaugurate civil war, and having done so, we will meet it in a spirit as determined as the Administration has exhibited toward the South."[12]

Despite the defiance exhibited by the governors of Kentucky, North Carolina, and Virginia, governors from the Northern states quickly stepped in, filling any deficit created by the untendered troop quotas. The war spirit had been loosed upon the fractured Union, and observers kept a careful eye on the border states as the replies of their executives continued to trickle into Washington City. On Wednesday, April 17, Governor Jackson apparently received the War Department's official communiqué through the mail. There could now be no doubt as to its authenticity. Having had several days to think through his response, Jackson wrote out a draft of his reply, made several alterations in it, and then produced his official response to the president's call for troops. The letter was terse, indignant, and defiant; it would be the most widely read public statement of his administration. Acknowledging receipt of "a call on Missouri for four regiments of men for immediate service," Jackson averred, "There can be . . . no doubt but the men are intended to form a part of the President's army to make war upon the people of the seceded States." The governor thus proclaimed, "Your requisition, in my judgment, is illegal, unconstitutional, and revolutionary in its object, inhuman and diabolical, and cannot be complied with. Not one man will the State of Missouri furnish to carry on any such unholy crusade."[13]

Jackson's closing declaration was clearly the most belligerent reply to the president's requisition so far. Obviously the governor was outraged, and to communicate the depth of that feeling, he selected his words with care. In an earlier draft of his response, the proud Missouri governor had objected, "Not one man will the State of Missouri furnish to carry on any such *unholy crusade against her Southern sisters*" (emphasis added). Two metaphors lay embedded in this draft of the declaration; there was literal and figurative truth to both. The first metaphor emphasized Missouri's ties of kinship and fealty with the South—a potentially potent link to be made because most Missourians were émigrés from the border South and, in all probability, still had relatives in those states. The matter was thus a familial one, and for Jackson, cooperating in a campaign against members of one's own family was unthinkable. Yet it was the very thing the Northern states were clamoring to do: the governors of many states in the North were literally begging the War Department to allow them to exceed their requisitions for troops. That brought into play the second metaphor. Like the great "crusades" of the Middle Ages that sent off eager European volunteers to cleanse and recover the "Holy Land" from the Middle Eastern followers of Mohammed, so now did the North appear bent on cleansing and recovering the Southland from the disciples of Thomas Jefferson and John C. Calhoun. To Jackson it appeared every bit an "unholy crusade" against kin and kindred. When it came time to finalize his stunning denial, however, the governor deleted the reference to Missouri's "Southern sisters"—perhaps in the interests of linguistic economy, perhaps to clarify the focus of the "unholy crusade" metaphor. For whatever reason he made the change, Jackson remained unwavering in one determination: Missouri would not comply with President Lincoln's call for troops.[14]

On the same day that Governor Jackson issued his stinging rebuke to the War Department, at least one border state was preparing to fall in line with the Lincoln administration's request—provisionally. Maryland, surrounding the District of Columbia on three sides, was naturally of enormous importance to the federal government, and Governor Thomas H. Hicks had been under intense pressure from Secretary of War Simon Cameron and Maj. Gen. Winfield Scott to tender the state's quota of troops. After negotiations Hicks cooperated, providing that Maryland's militia forces be "posted and maintained" in that state "for the defense of the United States Government, the maintenance of the Federal authority, and the protection of the Federal capital," not for an invasion of the South. Given these assurances from federal authorities, Hicks bowed to "the lawful demand of the United States Government," and promised the state's "effective and reliable aid for the support and defense of this Union."[15]

Although Maryland, like Missouri, was a border state, its situation was somewhat exceptional due to its unusually close proximity to the nation's capital. A state closer to Missouri in terms of its regional affinities was the Middle South state of Tennessee. Like Missouri, Tennessee was sensitive to the prospect of federal "coercion" of the seceded Southern states. On April 17 Governor Isham G. Harris curtly informed the War Department of that fact. "Tennessee will not furnish a single man for the purpose of coercion," Harris proclaimed, "but 50,000, if necessary, for the defense of our rights and those of our Southern brethren." Three days later the Tennessee governor, armed with passages from the Declaration of Independence, held forth once more, warning the War Department that military coercion would cause the Southern states to exercise their right to revolution, as might "the free people of every other sovereign state." Harris cautioned, "Tennessee can regard the present coercive policy of the

Federal Government in no other light than a wanton and alarming usurpation of power, at war with the genius of our republican institutions, and . . . subversive to civil liberty." Echoing Missouri's Governor Jackson, the Tennessee governor concluded, "In such an unholy crusade no gallant son of Tennessee will ever draw his sword."[16]

Two weeks after the Lincoln administration's call for troops, only two states remained unaccounted for: the Middle South state of Arkansas and the border state of Delaware. "A flying rumor" circulating in Missouri had the governor of Arkansas responding brashly to the president, "Yours received, calling for a regiment of volunteers from Arkansas. 'Nary one'—see you d[amne]d first." In comparison to the rumor, Governor Henry M. Rector's actual reply of April 22 was almost anticlimactic, being but a curt refusal to supply troops "to subjugate the Southern States. . . . The demand is only adding insult to injury," Rector complained. "The people of this Commonwealth are freemen, not slaves, and will defend to the last extremity their honor, lives, and property against Northern mendacity and usurpation." Two days after Arkansas's reply came the response from Governor William Burton of Delaware, who explained rather lamely that he had "no authority whatever" to tender troops in compliance with the War Department requisition. "There are volunteer companies formed and their officers commissioned by the Executive, and others are being formed," Burton explained in guarded terms, "but it is altogether optional with them to offer their services to the U.S. authorities."[17]

As responses from governors of border and Middle South states became known, an intriguing degree of similitude became apparent in their vocabulary and syntax. Colorful litanies of adjectives described President Lincoln's request for troops: it was "wicked" (Magoffin, Ellis), "inhuman" and "diabolical" (Jackson), "wanton" and "alarming" (Harris). In terms of its purpose, the request was viewed as an attempt to subdue or "subjugate" their kindred of the Southern States (Magoffin, Ellis, Letcher, Harris, Rector); it was "an unholy crusade" (Jackson, Harris), a "usurpation" (Ellis, Harris) "adding insult to injury" (Rector). In terms of the arguments advanced by the border South governors, there were also striking similarities. Governors Ellis, Jackson, and Letcher roundly complained that the request was in some way "unconstitutional"; Ellis and Rector argued that some form of "usurpation" of powers was involved; and Harris emphatically maintained it was "subversive to civil liberty." With the exceptions of Maryland and Delaware, then, the responses of the border state and Middle South governors were almost of a single voice opposing the federal government's call for militia forces and united in an expression of outrage and indignation.

While the border state and Middle South governors were venting their outrage and indignation, opinion leaders in Missouri were making their own positions clear. "The Governors who have refused to furnish troops have done right, and will be sustained," the editor of the *North-West Conservator* predicted. "The sympathies of the people of the border slave States are with the South, and they will not furnish men and money to fight their sister Southern States." On that much there appeared to be a consensus. "President Lincoln has called for 4000 volunteers from Missouri," the editor of the *Liberty Tribune* observed; "we now give it as our opinion that he will not get fifty." As for the propriety of President Lincoln's requisition for troops, editors across the state closed ranks as well. "Mr. LINCOLN has, in his attempt to become famous, become *in*-famous," John B. Williams of the *Fulton Missouri Telegraph* wrote. "He has, by duplicity, deceit, fraud and rascality, brought upon us a war which was unnecessary, unjust and inhuman. . . . Future history will hold him up to a glorious infamy," he claimed. "He will be remembered hereafter, but only to be cursed and derided as a liar, a coward and a bigot." Rather than cooperate in this "infamous attack" aimed at "*subjugating* the South," editor Williams fumed, "Missouri will protect herself," refuse the requisition for troops, and "keep a strict guard over our own interest." Concluded Williams: "A central or middle Confederacy must be formed—There is no hope now for a reconstruction of our government. Mr. LINCOLN's infamy has punched out all the marrow that ever was in that thought."[18]

Editor Williams's low opinion of Abraham Lincoln was shared by other Missouri opinion leaders, who likewise denounced the president's call for the state's militia forces. "There are none here for him," ventured conservative editor William F. Switzler of the *Columbia Missouri Statesman:* "Those who elected him ought to be required to do his fighting. Those who dance must pay the piper." As for the popular belief that the troops were intended for "the subjugation of the Southern States," Switzler offered, "We hope it will not be, and can scarcely conceive of such an act of atrocious wickedness and folly." If speculation proved to be true, however, he proclaimed that

it can never be accomplished. Armies of invasion whose ranks are filled with Black Republican troops from the North . . . may attempt to fight their way through the Border Slave States—for they will never get through unless at the point of the sword—and make war upon the Southern States, and lay waste our towns and fields and sack and burn our cities in the mad attempt to 'repossess' the forts, but the Southern people can never be subjugated, *try it who may*. . . . The position . . . of Missouri and the Border Slave States for the present is clear. Let them stand like a wall of fire between the belligerent extremes, . . . and with their strong arms and potential counsel keep them apart. . . . Let them stand pledged . . . to resist any attempt at coercion . . . [and to] stand by Virginia and Kentucky and our Southern sisters [in the event of Northern invasion] . . . sharing their dangers and abiding their fortunes and destiny in driving back from their borders the hostile feet of Northern invaders. . . . Of the South; we are for the South.

"No citizen of Missouri, who is not unloyal to the South," seconded C. P. Anderson of the *California News*, "could consent to furnish men or money for this unholy purpose. . . . We are unalterably with the South in the present attitude of affairs," Anderson concluded, "and today we are *first, last, and all the time for our brethren of the South*—'COME WEAL, COME WOE OR DEATH.' "[19]

Amid such solid declarations of Southern sympathy Governor Jackson's stinging rebuke to the War Department became known to the public. Suddenly—indeed, almost overnight—the governor became a popular hero, enjoying the hearty approval of almost everyone, except perhaps the Republicans. When Jackson had tried to rally Missourians in a bold public speech on the eve of the state convention's first session, urging them to prepare for the coming conflict and stand decisively with the South, he had drawn sharp criticism. Now, little more than a month later, many Missourians concluded that the governor was right after all: there was no hope left for compromise and no reason to believe that a Republican administration would seek reconciliation with the Southern states. Now, with a prescient hero to follow, Missourians hastened to rally around him.

The depth of Governor Jackson's popular support quickly became evident when, in county after county, mass meetings were held celebrating the governor's reply and expressing sympathy with the South. Resolutions soliciting popular approval became fixtures of these meetings and often used the very words or phrases of the governor's reply to the War Department. Citizens in Ray County assembled on Saturday, April 20, to announce their approval of "the prompt and patriotic response of Gov. Jackson to the demand upon Missouri for troops to be . . . used in the present unholy crusade against our Southern brethren." The citizens also passed resolutions proclaiming that they "disparage and condemn the action of the late Convention" and that they "held themselves ready to co-operate with the South in expelling from her soil the hordes of fanatical abolitionists [that] threatened to pour in upon her borders." That same day, two mass meetings occurred in Randolph County, one for the "Conditional Unionists," and the other for "States' Rights" supporters. The conservatives declared that they "cordially approve[d]" the governor's reply and deplored Lincoln's actions as "showing a disregard of Constitutional law equaled only by his atrocious recklessness for the lives of our people." The "States' Rights" party, meeting separately, assumed a much more radical stand. "It is now time for States and individuals to say which ye will serve," they proclaimed, "Abe Lincoln in prosecuting an unholy, unrighteous and inhuman war upon our brothers of the South, or . . . our brethren of the South in resisting an unchristian warfare."[20]

Even with the start of a new week Missourians continued to keep telegraph operators busy relaying the news of their public meetings. On Monday, April 22, residents of Benton County assembled in the town of Warsaw, where they passed resolutions "favoring immediate secession; endorsing Gov. Jackson's contemptuous treatment of Lincoln's demand upon Missouri for troops; denouncing the State Convention as in league with the Abolitionists"; and "repudiating our delegates to that Convention and requesting them to resign immediately." On the same evening in Clay County, "States' Rights" adherents met in Liberty to denounce hotly "the hellish designs" of Lincoln's "craven heart," as well as "his cold impudence in calling on the good citizens of Missouri to aid him in making widows and orphans of Southern sisters." "The bold, patriotic and gallant response" of Governor Jackson "has won for him a home in the hearts of the people of that State never to be obliterated," they proclaimed, pledging themselves to support and aid the governor, even "to shoulder our muskets and fight to the last extremity for the just rights of the Southern Confederacy." The more conservative citizens of Clay County met on Tuesday, April 23, choosing also to "approve and endorse" Jackson's reply "in refusing to furnish troops for the purpose of coercing our Southern brethren. . . . Secession is no remedy for evil," they further resolved, but if "reduced to the necessity" of such a move, "we will stand by and co-operate with our Southern friends."[21]

Governor Jackson's terse refusal to supply troops also earned him the approbation of the Missouri press. When the publishers of the *Richmond North-West Conservator* printed Jackson's letter to the War Department for their readers, their approval was evident by the bold headline, "The Insult Promptly Answered." Editor Francis M. Taylor of the *Randolph Citizen*, until this point a staunch critic of Jackson, praised the governor's reply as one that "will meet with the cordial endorsement of every true-hearted Missourian." Even an outspoken "Conditional Union" man like William F. Switzler of the *Columbia Missouri Statesman* found reason to praise the governor: "Well done Gov. Jackson! There is not a man in Missouri, untainted by the 'diabolical' heresy of Black Republicanism, who will not endorse you in this prompt and befitting refusal to respond to the unconstitutional and revolutionary call for troops by Mr. Lincoln."

Switzler continued, "His call, sir, is all you say it is—illegal, inhuman and diabolical, and deserves the execrations of every true son of the South."[22]

The furious dismissals of the president's call for troops and celebrations of Governor Jackson's reply were fast overwhelming any remaining pleas for calm in the Missouri press. One of the few papers not caught up in the frenzy offered only a sobering, if plaintive, appeal for conservative thinking. "Where the end of our national troubles is to be," the little *Bethany Star* lamented at the end of April 1861, "is beyond all human knowledge. . . . If fanaticism would but pause here and behold the abysm into which it is hurling our once happy country, [we] might be saved," its poetic editor offered, "for if the extremists of antagonistic parties shall once redden our hands in fratricidal blood, all the hallowed associations of old, all the enduring recollections of the peace and prosperity which blessed the days of our union, will be dissolved in a crimson tide, and we will fall to rise no more—for 'a house divided against itself cannot stand.'" Opinion leaders across the state had typically offered such sentiments three months before, but now the public mind in Missouri had changed remarkably. Far more common were exclamations of partisan loyalty, such as that exemplified by one young writer who decorated the outside of his correspondence with a bold "Hurrah for Jeff Davis!" "Nothing is heard of here but war," he wrote his brother. "The people are very much excited and secession is the word. . . . I am for secession, amediate [sic]," the youthful correspondent ventured; "I want to hear of Maryland Seceding and then that Jeff Davis is in the White House. Missouri will secede." The public mind had changed indeed.[23]

Governor Jackson's Rhetorical Estrangement

Claiborne Jackson and his advisors met the public drama over Fort Sumter with renewed energy, determined to prepare the once-reluctant state for war. The Missouri governor had privately concluded in early March that reconciliation would never occur between the North and the South and that armed conflict between the two sections was a distinct probability. Soon after the adjournment of the state legislature on March 28, Jackson hastened to St. Louis as soon "as his duties at the capital would permit" to prepare for the coming exigency. The governor's mission was twofold. First, he determined to reason with prominent proslavery Democrats who were having second thoughts in their Union resolve. Second, the governor also planned to confer with Brig. Gen. Daniel M. Frost, commander of the

First Division of the Missouri State Militia, and to cultivate a relationship with the Southern partisans of St. Louis, popularly known as the "Minute Men." His link with the group was Basil Duke, a young Kentucky-born attorney who had made himself conspicuous in the agitation of the "Minute Men" in St. Louis. So greatly had Duke impressed the governor, in fact, that when legislation creating a board of police commissioners in St. Louis allowed Jackson to appoint four persons who would "have absolute control of the police of the city," the youthful Kentuckian was one of his choices. Now Duke would provide the governor with the covert assistance he required from the pro-Southern element of St. Louis.[24]

The "Minute Men" required the help of Governor Jackson as well. Recent reinforcement and fortification of the St. Louis Arsenal, the largest such military repository west of the Mississippi River, had moved the leaders of the blustery Southern partisans to conclude that "the time had passed when the Minute Men could take the arsenal" without special assistance. "Minute Man" Colton Greene devised a plan to overcome the fortified St. Louis Arsenal using "arms from some of the arsenals which had fallen into the hands of our friends in the south"; but they still needed proper credentials to obtain them. As governor of Missouri, Jackson could furnish such credentials, so Duke and Greene communicated word of their "scheme" to Thomas Snead, a former St. Louis editor who was acting as the governor's aide. Jackson's conferences with other pro-Southern men in the city revealed support for such a plan of action, whereupon he decided that "the seizure of the arsenal should be attempted at the earliest possible date" to facilitate "arming and equipping the State Militia." For precise and trustworthy military advice in the matter Jackson looked to West Point graduate D. M. Frost, who promised to prepare a memorandum outlining the necessary details of the operation.[25]

Brigadier General Frost was working on his memorandum for the governor when news arrived in St. Louis detailing the fall of Fort Sumter and President Lincoln's call for troops. Amid the public outcry against the militia requisition, Frost took it upon himself to address not only the operation against the St. Louis Arsenal but also the larger strategic situation of Missouri. "The President . . . proposes to inaugurate civil war on a comprehensive plan," the distinguished West Point graduate warned Governor Jackson, counseling him as to likely federal troop movements and strategy. "Presuming that Mr. Lincoln will be advised by good military talent, he will doubtless regard [St. Louis] as next in importance, in a strategic point of view, to Charleston and Pensacola," Frost predicted. "He will therefore retain at the arsenal all of the troops now there, and augment it as soon as possible." Such action, the brigadier general warned, combined with the continuing efforts of the arsenal commandant to fortify the federal post, would rapidly "have this town and the commerce of the Mississippi river at his mercy."[26]

To prepare the state for such a prospect, Frost forwarded a detailed plan of action to the governor, addressing both the military and political exigencies of the moment. On the political front, Frost recommended reassembling the Missouri legislature, which had recently adjourned without having passed the long-debated "Military Bill," legislation that facilitated "placing the State in a condition to enable you to suppress insurrection or repel invasion." Frost also suggested that Governor Jackson issue "a proclamation to the people of the State, warning them that the President has acted illegally in calling out troops" and in secretly cooperating with the Unionists of St. Louis, "who have declared their intention to resist the constituted authorities" should these officials "adopt a course distasteful to them." In terms of military preparations Frost advised Jackson to "send an agent to the Governor of Louisiana, (or further, if necessary), to ascertain if mortars and siege guns" might be obtained for use against the now-fortified St. Louis Arsenal. To begin preparing the Missouri State Militia for possible action, the brigadier general also suggested recalling active brigades from the Kansas frontier, mobilizing those not active, and assembling them all in a "camp of instruction" in the St. Louis vicinity. The camp would serve as a central location "to muster military companies into the service of the State" and "to erect batteries" of artillery.[27]

On receiving Frost's memorandum Governor Jackson sprang into action. As Colton Greene later recalled, the dramatic events of the previous few days had sensitized the pro-Southern element in Missouri to "the necessity of striking a blow" against the federals. Time was limited, however. Hurrying back to St. Louis, Jackson secretly conferred with the arsenal operation's prime movers—Frost, Snead, Duke, Greene, and the other "Minute Men"—for their "final deliberations." Greene recalled that "The kind of arms and the uses they were to be put to were discussed at this meeting, and Frost made out a list of the particular kind" of arms needed by the state militia. The group also discussed Frost's suggestion of a state militia encampment, the offensive and defensive preparations it would require, and the most strategic point near the arsenal to locate it. To facilitate acquisition of the necessary arms, Governor Jackson appointed Duke and Greene "Commissioners—detailed Captains of the M[issouri] S[tate] G[uard] acting on the Governor's staff." Their orders were to travel to Montgomery, Alabama, provisional capital of the Confederate States of America, to confer with President Jefferson Davis concerning the situation in St. Louis and in the state. Verbally, Duke and

Greene were instructed by the governor to solicit "expressions of the views of the President upon the attitude of Missouri in the event of war, and particularly as to whether her alliance and adhesion was desired by the . . . Confederate States."[28]

As Missouri's "Commissioners" to the Confederate States, Duke and Greene were provided with Brigadier General Frost's memorandum outlining the types of arms that would be required in an operation against the St. Louis Arsenal and an official letter from Governor Jackson to President Davis that would act as their credentials. The letter was dated April 17, the very same day Jackson had issued his stinging rebuke of the War Department's requisition for Missouri troops. The governor's letter to President Davis was of a completely different tone, however. Announcing the two captains as officers of the Missouri State Militia authorized to negotiate "with the proper authorities of the Confederate States for the loan of a few large guns and mortars," Jackson related the state's military plight to Davis: "Missouri has been exceedingly slow and tardy in her movements hitherto, but I am now not without hope that she will promptly take her stand with her Southern sister States." Because "the Arsenal at St. Louis, now under an Abolition officer, it is feared, will be greatly in our way in the event of active hostilities being commenced against the Confederate States," Jackson explained, "it will probably become necessary to have a few large guns to batter down its walls and drive out our enemies. . . . Unfortunately for Missouri," he continued, "she has no guns of the proper kind, and our recent Legislature failed to make an appropriation for the purchase of any such." Therefore, the governor offered Captains Greene and Duke as his official emissaries, charged with discerning "whether the guns required can be had in the Confederate States." As the secret meeting concluded, all those present were sobered by the gravity of their plan. There was no turning back. That realization in their minds, Governor Jackson took leave of the "Minute Men" to return to Jefferson City; the two daring captains left St. Louis "incognito" the next day on their mission to Montgomery.[29]

When Claiborne Jackson returned to Jefferson City after several days in St. Louis, he found a letter waiting for him from David Walker, president of the Arkansas State Convention. Walker had been requested by the Arkansas convention to correspond with Missouri's governor regarding "the political affairs of the country and the proposed remedies for existing evils." Jackson replied to the Arkansan frankly and freely. "From the beginning, my own conviction has been that the interest, duty, and honor of every slaveholding State demand[ed] their separation from the Northern or non-slaveholding States," he confided. "Mr. Lincoln, the representative man of the

Northern mind, is the author of the sentiment that 'the States of the Federal Union cannot permanently endure, part free and part slave.' . . . This is the doctrine of the 'Irrepressible Conflict,' and though not of necessity a great philosophical truth, yet it is the belief of the Northern people and like all other people they act upon their belief and conviction of duty." Consequently, the North seemed to "believe the institution of slavery to be 'the sum of all villainies' " and thought it "their duty to their God and country alike" to "extinguish it from the face of the earth." "All of the South believe it to be the most damnable and hellish crusade that was ever waged against any people on earth," Jackson wrote, echoing his recent reply to the War Department. He observed that though the Northern people "have abolished slavery in all their own States, they still feel they are responsible for the sin of slavery, because they happen to live in the same Federal Union as we." "For my part," the Missouri governor concluded,

I am for relieving their tender consciences, by a full, complete and final separation. Missouri will be ready for secession in less than thirty days, and will secede if Arkansas will only get out of the way and give her free passage. Missouri and Arkansas have been called upon by an Abolitionist President for troops to Whip their Southern brethren and friends into the support of a miserable Black Republican, fanatical Administration, and the question is: Shall they assist in this hellish work, or like true and noble States stand by their friends, and perish with them if need be in the maintenance of their common rights? It seems to me that the time has come when all true Southern men should be united as a band of brothers against the common enemy. Public sentiment here is rapidly tending to this point. A few more days will determine all.[30]

While Governor Jackson was keeping a watchful eye on public opinion in Missouri, Basil Duke and Colton Greene were preparing to discharge their mission in Montgomery, Alabama. On reaching the provisional Confederate capital, the two Missourians embarked on what can only be described as a series of extraordinary conferences with Jefferson Davis and his cabinet. "We were questioned very closely about the conditions in St. Louis and Missouri," Basil Duke recalled, and differences of opinion cropped up in the cabinet as to how to respond to Governor Jackson's overtures. Secretary of War Leroy P. Walker expressed his initial misgivings concerning the request for arms at their first conference; he "distrusted the border States," according to Greene, "and thought he could get on without them." President Davis, Secretary of the Treasury Judah P. Benjamin, and Attorney General Robert Toombs were enthusiastic about the request, however, and reasoned with Secretary Walker until he "finally yielded" to their counter-arguments. "The President very cheerfully granted Governor Jackson's request," remembered Duke, "and gave us an order on the commandant of the arsenal at Baton Rouge for the guns specified on the list prepared by General Frost."[31]

As far as the military situation of Missouri was concerned, President Davis surprised the captains with his interest in and keen knowledge of the St. Louis area. As a fresh young West Point graduate, Brevet Second Lieutenant Jefferson Davis had been stationed at Jefferson Barracks, only a few miles below St. Louis on the Mississippi River, periodically from 1829 to 1833. Now as the chief executive of the Confederate States of America, "Davis took a lively interest in the proposed plans . . . of capturing the St. Louis arsenal," Greene recalled, actively suggesting several particulars of the defensive aspect of the operation. "He seemed informed of the topography of the ground near the arsenal and knew, *in particular detail*, what the arsenal contained," the governor's envoy marveled. Greene later discovered that Davis had a covert "agent in St. Louis" who added to the Confederate president's own familiarity with the area by keeping him informed about ongoing developments at the arsenal.[32]

Before Greene and Duke left Montgomery, Davis supplied them with a requisition for arms "written in guarded terms (quantity not limited)" from the arsenal in Baton Rouge, and a letter of reference to the governor of Louisiana "asking his aid and co-operation." He then verbally assured the Missourians that "the policy of the Confederate States would be to harmonize all the interests of all the slave-states," Greene noted, "and the adhesion of Missouri was urgently invited." "The President," he remembered, "said, that not only did he desire the adhesion of M[issouri], but that he believed that the Northwestern states, the Grain states, lying on the Mississippi river, would find it in their interests to join their fortunes" with the Confederacy. Davis also entrusted to Duke and Greene a "sealed communication" for Governor Jackson, expounding on the views he had expressed to them. With that, he bade them good-bye.[33]

As the Missouri envoys were embarking on their trek to Baton Rouge to secure arms, Governor Jackson continued his labors to insure that the state would be able to defend itself in the event of war. Taking advantage of his newfound popularity on April 22, Jackson recalled the Missouri legislature into "special session" to begin on May 2. Its purpose, he explained, would be twofold: first, for the "enacting of such laws and adopting such measures, as may be deemed necessary and proper for the more perfect organization, and equipment, of the militia of the State"; and second, "to raise the money, and such other means, as may be required to place the State in a proper attitude of defense."[34]

Several days after this proclamation was issued, Sterling Price, president of the Missouri State Convention, paused while passing through Jefferson City to confer briefly with the governor. Price was anxious to know whether Jackson deemed it advisable to immediately reconvene the state convention to consider the outbreak of hostilities. As he had with President Walker of the Arkansas State Convention, the governor held Price in his confidence. "I told him not to be in a hurry," Jackson related to a correspondent, "but to wait 'til the Legislature met, and to be here [Jefferson City] at that time." The governor further advised Price that "we should not go out of the Union until the Legislature had time to arm the state to some extent & place it in a proper position of defense." After a discussion of about ten minutes, the men closed their conference, Jackson to resume working on preparing the state, Price to resume his journey to St. Louis.[35]

When Governor Jackson read the *St. Louis Missouri Republican* several days later, he discovered to his horror that Price had shared details of their conference with senior editor Nathaniel Paschal. Governor Jackson "expressed to Gov. S[terling] Price the conviction that the State Convention ought not to be called together for the passage of a secession ordinance," Paschal wrote in his editorial of April 27; "he is in favor of retaining the present status of the State, leaving it to time and circumstances, as they may arise, to determine what is best for Missouri to do." From this the influential moderate editor arrived at a striking conclusion. "The sober second thought . . . is beginning to prevail," Paschal announced, "and as a sentinel on the watch-tower, we proclaim that 'all is well'—that Missouri will not secede from the Union, unless greater and more justifiable reasons than any which have yet been presented" come before the people. "There is not a man in the State . . . who will not agree with [Governor Jackson]" in the proposition that Missouri "should be put in a position to defend her Territory from aggression," the editor argued, but "we are not prepared for any such act as a dissolution of our connection with the Union, and every man knows it." "Missouri wants peace," the influential moderate wrote, "and the opportunity which a neutral position will afford to mediate between the opposing sections, and to restore amicable relations, or, if that cannot be done, to secure a cessation of hostilities."[36]

The doctrine advanced by Paschal was none other than "armed neutrality," and in the editor's construction of things, the governor of Missouri was its chief advocate. Jackson was incensed. "I know not when I have been so deeply mortified as on yesterday when I read the leading Editorial of the Republican," Jackson wrote another St. Louis editor. "If it is the purpose of Paschal and Price to make me endorse the position of the Republican and the miserable, base and cowardly conduct of Gov. Price's submission convention, then they are woefully mistaken. Lashed and driven as they have been by an indignant and outraged constituency from their position of 'unconditional union,' " he continued, "they are now seeking shelter under the miserable absurdity of 'armed neutrality.' " Still worse than the personal humiliation Jackson felt from Price's indiscretion was the prospect of having the editorial produce confusion in the public mind. "I do not think that Missouri should secede today or tomorrow," the governor confessed, "but I do not think it good policy that I should *publicly so declare*. I want a little time to arm the State, and I am assuming every responsibility to do it with all possible dispatch," Jackson explained. "Missouri should act in concert with Tennessee & Kentucky. They are all bound to go out and should go out and should go together if possible. My judgment is that N[orth] Carolina[,] Tennessee & Arkansas will all be out in a few days, and when they go Missouri & Kentucky must follow[.] Let us then prepare to make our exit. *We should keep our own counsels*," the governor warned, noting, "Every man in the state is in favor of arming the state. Then let it be done. All are opposed to furnishing Mr. Lincoln with soldiers. Time will settle the balance."[37]

As for the attitude of the pro-Southern press toward secession, Jackson counseled against public speculation as to "*the time or the manner* in which Missouri should go out. That she ought to go and will go at the proper time I have no doubt," the governor mused. "She should have gone out last winter when she could have seized the public arms and public property & defended herself. This she has failed to do & must now wait a little while." Declared Jackson, "The people of Missouri I must think understand my position," despite its misrepresentation by editor Paschal of the *Republican*. "Paschal knows the people are twenty to one against him and *hence* he seeks to drag me into his aid and support. . . . To frighten our people into the most slavish position, he parades before them from day to day our defenseless attitude & meanly makes it out a thousand times worse than it really is. Missouri can put into the field today twenty thousand men better armed than our fathers were, who won our independence." To counter such misrepresentations, the governor asked his friend to defend him from the "false positions in which Paschal & Price seem disposed to place me," and to remind Missourians that "I am fighting under the true flag. . . . Who does not know that every sympathy of my heart is with the South?" Jackson queried in exasperation. "I have not the patience or time" to address anything beyond the defense of Missouri, he declared: "Let us first preserve our liberties and attend to business affairs afterward. Let all our energies & all our means be applied to our defense & safety."[38]

The defense and safety of the state of Missouri was no doubt foremost in the minds of the legislature on May 2, when it dutifully reassembled in Jefferson City in "special session." The next day Jackson transmitted a message to them outlining the present state of affairs. "Since your adjournment, events affecting the peace and safety of the country, have been transpiring almost with the rapidity of thought," he told them. "Manifestations from every quarter, and of a character neither to be overlooked or disregarded, indicate but too plainly that our whole country, its Constitution and laws, are in imminent danger of disorder and destruction." The "Federal Constitution, the bond of union of a once united and happy people, was framed by the delegates of distinct and separate States" representing different sections, Jackson explained. "There has been no necessary conflict of interests between the North and the South, the East and the West." And yet such a conflict had been provoked, compelling them to gather in special session.[39]

"The progress of fanaticism, sectionalism and cupidity in the Northern States" has at last resulted in "the triumph of a purely sectional faction," Jackson declared, a party which "threatens to destroy the sovereignty of States, and practically convert the government of the United States into an overshadowing consolidated despotism." The attitude of the present executive toward the States represented "a perversion so monstrous and so dangerous" that "all wise and reflecting men foresaw [it] must end in a dissolution of the Confederacy, and that result has not taken us by surprise," the governor ventured. Should that dissolution become permanent, he claimed, it would not be the fault of the people of Missouri:

They have asked nothing which was not their right. They have done nothing in derogation of the rights of others. They have patiently submitted to many and great injuries for the sake of peace. They have ever counseled concord and fraternity. . . . They have been slow to believe that designs destructive to their rights and interests could be entertained by the Administration of Mr. Lincoln. They refused to see in his inaugural any purpose of introducing the horrors of civil war. They have cordially united in every effort of the people of the Border States to effect such a compromise as would secure the rights and honor of all, restore fraternal feeling, reconstitute the Union, and impart new vigor to the Constitution. Their counsels and their rights have been alike unheeded.

"The old Confederacy is broke," Jackson announced; "a new one has been organized by a portion of the States; and President Lincoln . . . has threatened a destructive war between the States" in his effort "to subdue the seceded States."[40]

Proof of this effort was to be found in Lincoln's April 15 proclamation calling for troops from Missouri, Jackson offered, adding, "I am sure I but gave utterance to the universal heart of our people when I replied, that Missouri would not furnish one man to assist in such a war." Then, taking Brigadier General Frost's advice, the governor argued, "The action of the President is evidently unconstitutional and illegal, and will only tend to still further alienate the people of the free and slaveholding States in their opinions and sentiments. . . . The President . . . has not only discovered the power in the *government* to make war on the States, but has assumed that the *Executive Department* can initiate that war. Neither Washington, nor Jefferson, nor Jackson ever for one moment imagined that they were clothed with such a despotic power as this." President Andrew Jackson had once ventured that neither the Constitution nor the Union could be maintained "in opposition to public feeling, by the exertion of the coercive powers confided to the government," the governor recalled, and President John Quincy Adams felt it "far better for the people of the dis-united States to part in friendship from each other, than to be held together by constraint." Surely, the bonds of Union are secured "in the love and affections of the people," the governor surmised. "But the lessons of wisdom taught by the older and purer statesmen of the country seem to be unheeded by the present Administration. Its policy is rapidly tending to revolution; and, unless speedily arrested, will end in ruin and disaster to the hitherto prosperous and happy people of the American Continent. The great and patriotic State of Virginia, after having failed in all her efforts to re-adjust the Union, has at last yielded in despair, and seceded from the old Federal Union," Jackson told the General Assembly, observing that the same resort seemed to be attracting the states of the Middle and border South. "Our interests and our sympathies are identical with those of the slaveholding States, and necessarily unite our destiny with theirs," the governor argued. The similarities of "social and political institutions," "industrial interests," "sympathies, habits and tastes," as well as "common origin and territorial contiguity," all indicated "our duty in regard to the separation which is now taking place between the States of the old Federal Union."[41]

Jackson urged that while the dissolution of the Union slowly ran its course, "it is . . . indispensable to our safety that we should emulate the policy of all the other States in arming our people, and placing the State in a proper attitude of defense." He cited the Militia bill—which had foundered in February during a wave of optimism—as an appropriate starting point so that "our rights can be defended by strong arms and willing hearts." "Missouri has, at this time, no war to prosecute," the governor cautioned them. "It is not her policy to make aggressions on any State or people; but in the present state of the country, she would be faithless to her honor, and recreant in her duty, were she to hesitate a moment in making the most ample preparation for the protection of her people against the aggression of all assailants." "Do nothing imprudently or precipitately," Jackson implored them. "We have a duty to perform. Let us . . . reason one with another" and "avoid all passion and all tendency to tumult and disorder," endeavoring "ultimately to unite all our citizens in cordial co-operation" for the sake of "honor," "the security of our property," and "all those high duties imposed upon us by our obligations to our families, our country, and our God."[42]

As Missourians paused to reflect on the governor's remarks, one aspect became clear: the state's relationship to the federal government had deteriorated badly—so much so, in fact, that the governor openly questioned whether its continuance was to be desired over amicable separation. Perhaps the bonds of union were indeed secured "in the love and affections of the people," just as "Old Hickory" and "JQA" believed, and perhaps the recent actions of the Lincoln administration had indeed caused those affections to wane. There was great import in Governor Jackson's declaration that "the old Confederacy is broke; . . . a new one has been organized by a portion of the States," for these were Missouri's "Southern Sisters," the kin and kindred with whom "our interests and our sympathies are identical." A new Union with these states was Missouri's future, Jackson suggested, a new Union preferably forged in peace but with vigilant military preparation if required. This satisfied the state's duty and honor—virtues yet esteemed in the border South. At this significant juncture in Missouri's relationship with the federal government, past history, present conditions, and future preparations were the vehicles of the governor's address. Such a past-present-future orientation made possible a reassertion of Missouri's collective identity: it enabled the public to cherish the state's past, to distinguish its political values from those presently held in the nation's capital, and to look forward to a new future with those of common values and interests. It was certainly cause for reflection.

One week after Jackson's address to the special session of the Missouri General Assembly, Captains Greene and Duke returned to Jefferson City, road weary but eager to consult with Governor Jackson about their mission.[43] With them they carried a letter from Jefferson Davis informing the Missouri governor that as president of the Confederacy Davis "most cordially welcomed the fraternal assurances" delivered by Captains Duke and Greene. "A misplaced but generous confidence has, for years past, prevented the Southern States from making the preparations required by the present emergency," the Confederate president graciously explained, "and our power to supply you with ordnance is far short of the will to serve you. . . . I concur with you as to the great importance of capturing the arsenal and securing its supplies," Davis wrote Jackson, agreeing with the governor's concerns about "the means taken to obstruct your commerce and render you unarmed victims of a hostile invasion." As to the Confederacy's future relations with the state, Davis was cordial and inviting. "We look anxiously and hopefully for the day," the Confederate president concluded in his most graceful form, "when the star of Missouri shall be added to the constellation of the Confederate States of America."[44]

Conclusion

The federal call for militia forces in the wake of Fort Sumter ushered in the denouement of Missouri's "Conditional Unionism," the final unraveling of the long-cherished affections of many Missourians toward the American Union. Their attachment to the Union was strong to a point, but when Missourians perceived that the whole idea of "Union" was undergoing subtle change, the tensions finally became too great. As a border state Missouri had become sadly and intimately acquainted with tension in recent years. But now, when something had to give, residents of the state discovered that only a slender thread of politics and commerce linked them to the North, whereas a woven cord of kinship, fealty, social habits, and "domestic institutions" bound them to the South. Naturally, their alienation did not occur overnight, although their furious expressions of latent estrangement might have made it seem that way.

Rhetorical estrangement in this case called attention to and emphasized a divergence in political opinion and collective values. An important function was served by such discourse, as it often praised leaders and values of the collective or blamed the public figures and principles of the opposition. Reactions among the Missouri public and in the press clearly demonstrated a tendency toward "praise" and "blame" in the aftermath of Lincoln's call for troops. A conspicuous addition to those discontented at this point were the "Conditional Unionists," those who had hoped to see the North and South reconcile their differences and had resisted Governor Claiborne Jackson's earlier call to rally behind the South. But Lincoln's call for troops achieved what the governor could not: the president forced a choice— a hard choice at that—between opposition to "coercion" and opposition to secession. With war staring them in the face, the "Conditional Unionists" who were unable to conscience the "coercion" of the South had a parting of the ways, not with the idea of "Union" but with what the present Union had become. Rhetorically, they disputed the premises of the federal relationship as enunciated by the Republican party, arguing for an interpretation of the idea of "Union" more along the lines of Calhoun or Jefferson. "Union," in their construction of the term, was fundamentally incompatible with "coercion." Having held out hope against "coercion" for so long, "Conditional Unionists" adopted a rhetoric of disaffection that was particularly striking and particularly embittered.

The rhetoric of disaffection and its consequent rhetorical estrangement ushered in a new manner of thinking about the state's relationship with the Union and the nascent Confederate States of America. The federal call for troops set Missourians in motion exploring unprecedented alternatives of response; they were willing to prepare for the worst and to consider ideas they had once rejected with some firmness. In effect, the federal call for troops brought forth the undoing of Missouri's affections toward the Union; it was the final blow that produced estrangement with the state's existing political relationship and encouraged efforts to secure more satisfactory political ties.

8

Civil Rights and the Cold War

A Rhetorical History of the Truman Administration's Desegregation of the United States Army

Steven R. Goldzwig

Rhetoric is associated popularly with demagoguery, bombast, empty words, "mere rhetoric." In its various emanations from the mouths of politicians, rhetoric is even more suspect—prima facie evidence for immediate and rancorous distrust and disdain. For people disposed to such popular interpretations of rhetoric, it is *deeds*, not words, that matter; and such folk often suggest that this is especially the case in politics. I will take issue with this point of view by arguing that rhetoric is action in the world, a very profound action that forms the basis of all human decision making and enactment. Rhetoric has ideological, social, and material implications. On the strength of persuasive words, people go to war, make peace, strengthen or weaken economies, pass programs or pass them up, act graciously or brutishly. To get anything accomplished, one must be persuaded that it is worth doing, worth the risk. Indeed, peaceful social change requires rhetorical struggle. Any prescription for individual or collective change must be *argued for*. And in argument there is *agon*, struggle.

An investigation of rhetorical history is especially suited to trace this peculiarly human contest because it allows us a special kind of knowledge about politics and political actors. By using the unique lens of history-through-speech (and speech-as-history), I hope to demonstrate the proposition that history, politics, and the contemporary presidency are usefully served by documenting and analyzing rhetorical practices. Because rhetorical history "takes rhetoric as its subject matter and perspective," it concerns itself with the role of persuasion in the history of ideas, politics, and society.[1] Rhetorical history, then, is a special lens for describing and assessing political actors, events, and cultures.

The rationale for doing rhetorical history is itself persuasive. First, rhetorical histories allow us a closer look at political actors as wordsmiths in action. The close textual analysis of letters, memoranda, logs, and other forms of recorded documentary evidence often can supply scholars with the best evidence of the individual motives, methods, beliefs, and values of political actors as they wrestle to shape public philosophy and implement public policy. The persuasive appeals launched by and directed at presidents, cabinet members, officers, advisors, friends, enemies, interest groups, and various other public and private constituencies provide an important nexus for the exploration of rhetorical history. It makes a difference who gives the advice, who takes the advice, who ignores it, and why. Second, rhetorical history is a lens for understanding political cultures. Rhetorical histories assess the sociopolitical and cultural legacy of particular administrations and help explain their impact on communal memory. In studying the rhetorical dimensions of past proposals and policies, we chart a common future. In sum, when they are well executed, narrative accounts of contemporary presidencies and administrations based on rhetorical history are sites for the production of further knowledge about the creations, motives, and policies of individual presidents and presidencies, the intricacies of the institutional-administrative arrangements involved, and the cultural significance of such legacies. In short, rhetorical histories mount their own unique narratives that leave us the richer for the telling.

I will demonstrate rhetorical history's utility through a case study of the Truman administration's historic efforts to desegregate the United States Armed Services. My particular focus will be on the Army, where the opposition to an integrated service was most entrenched and therefore the rhetorical struggle most telling.

Harry S. Truman and Civil Rights: Values and Public Philosophy as Discursive Performance

Harry S. Truman's views on civil rights are most accessible in his public address. His words help reveal his character, values, and public philosophy. The discourse also serves as a fair barometer of his expressed civil rights beliefs and therefore helps frame his public accountability. As William C. Berman notes, "Truman never hesitated to pronounce his steadfast loyalty to the ideas of justice and equality."[2] Moreover, "In practically every speech President Truman made on civil rights, he pointed out the necessity for Americans to practice what they preached, since the world was watching."[3] Indeed, the issue of civil rights was important not only in its own right but also because of its perceived consequences in international affairs. As Richard Dalfiume contends, "Cold War propaganda against the United States hit hard at the race problem; State Department experts estimated that nearly half of the Russian propaganda against the United States was focused on this issue alone."[4] With Truman's assistance Jim Crow was transmogrifying into a formidable diplomatic dilemma.

Truman's civil rights philosophy can be adduced in various public speeches and commentaries. During the 1940 election year, for example, Truman stated: "In giving to the Negroes the rights that are theirs, we are only acting in accord with ideas of a true democracy."[5] Berman judged such discourse "a model of sobriety and good taste," especially "when measured against typical southern utterances on civil rights" at the time.[6]

The Truman presidency was witness to events, however, that seemed to erode both the law and social relations. The president became increasingly convinced of the need for a major civil rights initiative. On June 26, 1946, President Truman sent a message to the NAACP's annual convention. He assured participants that the ballot was a sacred right and that any form of organized terrorism against the franchise was nothing less than intolerable in a free democratic society. Yet the South would not become, by any stretch of the imagination, a willing partner in equal citizenship for African Americans. Indeed, vigilante violence and murder perpetrated by white southern nightriders seemed a chilling reminder of the vengeance of those who opposed the gathering forces of social change.[7]

After the crushing off-year election defeat of Democrats in the 1946 Congress, Truman issued Executive Order 9008, which created a presidential civil rights committee. As Berman indicates, Truman "undoubtedly wanted to see 'fair treatment' extended to all citizens. It is not likely, however, that he wished to upset his working relationships with the South in December, 1946, in order to support such an objective. Yet by establishing a civil rights committee, Truman inadvertently built up political pressure that could spell trouble for him in the future."[8]

In his State of the Union Address on January 6, 1947, Truman announced that present civil rights abuses would require federal legislation: "We have recently witnessed in this country numerous attacks upon the constitutional rights of individual citizens as a result of racial and religious bigotry. . . . I have, therefore, by Executive order established the President's Committee on Civil Rights, with a view to making recommendations to the Congress."[9] Not coincidentally, in this same address Truman declared that despite having demobilized the armed services in 1946, the nation still would "need well-equipped, well-trained armed forces and we must be able to mobilize rapidly our resources in men and material for our own defense should the need arise." Significantly, the president noted, "We are encountering serious difficulties in maintaining our forces even at these reduced levels." Truman's military advisors were warning him that he might have to reinstitute the draft. The Selective Service law in force at the time was scheduled to expire on March 31.[10]

On January 15, 1947, the president commissioned his civil rights committee; on January 16 he announced that the three services had reached an agreement on the plan to unify the armed forces. At first glance these two activities would seem to be unrelated. However, on March 12, 1947, Truman delivered his "Special Message to Congress on Greece and Turkey: The Truman Doctrine." Therein Truman declared the United States ready, willing, and able to take up its role as the defender of the free world. As a result the state of military preparedness would become one of the key foreign policy issues of the Truman administration. Because civil rights abuses now constituted an obstacle to an efficient and effective fighting force, they now took on added urgency.

The convergence of civil rights, the emergent cold war, and U.S. armed forces preparedness is perhaps best elaborated in Truman's historic June 29, 1947, address to the NAACP. In this landmark speech the president would stake out an unprecedented role for the federal government in the civil rights arena. Truman spoke of a "turning point in the long history of our country's efforts to guarantee freedom and equality to all our citizens." Truman stated, "the extension of civil rights today means, not protection of the people *against* the Government, but protection of the people *by* the Government." The president clarified the mission: "Our immediate task is to remove the last remnants of the barriers which stand between millions of our citizens and their birthright. There is no justifiable reason for discrimination because of ancestry, or religion, or race, or color." Truman declared emphatically, "Our National Government must show the way!"[11] Truman underlined the foreign policy implications of vigilance toward civil rights at home: "Our case for democracy should be as strong as we can make it. It should rest on practical

evidence that we have been able to put our own house in order. . . .
We can no longer afford the luxury of a leisurely attack upon prejudice and discrimination."[12] Given Truman's prior public statements
and the president's own predilections in foreign affairs, it seemed
natural to cast civil rights in this light. As the president saw it the
United States's first obligation was to "put our own house in order."
Only then could Americans credibly promote Western-style democracy and confidently solicit the allegiance of the world community
to democratic principles and practices. The link between practicing
civil rights at home and fostering democratic principles abroad would
have profound implications for generations of Americans in their
thoughts on war, peace, and race relations in the United States.

On February 2, 1948, basing his policy on the recommendations
of his October 1947 civil rights committee report, *To Secure These
Rights,* the president delivered yet another unprecedented civil rights
address. Striking a calm, dignified, humane tone, Truman asked Congress for additional authority to act on pressing issues, which included establishing a permanent Commission on Civil Rights,
strengthening existing civil rights laws by securing federal protection against lynching, insuring voting rights protections, impaneling
the long-delayed Fair Employment Practices Commission, and enacting measures prohibiting discrimination in interstate transporta-
tion.[13] The president also indicated his resolve to fortify federal non-
discrimination policy. Regarding U.S. armed forces, in particular, the
president remarked pointedly: "During the recent war and in the
years since its close we have made much progress toward equality of
opportunity in our armed services without regard to race, color, religion, or national origin. I have instructed the Secretary of Defense to
take steps to have the remaining instances of discrimination in the
armed services eliminated as rapidly as possible. The personnel policies and practices of all the services in this regard will be made consistent."[14] Recognizing its propaganda potential, the government carried the president's address over Voice of America. Berman observed
that "the civil rights message now entered the cold war arena as a
document of diplomacy. At home it immediately became a source of
major political controversy."[15]

Although the president's civil rights legislation would founder on
the shoals of powerful, at times virulent, southern opposition in Congress, the military reform he contemplated was a matter of executive responsibility; presidential action required no congressional approval. Truman's authority to issue an executive order would enable
him to make his most indelible mark on civil rights policy by target-
ing continuing forms of discrimination in the military.

The Fahy Committee:
A History of Institutional Warfare

On July 26, 1948, a day prior to convening a special session of Congress to attend to ongoing national problems of inflation and housing, Truman issued Executive Orders 9980 and 9981. As Berman notes, both orders were directly tied to the upcoming campaign and election: "The Truman orders were timed perfectly . . . to focus attention on Congress. And, concurrently, to undercut [Progressive Party candidate Henry] Wallace's standing with many Negroes."[16]

Executive Order 9980 authorized a federal review board for investigating discrimination in federal government employment practices. The Fair Employment Board was set up as an arm of the Civil Service Commission. It sought to review cases, supervise compliance, and adjudicate appeals. It had no direct enforcement powers—save imploring the president to take additional action whenever and wherever he deemed necessary.[17] Executive Order 9981 directed new efforts at equal opportunity in the armed forces and created the President's Committee on Equality of Treatment and Opportunity in the Armed Services, which was authorized to begin oversight tasks. Significantly, the order made no mention of segregation. It was impossible to tell whether the order was intended to achieve an integrated armed services. The executive orders predictably raised the ire of southern Democrats for going too far and the suspicions of the black community for not going far enough.[18] After issuing the two orders Truman appeared in person before Congress the next day to outline his eight-point legislative package, which also included civil rights provisions. The response was "noticeably cool."[19]

At the time Harry S. Truman signed Executive Order 9981, "the racial scene in the services was scandalous, if viewed from any perspective of fairness."[20] The order read in part: "There shall be equality of treatment for all persons in the armed services without regard to race, color, religion, or national origin. This policy shall be put into effect as rapidly as possible, having due regard to the time required to effectuate any necessary changes without impairing efficiency or morale." Truman directed his committee "to examine the rules, procedures, and practices of the armed services in order to determine in what respect such rules, procedures and practices may be altered or improved with a view to carrying out the policy of this order." The committee was charged with executing its duties "until such time as the President shall terminate its existence by Executive order."[21] As Dalfiume notes, "Basically, the President's committee was a liberal one."[22]

What came to be known as the Fahy Committee would work with

the various branches of the armed services in planning and implementing a fair and equitable process for eliminating the entrenched apartheid of the status quo. The Navy and Air Force were already making substantial progress toward integration, so the main stumbling block resided with the Army. Whether or not it was admitted, or even foreseen, the president's order would become the opening salvo in a great social experiment. The daunting task before the committee was simple in its complexity: to see if people serving in a democracy could get along with each other and to erase the longstanding color line in the nation's military. As directed by President Truman, this experiment in human relations was now a federal mission and responsibility.

EARLY STIRRINGS OF ARMY OPPOSITION. One month before the formal appointment of the Fahy Committee membership, the Army was preparing to release its own report, "The Negro in the Army." In late August of 1948 the Army pressed to have this report released immediately in an effort to upstage a report with recommendations to be issued by black leaders, such as Lester Granger of the Urban League, who had met with Secretary of Defense James V. Forrestal in late April to discuss means of redressing ongoing racial problems in the military.[23] Presidential advisor Philleo Nash informed Clark Clifford that the Army's report was "carelessly executed" and contained "several deficiencies" and "old statistics." Even more damning from Nash's perspective, the Army's report made no mention of the president's newly announced committee.[24] Clifford, also fretting over the Army report's contents, timing, and reception, issued a memo to Secretary of the Army Kenneth C. Royall: "Since the Defense Establishment seems to feel strongly that this report should be made public in advance of the recommendations of the Granger group, we will not object . . . provided that it is accompanied by a statement that it covers the situation prior to the issuance of the recent Executive Order on Equality and Treatment of Opportunity in the Armed Services. . . . My personal recommendations would be that the Granger recommendations and this report be released simultaneously."[25]

Although the Committee would not meet formally until January of 1949, the effect of the president's order was immediate and profound. On the positive side of the ledger, Donald S. Dawson, an administrative assistant, would inform the president, "Since your Executive Order was issued, all important opposition to the draft on the basis of the Army's race policy has disappeared. . . . Negro leaders and their white friends have been universal in their praise."[26]

Secretary of the Army Royall, however, was worried about the composition of the president's committee. He complained to Truman:

"[A] number of [those] being considered . . . have publicly expressed their opinion in favor of abolishing segregation in the Armed Services. At least one of them, Lester Grainger [sic], has been critical both of the Army and of me personally on this particular matter. I feel strongly that no person should serve on this Committee who has formed a fixed opinion on this subject on either side. . . . I would like an opportunity to discuss this matter with you personally before appointments are made."[27]

On October 21, 1948, Secretary of Defense James Forrestal notified the military service secretaries of the Fahy Committee plans. At that time the president's committee expected to meet for the first time in mid-November and anticipated completing its work within two months. Meanwhile, as chair, Judge Charles Fahy had requested background materials. Forrestal directed "each Department [to] designate one of its Assistant Secretaries as the official point of contact for the Department with Mr. Fahy's Committee." He also advised the assistant secretaries to work with "one ranking Negro officer" and with the members of the Armed Services Personnel Board.[28]

A NEW PLAN.   On December 2, 1948, after a series of delays, Secretary of the Army Kenneth C. Royall submitted to Defense Secretary Forrestal an experimental Army integration plan: "I propose, but only if similar action is taken by the Navy and the Air Force, to establish a completely non-segregated Army post with approximately 5,000 officers and enlisted personnel assigned to the following units: (1) One infantry regimental combat team. (2) One engineer battalion. (3) One station hospital and medical complement. (4) One post headquarters. Of the enlisted men, roughly 10% will be Negro, this being approximately the average proportion in the Army at present." Royall thought it important to create "widespread understanding of the project" while simultaneously preventing "too much publicity or non-representative publicity." He advised Forrestal to limit press visits. The experiment, which became known as the Royall Plan, was meant to test the willingness of troops to serve in integrated units, the efficiency and combat value of such an arrangement, the implications for the command structure, any ensuing social, morale, or discipline problems, opportunities for African American advancement, and finally, whether the experiment could be generalized to the Army as a whole.[29] Designed to demonstrate "progress" on the race issue and to counteract the Fahy initiatives, the Royall plan was distributed to the other branches of the service for review and comment.

Secretary of the Air Force W. Stuart Symington, in responding to the Royall Plan, was less than enthusiastic. In a memorandum to Forrestal he observed: "The experiment will not be conclusive. There are so many artificial features involved that success or failure of this experiment would not be predictive of success or failure under other conditions. . . . The public relations aspects . . . are particularly undesirable. By its very nature, the attention and searching scrutiny of the Negro press and various pressure groups would be focused upon this activity which, through its artificiality, is of minimal military significance but of major significance in the current public controversy on purely racial issues." Symington contended, on the other hand, that the Air Force was in a position to conduct such an experiment because it already had trained black technicians in place to meet the call for 10 percent representation and he anticipated no social or morale difficulties.[30]

Acting for the secretary of the Navy, John Nicholas Brown's response was similar to that of the Air Force. The Navy felt the experiment "will certainly create widespread publicity . . . [that would be in] large portion . . . adverse and non-constructive in nature. With regard to the Navy the assignment of Negro personnel is made without reference to the race of the individual. [Indeed,] very satisfactory progress has been made in the Navy and the Marine Corps without creating problems of morale and discipline or lowering the esprit de corps."[31]

Because both the Air Force and the Navy seemed to be moving forward on the president's executive order without much prodding, even before the Fahy Committee formally convened, the Army seemed, by contrast, all the more mired in the so-called "Negro problem." Much of its trouble seemed to stem from inflexibility. The officers themselves seemed most intransigent. Whether Secretary of the Army Royall knew his plan would be unacceptable to his sister services is unknown. Royall may have insisted that the Air Force and the Navy had to go along with *his* plan knowing that, given their different situations, there would be little agreement. In this way the "experiment" would be scuttled.[32]

The Rhetorical Battles of 1949

The symbolic import of Executive Order 9981 was widespread. Yet the mere proclamation of equality in the armed forces did not make it a reality. Six months had passed and it was still unclear whether Truman had partial or total desegregation in mind. Nor was it entirely clear what impact the order might have on the armed services. Another hard round of persuasion was about to begin as the Fahy Committee began the arduous task of implementing Truman's order. The president met with the Fahy Committee on January 12. A text drafted for Truman's use in addressing the committee is instructive regarding the administration's philosophy:

Our total national economy demands the most effective utilization of every citizen. Likewise it is the privilege and responsibility of every citizen to make the maximum possible contribution to our national strength. The concept of democracy that our nation represents to the peoples of the world demands that there be equality of treatment and opportunity in the armed services as well as in other phases of our national life. The Committee will wish to make a comprehensive survey of the past and present status and service of the Negro citizen in the armed services. . . . It is my profound desire that the work of this Committee shall yield results which will not be simply a report, but a set of operable plans, a blueprint, for constructive action. The national security requires that you make your contribution, consistent with the fundamental rights of all men, toward the full development of the strength of our country.[33]

In highlighting the economic and national security aspects of the committee's responsibilities, Truman rhetorically subordinated individual civil rights to the collective national welfare. Post–World War II national pragmatics trumped the larger moral questions. These arguments also were uniquely tailored to counteract military opposition.

At the actual January 12 meeting, which lasted ten minutes, Truman told the committee: "I have asked you . . . to serve on this commission in an effort to expedite the thing in the Government Service so that you can actually carry out the spirit, as well as the letter of the order [no. 9981]. . . . I'm satisfied that with this sort of setup we can get the thing working as it should work." In requesting a unified and consistent policy, Truman seemed to have in mind something beyond a simple concern with the armed services. His vision for civil rights in America was expansive: "I want this rounded out a little bit. I want the Department of the Interior, the Commerce Department, the Treasury Department, interviewed on the subject [of] why you are in existence, and let's make it a Government proposition, as well as an Armed Services [one]." Indeed, Truman's expressed intention was decidedly not to merely "limit it to just one branch of the Government. That's what I have in mind all the way down the line. Not only that, I think we've got to go further—not at this time, but later—and see that the state and local governments carry out the spirit of the laws which we hope to get on the books down here during this session of Congress." As envisioned by the president at the time, the armed services would become a model for the nation.

The president appeared wary of the negative publicity that could follow the committee's formal and informal investigative work: "I want it done in such a way that it is not a publicity stunt. I want concrete results—that's what I'm after—not publicity on it. I want the job done and I want to get it done in a way so everybody will be happy to cooperate to get it done. Unless it is necessary to knock somebody's ears down, I don't want to have to do that, but, if it becomes necessary, it can be done. But that's about all I've got to tell you."

Truman's was a tall order given the history of the services and their demonstrated lack of cooperation with each other in prior encounters over the desegregation issue. Still, the tone had been set. A no-nonsense approach would be adopted by the Fahy Committee. The president "hoped" the committee could get back to him with a report by June 1, "and then," he said, "if it is necessary to continue, why, we can go on from there, in order to give you plenty of time. I'd like to have the outline of the situation before the Congress adjourns in case we need to ask for any legal amendments to the law because, in that hearing, at that time, we will endeavor to pass the Civil Rights Program as outlined in my message on the subject in the last Congress. I hope to get some concrete results of that in the Eighty-first Congress."[34]

On January 18 E. W. Kenworthy, executive secretary of the Fahy Committee, voiced confidence in the ongoing informal developments since the issuance of the president's executive order: "I think the President's Committee has done pretty well on this. The Army has now accepted three of our four recommendations—on opening schools and jobs, and on assignment to any unit—and there remains now only the fourth recommendation, the elimination of the 10 per cent quota. I am sure we will get that too."[35] Kenworthy had engaged in a bit of wishful thinking; a much longer struggle lay ahead. This was brought home most forcefully to the Fahy Committee at its March 28 meeting.

"EXCEPTIONALLY AND PECULIARLY QUALIFIED." On March 28, 1949, Judge Fahy's committee was anxious to talk with the service secretaries on a number of items, including (1) whether the earlier Gillem Report (WD Circular 124) "envisage[d] the eventual elimination of segregation"; (2) the secretaries' interpretation of Executive Order 9981; (3) whether there was a need for a "unified policy on utilization of Negro manpower"; (4) whether the Fahy Committee should hear testimony from the joint services' Personnel Policy Board; (5) the secretaries' ideas and suggestions regarding administration and implementation of new policy; and (6) specific questions for Secretary Royall on the "policy and practice" of Generals Clay and MacArthur.[36]

At the meeting Secretary Royall, armed with a lengthy statement, reiterated Army arguments for continuing segregation. He rehearsed the long-standing racist viewpoints common at the time:

The Army is not an instrument for social evolution. . . . Applied to the question of segregation, the criteria must be what produces the greatest and most effective use of all our manpower . . . so that we may place a winning Army on the battlefield. . . . The history of two wars has demonstrated that in general Negro troops have been less qualified than white troops for the performance of certain types of military service, for example, service with the infantry or with other units requiring troops "close with the enemy."

On the other hand, there are undoubtedly other functions for which Negro troops are exceptionally and peculiarly qualified. Motor or ship transport service might be given as examples. It follows that in the interest of efficient national defense certain types of units should be entirely or largely confined to white troops, and that where Negroes are assigned to any of those units, they should be carefully selected.

Royall also maintained that an integrated Army posed morale problems. He argued that troops engaged in war must "have confidence both in their leaders and in the men that are to fight by their sides"; thus, "in close personal relationships such as exist in an Army unit, voluntary segregation is normal in ordinary civilian relations. And this is true even in those localities where no type of segregation is required by law." Royall contended, "In this connection we must remember that a large part of the volunteers in the Army are southern-ers—usually a larger proportion than from any other part of the country. Whether properly or not, it is a well known fact that close personal association with Negroes is distasteful to a large percentage of Southern whites." Therefore, "abandonment" or "sudden change in . . . the Army's partial segregation policy would . . . adversely affect enlistments and reenlistments not only in the South but in many other parts of the country, probably making peacetime selective service necessary." Royall thus raised the specter of racial resistance weakening military preparedness.

According to Royall one of the "most difficult" problems was getting white soldiers "to serve under Negro officers or particularly under Negro non-commissioned officers." He argued that black enlistments did not suffer under the present policy and that the Army was taking steps to improve opportunities for advancement. "As a matter of fact," Royall boasted, "the progress of the Negro in the Army—and his present status—is superior to that which he occupies in any other department of the Government—military or otherwise. Nowhere else does the Negro hold as many positions of importance and responsibility." This latter argument had been an old saw.

Despite his negative declarations, Royall said the Army was still willing to make "such adjustments as are necessary from time to time to meet changing conditions." Royall concluded that the Army had initiated "the best practical method of handling—and gradually narrowing—the segregation problem." He thought it inappropriate "to force a pace faster than is consistent with the efficiency and morale of the Army—or to follow a course inconsistent with the ability of our Army, in the event of war, to take the battlefield with reasonable assurance of success."[37] Royall's testimony must have shaken all but the most inveterate optimists on the Fahy Committee. Members had thus far demonstrated themselves to be steely-eyed realists, however, so it was also highly unlikely that they would fold up their tents. They were committed for the duration. And change was in the wind.

That same day, March 28, Louis A. Johnson formally replaced an ailing, overworked, and increasingly befuddled James Forrestal, who had submitted his letter of resignation as Secretary of Defense on March 1, 1949.[38] On April 6 Secretary Johnson issued a memorandum to all secretaries of the armed services and the chair of the personnel policy board announcing some "supplemental" policies pursuant to equal opportunity. Provision 1b. (3) seemed to add a new wrinkle: "Some units may continue to be manned with Negro personnel; however, all Negroes will not necessarily be assigned to Negro units. Qualified Negro personnel shall be assigned to fill any type of position vacancy in organizations or overhead installations without regard to race."

The new policy proved controversial. The pivotal word here was *organizations*. Army policy had previously limited the employment of blacks in desegregated units to "overhead" tasks, which included menial duties such as housekeeping, laundry, commissary duty, and the like. The word *organizations* could be interpreted as increasing opportunities, and as written the new directive seemed at odds with existing Army policy; however, the Fahy Committee only learned of its existence from Johnson on April 18, when he declined an invitation to testify at the committee's April 26 meeting. Johnson argued that his appearance would be "premature" and "unprofitable" because he had not had time to assimilate "the details of this difficult problem." Johnson did promise to examine present policies, to solicit statements from the service secretaries, and to have them reviewed by the personnel board "to determine their adequacy."[39]

Johnson's new order proved vexing to the Fahy Committee, which not only suffered such unilateral action but now risked being preempted. Johnson's directive inspired increased vigilance as the committee pondered counter moves and carefully calibrated the public relations ramifications involved. Johnson's order also induced a healthy skepticism toward continuing the present course of action, a skepticism further encouraged by the evolution of the negotiations with the Army, the suspicion that the numbers submitted by the Army did not convey the full extent of the ongoing problems, and the Fahy Committee's own investigations. As one thoughtful person in an unsigned memorandum to Charles Fahy suggested, "I now think that we better jump from battalion to man-to-man integration. . . . The new policy is nothing but the old practice in small print. . . . Our visit to Meade convinced me that while Negroes are indeed being put into overhead installations, they are not being assigned in anything like the numbers they could be." The author seemed to have his hand on the true pulse of the dilemma:

Secretary Johnson's memo raises real problems for the Committee. . . . Except for a flat statement eliminating all segregated units, there is not much by way of a policy statement that the Committee could make which would go beyond the Secretary's. Therefore, the Committee must concentrate on procedural matters in its recommendations. I do not know what procedures the three services will propose in reply to Johnson's memo—I daresay nothing very revolutionary. But I think it would be very bad if the Fahy Committee proposed concrete steps which seemed to fall short of the Johnson policy. . . . Perhaps it isn't a policy. . . . But the press and the public think it is a policy, and they think it is a promise. . . . We have been put in a tough spot.

In anticipating an upcoming interim report for President Truman, the writer advised Fahy to issue "recommendations on the Army only. The reason . . . is that our thinking is likely to be pretty conclusive on the Army. Therefore, if there are leaks—and there are bound to be—at least the recommendations will stand examination. I would want to know a lot more about the Navy and the Air Force before I submitted any recommendations, even in an interim report."[40] Nevertheless, under the committee's continuing pressure, the "yeast . . . [seemed] to be working." The Army was now "considering the abolition of quotas." Moreover, "if men . . . [were] assigned on the basis of their MOS [Military Occupational Specialties], regardless of race," then reason argued that segregation would "come tumbling of its own weight."[41]

INITIAL RECOMMENDATIONS AND INTERIM REPORT. The initial recommendations drafted by the Fahy Committee on May 24 detailed the process of prying open the closed opportunities in the present system. Perhaps most important, and most difficult of all, was the committee's call for the abolition of racial quotas as promulgated by WD Circular 124 (a.k.a. the Gillem Board Report) and the substitution of intelligence test classifications (a.k.a. General Classification Tests, or GCTs). As the Fahy Committee noted, "The [present] quota system does not implement, but goes far to defeat, the Army's declared policy in Circular 124." The Army complained that the higher enlistment scores required by the Navy and the Air Force resulted in the Army's securing a higher percentage of men in the two lowest test score categories (Class IV and Class V). One preferred solution was simply to make "the entry intelligence score for the three services . . . the same."[42]

Responding to Defense Secretary Johnson's call to reexamine service policies, Acting Secretary of the Army Gordon Gray, who served as Royall's successor, issued a vigorous defense of Army implementation of policies under the Gillem Board regulations. Gray was especially wary of changing the quota system based on test scores, arguing that this would reduce the number of recruits dramatically: "The Army currently limits Negro enlistments to their civilian population ratio, about 10 percent. . . . There is a definite limit to the number of men with low GCT's that the Army can absorb. . . . Without a quota system of any kind, Negro membership could rise easily to 30 or 40 percent." Gray advised Johnson: "There is a growing concern among many senior officers . . . that we are weakening to a dangerous degree the combat efficiency of our Army. These officers are familiar with the combat performance of Negro troops during war and feel that we have already gone too far in inserting colored organizations in white combat units."[43]

On June 7, in a follow-up report to the president, the Fahy Committee indicated it had made "considerable progress." Admitting that the Army's second plan "did not go beyond the framework of its present policy and practice," the committee assured the president that it "[expected] to have further conferences" and asked for a delay in issuing their required interim report while they tried to negotiate pending matters. Truman granted this request.[44]

Army intransigence was much more serious than the progress report indicated. As Kenworthy complained to Fahy, "The Army is determined to do nothing about guaranteeing that Negroes completing school courses will be used regardless of race." Kenworthy lamented, "I do not see how the Army can expect to keep its segregation policy inviolate when the Navy and the Air Force have abandoned segregation as a policy. The beginning on integration which the Committee has recommended, it seems to me, is modest, gradual, and calculated to improve the Army's use of manpower. I cannot see how it could cause the Army any embarrassment or lower its efficiency."[45]

Kenworthy's frustration was based on both short-term and long-term concerns. Achieving cooperation on desegregating the services was in the interest of African Americans and in the national interest of efficient use of personnel; however, this issue also had a direct bearing on the reorganization of the postwar military establishment.[46] The monumental postwar restructuring of the American defense system was materially jeopardized by an unfathomable, unwieldy, and, for many, embarrassing resistance to change. At the dawn of the cold war the Army's recalcitrance created an immobilizing effect. In rejecting a third Army plan, dated July 6, the Fahy Committee informed the secretary of the Army that, among other flaws,

the abolition of quotas to major commands for school selection is profligated by the retention of quotas in assignment to units, and thereby intensifies rather than eliminates *unequal treatment* and *opportunities*. . . . The proposed improvement of numerical utilization of Negroes in MOS of each field is dissoluted by the *restricted utilization of the individual* to the opportunities offered on a fixed basis to persons only of his race. . . . It is this Committee's best judgment that the . . . proposal fails to meet in any reasonable manner the spirit and letter of the President's Order.

This intransigence was accompanied by an annoying tactical delay. The Army had proposed appointing a board to look into ongoing matters and encouraged the committee not to make a report to the president until it convened and issued its own recommendations. From Kenworthy's perspective this request was a slap in the face: "Now suddenly the Army suggests that the problem, which was being discussed at what amounts to a cabinet level, be turned over to a board of Army officers for review. The plain intimation is that the Army can handle this matter unilaterally, without further interference from the President's Committee."[47] Given the meager prospects indicated by these stifling developments, it was anyone's guess how long true conversion to a fully integrated Army might take. By July of 1949 Kenworthy and Fahy were taking no bets.

The Fahy Committee sent Truman its interim report on July 27. The committee advised the president that the Army had met "some parts of our recommendations" but had not yet met the full requirements of Executive Order 9981. The committee had proposed four major revisions in the Army's present policy:

1) Open up all classes of Army jobs to qualified personnel without regard to race;

2) open all courses in Army schools to qualified personnel without regard to race;

3) assign and use personnel upon completion of school courses without regard to race;

4) abolish the racial quota, substituting a quota system based on the distribution of mental grades as determined by the General Classification Test.

This four-point program, long the benchmark for Army compliance with Executive Order 9981, continued as the basis for controversy. The fourth demand remained least amenable to change.

The committee informed the president that the racial quota issue had proven particularly vexing because the Army had previously agreed to drop the quota only if all three services were to adopt the same minimal standards of acceptance. Nevertheless, the interim report remained adamant on this issue: "The Committee is of the opinion that the Army should abolish the racial quota now."[48]

The Army's continued resistance may have given the committee pause for additional reflection. On August 8, 1949, Kenworthy assured Fahy that the committee's proposed policy was appropriate. After going over the files of the old McCloy Committee operations during World War II, the Fahy Committee's executive secretary, perhaps self-servingly, said he had found "a history of unrelieved headaches." He lamented: "I cannot understand how the Army can defend its racial policy by appealing to experience. I was never more certain that we are on the right track. If our recommendations had been in effect in the twenty years between the wars, I feel certain that the Army would have had more efficient Negro troops."[49] The committee still understood itself as making no more than sensibly moderate demands. Its Army directives were never meant to "break up immediately its segregated units." All proposals were merely directed at "getting the best utilization out of more highly qualified Negroes in the Army."[50] This rhetorical tack was repeated over and over.

A NEW INITIATIVE. On September 26 Judge Fahy informed the president that there seemed to be agreement on all issues except the quota, and if actual implementation proceeded in accordance with the committee's intentions, then "great progress" was within reach. On September 30 Secretary of the Army Gray advised Secretary of Defense Johnson that he had developed new regulations, subject to the service secretary's concurrence, that would accede to the Fahy Committee's demands. Military Occupational Specialties would seemingly be opened to qualified personnel regardless of race; quotas for attending Army schools would ostensibly be abolished; promotions would be handled on an "equal merit" system; ROTC students would train and remain together without racial reference; and a new board of senior Army officers would meet on a regular basis to review progress on the new policies. This new policy initiative did not immediately break up existing segregation; rather, it seemed to assure equal opportunity for qualified enlistees and personnel in existing units. Johnson issued a press release announcing these changes. The Fahy Committee, however, was unsure whether the new Army directive went "far enough" and implored the president not to comment publicly until a full committee assessment could be undertaken.[51]

Trying to sort out the implications of the newest Army proposal and the defense secretary's subsequent public endorsement proved, like everything else associated with these efforts, to be a bit of a trial, as minority affairs aide David K. Niles made clear in an October 5 memorandum to Truman: "Fahy['s] committee reached an agreement with the army that assignment of qualified personnel to specialist occupations would be on the basis of merit and fitness without regard to race or color. Yet the Army's program is evasive on this point, which the Fahy Committee feels is key to their entire objective. . . . [Moreover,] Secretary Johnson's [press] release, covering this program, is arousing a good deal of controversy, and has resulted in inquiries from a number of reporters, and letters and telegrams from interested organizations."[52]

A "Further Interim Report to the President" reinforced Niles's assessment. Issued on October 6 by Fahy on behalf of the committee, this report was directly occasioned by Johnson's announcement of the new Army policy. Fahy observed, "It is true that the new program is a step forward, but its effectiveness is seriously impaired by the omission to provide that, after the men have acquired their Military Occupational Specialties and have completed their school courses, they shall be assigned according to their qualifications and without regard to race or color." Although all parties anticipated a "slow process," Fahy argued, "that should not be a deterrent to the adoption of the assignment policy we have urged."[53]

The Further Interim Report addressed the problem of assignments bluntly. The opening of the Military Occupational Specialties would

be nullified to a considerable degree by the failure of the program to provide that personnel, to whom these opportunities will be accorded, will be assigned without regard to race or color. Unless assignments are so made, and are not restricted as at present to Negro and overhead units, the principle of equality of treatment and opportunity is not carried forward and the manpower of the Army is not utilized to best advantage. The Committee feels that this further logical step is required to effectuate the President's Executive Order 9981 and the statement of the Secretary of Defense of April 6, 1949.[54]

Meanwhile, abolition of the quota system was still a bone of contention. The intricacies of abolishing the racial quota are perhaps best exemplified in Kenworthy's memorandum of October 29. He told the committee he was now in "an impossible situation" and described a breakdown in the "firm understanding with Gray and [Special Consultant to the Secretary of the Army] Bendetsen and MacFadyen [sic] that P & A [Army Personnel and Administration] would work with the staff to try to solve the quota problem. The bottlenecks are General Brooks, Director of P & A, and his number two, Colonel MacFadyen [sic]." Probative evidence of Army obstructionist policies was found in a "statement sent out by P & A to all commanding generals forbidding them to use Negroes except in Negro units and in 'Negro spaces' in overhead installations." Kenworthy concluded: "I know from the best authority within P & A that its hope is that the Committee will submit its final recommendations—what its recommendations are they don't much care—and disband."[55]

"A SLOW AND PRACTICAL PROCESS." An immoral and nefarious policy had become an albatross for the executive secretary. His enthusiasm and creativity in trying to circumvent, if not overcome, the forces against change were beginning to wear thin. Kenworthy and company were determined, however, to make sure that the long, hard road traveled thus far would indeed lead to the destination they had targeted. The import of their duties had been reinforced by a demonstratively committed and straightforward president. Because each skirmish in the battle had been hard won, there was little else to do but press ahead.

Neither the utilization and assignment problem with Army occupations and schools nor the general racial quota would slip away into the quiet night. Gray wrote Fahy on November 17: "I have repeatedly declared that the Army is prepared to adopt a substitute for the numerical quota if one could be devised which afforded assurance against a disproportion between Negro and other personnel within the Army in peace as well as in war time. After a most careful examination into the subject, I am compelled to conclude that nothing has been suggested by your committee which approaches this requirement."[56]

Kenworthy remained adamant on the continuing inadequacy of the Army's schools policy: "The Committee very definitely stated to the President in its interim report of 11 October that it opposes further creation of Negro units and that its objective is 'the beginning of integration by a slow and practical process.'" Furthermore, Kenworthy complained, "The officer detailed to write the . . . special regulation has conceded that the regulation does not affect appreciably the Army's present policy on assignment and does not reflect the Committee's recommendations to the Army."[57] Kenworthy argued that "the only way to make the opening of MOS and schools effective is to infiltrate gradually the qualified, school-trained Negroes into white units." The only remaining question was, "Does the Army intend to do this by the revised 124?"[58]

RAW POWER POLITICS. The intense wrangling continued until it sometimes spilled over into raw power politics pitting military against executive authority in particularly vexing, and sometimes excruciating, encounters. For example, Karl Bendetsen telephoned Charles Fahy on November 27 to inquire whether the committee

would agree that the revision of 124 accurately reflected the policy statement issued by Secretary Gray and approved by Secretary Johnson on September 30. Mr. Fahy replied . . . that he would by no means agree to such a procedure, and he added that if the Army issued a revision of 124 to commanders, he would notify the White House of the Committee's disapproval; and furthermore he would issue a statement to the press making it clear the Committee had not approved the Army's policy. If this were done, Mr. Fahy said, then a situation would arise which had so far been successfully avoided; i.e., a controversy in public.

After this exchange,

Mr. Bendetsen then asked whether Mr. Fahy meant that the Committee had the authority to prevent the Secretary of Defense from approving the Army's policy. Mr. Fahy replied that he was not trying to usurp the prerogatives of either Secretary Gray or Secretary Johnson, and that they, of course, had the right to issue an approved policy statement. The point he wished to make, however, was that the Committee operated under an executive order of the President, and that in the Committee's view the Army's policy did not meet the requirements of the policy expressed in the president's Executive Order 9981.[59]

As November 1949 drew to a close committee members were increasingly anxious to produce public results. They feared additional encroachments on their power, not only through the now continuous Army subterfuges but also by the second-guessing they were receiving from Truman's advisors and an increasingly impatient Congress. It was a delicate, damnable, precariously frustrating enterprise. The committee's presidentially mandated low profile was now proving a liability rather than an asset. Many committee members pined for a public relations counteroffensive.

The intricacies of the power relations are best revealed in the ongoing correspondence. Committee member Dwight R. G. Palmer wrote Kenworthy:

There is every evidence that Secretary Gray and all his people think along the line of a "disproportionate" number of Negroes vs. whites. Well, this is the quota business. We discuss elimination of quota and they pull this "disproportionate" angle. If you are going to continue to hold sessions with the Army people (and I think you should) keep us advised in report form and look out you don't even halfway commit us to any subtle schemes of the Army. To date I have not seen a revised "124" nor any further comments since Judge Fahy referred to remarks by a Mr. Nash. Frankly, I am not sold on these "second string opinions." Such fellows have no responsibility to us nor can we sit by and let them "opinionize" about how we ought to handle our job. We have members who believe some publicity must be forthcoming. Is such a suggestion to die on the vine? We ought to do something.[60]

Palmer's misgivings did not preclude White House advisors from issuing opinions on unresolved matters. The administration still favored quiet diplomacy. On December 9, 1949, Nash advised Kenworthy that "a public statement should be avoided" and that if the committee were still intent on making one, "then it should be as mild as possible." The committee's dissatisfaction with the matter of "assignment" in the proposed revisions to WD Circular 124, Nash advised, should be addressed in a memorandum to the Army and copied to the White House, whereupon the White House "would indicate to the Army that it should move to meet the recommendations of the President's Committee."[61]

Having publicly commissioned the Fahy Committee and having defined its mission, the president, of course, ultimately was held accountable for the impasse. For example, Senator Ralph E. Flanders of Vermont wrote Truman: "From various sources I get the impression that your plan for doing away with racial segregation in the armed services is not making very much headway, particularly in the Army." Flanders issued what amounted to a threat: "The matter should, I believe, be looked into by a Congressional investigation if conditions are as I understand them to be and if they continue. It would seem better if you could make another effort to have your desires followed so that a public investigation would be unnecessary." The president issued a curt reply: "I read your letter of the 13th with a great deal of interest. For your information, the program as outlined in the matter to which you refer, is proceeding very satisfactorily. Efforts are being made, of course, to cause us all the trouble possible in getting the plan to work. There are certain conditions which have to be met on a gradual basis. Eventually we will accomplish the purpose, if the busybodies will let us alone."[62] Other "busybodies" entered the fray. Appearing on *Meet the Press*, Secretary Gray was asked to explain why the Army, unlike its two sister services, had failed to reach resolution with the Fahy Committee. In a somewhat self-serving defense, Gray denied he was making "trouble" for the president and argued forcefully that he was actually trying to revivify a process that had reached a "virtual standstill."[63]

Denouement—1950

With the growing public perception that the president's committee seemed stymied, Congress moved to resolve the matter on its own. Truman and the defense establishment steeled for additional rhetorical pressure. On January 12, 1950, Representative Jacob Javits (R-N.Y.) introduced a resolution to create a Congressional Select Committee investigation of discrimination and segregation in the armed services. Javits complained that the services had been developing separate policies: "Persistent charges have been made that practices of segregation and discrimination continue in the Army. Nothing could be more useful as propaganda material to the Communist propagandists in the 'cold war.'" In particular Javits maintained that communist propagandists in West Germany, Western Europe, Asia, and Africa were having a field day over the dispute. And, he noted pointedly, "With Communist China as a propaganda base, segregation and discrimination on grounds of race, creed or color in the United States can be used to win tens of millions to the Communist cause."[64]

On January 16, 1950, the Army finally acquiesced, announcing its long-awaited revisions on WD Circular 124. The committee was pleased with the final wording of section 10 and subsections 10a, 10b.1, and 10b.2, which addressed the contested issues of assignment and utilization. Fahy informed the president of these latest developments and attached the Army's revision. Three of the committee's four major recommendations had now been adopted. The final obstacle to full implementation was the Army's racial quota system.[65]

Secretary of Defense Johnson felt the Fahy Committee, having served its purpose, should now be abolished. Johnson asked Truman to turn the remaining issues over to the Defense Department, which would be responsible for submitting "semi-annual progress reports." Opposed to abolition, the president's advisors issued a spirited defense. Clark Clifford offered the president the following advice: "The elimination of racial quotas upon enlistment is still under discussion between the Committee and the Army. Even after a successful solution to that problem is agreed upon, Dave Niles and I think that the Fahy Committee should be continued, possibly on an advisory rather than an operating basis, for an indefinite period, so that it will be in a position to see that there is not a gap between policy and an administration of policy in the Defense Establishment." Truman, in a marked demonstration of leadership, decided to continue the committee's mission until the quota issue was resolved.[66]

On February 7, 1950, David Niles informed the president of "friendly and encouraging talk on the Fahy Committee's remaining recommendation—the substitution of an achievement quota for the present racial quota." Niles reported the latest committee proposal would now require all recruits to score a minimum of 90 on the GCT test, make it difficult for low-score personnel to reenlist, and eliminate the racial quota of "one Negro for every nine whites." Niles deemed the proposal "fair," "sensible," and "gradual" because "Negro units . . . would not be abolished overnight." Such rhetorical characterizations were in keeping with Truman's stated goals. Thus, this latest report must have been most welcome.[67]

Truman, however, seems to have hedged his bet a bit regarding the outcome of the final agreement between the Fahy Committee and the Army. Secretary Gray seems to have requested and received approval from the president and Secretary Johnson to return to the old system if it became necessary. On March 1, 1950, Gray wrote Truman: "If, as a result of a fair trial of this new system, there ensues a disproportionate balance of racial strengths in the Army, it is my understanding that I have your authority to return to a system which will, in effect, control enlistments by race."[68]

Nonetheless, on February 24, 1950, even before the final agreement between the committee and the Army was reached, Kenworthy would exuberantly inform Eric Severeid of CBS News that

What is going on is a kind of quiet social revolution about which the country knows nothing. We feel that over a period of time this opportunity for whites and Negroes to live and work together is going to have an incalculable effect upon the civil population. And it has all been done by concentrating on the business of job opportunities, and also by not making a public hue and cry, but sitting down with the services and persuading them that they were making inefficient use of the manpower they had. The Committee maintained that the services could not afford this human wastage.[69]

On March 13, 1950, Fahy informed Niles that a confidential agreement had been reached with the Army on March 6 to abolish the racial quota and that the committee was now in the process of preparing its formal final report.[70]

The final Fahy Committee report, *Freedom to Serve*, outlined the monumental struggle to desegregate the armed forces and the Army in particular. By defending and supporting the Fahy Committee, Truman helped overturn Jim Crow in the federal government. The president's victory demonstrated a pronounced acumen: "politics and morality merged to produce justice."[71] Dalfiume summarizes:

Truman's issuance of the executive order and his insistence that its purpose was to end segregation weakened resistance in the armed services. Furthermore, the President's backing for all of the Fahy group's recommendations to the Army enabled the committee to overcome the almost total opposition to integration in this service. Throughout this period it was the support of civilian leaders within the military establishment for integration that proved decisive. The significance of the committee's achievements is that at its beginning the Army had an official policy of segregation and at its conclusion the Army was officially committed to integration.[72]

The president was quite pleased with the Fahy Committee's accomplishments. Truman observed that equality of opportunity in the armed forces would improve "military efficiency" and "strengthen . . . our entire national life." This was a decisive step because it helped establish the fledgling Truman Doctrine: "The free nations of the world are counting on our strength to sustain them as they mobilize their energies to resist Communist imperialism."[73] Thus opened the widening gyre of civil rights and the cold war.

Sociopolitical and Cultural Legacy

Powerful political and social forces in effect at the end of the Second World War made it impossible to ignore or perpetuate the *status quo* in U.S. race relations. Blacks were becoming an important political force at the ballot box and were growing increasingly unhappy with the abrogation of their civil rights at home and abroad. Their pleas for civil rights soon became entangled in the larger propaganda chips of cold war diplomacy. This process was a creation of presidents, advisors, politicians, and black leadership alike. For Truman these developments had profound consequences. Even if his political instincts told him to avoid African American rights, historical fortunes flung him into the vortex.

Truman, palpably aware that his presidential responsibilities called him to a new and greater accountability, understood that constitutional protections had to be afforded to each and every American regardless of race, creed, or color. Early on the president seemed to sense that the separate-but-equal doctrine was a method of enshrining discrimination and, therefore, had become a "contradiction" that had no place in contemporary American society. Truman's role in the federal government's extension of civil rights to its citizens was clarified in his efforts to introduce civil rights legislation and, failing the substantive congressional hurdles at the time, was codified through executive action ensuring equal opportunity in the armed services. Civil rights legislation almost cost Truman the 1948 election. Executive action earned him an eminent place in civil rights history.

With the May 22, 1950, issuance of its final report, *Freedom to Serve*, the Fahy Committee disbanded at the president's request. The Korean War began in June of 1950. During that war, unlike those that preceded it, the old bugaboo of inferior black units was displaced as field commanders pushed *toward*, rather than away from, integration. As William Pemberton recounts, "By October 1953, 95 percent of black soldiers served in integrated units."[74] The groundwork laid by the Fahy Committee made this significant development possible. For all practical purposes, "by the end of 1954, segregation and discrimination were virtually eliminated from the internal organization of the active military forces."[75] As Berman summarizes, Executive Order 9981 "was undoubtedly President Truman's greatest civil rights achievement—and it illustrates the intelligent use of executive power to change, within admittedly narrow limits, a racist structure."[76] As Milton Konvitz notes, "in the history of civil rights in the United States this order ranks among the most important steps taken to end racial discrimination."[77]

Just as important, the move to reorganize and unify the military service to set up the postwar defense establishment, when writ large, became a test of the United States's ability not only to rebound from the war but also to assume its *symbolic* role as the undisputed leader of the emerging new world order. Under the heady aegis of a dawning Pax Americana, successive administrations assumed that if democratic principle ruled, then global democratic participation would follow. In hindsight, this political premise proved a recurrent, sometimes monstrously hazardous, rhetorical theme in much cold war diplomacy. For in Truman's inauguration of the cold war, we find one of the early rhetorical links to U.S. civil rights as central to the image and consistency of American foreign policy. This argument was introduced by Truman, used in his rationale for his appointment of the Fahy Committee, and employed by successive administrations and civil rights advocates alike. Preserving human rights at home became a linchpin for the attractive presentation of Western-style democracy and rhetorical themes underlining, if not exacerbating, the emerging global competition with the Soviets. Thus, the familiar dualist nature of cold war foreign policy address, and the attendant bipolarities of arguing good and evil systems of government, received some of their first rhetorical rehearsals in the struggle to integrate the armed services.[78] Civil rights was a part of the cold war before *Brown v. Board of Education.*

In the great tradition of American pragmatism, the president, the Fahy Committee, and the Army would finally converge on rhetorical values all parties held in high esteem: maximum efficiency as the key to national security. The effective utilization of manpower reigned uppermost in the arguments from all directions. Such normative criteria helped push principle into implementation and action. The integration of the armed forces, perhaps little understood for its enormity at the time, is now perceived as a monumental step that paved the way for the civil rights movement in the 1950s and 1960s.

On the other hand, the Achilles' heel of contemporary civil rights discourse is perhaps also traced to the cold war. The cold war imperatives toward "maximum efficiency" and the preservation of "national security" no longer buttress today's civil rights arguments. The contemporary assault on affirmative action programs, for example, may be a part of the post–cold war, post–Soviet Union environment. Without an "enemy" to hate, we may be prone to lose our grounding. When Americans are persuaded to moral action based on xenophobic and nationalistic sensibilities, the moral moorings securing civil rights seem rather tenuous. Moreover, once the "enemy" is vanquished or disappears, the individual may have a hard time supporting a positive personal ideology and endorsing any governmental program of action. And the collective, having grown weary of the discourse of individual civil rights, may retreat from any discussion of human rights. Having known for so long what to be against, it may be decidedly harder now for Americans to discern what one can and must be for, individually and collectively. The recent court cases signaling a rollback on affirmative action may be harbingers that we as a nation are ready to fold our social tent on civil rights and traverse a long desert of the soul that may have little to do with the so-called abuses in the present system. Of course, such speculation needs further development, refinement, and support.[79]

Arguments against desegregating the armed services bear similarities to contemporary arguments against having gays in the military, women in combat roles, and, of course, affirmative action and the use of quota systems. What is perhaps startling is that many of these arguments have changed little in over fifty years. The rhetorical history documented here echoes the early roots of discussions on affirmative action and the use (and abuse) of quota systems. It also helps explain how affirmative action, as a concept, gradually but perceptibly gained a foothold in the country's conscience and in its institutions as a viable method of ensuring equality of opportunity for all Americans. Finally, I would like to address briefly a larger cultural legacy. With the fiftieth anniversary of the age of thermonuclear weaponry, inaugurated by the U.S. bombing of Hiroshima and Nagasaki, Harry Truman and his administration became the subjects of renewed controversy, especially under the recent scrutiny of revisionists. But one might contrast those disputes with Truman's accomplishments as outlined in this chapter and reflect a bit further. The nation also recently celebrated the fiftieth anniversary of the Truman presidency. Like most people, Harry S. Truman experienced success and failure—and mostly with mixed results. On his efforts to integrate the armed services, however, there was a particularly happy alchemy. Both immediate and long-term good was achieved, and that is a legacy anyone can applaud.

9

"The Deciding Factor"

The Rhetorical Construction of Mansfield's
Credibility and the Eisenhower
Administration's Policy on Diem

Gregory Allen Olson

"Mike arrived in Washington a few years after Ev and I did, but he
came with impressive credentials. The first day he entered the Senate he was appointed to the Foreign Relations Committee and was
considered the only authentic eastern expert on the committee. My
how things have changed. He's got plenty of company now."[1]
—Anecdote prepared for President Johnson in 1968 for a dinner
honoring Everett Dirksen and Mike Mansfield

Majority Leader Mike Mansfield is best known as a critic of U.S. involvement in Vietnam during the administrations of John F. Kennedy,
Lyndon B. Johnson, and Richard M. Nixon. In Oliver Stone's controversial movie, *JFK*, the premise that Kennedy had decided to withdraw from Vietnam after his expected 1964 reelection is based on
Kenneth O'Donnell's account of a meeting between Mansfield and
Kennedy.[2] After Johnson expanded the war, journalist John W. Finney
suggested that Mansfield became Johnson's "most troublesome critic
on the Vietnam war," a role he maintained during the Nixon administration.[3] Yet during his sustained criticism of three administrations, Mansfield was unsuccessful in reversing this nation's course in
Vietnam. Indeed, the senator considered it his greatest failure.[4] Few
now remember that Mansfield did exert influence in the early days
of America's efforts at nation building in South Vietnam. When the
U.S. was funding the French effort in Vietnam and working behind

the scenes, but had not yet committed military forces, "influential politicians like Senator Mansfield" convinced Eisenhower that Diem was the only man who could lead South Vietnam.[5]

No one has posed the question of how a first-term Democratic senator from Montana could influence a Republican administration on such a vital issue. This essay argues that the answer to that question is that Mansfield successfully created the perception that he was *the* Senate expert on Vietnam. Once the idea of his credibility was established, it was never seriously questioned. In a period when few Americans were knowledgeable about that part of the world, that perception translated into influence. Aristotle believed ethos to be the strongest means of persuasion;[6] this essay will examine how Mansfield developed the perception of his credibility over a period of time.

Building Ethos: Personal Background and the Press

When Mansfield came to the Senate in 1952, he already had a reputation as an expert on Asia. The Montanan had spent time in the Philippines and China as a marine after World War I and became interested in the Far East. After earning bachelor and master's degrees at the University of Montana, Mansfield stayed at his alma mater, becoming a professor of Far Eastern and Latin American history. Charles E. Hood quotes one University of Montana official as saying that even with that background in Asia, when Mansfield was elected to the House of Representatives in 1942, he "simply made himself an authority on the Far East by proclaiming himself one." Whether his expertise was real or not, his knowledge of Indochina—the three former French colonies of Vietnam, Laos, and Cambodia—was limited, a fact illustrated by his lecture notes, which are comprehensive when dealing with Japan and China but contain only one and one-half pages of material on Indochina.[7]

Both Mansfield and the press contributed to the exaggerations about the Montanan's expertise. For his part Mansfield often overstated his experience in the Far East. In a 1947 letter to President Harry Truman, Mansfield claimed to have completed "three-quarters of post-graduate work on my Ph.D.," even though he spent only two summers at UCLA, completing six courses without starting work on his dissertation. In that same letter, Mansfield asserted that he "served overseas in the Philippines, Japan, and China," but his stay in China was only twelve days and his time in Japan consisted of a one-day fueling stop.[8]

In addition, the Montanan tended not to correct errors in the media concerning his academic background and time spent in the Far East.

Drew Pearson started it all in 1944, suggesting that Mansfield spoke Chinese. These errors were repeated; in 1958, for example, the *New York Times* called Mansfield "one of the few Chinese-speaking members of Congress." One scholar speculated that Mansfield picked up "some skill in the Chinese language" from his brief stint there in the 1920s. In 1983 a book suggested that Mansfield had "long been familiar with Asia as a resident." As recently as 1993 a book on Kennedy goes so far as to assert that Mansfield "was an intelligence officer in World War II."[9] Once these perceptions found their way into print, journalists merely consulted their clip files and never challenged Mansfield's expertise.

Mansfield found such coverage useful and cultivated his relationship with the press beginning in his House years.[10] An examination of Mansfield's correspondence suggests that Mansfield built his credibility as an expert on the emerging issue of Indochina by successfully courting members of the press. Francis Valeo, Mansfield's top aide and an Asia specialist, commented that Mansfield used the press to glean information not available through official channels: "In traveling abroad, it was Mansfield's habit to pick the thoughts of newsmen [*sic*], in reverse informal press conferences, if you will. This was especially so in places where he believed that the United States government was not reading the situation accurately, as was the case in Vietnam . . . throughout the American involvement."[11] One journalist concludes that few politicians have been "respected more and criticized less" by the media than Mansfield.[12]

Early on Mansfield acknowledged, "Unfortunately, I do not know too much about the Indochinese situation. I do not think that anyone does." Mansfield was correct; in 1954 there were no U.S. books on Indochina and one estimate put the number of American scholars who were experts on the area at fewer than five.[13] Given that lack of knowledge on Vietnam, Mansfield faced little competition in establishing himself as the Senate expert on the region.

Building Ethos: Site Visits, Reporter Contacts, and Reports

Mansfield won election to the Senate in a bitter election in which he was branded "China Mike" and was held personally accountable for the loss of China. This was the only charge that Mansfield was ever "really afraid of," according to his top aide.[14] Mansfield needed an issue to dispel such attacks, and he found that issue on May 7, 1953, when Supreme Court Justice William O. Douglas hosted a luncheon at the Supreme Court Building and introduced Mansfield and John F. Kennedy (D-Mass.) to Vietnamese nationalist Ngo Dinh Diem. Already intrigued by the Far East, Mansfield became interested in Indochina as a potential prize in the cold war. The Montanan was so unknown at the time of this meeting that the State Department thought he represented Ohio![15] Based on Mansfield's later commitment to Diem, he must have left this meeting impressed with the Vietnamese nationalist. Valeo said that Diem was "a name he [Mansfield] carried" after the Douglas introduction.[16] Indeed, many American Catholics were infatuated with Diem, a Catholic nationalist in a nation that was largely Buddhist. Ellen J. Hammer writes that "Diem's fervent Catholicism opened many doors."[17] Clearly, Mansfield, Kennedy, Douglas, and many American Catholics were drawn to Diem by a common religious bond. Yet Diem's Catholicism was only part of the attraction; in the midst of the McCarthy era, Diem appeared to be concerned with social and political reform, which pleased liberals, and yet he was dogmatically anticommunist, which pleased liberals and conservatives.[18]

Mansfield's interest in Diem led him to use his seat on the Foreign Relations Committee to undertake a trip to Indochina in September of 1953. This was a period when foreign travel for a senator was a novelty and a visit to Indochina unique.[19] The New York Times considered this trip important because the Foreign Relations Committee was sending a member who was "the earliest and most persistent backer for heavy aid to the French, short of the involvement of United States troops against the Communist-led rebels in Indo-China." The newspaper made no claim of Mansfield's expertise.[20] By the spring of 1955 Mansfield had changed the New York Times's perception.

The trip proved "an eye opener" for Mansfield. In his written report Mansfield expressed his cold war view by linking Indochina to Korea: "World peace hangs in the balance along both these avenues of Communist expansion. Hence, the security of the United States and of other free nations is no less involved in Indochina than in Korea. Indochina is the key to control of southeast Asia, rich in the raw materials of war."[21]

The Montanan promoted his report by sending copies to prominent business leaders, military officers, educators, government officials, and members of the press. Mansfield always valued the press, which is illustrated by his files relating to the 1953 trip. Prior to departure the senator had a list prepared of members of the press stationed in the cities that he visited. Mansfield met with many of these reporters on this trip and then continued to correspond with them, making sure they received his report to the Foreign Relations Committee. Mansfield was seeking answers and was probably promoting himself as a Far East expert as well. While in Paris Mansfield took Volney Hurd of the *Christian Science Monitor* to lunch; Hurd wrote Mansfield to thank him for lunch and praised the report as "excellent" and "useful." Arnaud de Borchgrave of *Newsweek* covered Vietnam from Paris and called the report Mansfield sent him "immensely interesting." In Mansfield's responses to both correspondents, he asked that they continue to share their thoughts with him "because it will help me greatly in trying to put across my views on this perhaps most critical area in the world today." Both men continued to correspond with Mansfield, as did other contacts that Mansfield made on this visit. For example, Mansfield requested and received de Borchgrave's cables to *Newsweek*.[22]

Mansfield cultivated friendships with government officials as well as with members of the press. Douglas MacArthur II of the State Department sent Mansfield a letter praising the report's "clarity" in stating the problems and estimating "future possibilities." Assistant Secretary of State Livingston Merchant wrote Mansfield that the report was "a remarkably clear and concise statement of the problem in that area of the world." Frederick Nolting Jr., then Special Assistant to the Secretary of State and later President Kennedy's ambassador to South Vietnam, called the report "heartening because of its general endorsement of U.S. policy toward Indo-China" and because of the report's conclusion that "the probability of success warrants the very large contribution that the United States is making." The report was more influential with Secretary of State John Foster Dulles and the State Department than with the Foreign Relations Committee, where there was little interest in Indochina.[23]

Mansfield used his 1953 report as the basis for several speeches on Indochina early in 1954, carving a deeper niche for himself as the congressional expert on Indochina. The report had moved Mansfield into the center of the nation's discussion on Indochina. Mansfield continued to seek information from people he met on his 1953 trip to Indochina, mainly members of the press. In February, as one example, Charles Collingswood had Edward R. Murrow wire Mansfield a transcript of Murrow's Paris interview with journalist David Schoenbrun on the situation in Indochina.[24]

On February 8 Mansfield delivered his first 1954 Senate speech on Indochina. This marked the beginning of congressional debate on Indochina, as there had been virtually none until Eisenhower dispatched Air Force technicians on January 29. The Montanan started the speech by building his credibility, based on traveling "several thousand miles in the three states of Indo-China" the previous September.[25] Mansfield sent a copy of his February 8 speech to Volney Hurd, and they continued to share their ideas through a series of letters. Hurd called Mansfield's speech "right on the line" and further suggested sending German troops to Indochina because the U.S. could not commit troops. Mansfield refuted Hurd's idea, and Hurd responded to the Mansfield rebuttal by writing: "I bow before the keen thought which produced the exceptional memorandum you enclosed in your letter on my thoughts about German divisions for Indo-China! It was a first-class and brilliant weighing of the pros and cons and you have become my favorite candidate for Secretary of State." In another letter Hurd quoted his wife: "We believe in majority rule and people having the government they want, don't we? What right have we then to help bombard (with napalm) people who represent the majority in their country? Have we any right to stop a country from even going Communistic if that is the wish of the majority—for today with the radio everyone in Vietnam knows Ho [Chi Minh] is a Communist leader?"[26]

A constituent wrote Mansfield concerning the February 8 speech to suggest that the senator was becoming "a powerful man in Washington." Mansfield modestly denied that, but media coverage of Indochina was giving that impression.[27]

Another contact that Mansfield had made on his 1953 trip was an assistant to the U.S. ambassador to Thailand, William vanden Heuvel. On March 8, 1954, vanden Heuvel sent Mansfield a letter that included a nonclassified paper. Although that paper is not extant a later letter indicated that it contained an argument in favor of bringing Diem to power in Vietnam. Vanden Heuvel chose Mansfield to receive the paper because "I have long admired your judgment and recently known your friendship." Mansfield "incorporated some of the material" from vanden Heuvel's paper in a speech he wrote; the rough draft is dated March 18, and it was delivered in the Senate four days later. Mansfield believed it "almost mandatory that something be said on the Senate Floor at this particular time" about the situation in Indochina. In the speech Mansfield once again alluded to his September trip to establish credibility, mentioning that he had "crossed paths in India" with majority leader William Knowland (R-Calif.) the previous fall.

Mansfield again sent copies of his speech to ingratiate himself with members of the press and others; he wrote vanden Heuvel that he would appreciate "yours and the Ambassador's comments or criticisms. I value your giving me the benefit of your thoughts because you are so much closer to the scene than I am and evidently you are seeking a solution."[28] Jack Dowling of Time-Life referred to his meeting with Mansfield in Saigon and talked of the "clarity" of the Montanan's views on Indochina, adding, "I am delighted that you had the opportunity and took the time to study these conditions carefully on the spot and so are in a position to impress upon your fellow senators and Congressmen [sic] the realities of Indo-China and the problems that we must face there. Also I am deeply honoured that you should keep me informed on your progress in this growing debate and that you should find my opinion is worth noticing."

De Borchgrave called the speech "first rate" and gave Mansfield some information, including his belief that Dienbienphu would fall because the U.S. had not sent B-26s quickly enough. When David Schoenbrun was sent to Saigon to report on the war, he asked Mansfield who his best sources had been. Mansfield recommended Larry Allen of the Associated Press, another correspondent who Mansfield took the time to meet while in Indochina. Allen called Mansfield his "favorite Senator" and agreed with Paul Douglas's (D-Ill.) comment, after the March 22 speech, that Mansfield was performing a "public service of great magnitude." The correspondent offered Mansfield access to the incoming file at the Washington bureau of the AP and agreed to answer any of Mansfield's questions as long as Mansfield didn't quote the source, an arrangement that continued at least into 1955. Mansfield already had praised Allen in the *Congressional Record* and Allen asked him to write a letter to his boss sharing that praise. Of course Mansfield did, and in May he enclosed another Allen article in the *Congressional Record* with his praise.[29]

Mansfield next spoke in the Senate on April 14. Once again he sent copies of his speech to a number of people. Chester Bowles called it an "excellent statement"; Hurd wrote it was "pretty hard to criticize a speech of yours because you are so thorough, so clear thinking and so objective"; and vanden Heuvel proclaimed, "I would have jumped to my feet and cheered until hoarse at the conclusion of your speech of 14 April. It was a superb job and done in the best tradition of American bipartisanship."[30]

The Montanan's contact with Hurd proved useful when the journalist wrote Mansfield about a communist massacre of civilians in Cambodia: "Who better than you could launch it [publicity about the incident] with a strong Senate speech for your speeches are all getting excellent coverage here [Paris] these days—and deservedly so." Mansfield followed Hurd's suggestion, blaming the incident on "Ho Chi Minh and his Communist masters in Red China." The senator sent copies of this speech to the Cambodian and Vietnamese ambassadors in Washington. The former, Nong Kimny, wrote back thanking Mansfield for "your cooperation, your sympathy and the great interest you have always shown for the cause of my country." The latter, Tran Van Kha, expressed his gratitude and added, "I have seen you yesterday on Television . . . when you have once more defined our situation and talked so eloquently in favour of our country."[31]

Mansfield's strategy to build his credibility as the Senate expert on Indochina was working. For example, the *New York Times*, which had not commented on Mansfield's expertise at the time of his 1953 visit to Indochina, referred to him as an "outstanding Congressional authority" on the Far East by May 1954. In that month the editor of the *Washington Post* wrote Mansfield seeking corroboration of a statement made by journalist Howard K. Smith.[32]

Given such systematic cultivation, it is not surprising that Mansfield was treated well in the press or that his contacts helped increase the perception that he was the Senate expert on Indochina. That perception proved helpful when Secretary of State Dulles invited Mansfield to attend the Manila Conference in September 1954, where the Southeast Asia Treaty Organization (SEATO) was created.

Before the beginning of the Manila Conference in September, Dulles made it a point to call Alexander Wiley (R-Wis.), chair of the Senate Foreign Relations Committee, to discuss Senate appointments to the conference. Wiley recommended Mansfield as one member because the Montanan would be in the Far East anyway on his second trip to Indochina. When Dulles checked with Walter George (Ga.), the ranking Democrat on the Foreign Relations Committee, George agreed: "He would be good, he is developing and will be a great fellow in the Senate."[33]

Mansfield was selected partially because of his availability. It was more than that, though. Dulles trusted Mansfield not to play partisan politics with foreign policy. The secretary of state believed strongly in bipartisanship and valued Mansfield because the Montanan was rarely partisan. During the Truman administration Dulles had been chief negotiator for the Japanese peace treaty and worked closely with the House Far East Subcommittee, of which Mansfield was a member. The two men came to know each other, and Dulles wrote of Mansfield: "I always had the feeling that we worked together in a spirit of cordial cooperation."[34]

By including members of the Foreign Relations Committee, the administration increased the likelihood of quick ratification in the Senate, which is what happened. Of course, the administration needed a Democratic member of the committee. Mansfield's selection may have also been an attempt to co-opt him as a potential critic of SEATO. The Montanan had spoken against such a pact in the past because it involved largely white nations defending Asians and did not have India as a member.[35]

Both Mansfield and H. Alexander Smith (R-N.J.) signed the Manila Pact, creating the Southeast Asian Treaty Organization. With the exception of the United Nations Treaty, this was the first and only time that members of Congress have been treaty signatories. It was made more unique because the Republican administration invited a Democrat.[36]

Mansfield's historic role thus furthered perceptions of his ethos on Asia with government and media alike. Mansfield and Dulles developed some closeness and "mutual respect" that would have significant consequences.[37] As one example, when Dulles met with Eisenhower on October 18 about a mutual security treaty with Nationalist China, the secretary wanted to touch bases with Senate leaders, including Mansfield, even though Mansfield was the only first-term senator on the list and did not hold any leadership post.[38]

The Montanan's involvement with the Manila Pact further enhanced the public perception of his expertise. Ernest K. Lindley praised Mansfield's bipartisanship in *Newsweek* and referred to him as "the leading Democratic Senatorial expert on Southeast Asia."[39] Perhaps Mansfield's cultivation of de Borchgrave was paying off in positive reporting from *Newsweek?*

Bracketing the Manila Conference and further enhancing perceptions of Mansfield's expertise on Asia were visits to Vietnam. In his second set of sojourns to Indochina Mansfield met with Diem; in typical fashion he also sought out members of the press. Each leg of his trip held significant events. On his way to the Far East Mansfield stopped in Paris and met with Guy La Chambre, the French minister for relations with Indochina. La Chambre had met with Dulles in Manila two days earlier, where the minister of state had pushed for the replacement of Diem. Dulles had told La Chambre: "Senator Mansfield had recently been in Indochina and had expressed the view that Diem might possibly be the last chance of a Prime Minister who could be effective." In his September 8 meeting with Mansfield, La Chambre said that "if Diem is not able to create an effective Government" and produce a program of action "within two or three weeks, he will have to go, as time is so short we cannot afford to wait." La Chambre quoted the French ambassador as calling Diem "totally ineffectual." Despite the French minister's opposition, Mansfield concluded the meeting by asserting "that a change in Government every few weeks in Viet Nam would be disastrous. In the absence of a good alternative to Diem, we believe that his Government must be supported and encouraged to broaden its base so as to make it truly effective."[40]

On his way home Mansfield received the following message from the State Department: "The Secretary of State requests you to advise him what you think about the Vietnamese situation and especially your judgment of the ability of Diems [sic] to form a government worthy of our support."[41]

Dulles was using Mansfield's strong support for Diem in conversations with the French and within the administration to justify continued U.S. support for the prime minister. Kenneth Young, assistant secretary of state for the Far East, recalled, "Mansfield was an old friend of Diem's and we knew what the answer would be in advance, of course, but it stunned the French."[42] Mansfield's cable from Berlin shows that his recent trip hadn't lessened his confidence in Diem:

The political crisis in south Vietnam arises from the insistence of Diem on forming a government that is free of corruption and dedicated to achieving genuine national independence and internal amelioration. . . . Ironically, however, only a government of the kind Diem envisions . . . has much chance of survival, eventually free of outside support because only such a government can hope to achieve a degree of popular support as against the Viet Minh. If Diem fails, the alternative is a government composed of his present opponents, no combination of which is likely to base itself strongly in the populace. Such a government would be indefinitely dependent on support of the French and could survive only so long as the latter are able to obtain Viet Minh acquiescence in its survival. The fundamental question, therefore, may well be not can Diem form a worthy government but do the French really want Diem and what he stands for to succeed . . . ?[43]

In a Washington meeting with La Chambre and the French the day after receiving this telegram, Undersecretary of State W. Bedell Smith read Mansfield's telegram and added that Mansfield was "a powerful Democratic Senator in opposition who believes that Diem is the best hope there is." In an administration meeting the next day, Dulles referred to Mansfield's appraisal: "the Senator's views would carry a lot of weight in the Foreign Relations Committee, especially with the Democrats." That became the standard administration line. For example, in talking with the French in October Young said that "Senator Mansfield is particularly well informed on Indochina and that his views may be expected to be influential when the subject comes up in Congress." The administration's use of Mansfield's position ended French opposition to Diem until after the American elections in November.[44]

Using Ethos: Influencing Eisenhower's Policy on Diem

Having temporarily halted the French effort to depose Diem, Mansfield wrote a pessimistic report for the Foreign Relations Committee based on his 1954 visit; he started it by saying that U.S. policy had "suffered a serious reversal" in the past year. The most far-reaching part of the report said, "In the event that the Diem government falls, therefore, I believe that the United States should consider an immediate suspension of all aid to Vietnam and the French Union forces there, except that of a humanitarian nature."[45]

In editorializing about Mansfield's report, the *Milwaukee Journal* called him "one of the best informed congressmen on that part of the world." Hammer concluded that Mansfield "had become the Senate authority on Indochina" by the time of this report.[46]

As a result of that snowballing credibility, David L. Anderson claimed that Mansfield's report "immediately became the cornerstone of the pro-Diem position." Chester L. Cooper agreed: "Mansfield's report had an important influence on the Administration's decision to move forward with an aid program for the struggling Saigon Government. On October 23, 1954, President Eisenhower sent a letter to Premier Diem, and it was that letter that was cited by the members of the Kennedy Administration and . . . by officials in the Johnson Administration to relate the origin and continuity of U.S. policy in support of Diem."[47]

Although sent in late October, Eisenhower's letter to Diem was planned in August and drafted in early September. The interval between the drafting of the letter and the decision to finally send it indicates Eisenhower's hesitancy. The release of the letter so soon after Mansfield's report is more than coincidence. On October 22 Undersecretary of State Herbert Hoover Jr. indicated to Dulles and the U.S. ambassador in Saigon, Donald Heath, that Eisenhower's letter was being released and that the "conclusions of Senator Mansfield are relevant" as to aid. Dulles and French Premier Pierre Mendes-France had agreed in September to support a successor government if Diem should fall from power. Mansfield's report undercut that agreement because of the perception that the Montanan had the influence in Congress to cut off aid if Diem were purged.[48]

Although Mansfield had earlier criticized the administration for failure to consult with Congress, no such criticism was forthcoming when Eisenhower committed U.S. support to Diem without direct congressional input. Victor Bator wrote that by November 1954, "Policy in Vietnam was no longer determined in the State Department. It followed the direction of Congress, more particularly that of Senator Mike Mansfield, . . . who associated the unconditional support of Diem with resolute policy to eliminate 'colonialist' France."[49]

On October 25 Pierre Millet of the French Embassy in Washington asked Young if he thought Mansfield's report went "too far." Young reiterated that Mansfield had influence in Congress where Diem was concerned and that congressional reaction would be "adverse" if Diem were replaced. On November 5 Dulles instructed the U.S. ambassador to France, C. Douglas Dillon, to tell Emperor Bao Dai that Mansfield's conclusions about cutting aid if Diem were deposed were "relevant." Dillon, too, "reminded Mendes of Senator Mansfield's report and the importance it would have on congressional opinion and decisions regarding further aid to Indochina."[50]

When Mendes-France visited Washington in mid-November, Dulles urged the French premier to find time to meet with Mansfield, emphasizing Mansfield's knowledge of the area, influence in the Senate, and strong conviction that Diem was the best hope for Vietnam. Mansfield's stature had grown since his August trip to Paris when Dulles had written the Senator: "I am telling Paris not to press Mendes-France for an appointment in view of his very heavily burdened schedule."[51]

Besides influencing the administration, Mansfield's report gave a boost to Diem. Diem distributed one hundred thousand copies of the report, and the *Pentagon Papers* claimed: "The Mansfield Report elated Diem, subdued the French and annoyed Paris."[52]

Even with U.S. support—and Mansfield's—Diem's government was in trouble at the end of 1954. Eisenhower turned to a military man to solve the numerous problems the Diem government faced. In early November General J. Lawton Collins traveled to Saigon as Eisenhower's personal emissary and a temporary replacement for Ambassador Heath. Dulles told Collins that the Mansfield report "deserves serious consideration." The secretary of state said that Mendes-France was "aghast" when told that aid would likely be cut off if Diem fell from power, and Dulles emphasized to Collins that the French must be reminded of Mansfield's position. Collins's briefing book included copies of Mansfield's 1953 and 1954 Indochina reports. General Collins's two- to three-week assignment stretched to over six months, and the temporary ambassador spent most of that time battling Mansfield and others for influence over the administration's Vietnam policy.[53]

Collins quickly came to agree with the French that Diem was not capable of leading. On December 6 Collins cabled the State Department that Diem must be replaced if he didn't change in the next several weeks. Quite remarkably, Young and Assistant Secretaries of State Walter Robertson and Thruston B. Morton visited Mansfield on December 7 to ask his advice on Collins's telegram. Mansfield strongly disagreed with Collins's conclusion, and his reply was cabled to the ambassador. For the next five months Mansfield lobbied intensely to retain his friend Diem.[54]

Young and Robertson sought out Mansfield because they shared his support for Diem; the three men became allies on the issue. These regular consultations also occurred, as Anderson points out, because Mansfield was perceived to be "the Senate's expert on Indochina."[55] In a conversation with Robertson on December 15, Mansfield repeated his support for Diem but emphasized the need for Diem to cooperate with the U.S. as well, which meant broadening his government and not ruling through his family. If Diem failed to make those changes, the U.S. should terminate support. That message was cabled to the U.S. embassy in Saigon for possible use with Diem, since Mansfield was a "good friend" and considered "impartial" and "objective" by the South Vietnamese leader. Young wrote Collins one week after meeting with Mansfield: "Of course Senator Mansfield believes that there isn't much else besides Diem and the process of replacement would create far more chaos and confusion than is even present today in Free Viet-Nam."[56]

On December 17 Robertson once again shared State Department documents with Mansfield and sent the senator's reactions to Collins.[57] All of this attention and influence had to be heady for a first-term senator from Montana. William Conrad Gibbons refers to "the *pas de deux* between the State Department and Senator Mansfield."[58] As Mansfield noted of his dealings with Dulles, they were

very close and fairly intimate dealings. He called on me many times for advice and counsel as to what should be done in Diem's early days. For a while I was quite free with my information and advice.

I think it was a new area for Dulles—and for Mr. Young, too. I suppose they were looking around for advice from people who may have been there in order to get some guidance until they got their feet firmly on the ground and made up their minds definitely.

I think he [Dulles] leaned a little bit too heavily on me in the matter of Diem and some of the moves he made after taking over South Vietnam—to such an extent that I felt it had to be broken off, because it was outside the ken of my responsibility and entirely within the purview of the Executive branch under the Constitution.[59]

Despite these efforts to distance himself, it was because of Mansfield's persistence that the U.S. policy became one of supporting Diem until a more suitable candidate could be located. Dulles made that point at a meeting with French chief of staff General Paul Ely and Mendes-France on December 19, adding: "Congressional committees, particularly the two foreign affairs committees, led by Mansfield and [James P.] Richards (D-S.C.), were intensely interested in [the] problem and would have to be consulted. . . . Mansfield believes in Diem." Dulles cabled Collins on December 24: "Under present circumstances and unless situation in Free Viet-Nam clearly appears hopeless and rapidly disintegrating, we have no choice but [to] continue our aid [to] Viet-Nam and support of Diem. There [is] no other suitable leader known to us." Collins responded that although he was not "ready to throw in the sponge," he doubted that Diem had the leadership qualities needed to succeed. So at the end of 1954 Dulles reaffirmed U.S. support for Diem—support that was tenuous and influenced by the perception of Mansfield's expertise.[60]

Using Ethos: Mansfield Becomes "The Deciding Factor" in Saving Diem

When Dulles met with the Foreign Relations Committee early in 1955 to report on a trip to Vietnam, he clearly granted Mansfield's expertise on Vietnam. The secretary of state asked for factual corroboration by saying, "you know the situation," and once invited Mansfield's questions because "Southeast Asia is your part of the world."

In this session Dulles also described the problem Diem faced with the sects, who had "exercised virtual sovereign rights in the areas of the country which they occupy. They have their own armed forces, their own police. They collect the taxes, and operate quite independently of the central government."[61]

The three sects were the Cao Dai, the Hoa Hao, and the Binh Xuyen. The Cao Dai were an exotic mixture of Confucianism, Buddhism, spiritualism, and Catholicism, with their own Pope, female cardinals, and saints including Victor Hugo, Christ, Buddha, Joan of Arc, and Sun-Yat-Sen. The Hoa Hao were a fundamentalist Buddhist group, while the Binh Xuyen were not religious, for they were originally river pirates who dominated gambling, prostitution, and opium in the Saigon area and ran the police through payments to Emperor Bao Dai. The three sects could not be ignored because together they controlled more than 10 percent of the population and each group had a private army, totaling forty thousand to fifty thousand.[62]

In January Diem had closed down the gambling casinos, depriving the Binh Xuyen of their major source of income. On March 10 Collins warned Bao Dai's representative of the danger of any Binh Xuyen/Bao Dai attempt to unseat Diem, once again using Mansfield's October report to reinforce the threat. With the aid of Colonel Edward Lansdale of the CIA, Diem bribed members of the Cao Dai and Hoa Hao to join his government. Gibbons speculates that the U.S. spent as much as $12 million in bribes during March and April of 1955. At the same time, Diem cut subsidies to the sect armies, which forced many troops to desert. Alarmed by the defections, the three sects united. In the third week of March Diem refused a sect demand that he reorganize his government, and the Cao Dai and Hoa Hao ministers left Diem's cabinet. The three sects then formed the

United Front of Nationalist Forces. On March 29 fighting broke out between Diem's forces and the Binh Xuyen. The French quickly arranged a truce, but Collins cabled Dulles that he did not think Diem could survive the crisis.[63]

When Dulles called Eisenhower on April 1 to talk about Diem's crisis in Vietnam, the conversation turned to Mansfield and the fear that he would attempt to cut off U.S. aid if Diem were replaced:

The Sec. said Mansfield is devoted to Diem. He thinks we ought to talk with him about it to see what line he will take. The Pres. said he does not know that we should. The Sec. might tell Collins that he is on the spot and will have to play it by ear. His telegram comes as a surprise because we bet pretty heavily on him [Diem]. Let us know if we can do anything. The Sec. said he still thinks we should talk with Mansfield, and the Pres. indicated assent. The Sec. said though we should not be controlled by his [Mansfield's] judgment.[64]

Later that day Mansfield met with Dulles, Robertson, and Young and once more fought for the retention of Diem.[65]

On April 4 Dulles cabled Collins expressing his confidence in the ambassador but indicating that he and Eisenhower believed it was time to see if Diem could survive with French and U.S. logistical and moral support. The secretary of state complained: "I thought we felt when I was in Saigon that the decision to back Diem had gone to the point of no return and that either he had to succeed or else the whole business would be a failure." Dulles once again reminded Collins of congressional opposition to a shift in leadership.[66]

When General Paul Ely of France decided that he couldn't support Diem any longer, Collins cabled Washington on April 7 that Diem would have to be replaced. Once more Young shared Collins's cable with Mansfield; once more the senator was allowed to refute it.[67] Not surprisingly, Collins was not persuaded; on April 9 he sent several telegrams to Dulles pushing for Diem's removal. Dulles replied to Collins that the secretary of state and Eisenhower were "disposed to back" Collins's decision. Yet Dulles remained cautious, fearing loss of U.S. prestige: "We will be merely paying the bill and the French will be calling the tune." Dulles warned, "Mansfield, who is looked upon with great respect by his colleagues with reference to this matter, is adamantly opposed to abandonment of Diem under present circumstances." Collins responded by challenging the basis for Mansfield's expertise: "I have no way of judging Mansfield's position *under present conditions*. These conditions are rather different than those existing when he visited Vietnam in Sept., 1954 when he feared military dictatorship as [the] only alternative to Diem. . . . As practical politicians, I would think that Mansfield and his colleagues . . . would give considerable weight to the arguments I have advanced."[68]

Dulles became equivocal in his support for Diem but continued to fear Mansfield's ability to cut U.S. aid. He told the French ambassador that the administration would have difficulty obtaining appropriations if Diem were replaced, asserting: "Senator Mansfield, who was very influential in these matters, felt strongly that Diem should be backed to the limit and that there was no adequate substitute for him." Later on April 11 Dulles cabled Collins and agreed with the need to replace Diem. Dulles expressed concern about Mansfield's position in a conversation with Senator Walter George, and the secretary of state had Robertson talking to Mansfield about replacing Diem. On April 20 the secretary of state cabled Collins: "Among other things that need to be explored in this connection is the question of what change can obtain financial backing from the United States comparable to that which we are prepared to give Diem. This is a matter not just for the Executive but for the Congress and those who have leadership in this matter, such as Mansfield . . . [who is] very strongly opposed to any shift. As things now stand, they would . . . throw their influence . . . against backing any substitute that now seems in sight."[69]

On April 22 Pierre Millet, minister of the French embassy in Washington, visited Mansfield to discuss the possibility of replacing Diem. Millet pointed out that both Collins and Ely had concluded that Diem must be deposed. Mansfield recalled:

Evidently, he was here to pressure me into changing my position on Diem but I still feel he is the only man who stands a chance and it is a long chance of keeping South Vietnam free. It appears to me that the Administration in discussing the Indo-China situation with the French Ambassador here _is in effect putting the major responsibility on me._ As to what our future decision will be vis-a-vis the retention or overthrow of Diem, I pointed out to Mr. Millet that the responsibility lay with the President and Secretary of State and that it was up to them to assume that responsibility. All I could do was to make my views known [emphasis added].[70]

Having systematically worked to establish his expertise on this issue, Mansfield now chafed under the responsibility. } bullshit

While Millet was pressuring Mansfield, Collins, now back in the United States, met with the Vietnam Working Group headed by Young and comprising members of the State Department, Defense Department, and CIA. During this meeting Collins went to the White House for lunch with Eisenhower. No decision was made at the luncheon except that the group would continue studying the matter and "that Mansfield would be asked in." Young and the members of the Working Group proposed alternatives, but Collins was adamant: Diem must be replaced. Young recalled: "We seemed to be confronted with a *fait accompli*; . . . it appeared to be a Presidential decision that Diem had to go."[71]

On Monday morning, April 25, the Working Group reluctantly accepted the need for a change in government and decided on a provisional government with Diem as chair of a consultative council until a national assembly could create a permanent government structure. Dulles and Collins conferred over lunch, and the secretary of state accepted the compromise.[72]

Pursuing the ouster of Diem, Collins met with the Senate Foreign Relations Far East Subcommittee and had a private meeting with Mansfield on April 27. Valeo, who remained in the hall when Mansfield met with Collins, remembers Mansfield's telling him that "Collins really doesn't know much and he just bought what they [the French] handed to him."[73]

A number of histories conclude that Mansfield was eventually persuaded to accept the compromise to depose Diem, but this author found no proof to support that claim. Mansfield maintains he never favored deposing Diem. The senator wrote this author that "I did not accept a compromise suggested to me by General Collins acting, I presume, with Secretary Dulles' support to replace Ngo Dinh Diem as Premier of South Vietnam. At no time, to anyone, did I or ever would [I] have accepted such a proposal."[74]

While the decision to replace Diem was being made in Washington, Diem dismissed the Binh Xuyen head of police, and fighting broke out on April 27. Collins met with the National Security Council on the twenty-eighth and told them that "Diem's number was up." Meanwhile Dulles instructed Saigon to "hold up action" on replacing Diem because the battle could lead to Diem's "emergence from the disorder as a major hero." Eisenhower sided with Dulles, saying "that it was an absolute sine qua non of success that the Vietnamese National Army destroy the power of the Binh Xuyen."[75]

Diem's forces were victorious. Mansfield issued a long statement in support of Diem on April 29 that he delivered in the Senate on May 2. The Montanan charged a French-Bao Dai conspiracy and denounced Diem's opponents as "the black hand, the pirate, the mercenary, the racketeer and the witch doctor."[76] On April 30 Young wrote Robertson: "If Diem is forced out, Mansfield would have us stop all aid to Viet-Nam except of a humanitarian nature. Senators Knowland and [Hubert] Humphrey (D-Minn.) have also backed Diem. A large number of members of the House Foreign Affairs Committee . . .

have informed the Department . . . that they would not favor the State Department withdrawing support from Diem. In fact there are going to be real difficulties on the Hill if Diem is forced out by what appears to be French-Bao Dai action."[77]

On that same day, Dulles sent instructions for the Paris embassy to inform Bao Dai of the likely termination of aid if Diem were replaced: "Senator Mansfield's statement is clear evidence [of] this position." Dulles cabled Collins on May 1: "There is increasing congressional support for Senator Mansfield's views with which you are already familiar."[78]

The perception of Mansfield's expertise was firmly established by this time. The contact with Volney Hurd paid dividends as the *Christian Science Monitor* called Mansfield the "Senate's chief Indochina specialist." The *New York Times* referred to Mansfield as the "Senate's leading authority on Vietnam" in their coverage of Diem's victory over the Binh Xuyen. One week earlier the same *New York Times* reporter merely referred to Mansfield as "a member of the Senate Foreign Relations Subcommittee on the Far East."[79] The perception of Mansfield's expertise seemed to grow with Diem's victory.

The secretary of state met with the Foreign Relations Committee on May 17, saying he was "encouraged" by Diem's ability during the crisis. Mansfield and Dulles praised each other for actions taken during the Battle of the Sects. In 1966 Mansfield recalled this incident: "It was because of the impetus given by some of us—I hope I'm being modest enough when I make this statement—in behalf of Diem that gave the President [Diem] the initiative to wipe out the Binh Xuyen and to put down the Cao Dai and the Hoa Hao."[80] Mansfield had won his battle with Collins to keep Diem, but Collins's predictions about Diem's limitations proved accurate.

Diem understood Mansfield's role in continued U.S. support and wrote a warm letter to the senator on May 4: "If I am permitted to quote Confucius, the sage said: 'Only in winter do we know which trees are evergreen.' Figuratively speaking, you are the evergreen, as luxuriant as always; not only have you been the stark fighter for democracy and human rights but also the true friend of the Vietnamese people."[81]

Mansfield's role in Diem's victory over the sects led to his being called the "Godfather" of Diem. Journalist Joseph Alsop called Mansfield's support for Diem at this time the "deciding factor" in the Eisenhower administration's decision to continue supporting the South Vietnamese leader. Thomas Boettcher considers Mansfield's support for Diem the most crucial because "his views on Vietnam were accorded greater weight" due to his academic background.

Townsend Hoopes claims that Mansfield caused a "national self-imprisonment" with Diem because Mansfield had the influence in the Senate to terminate aid if Diem were replaced. Thus, Dulles was forced to back Diem to keep Mansfield's support.[82] *Harper's Magazine* concluded: "Few Americans realize that Senator Mike Mansfield of Montana is widely regarded abroad as the chief architect of U.S. foreign policy for Southeast Asia. Senator Mansfield's first-hand reports from Indochina did carry great weight in shaping American policy and his steady support has been largely responsible for keeping Diem's government afloat, when newsmen [*sic*] were predicting that it would sink in a matter of days."[83]

Conclusion

Mansfield's main accomplishment in 1953–1955 was to help gain and keep U.S. support for Diem. John D. Montgomery wrote that it is "unquestionable that the Senator's intervention was an essential element" in that achievement.[84]

The question for this study is how did a first-term senator from a sparsely populated state achieve such influence in 1954–1955? Mansfield entered the Senate with the reputation of being an Asian expert. Once in the Senate he set out to build his credibility by creating the perception that he was an expert on Vietnam. Was Mansfield an expert? Certainly he was not in 1953 when he decided to become one. But Mansfield wanted to avoid future attacks similar to those waged against him in his 1952 Senate election, and the emerging cold war contest in Vietnam gave him his issue. Mansfield found little competition in the State Department because experts on Southeast Asia had been purged during the McCarthy "hysteria."[85] U. Alexis Johnson wrote that he was surprised in 1954 to be selected for the Indochina phase of the Geneva Conference because he "knew comparatively little about Indochina, [yet] I discovered when I returned to Washington that this did not automatically disqualify me, since none of my State Department colleagues seemed to have any clear notion of what we could hope to get out of the conference, and I did not hear of anyone competing for my job."[86] With that lack of competition, Mansfield "grew" in the realm of foreign affairs and emerged as one of the nation's few experts on the region.[87] By 1955 the perception of his expertise was undoubtedly valid.

Mansfield created the perception of his expertise through site visits, through correspondence with important opinion makers in and out of government, and by sending copies of his reports based on his site visits to many of these people. He then used the material from his reports and information gleaned from his contacts and visits to Indochina to deliver a number of speeches on the situation. This rhetorical strategy paid dividends. For the remainder of Mansfield's Senate career, he was considered an Indochina expert by the media and his peers. Virtually any article written about Vietnam, Indochina, or Asia that mentioned Mansfield commented on his own expertise. In Senate debate colleagues often referred to and deferred to that expertise.

The Eisenhower administration, too, conceded Mansfield's expertise on that part of the world. One indication that the White House considered Mansfield an expert on this region is the existence of an early 1955 document in the Eisenhower Library that reveals some consideration was given to offering Mansfield a diplomatic post in the Far East.[88] After Mansfield's 1955 visit to Indochina, Robertson wrote Hoover about a Mansfield suggestion: "This is a recommendation of one of the *most influential and knowledgeable* Senators with respect to Viet-Nam" (emphasis added).[89]

Mansfield's credibility with Dulles was further strengthened because of the dimension of trust. Dulles had confidence that Mansfield would not be partisan. The secretary of state had liked Mansfield when the Montanan had served in the House, and the relationship was strengthened when both men represented the U.S. at the Manila Conference.

Like almost all Americans Dulles was ignorant of Indochinese culture and history. Dulles, too, was seeking answers and accepted Mansfield's expertise. Mansfield's 1954 report forced the Eisenhower administration to support Diem over France's objections because it was believed that Mansfield had the clout to convince his Senate colleagues to cut off funds to any successor government. That a first-term Democrat could exert that influence is all the more remarkable because Republicans held a majority in the Senate until the start of the 1955 session. Dulles and important members of the State Department came to agree with Mansfield on Diem, and the senator had allies in his battle with Collins. But Mansfield's refusal to agree to dump Diem was pivotal in keeping the Eisenhower administration's support behind the prime minister.

Rarely has a first-term senator exerted such influence, and although histories of the period comment on Mansfield's role, none speculate on how he was able to gain such power. An examination of Mansfield's papers provides an excellent case study of how one public official was able to successfully create the perception of credibility for audiences within and outside of government. Propelled by that reputation, "Mansfield was able to influence American policy at decisive moments, and perhaps change the course of Southeast Asia history."[90]

This case study provides an explanation for why an obscure first-term Democratic senator was able to sway a Republican administration and change the course of American history. Careful examination of archival resources reveals the complexities of ethos in action.

10

Declining Honors

Dorothy Day's Rhetorical Resistance to the Culture of Heroic Ascent

Carol J. Jablonski

I came to Dorothy Day as an analyst on assignment. I had been asked to write a chapter on Day for an edited volume on contemporary women orators.[1] I knew that Day was involved in the Catholic Worker movement and that her career spanned the depression and cold war eras. But I had only a vague sense of who she was until I began to study her papers at the archives at Marquette University in the spring of 1992.

It was cold and rainy in Milwaukee during my first visit to the collection. The weather fit my state: after four days working on Day's papers, I was to fly to Pennsylvania to see my father. I knew it would be the last time I saw him; I traveled with funeral clothes in case he died before I got there.

I hadn't thought about the connection between my father's origins and Dorothy Day until my plane came into the snowy Milwaukee sky. His parents immigrated to the United States from Poland at the turn of the century. They met in Milwaukee, married, and had six children. My father was their fourth. Dad's stories about growing up in Milwaukee emphasized the joys and struggles of a gifted and gregarious child. He worked nights to help support the family and to pay his college tuition. He reveled in campus life: he lettered in several sports, was elected class president, and maintained a high grade point average. He played professional basketball and got a master's degree from Marquette. He told these stories often: they defined him for himself and for others.

My father's stories were part of a larger immigrant narrative that many of his generation helped to sew into the fabric of American culture: assimilation through hard work and achievement; courage to take risks and to make changes in one's life; mobility that took one not only upward but outward from the immigrant enclave. Neither the private tellings nor the public expressions of this narrative dwelt much on the stresses of immigrant life: the limited work available to those whose speech was thickened by eastern European dialects; the difficult conditions under which immigrants were forced to work and to live; the alcoholism that became a part of everyday life and that left its worst victims homeless; the resistance of some immigrants to the culture and practice of American capitalism despite enormous pressures to assimilate.[2] On the contrary, most narratives about immigrant life in the late nineteenth and early twentieth centuries emphasized overcoming adversity.

Michael Dukakis's speech at the 1988 National Democratic Convention accepting the nomination for president is a case in point. Dukakis used the story of his father's immigration from Greece and the difficulties his family had faced—and *overcome*—to demonstrate Dukakis's own authenticity and patriotism as an American.[3] In telling his father's story and in accepting his party's nomination for president, Dukakis tapped into cultural logics that privilege the successful assimilation of immigrants and their progeny into the American way of life. One is to infer from this narrative that the American way of life was perceived by immigrants (and other Americans) as unquestionably good, just, and desirable—and that the best way for the immigrant to take part in it was to get along while trying to get ahead.

For some, however, the immigrant experience pointed up the need for fundamental changes in American life. Dorothy Day, journalist, radical, and convert to Catholicism, embodied this "other" story. My work in the Dorothy Day–Catholic Worker collection at Marquette University in April 1992 took me into a world my father and his family had known in the 1930s, a world of conflicts and choices now obscured by the social and economic ascendance of second- and third-generation Catholic Americans. I remembered the murmurs among family members about my grandfather being a radical socialist. I talked with my father's sisters, still living in Milwaukee. Recalling Dorothy Day with admiration, they told me about the Catholic Worker house that still stands in Milwaukee. I began to imagine my father emerging from a milieu of ideas and passions that may not have engaged him long, if they engaged him at all. As I contrasted the values my father embraced with those he did not, I began to understand the significance of Dorothy Day's protest. Day resisted heroic ascent. She opposed the culture of American Catholicism that encouraged people like my father to assimilate into—and contribute to—the capitalistic state as a matter of religious principle. For Day, transcendence was found not in social and economic advancement but in voluntary poverty. Her "downward ascent" not only brought her closer to the poor but, she believed, closer to God.

The contrast in values and choices I so poignantly realized during my first visit to the Dorothy Day–Catholic Worker Collection provide an interesting point of departure for analyzing a compelling rhetorical problem Day faced, particularly in her later years. A deeply devoted convert to Roman Catholicism, Day sought spiritual perfection, or saintliness; yet she overtly eschewed being canonized a saint in the Roman Catholic Church. Norman Lifton suggests that Day's "saintly deviance" (as perceived and constructed by others) was central to her success as a social movement leader. Externally, Day's "saintliness" helped to moderate the threat her radical views posed to existing institutions and individual self-interest, while her "deviance" kept pressure on for social change. Internally, Day's "saintliness" provided a spiritual standard that attracted and motivated movement members, while her "deviance" satisfied them that the movement was "on the cutting edge."[4] Canonization might compromise or eliminate the threat Day's legacy would pose to existing institutions and individual self-interest after her death. Talk of canonization during her lifetime would also undermine her persuasive goals.

Thus honors bestowed during her lifetime were problematic for Day. Although she accepted a number of awards and prizes, Day declined honorary degrees and other honors that she felt would compromise her position as a religious radical. In this essay I use Day's declined honors as a focal point for illustrating her struggle to construct and maintain a persona of one who, although saintly, resisted the culture of heroic ascent. Letters she wrote declining honorary degrees provide a revealing picture of Day as a persuader. She carefully avoids giving the impression that she judges the institution as morally inferior to herself, yet she uses the opportunity to explain her position and that of the Catholic Worker movement. This strategy, I propose, is compensatory for the potential loss of influence that would have been available to her had she accepted the honors she declined.

After examining the letters refusing honorary degrees I turn to a letter stored in the "honors declined" file that was marked "not sent." Addressed to Father Theodore Hesburgh, president of the University of Notre Dame, the letter appears to be a refusal of the university's coveted Laetare Medal in 1972. Day, approaching her seventy-fifth birthday, was ill at the time; the letter appears to ramble and breaks off after ten handwritten pages. Analysis of the letter in light of others she wrote declining awards suggests that Day was inclined to refuse the Laetare Medal but finally could not find the rhetorical means to do so. The letter "not sent" provides a context for explicating the rhetorical difficulties inherent in Day's posture of saintly deviance. In the course of describing Day's rhetorical inclinations from this vantage point, I touch on several issues of note for the rhetorical historian: the value of research in collections and archives; the relationship between researcher, primary materials, and subject; and the researcher's dual obligations to her subject and to "history." Let me begin, however, by providing a brief overview of Day's life.

Rhetorical Biography

Born in Brooklyn, New York, on November 8, 1897, Day was attracted at a young age to the poor and the destitute. Her family was living in San Francisco in 1906 when a devastating earthquake hit that city. Day witnessed the intense suffering of earthquake survivors and was touched by the generosity and sense of community that emerged among them. The family soon moved to Chicago, where Day lived until she went to college at sixteen. Despite her father's antipathy toward "foreigners" and "agitators" and his restrictions on bringing guests into their home,[5] Day developed a strong social consciousness. "Although my only experience of the destitute was in books," she would later write in her autobiography, "the very fact that [Upton Sinclair's] The Jungle was about Chicago where I lived, whose streets I walked, made me feel from then on that my life was to be linked with theirs, their interests were to be mine" (LL 38).

Day spent two years at the University of Illinois, where she wrote for the Daily Illini and joined the Socialist party. By then, by her own account, she "was in love with the masses" (LL 46). After moving to New York to follow her family, Day took a job as a journalist with the socialist paper the New York Call. Over the next few years she would write for two other radical publications, The Masses and The Liberator. Opposed to war but moved by the suffering of the wounded, Day turned to nursing during World War I. She left hospital work in 1920, however, to resume writing. The next few years were difficult for Day, although how difficult was not known until after her death in 1980. A disastrous affair ended when she got pregnant. Day's biographer, William Miller, revealed in 1982 that Day's paramour insisted that she have an abortion, which she did.[6] Day married on the rebound, went to Europe with her new husband, and divorced soon after her return to the United States. Although she traveled between New York, Chicago, and New Orleans, Day eventually returned to New York, where she kept company with a group of literary radicals, including Malcolm Cowley and Kenneth Burke. In 1927, approximately a year after she started living with Forster Batterham, who was a biologist and anarchist, Day gave birth to a much-wanted daughter, whom she had baptized over Batterham's objections. Day's relationship with Batterham ended shortly thereafter, when she announced that she, too, would be baptized Roman Catholic.

The religious culture into which Day was baptized in 1928 was anything but hospitable to the radical ideas and programs she had been reading and writing about since her adolescence.[7] Although convinced that converting to Roman Catholicism was the right thing for her to have done, Day was distressed by what she saw as the church's inability to address pressing social and economic problems. Not until December 1932, when she met Peter Maurin, did Day find a way to reconcile her radical social leanings with her religious faith. Maurin was an itinerant French theologian who drew on Catholic doctrine, including statements by recent popes, to oppose the ideas, practices, and consequences of the capitalist state. A personalist, he advocated individual responsibility, justice for workers, communal sharing of goods, a return to the land, and practice of the corporal works of mercy. Day took Maurin's ideas and put them into a newspaper, which they sold on New York's Union Square on May Day 1933 for a penny a copy. Within weeks, the *Catholic Worker* had attracted a large enough following to warrant an expansion of working space and the opening of a soup kitchen. Catholic Worker hospitality houses soon sprang up, offering poor and unemployed workers food, shelter, and an opportunity to learn and discuss Catholic Worker ideas.

Although labor concerns dominated Catholic Worker rhetoric in early years, they soon were eclipsed by the attention Day paid to the cause of pacifism. Day refused to endorse U.S. support of Franco during the Spanish civil war, a position that drew fire from mainstream Catholics. She opposed the entry of the United States into World War II after Pearl Harbor, a move that lost her significant support within and outside the movement. During the 1950s she was arrested and jailed in New York for refusing to participate in civil defense air raid drills. Although some Catholics saw Day's civil disobedience as immoral, the civil defense protests won her increased respect from individuals within and outside the church.[8]

Day's reputation as a nonviolent religious pacifist helped to define her as an important adjunct to the early civil rights and anti–Vietnam War movements. A longtime advocate of nonviolent resistance, she appeared at civil rights rallies and wrote about her experiences for the

Catholic Worker. As one who had publicly supported war resisters during World War II, Day brought moral credibility to demonstrations opposing the war in Vietnam. Two Catholic Workers initiated draft card burning as a form of protest against the Vietnam War; Day stood behind them. In addition, Daniel and Philip Berrigan had also been affiliated with the Catholic Worker movement prior to their protests against the Vietnam War.

Although her public profile was that of a pacifist, Day relentlessly championed the cause of employed and unemployed workers and the poor. Piehl suggests that Day was concerned that the Catholic Worker movement not be seen as strictly a pacifist movement but as a broader movement for social and economic justice.[9] Indeed, Day's views of the poor—and of the need for believers to serve the poor—provided the spiritual mainstay for the Catholic Worker movement. In contrast to views that shame and condemn the poor while elevating those who serve them, Day and Maurin held that service to the poor humbled— and hence saved—the server. Day embraced voluntary poverty and service to the poor in hopes of improving the material and social conditions of the poor *and* of achieving mystical communion with the divine. Day's practical and spiritual use of voluntary poverty made her a stunning symbol of resistance in and to twentieth-century American culture.

Coming to Terms with Dorothy Day

One could go a long way toward understanding Dorothy Day and the Catholic Worker movement without ever stepping in the Marquette University archives. Much of Day's writing explains the movement and chronicles its history. Often autobiographical, her works illustrate Day's rhetorical efforts to construct a "life" that enacted her beliefs and that appealed to various readerships. Klejment and Klejment's 1986 bibliography and index lists ten books authored by Day,[10] including an autobiographical novel, which in her later years she tried to suppress;[11] an account of her conversion and defense of the faith, written to show radical atheists why she embraced Roman Catholicism;[12] two volumes of essays drawn from Day's *Catholic Worker* columns;[13] an account of life in a Catholic Worker hospitality house;[14] an official autobiography, which tells the story of the retreat experiences of Day and Maurin during the 1940s;[15] a biography of St. Thérèse, which contains autobiographical material about her own struggles in faith;[16] and the story of the *Catholic Worker.*[17] According to Klejment and Klejment, Day authored over nine hundred articles and columns for the *Catholic Worker* and other publications. Fifteen years after her death Day's work may not be well known outside religious and pacifist circles, but much of it is accessible to the library researcher.

Supplementing Day's own writings on the movement are the published works of several Catholic Workers, including cofounder Peter Maurin's *Easy Essays*[18] and narratives by other prominent movement figures.[19] Additionally, scholars from a variety of disciplines have examined the Catholic Worker movement[20] and the life and works of Dorothy Day.[21] At times critical of Day and the movement, the literature is also reverential, both qualities encouraged, it seemed to me, by the archives that hold the Dorothy Day–Catholic Worker collection.

The Dorothy Day–Catholic Worker collection at Marquette University started as Day's own files. Day requested that access to her personal correspondence, diaries, retreat notes and other personal materials be restricted for twenty-five years after her death. Miller's 1987 book *All Is Grace*, written at Day's request, contains materials from her diaries and retreat notes that would otherwise not be accessible until 2005.[22] The Dorothy Day–Catholic Worker collection also includes manuscripts, articles, press clippings, correspondence, oral history interviews, diaries and other materials from Catholic Worker houses, audio and video tapes, and a box of memorabilia. On my 1992 visit to the archives, I examined files containing correspondence and other materials pertaining to her public activities, including her funeral in 1980 (series D-5), oral history and other materials that shed light on her as a public speaker (various series), and the clothing that was contained in the box of memorabilia (series D-9). A second visit to the collection in 1993 was spent examining her book manuscripts (series D-3) and other materials pertaining to Day, primarily reviews and news clippings (series D-8).

My background as a Roman Catholic no doubt enhanced my feelings of reverence as I worked in the Dorothy Day–Catholic Worker collection. Shortly after her death and over the objections of her family and closest followers, efforts to have Day canonized as a saint were initiated.[23] Day had often been referred to as a saint.[24] It was a moniker she resisted because, she felt, "saints are not taken seriously enough by Catholics."[25] Day wanted to be taken seriously; she also resisted being co-opted by or absorbed into mainstream American Catholicism. Sainthood would mainstream her religiosity, reducing its prophetic call for fundamental change in American Catholics' embrace of capitalism and militarism. Furthermore, being recognized as an "American saint" would reinforce cultural values she resisted, that is, those that privilege heroic ascent.[26] Those who insist Day be canonized, of course, feel differently: "St. Dorothy" would represent the poor and be a much-needed model of spirituality for believers who traditionally have turned to the saints as exemplars of Christian living.[27]

As a Roman Catholic I am conscious of the fact that, if she *were* canonized, Day's materials would be considered sacred relics. This could result in a limitation of researchers' access to original copies— anything Day may have touched. As I read and touched page after page of her handwritten materials, I was filled with a sense of awe for her "practical mysticism": like many mystics, Day found and struggled with the sacred in the details of everyday existence. I also found myself caring a great deal for the person who resisted canonization. As a researcher, I wanted to honor her request not to be sculpted into the cathedral of history with stories that emphasized her piety while suppressing her politics.

My experience with Dorothy Day confirms what many scholars who work in archives know: one cannot work in another person's papers without developing a relationship with the subject. In describing the work qualitative researchers do with personal life documents, Denzin points up the irreducibly relational nature of working with another's story: "The lives and stories that we hear and study are given to us under a promise . . . that we protect those who have shared with us. And, in return, this sharing will allow us to write documents that speak to the human dignity, the suffering, the hopes, the dreams, the lives gained, and the lives lost by the people we study."[28] Denzin suggests that as reader and then as writer the researcher effectively puts herself into the narrative as she interprets the subject's life story: "Along the way, the produced text is cluttered by traces of the life of the 'real' person being written about."[29] The relational and autobiographical qualities of historical research, traditionally downplayed in favor of more "objective" or detached renderings of history, remind us of history's fundamentally humanistic character as a means through which we discover and express ourselves and our place in time in relation to others and their place in time. Dorothy Day's efforts to shape the reading and the telling of her story should make us more aware of and, perhaps, more uncomfortable with history that unreflexively records and privileges heroic ascendance.

Declining Honors

Near the end of my first visit to the Dorothy Day–Catholic Worker collection, after I had reviewed almost all of Day's public affairs materials, I came across a folder with the title, "Honors Declined" (series D-5, box 4). In the folder were a number of letters declining honorary degrees. Most of the letters were apologetic. In 1968, for example, Day penned a letter to Father Leo McLaughlin, S.J., at Fordham University, in which she noted the difficulty in writing the letter and recounted the ways in which she and the movement had benefited from the Jesuits:

I owe so much to the Jesuits, whose wisdom and understanding have guided us in so many ways, beginning with Father Parsons in 1933, Fr. Lord, who first persuaded me to speak and whose Catholic action a [*sic*] schools taught me the beauty and depth of the Liturgy, and the little way of the co-operatives; and Father Carrabine of Chicago whose faithful friendship for the Catholic Worker group there, gave leadership and directions to such old friends and fellow workers as Jim O'Gara, John Cogley and Tom Sullivan, not to speak of Fr. Becker of St. Louis and now Boston, not to speak of Fr. LaFarge, our very dear counselor as early as 1935 and 1936, and your own Father Roger, at Fordham, who knew Peter Maurin before the Catholic Worker began.

Day's letter reflects a common characteristic in her writing: a tremendous capacity for personal detail, crafted in ways that dramatize her point and that ingratiate her to readers. Her use of the serial example in this letter demonstrates her knowledge and appreciation of the extensive support priests from the Society of Jesus had given the movement. The listing of individual names creates a sense of personal acquaintance between Day and the individuals, as well as between Day and Fr. McLaughlin, who may have known several of the priests and Catholic Workers. The list of names and reference to the Jesuits also separates them from the institution (the university) that invited Day to receive the honorary degree.

The letter continues: "But the fact is, I cannot receive honorary degrees, and have refused four others, for the simple but very deeply felt reason of my pacifism and my attitude toward the State, 'the all encroaching state,' as the bishops have termed it. The existence of ROTC in the colleges and universities makes it impossible for me to accept. I realize that this is an extreme position, but I must take it, assuring you that I consider myself honored indeed at having received such a letter as yours." Day's gracious refusal to Fordham illustrates another characteristic of her rhetoric: she consistently avoided presenting herself as imposing her views on the reader or hearer. Throughout her papers one finds references to instruction and example as Day's preferred modes of persuasion.[30] Her cofounder, Peter Maurin, had taken a different tack, arguing to "make his points."[31] Day, on the other hand, sought to establish and maintain common ground with receivers, even when she disagreed with them.[32] In the Fordham letter, Day separates individuals and the Jesuits from the institution she sees as complicitous with the federal government (colleges and universities); she avoids mentioning Fordham as engaging in activities she regards as offensive.[33]

In a similar letter sent to the Catholic University of America in 1971, Day again separated the personal from the institutional. She noted her affinity for something about the university without specifically praising the institution: "It hurts me to say it to you, with the feeling I have had for all things Catholic and especially for the shrine [located on the campus] where I prayed in 1932 . . . for guidance (the answer God sent meant the beginning of the Catholic Worker movement). It is with all humility that I must refuse your generous offer of an honorary degree." Day took the opportunity in this letter to provide some instruction on the Catholic Worker movement:

The Catholic Worker stands in a particular way for the poor and the lowly, for people who need some other kind of schooling than that afforded by universities and colleges of our industrial-capitalist system. I have had to refuse seven other colleges and universities for the reason that they had ROTC, and one way or another closely allied to [the] Federal government. In many cases they receive research grants, many of which have to do with war and defense. We very definitely are working for the new man [sic] and the new way so often spoken of in the Gospel and book of Acts, and we would like to see the kind of an educational system envisioned by a Julious Nyerere, Catholic president of Tanzania. We talk of these things when invited to speak at Colleges around the country and try to stimulate the young to study ways by which they can change the social and educational system nonviolently.

Besides providing a lesson on the Catholic Worker movement, the correspondence implies a willingness on Day's part to come to the campus for a lecture rather than for a celebration honoring her with an honorary degree. Yet the suggestion is indirect. Despite her public stature in 1971 as a "saintly" servant of the poor, Day does not display the persona of a celebrity. In fact, as the CUA letter illustrates, Day's rhetoric shows a pattern of citation that downplays separateness and achievement as a "self" in favor of creating a semblance of connection between her ideas and programs and those of others. Although this pattern indicates both what Hart identified as characteristic of "true believers" (where the inclination is to downplay personal inventiveness in favor of doctrinal authority) and what Campbell associated with women's ways of speaking (where the tendency is to connect oneself with others),[34] it is also consistent with Day's spiritual "self" discipline. As mystics had done for centuries before her, Day negated the "self" as a part of her quest for "self" perfection. Her tendency to meld her own thoughts and words with those of others effectively disciplined her "I" (and the tendency to "selfishness" that might be implied by the authoritative first-person) and brought her closer to "perfection," that is, loss of self and absorption into the divine. In this sense Day's rhetoric enacts her search for communion through the evocation of rhetorical community.[35]

Day was not without sharp edges, however. One letter, sent to the University of Santa Clara in 1976, expresses frustration that she had not been able to get her message across: "I wish colleges would stop offering me honorary degrees which I must in conscience refuse, but wish to refuse with all respect and gratitude. Whoever is responsible for making such an offer to me certainly knows nothing of the philosophy of the Catholic Worker movement, nor of its aims. . . . The very offer of an honorary degree means that in a way I have failed to convey—to popularize Peter Maurin's teaching." The letter offers a tightly written account of Maurin's teachings and the slogans by which they were conveyed: "He was an advocate of the personalist and communitarian revolution. . . . The slogans of this revolution used to be 'War is the health of the State' and 'Property is Theft.' . . . We must keep in mind these slogans . . . recognizing what the United States stands for in the world today. We must also resist 'funding' by our government, as well as honors from colleges, many of which are so 'funded' in one way or another, for R.O.T.C. and research (often, if not always, military)."[36]

Day's refusal to accept honorary degrees was direct and uncomplicated; she did not want to support, nor did she want to be seen as symbolizing, institutions that contributed to militarism. In several letters Day expresses a sense of failure as a communicator: if she had gotten her message across, universities and colleges would know better than to invite her to receive honorary degrees. There is some evidence to suggest that Day saw an honorary degree as rewarding a person for work *not* done, that is, the work students do to qualify for a degree.[37] Her letters indicate discomfort with the relatively affluent lifestyle of college students, but that did not prevent her from accepting honors from some religious colleges and universities when they did not compromise her pacifist position.[38]

The University of Notre Dame's efforts to award Day the Laetare Medal in 1972 as an outstanding American Catholic might well have presented Day with a difficult situation because of the presence of ROTC at the university. In crafting a response to Father Theodore Hesburgh, Day chose to emphasize the embarrassment she could have caused Notre Dame by citing her own problems with the IRS as the major reason for not accepting the award. In a letter dated

March 10, 1972, Day states her "deepest regret" at having to "write and refuse the great honor that Notre Dame wished to bestow on me, and I am afraid would only be an embarrassment to you."[39] Day's use of the past tense suggests that she is not intending to accept the honor: the award will not be bestowed as the university "wished." She excuses herself from receiving the award because the IRS said she and the Catholic Worker movement owed $300,000 in back taxes. "It is a most complicated affair since it involves a debate as to whether we are political or charitable. They judge us as a political group." This brief account offered in response to the news that she was to be awarded the Laetare Medal might have been seen as ungracious, so Day provides an explanation: "Right now I cannot be coherent about all this since flu has left me with a heart murmur and bad pulse etc. and doctors orders are a rest at Tivoli where our farm is located." Before closing, she lets Hesburgh know that she remembers "with pleasure" their meeting in Jackson, Mississippi, during the civil rights movement; she mentions the enclosure of a recent edition of the *Catholic Worker* that contains an article about her recent meeting with Charles Evers.

Hesburgh replied on March 24, stating that he "would certainly hope" that Day would "accept the Laetare medal, since we are not at all embarrassed because of the IRS suit. Everyone has been overjoyed at your nomination for the award this year, and I think it would rob many people of their legitimate joy not to have you receive the medal." In published works, Day had written of how her work had made it difficult for her to be as joyful as a Christian should be. Conceivably, Hesburgh's reference to "robbing" others "of their legitimate joy" could persuade a person who would recognize the inability to experience joy as a personal shortcoming and who would not want to deprive others of that experience on her account. In response to Day's concerns about her tax situation, Hesburgh states that "the only real embarrassment would be for you not to receive the Medal, so I do hope you will."[40]

On March 27 Day composed a letter marked "not sent" that ran nearly ten pages in stationery-size handwritten copy.[41] In it she mentions that Hesburgh's "telegram arrived to find me on a sick bed and totally unprepared, even shocked at such an honor being offered me."[42] Day's reference to being "shocked" might have been an act of self-deprecation,[43] but it also signals distress, even anger. She notes that the award was "Not offered, really, since that would have given me a chance to refuse it, but bestowed on me." If Day was put off by the presumption that she would accept the award, she did not express it any more directly than in this statement.

The letter moves to Day's concern that her tax situation would put

Notre Dame in a "peculiar position," without directly addressing Hesburgh's rejoinder. It is a curious reversal. It would be difficult to imagine how awarding Day the Laetare Medal could embarrass the University of Notre Dame. Recognizing an alleged tax evader[44] would probably not injure the university's reputation with the "all-encroaching state," as Day so often referred to the government. Neither would the university's reputation as a Roman Catholic institution be damaged by honoring her, given her reputation as a religious activist. Accepting an award that might domesticate her religious and political radicalism could, however, put Day in a "peculiar position." But Day does not mention this as a problem, nor does she acknowledge the presence of ROTC at Notre Dame. Instead, she launches a historical narrative whose "lessons" point to the importance of "abjuring power" and opposing federal subsidy.

Day begins by affirming her stance as a Christian personalist against the prevailing reality of a "strong centralized state." "The Federal Government has taken on functions which are not proper to it," Day argues; hence "we ignore the principle of subsidiarity." The principle of subsidiarity affirms that people help one another in need, rather than expecting the government to do it on their behalf. Locating her motives in divine rather than human authority, Day writes that she has "spoken of myself as a Christian anarchist . . . to emphasize the personalist approach of our Lord who washed the feet of his followers and told them to do likewise. St. Paul and St. Francis (so different) spoke of 'being subject to every living creature' abjuring power."

Day carefully sets the stage for stating her opposition to federal subsidy. Characteristically, she uses Maurin's teachings to explain and to legitimize her position. But before stating his admonition against depending on Washington to solve many social problems, she calls to mind his concern that the movement be a positive force: " 'Be what you want the other fellow to be,' rather than criticize; . . . emphasize the personalist approach, starting with the 'I' and the 'We.' " The reminder seems calculated to moderate Day's oppositional posture without blunting the effect of her criticism. She also mentions a connection between Notre Dame and Maurin: he translated a book published by the Notre Dame Press entitled *The Personalist Manifesto* by Emmanuel Mournier. The sense of commonality this reference is expected to engender seems designed to increase the salience and palatability of the critical arguments that follow. Day writes at length about the consequences of losing the principle of subsidiarity:

Of course it is not so simple (I do truly understand that) but the fact remains that individuals and families, communities, parishes and neighborhoods have to a great extent given up their responsibility . . . and have waited to be funded, etc. by Washington. And corruption has grown, and great masses of the poor and destitute have been neglected, and corrupted too. We see it in our soup lines where the first of each month men of Skid Rows get a check, not enough to house them and feed them for a month ahead. We see no housing built for the poor. . . . Who ever hears of the principle of subsidiarity?

In contrast to the circumstances that have created such dependency and corruption is the position of Christian anarchism, which supports the efforts of cooperatives, credit unions, unions for industrial workers and craftsmen, and other organizations to channel member resources into member assistance. The principle of subsidiarity does not remove the obligation of the individual to take care of himself or herself, however; as Day notes, it often means "doing with what one has or doing everything [for] one's self as far as possible before calling on the community."

Day's decision to frame her narrative about the Catholic Worker movement around the principle of subsidiarity is an interesting one. It complicates the letter, requiring more effort by a physically weakened Day to compose. Why would she go to the trouble of writing such an involved letter? The letter "not sent" suggests that Day wanted Hesburgh to see that her tax problems stemmed from, and were symbolic of, the movement's fundamental opposition to federal involvement in the lives of individuals and communities. The contrast between the hegemony of the welfare state and Christian anarchism's embrace of the principle of subsidiarity seems to anticipate an argument that Day does not get to or perhaps chooses not to make, namely, insofar as Notre Dame accepted federal funding, it represented a view of the state that was morally inconsistent with the religious principles for which Day stood and for which the university was honoring her with the Laetare Medal. Given the pattern we have observed in other letters Day wrote declining awards, a logical next step might have been for her to refuse the award.

Two days later, on March 29, Day wrote another letter, which she sent to Hesburgh.[45] She mentions having tried to call him at the number he had given her, suggesting that Hesburgh may have spoken to her on the phone. She says she "tried to write again, but did not feel very coherent, so it made me very happy to get your letter this morning, forwarded to me from New York." Referring again to their meeting in Jackson, Mississippi, where she "felt your kindness and compassion," Day comments that she "was sure you understood my incoherent letter, which was really trying to forestall your generous offer of the Laetare Medal." Day may have been referring to the letter she did not send, or she may have been disclaiming her first letter of refusal so as to make her acceptance of the award seem something she would do if she were coherent. Whatever the case, she informs him that she will "accept of course, especially since you say I can receive it quietly." Although the letter and later correspondence discuss her health (and "Dr's orders") as impediments to receiving the award in person, Day recovers enough to receive the award in person at Notre Dame's commencement ceremonies on May 21.[46]

Conclusion

Clearly, Hesburgh's letter of March 24 was instrumental in Day's decision to accept the Laetare Medal, as were his later letters in convincing her to travel to Notre Dame for commencement. Day apparently had been impressed with Hesburgh when they met in Jackson, Mississippi; she would have been deferential to him as a priest and as president of the University of Notre Dame. Although she described herself as an "angry daughter" of the church, Day's obedience to church authority was legendary.[47] She may well have seen the Laetare Medal as something she could not refuse when pressed by Hesburgh to accept. The evidence available in the Dorothy Day–Catholic Worker Collection suggests that Hesburgh may have been the only university president not to take "no" for an answer; other presidents had written Day to express their respect for her decision not to accept their honors.[48] Of course the honor Hesburgh offered was *not* an honorary degree, which may have lowered Day's resistance to receiving the prize. She would not be considered an honorary "graduate" or product of the university, presumed to accept or endorse its position relative to the federal government. Hesburgh's letter of April 3, 1972, offers additional incentives for her acceptance of the award, including shaming the United States government for pursuing her for back taxes. He also suggests that a visit to Notre Dame would enable her to see old friends who would assemble for "a quiet and friendly reunion here at the university."[49] The thought of seeing friends from the Chicago Catholic Worker, some of whom had written to encourage her to travel to Notre Dame, apparently convinced Day to attempt the trip.[50]

And what of the letter "not sent"? It would be possible, I suppose, to accept Day's explanation that it was written when she did not feel coherent, although my analysis of the letter indicates that Day wrote a remarkably coherent, yet incomplete, argument for refusing the award. Miller states that Day declined awards principally because of her ill health but acknowledges that she sometimes declined awards when she felt the "would-be donor . . . had supported the military."[51] It is also possible that the "embarrassment" I attribute to Day stemmed, at least in part, from her own sense of unworthiness. An associate from the Catholic Worker, Jim Forest, notes that Day "was embarrassed by admiration, most of all from those she herself admired. She felt that she was far from being the person she ought to be: less irritable, less judgmental."[52]

Yet the letter "not sent" appears to be more than a deflection from Day's health problems and her sense of moral failure. When read in context with other missives she wrote to decline awards, the letter can be seen as Day's attempt to make a case for refusing the award on principle. Moreover, the letter illustrates Day's larger awareness of the predicament facing her as a "saintly deviant." Accepting such an award put her in what Branham and Pearce have called the "radical's paradox": "from the radical's perspective, even the opportunities provided by social and intellectual systems for the orderly expression of discontent are ensnaring traps that assimilate revolutionary intentions into channels which reify existing contexts."[53] Day could not finally escape the paradox. Despite her status as a symbol of radical Catholicism, her acceptance of Notre Dame's highest honor would have reinforced the existing context of university life on that campus. Yet the letter "not sent" illustrates her sensitivity to, and attempt to circumvent, the logical force of what Branham and Pearce would call a "charmed" communication system.[54] Because it was not destroyed but archived with her papers, the letter "not sent" provides an important piece of evidence about the communicative sensitivity and the ambivalence Dorothy Day experienced, particularly in her later years, as she struggled both with her own desire for saintliness and against the perils of sainthood.

11

History and Culture as Rhetorical Constraints

Cesar Chavez's Letter From Delano

John C. Hammerback and Richard J. Jensen

When Cesar Chavez started the United Farm Worker (UFW) in 1962, he faced the daunting task of organizing powerless individuals in an industry that had effectively crushed past attempts to unionize workers. To create a successful union Chavez had to recruit members while at the same time gaining support for his cause from the public. To achieve that goal Chavez relied heavily on his skills as a communicator: "He conducted many speaking tours, wrote articles, went on well-publicized fasts, addressed Congressional committees, television audiences, political gatherings, and consistently worked to spread his message directly to live audiences and indirectly through the mass media."[1] Chavez was an effective persuader who believed that his major task was to "state his case before the entire nation and stir its conscience."[2]

In most of our previous writings on Chavez we have focused on his public speeches, but we also have recognized that Chavez often employed written rhetoric for support and propaganda. In particular, his "frequent 'open letters' to students, churchmen, workers" and others sought to educate readers, build solidarity among followers, and gain supporters.[3] As we analyzed Cesar Chavez's public letters, we found that few guidelines exist for the analysis of such documents. Although "the public letter . . . has long been a means of persuasion by reformers and politicians, writers, and prisoners," communication scholars rarely have focused on that rhetoric.[4]

Although we have not discovered any statement by Chavez to indi-

little focus on letters

cate why he chose to issue public letters, we do know that he relied on that form often as a powerful means of conveying his message to his supporters and to the general public. We also know that such written documents have long been used by Mexican Americans, who learned the power of such documents from their ancestors in Mexico.

One letter seems to capture the essence of Chavez's attempts to stir the country's moral conscience. On Good Friday in 1969 he issued a public letter to E. L. Barr Jr., the president of the California Grape and Tree Fruit League. Chavez's "Letter from Delano" appeared in both the *Christian Century* and the *National Catholic Reporter*. One small salvo in an ongoing battle between Chavez and the growers, the letter clearly outlined Chavez's perception of key issues in his union's battle with the growers. This fight between farmworkers and growers began in 1962 when Chavez started organizing crop-pickers in and around Delano in central California, escalated in 1965 when the union initiated a strike and a subsequent series of boycotts against grape growers, and brought Chavez national acclaim during the mid-1960s as the leader of the nation's first successful farmworkers union, a union that won a series of unprecedented victories over the growers.[5] By 1969, with his leadership expanded into the civil rights and Chicano movements, Chavez had established his reputation as a hero in many segments of American society.[6] Placing the letter into a historical context sympathetic to Chavez and his goals, the *Christian Century* described it as a "statement on nonviolence" by the "leader in the struggle to obtain justice for those who have labored in California's vineyards; it is in the form of an open letter to the head of the growers' league which has opposed unionization of the grape pickers."[7]

On June 11, 1968, the *Christian Century* published a rebuttal of Chavez's letter by Barr and his successor, R. K. Sanderson, entitled "Why Grape Growers Do Not 'Render unto Cesar.'"[8] The letter personally belittled Chavez, questioned his motives in creating the union, and made clear that the growers did not share Chavez's rhetorical heritage, his views of the world, or his conception of the struggle.

The rhetorical dynamics of the "Letter from Delano" resist an easy explanation because Chavez's letter is in part a product of its ethnic rhetorical heritage.[9] To understand the letter and thus the debate between Chavez and the growers, it is crucial to understand the rhetorical history of Mexican Americans, of the public letter and other written documents as a rhetorical form of historical significance for those of Mexican descent, and of the discourse and person of Cesar Chavez.

Communication and Cultural Legacies

MEXICAN AMERICAN RHETORICAL CULTURE. Drawing on the insights of Mexican writers and from field work and interviews in northern Ohio, Alberto Gonzalez found that the history of Mexicans and Mexican Americans has yielded a "significant cultural inheritance" for Mexican Americans that explains much about their communication. The ethnic group's long history of calamitous events and deadly betrayals, ranging from dominance by Indian groups before the Spanish Conquest to the bloody conquest and later the colonization of northern Mexico by the United States, has often separated them from their history. These fragmented people developed a "self-conscious and resigned ambivalence that desires Oneness yet fears its certain fragmentation." Thus Mexican Americans sought to assimilate with the established culture even as they strove for "otherness" by reconciling with their history to achieve identity and unity in a dominant culture that threatens them and their culture—just as they were previously threatened by outsiders or historical intrusions. Gonzalez found that Ohio Mexican Americans resisted the pain of their otherness and their history by clinging to their history and culture; many scholars have noted the simultaneous drives among Mexican Americans toward inclusion and exclusion.[10]

Octavio Paz, Carlos Fuentes, and other major literary figures in Mexico believe that Mexicans responded to the opposing forces of exclusion and inclusion by forming a mask that allows them to ward off rejection from outsiders by uniting in race and culture and by diverting attention from the self. The contrary goal of inclusion, according to Gonzalez, takes form in expressions of powerful cultural values such as sacrifice and pride, especially pride in courage and other manly qualities, values sometimes expressed indirectly through images of blood or the pre-Columbian legacy of "ancient sacrifice" that features blood.[11]

We believe that rhetorical history may be especially important when studying the discourse of ethnic minorities or other groups apart from the dominant culture. These ethnic groups carry a history and worldview that rarely duplicate those of the majority and that consequently place critics at risk of projecting their own mainstream experiences and viewpoints onto a minority group. In Mexican American discourse, where the past is closely linked to the present, the dangers of an ignorance of history are particularly potent. This link to the past illustrates Jamieson's view that "some groups are more constrained by genre [in their rhetorical discourse] than others because of their sense of the presentness of the past."[12] We argued elsewhere that this historical sense was pervasive in the broad Mexican American protest movement of the 1960s and 1970s that "sought to build a positive image for Mexican Americans, in large part by discovering, maintaining, and revering large pieces of their Mexican heritage."[13]

In part because they attempt to reconcile the present with their past, wrote a Chicano author, the writings of Chicanos are "best understood within the framework of the history of the Mexican American people in the United States."[14] Another Chicano writer claimed that "history turns out to be the decisive determinant of the form and content" of Chicano discourse.[15] As we concluded in an earlier study, the rhetorical aspects of Mexican American discourse become "clear only within the context of their own rhetorical tradition, a tradition anchored in Mexican history and developed from the Mexican-Americans' culture and experiences."[16] We believe that Chavez's "Letter from Delano" clearly illustrates how rhetorical history illuminates the public communication of Mexican Americans in general and Chavez in particular. Chavez's public discourse grew out of his culture and his experiences. The Mexican American culture in the United States and that culture's roots in Mexico had a profound effect on Chavez's rhetoric. He drew on rhetorical forms and tactics that grew out of the Mexican past. He then adapted those forms and tactics to the United States.

To illustrate Chavez's use of his rhetorical history, we explore the traditional Mexican form of the plan as a rhetorical resource and then examine Chavez's worldview and his perception of the role of public discourse.

THE PLAN AS RHETORICAL FORM. Although to our knowledge Cesar Chavez never explicitly acknowledged the connection between his public letters and a specific rhetorical tradition, the rhetorical strategies he employed in the "Letter from Delano" clearly echo those exemplifying the Mexican rhetorical form of the plan. Mexican Americans have inherited and relied on the plan as a form of public address with deep roots in Mexican history. In Mexico these written documents, meant to be read and heard, were commonly issued in the unsettled period of Mexican history between 1821 and 1941. They ceased being circulated when the national government stabilized in 1941. The plans proclaimed their authors' revolutionary principles, justified their seizures of government, and sought to win supporters and public approval for their movement.

The typical plan—also called an edict, manifesto, act, decree or declaration—embodied rhetorical qualities that appear in the most famous document issued by Chavez's farmworker movement, "The

Plan of Delano" (1966), as well as other influential statements in Mexican American protest movements. The Chicano leaders of the 1960s and 1970s were well aware of earlier plans and their rhetorical power.[17]

The "Letter from Delano," like "The Plan of Delano," illustrates clearly the power of Mexican rhetorical history as enacted in contemporary written proclamations by Mexican Americans. Both the framework of expectations by Mexican American audiences and many of the most prominent rhetorical choices reflected in Chavez's letter drew from the tradition of such written documents in Mexican history as the plan, as the analysis in the next major section will show.

CHAVEZ'S WORLDVIEW AND DISCOURSE. As we have chronicled elsewhere, Chavez's eventful and unusual life afforded him a worldview that featured God, reform, and public address.[18] As a Mexican American and devout Roman Catholic, he believed that God had a millennial plan that required spokespersons to present arguments and facts for justice to a public that, when sufficiently informed, would inevitably redress injustices. To Chavez, farmworkers were but one part of the broad struggle for social justice that intensified in the 1960s, and his union was part of a social movement that God would bless with success once spokespersons had educated the public. Chavez devoted his life to enacting his deep commitment to moral issues and the public address necessary to reach his goals.

Chavez's worldview and extensive experiences as a union organizer and persuader shaped the rhetorical qualities, both stylistic and substantive, that characterized his speeches, writings, and interviews. He emphasized moral issues. He relied on, and thus showed his own faith in, well-reasoned arguments illustrated and supported by a plethora of facts; and he reified his belief that his message must be delivered, organized, and worded clearly, frequently going to painstaking efforts to achieve that clarity. He rejected a poetic and complex style, flamboyant delivery and writing, and claims of his own importance, virtue, powers, or skills. Moreover, he focused on substantive reasons and pertinent information rather than shifting attention to himself. Throughout his long rhetorical campaign he acted out his conviction that his message must be presented persistently, regardless of immediate reactions by audiences. The numerous public letters were a powerful part of that persistence.

Chavez's resulting rhetorical profile is appropriate for one who believes that God will ensure the triumph of a righteous cause by having spokespersons inform a public that will inevitably right the wrongs of society. Such spokespersons would not need to display rhetorical talents that call attention to their skills but instead would only need to present a well-supported righteous case clearly and indefatigably. They could be quiet teachers of moral truths who relied on higher powers for their influence rather than star rhetors whose rhetorical virtuosity ensured their electrical effects on auditors and their place in the galaxy of celebrated spellbinders. A historical study of Chavez and his discourse thus reveals both the reasons for and the development of his rhetorical profile. An application of this historically derived understanding helps the analyst to discover the rhetorical intent and meaning of his letter as well as its rhetorical dynamics with audiences who possessed little, most, or all of Chavez's rhetorical orientation.

The "Letter from Delano"

The "Letter from Delano" clearly draws from its Mexican American rhetorical heritage, the rhetorical form of the plan, and the rhetorical upbringing of Cesar Chavez in creating meaning. Although the "Letter from Delano" does not seek to achieve the identical goals of Mexican plans or of the other plans of the Chicano movement, it shares their purpose of gaining public support in a moral struggle against the established order—and hence it fits into the Mexican American rhetorical legacy of this form. The letter also reflects Fernando Delgado's view of the essence and purpose of plans as rhetoric: "Their enduring quality is how they succinctly and powerfully articulate a Chicano identity and offer motivations and strategies for action rather than stagnation."[19]

Particular rhetorical characteristics of plans included being named for a symbolically significant village or city where it was composed, a justification early in the document for the cause and the need for change, a set of reforms and means to achieve them, a depiction of the much-improved future once the cause triumphed, references to the church, and a deep belief in persuasion. Plans also conformed to their ethnic rhetorical heritage through their formal tone, a tone that both reflected the Spanish tradition of formality and was appropriate to documents read in the context of the life-and-death consequences of the revolutionary struggles in Mexico. In these documents ideas were typically expressed as "high sounding principles" with the "appeal to a noble purpose." The struggle was always described as one between starkly opposed forces, good versus evil or us against them.[20] Like Chavez, the writers of Mexican plans believed that words could persuade and that consequent shifts in public opinion could lead to triumph. Unlike Chavez's belief, plans put faith in leaders who could drive a movement to success.

That the "Letter from Delano" places great faith in words was illustrated earlier in the document. The letter also immediately fits itself into the tradition of plans by taking the symbolically charged name of a special city, in this case the city where Chavez's union was housed and his famous strike and pilgrimage to Sacramento began in 1966. The early paragraphs justify his movement, infuse it with morality, and picture the struggle as one between contrasting forces. The letter maintains that the "poor and dispossessed" have suffered from racial discrimination, inadequate educational opportunities, and exclusion from the democratic process. They have been subjected to disproportionate dangers and hence casualties in the military during wartime and are now in a "death struggle against man's inhumanity to man in the industry that you [growers] represent." Strikers in Delano "and those who represent us throughout the world" have been "under the gun, . . . kicked and beaten and herded by dogs, . . . cursed and jailed, [and] . . . sprayed with the poisons used in the vineyards"—all by the "rich and the powerful" who own the land. The future would see the "agribusiness system" reformed "not by retaliation or bloodshed but by a determined nonviolent struggle carried on by those masses of farm workers who intend to be free and human." The tone of the letter is serious and somber, lacking any humor, wit, or mock seriousness, devoid of personal attacks and casual asides. When Chavez briefly cites Gandhi's nonviolence as a model for his actions and then refers to his own twenty-five-day fast, for example, he uses these weighty words: "I repeat to you the principle enunciated to the membership at the start of the fast: if to build our union required the deliberate taking of life, either the life of a grower or his [sic] child, or the life of a farm worker or his child, then I choose not to see the union built."[21]

The letter stresses the importance of God and morality, discourse, and the social revolution for justice. These themes emerged in the very act of issuing it on Good Friday, the commemoration of the suffering and death of Jesus, for that day also represented the harsh treatment of farmworkers at the hands of growers.

In his opening paragraph Chavez cites the "tremendous moral force of our movement" and points out, in response to charges that the Union engaged in "violence and terror tactics," that Barr has "an awesome moral responsibility, before God and man, to come forward with whatever information you have so that corrective action can begin at once. . . . If for any reason you fail to come forth to substantiate your charges," he continues, "then you must be held responsible for committing violence against us, albeit violence of the tongue."

[Thus Chavez begins by setting the moral context for his movement and emphasizes the importance of factually supported argument to resolve issues.

The next two paragraphs reiterate and expand the themes of the opening paragraph. The second compares Chavez's strike and boycott to Martin Luther King's "nonviolent struggle for peace and justice" and cites King's "Letter from Birmingham Jail," the letter that served as a model for Chavez's message: "Injustice must be exposed, with all the tension its exposure creates to the light of human conscience and the air of national opinion before it can be cured." Consistent with his own view of the role of public communication to inform public opinion, Chavez then adds that in order to reach farmworkers' goals, he has "seized upon every tactic and strategy consistent with the morality of our cause to expose that injustice and thus to heighten the sensitivity of the American conscience." Chavez argues that Barr is lying about the farmworkers' movement and thus not meeting the need for accurate communication. Chavez accuses him of "working against nonviolent social change" and consequently inviting violence. Chavez begins the next paragraph by disclosing that his goal as a rhetor is to build a righteous case based on already presented facts: "Mr. Barr, let me be painfully honest with you. You must understand—I must make you understand—" the nature of the farmworkers' struggle. After citing a brief history of their struggle, he again places his cause in a sacred context: "But God knows that we are not beasts of burden, agricultural implements or rented slaves; we are men."

Subsequent paragraphs continue the theme of the need for a sustained campaign of discourse in a righteous reform. After reciting a list of unfair tactics employed against the people in his movement, Chavez proclaims that farmworkers will stay on the high word-road of nonviolent tactics, including "truth and public appeal," to reach their goals; and his movement will be persistent and patient, for time "accomplishes for the poor what money does for the rich." His broad worldview emerges more succinctly in his millennial claim: "We know that our cause is just, that history is a story of social revolution, and that the poor shall inherit the land." In the seventh and next-to-last paragraph he reiterates his faith in public opinion by asserting that "free men [sic] instinctively prefer democratic change and even protect the rights guaranteed to protect it."

The "Letter from Delano" embodies the sacrifice, the suffering, and, more broadly, the importance of the past. It describes farmworkers as "men and women who have suffered and endured much," who are engaged in a struggle that "gives meaning to our life and ennobles our dying," who have been "ridiculed," "kicked," "stripped and chained," and otherwise abused. Twice the word "bloodshed" is applied to their opponents, referring to a violent response that farmworkers are trying to avoid. Linking the central cultural value that encompasses courage, a will to resist, and a willingness to give all for an honorable cause to the nonviolent movement, Chavez labels the protest campaign of farmworkers "manly" and describes it as requiring "hard work and longer hours, with stamina and patient tenacity, . . . with prayer and fasting." Given the letter's release on Good Friday, such language resonates with the theme of physical sacrifice as a precursor to redemption. Despite the powerful forces against them, they "are not afraid nor do we cringe from the confrontation. We welcome it!" Turning to his opponent Mr. Barr, Chavez asks, "Once again, I appeal to you as the representative of your industry and as a man."

Throughout the letter Chavez projects the persona of one who believes that if his case is heard and understood, it will be part of the necessary broad campaign to change public opinion to ensure justice—a campaign that in this case would meet the needs of growers and workers alike if both sides talked together. Chavez accordingly focuses on his message and projects a modest picture of himself, acknowledging that he had made mistakes and that Martin Luther King describes better than he could express the farmworkers' "hopes for the strike and boycott." And just as Chavez places the higher morality of his cause over his own contributions, he refuses to engage in personal attacks on his opponents but instead treats them humanely and respectfully throughout the letter. To Barr he says, "I am convinced that you as a human being did not mean what you said but rather acted hastily under pressure from the public relations firm that has been hired to counter the tremendous moral force of our movement. How many times we ourselves had felt the need to lash out in anger and bitterness." Chavez implicitly contrasts the morality of his nonviolent grassroots movement with the inappropriate statements pushed by the "hired guns" brought in to handle the ensuing publicity, as distinct from Barr himself.

Depicting himself as less than a rhetorical expert, Chavez uses his concluding paragraph to make clear once again that he does not wish to denigrate Barr: "This letter does not express all that is in my heart, Mr. Barr. But if it says nothing else, it says that we do not hate you or rejoice to see your industry destroyed" but instead seek only to change agribusiness through nonviolent means. This change, he instructed earlier in the letter, called for growers to bargain face-to-face with the union or "to at least sit down with us to discuss the safeguards necessary to keep our historical struggle free of violence."

Chavez thus drew from the history of Mexican Americans, the rhetorical form of plans, and his own rhetorical character to craft the "Letter from Delano" as a carefully considered statement of principles and call for support. Chavez's moderate pleas were not met with equally moderate words from his opponents.

The Growers' Response

The response to Chavez's letter by the president and past president of the California Grape and Tree Fruit League offers an alternative perspective on the battle between the union and the growers. Their letter tells a great deal about how establishments tend to react to activists. Rather than respond directly to attacks, the establishment unleashes a variety of attacks to undermine the dissenter. Thus the letter by Barr and Sanderson reveals much about establishments in general and about the Chavez/growers dispute in particular.

The thirteen-paragraph letter is different in tone and content from Chavez's. It does not attempt to deal with the moral issues raised by Chavez but focuses on Chavez and his shortcomings. It advances three primary claims: Chavez has engaged in or is responsible for violent or immoral acts, and thus both his cause and his claim to lead a moral movement must be rejected; he has associated and been associated with a variety of disreputable people and organizations and should thus be defeated; and grape pickers are the best-paid and best-treated farmworkers in the country and thus undeserving of support. The growers' response is replete with sarcasm, personal attacks, cynicism, and clever language, all in sharp contrast to Chavez's formal, serious, and respectful tone.[22]

The essay begins with this unflattering description of Chavez: "How are mere mortals to attempt to reply to the charismatic leader who writes in flawless prose of his devotion to nonviolence, calls attention to his miraculous and marvelously publicized 25-day fast and draws comparison of himself to Gandhi? How does one cope with an adversary so determinedly bucking for sainthood?" Two paragraphs later the writers charge that "Poor Cesar has few followers among farm workers, but is blessed with many rich and powerful friends," including the AFL-CIO, the California Rural Legal Assistance Program, the Roger Baldwin Memorial Foundation of the American Civil Liberties Union, and writer George Plimpton, who as a supporter of "a favorite cause of the New Left branch of New York society" hosted a party to benefit farmworkers that was attended by the "fashionably dressed Dolores Huerta, Chavez' chief lieutenant." The response also maligns Chavez for being indirectly responsible for violent acts that union supporters or workers allegedly committed against stores, workers, and customers. Although "Chavez may disclaim responsibility for these violent actions," the growers explain, "the fact remains that the boycott is sponsored by UFWOC, not by the Campfire Girls, and the UFWOC is Cesar Chavez, not Mary Margaret McBride."[23] The use of such sarcasm to vilify opponents is typical of establishments under attack. As Andrew King states, "It is hoped that sarcasm will undermine the self-confidence of the challenger; it will strengthen the club spirit of the old group by flattering its weakened sense of superiority. It will cause third parties outside either group to see the emergent group as an aggregation of social clowns."[24] If Barr and Sanderson succeeded in their attack, Chavez would lose his standing as a moral leader. He would become merely one more individual who is only concerned about his own standing and his desire to get ahead in the world, not a defender of the poor but one who uses the poor to achieve his own questionable goals.

The attacks on Chavez's character continue in two long paragraphs depicting grape workers working in the best conditions and receiving the highest wages of any farmworkers. Rather than acknowledging the low wages received by workers, the growers engage in a diversionary attack on outsiders by attributing "base motives" to Chavez.[25] "Could it be," ask the authors cynically, "that the real prize in this effort is the union dues that could be collected from the workers?" If the authors of the letter could convince readers that Chavez was using the workers to achieve his own selfish ends, it would tarnish the public image of both him and his organization. It would also deflect attention from their lack of proof for claims that strikers committed crimes and from the easily available evidence that Chavez and his coworkers were living on subsistence wages at or below the level of the economically poor.[26]

The growers challenge Chavez's reasoning in several ways. They contend that his depiction of a struggle between rich and poor is in- *(1)* accurate, asserting that many growers are not wealthy and that Chavez has "rich and powerful friends"; that Chavez's commitment *(2)* to "organize, work, and communicate come first—before such secondary considerations as human life and the safety of others"; and that Chavez's goal of a "social revolution," a goal shared by his "early *(3)* mentor, the professional radical Saul Alinsky," violated the goals of secret balloting and the "free flow of food to the American public." Here, as when they poke fun at Chavez for seemingly seeking sainthood, the growers do not accept Chavez's view of the place of public address in reform, his serious study of Gandhi to understand the successful use of nonviolence in a moral cause, or his view of history as a series of social movements for justice that God oversees and guides to success by having rhetors inform a fair-minded public. Thus growers find Chavez to be a typical union leader motivated by power, fame, and greed or by lust for applause from the left elite, a leader whose commitment to communication is a clever tactic and whose proclaimed intentions and rhetorical invention and style must be viewed cynically. Ironically, it is the growers who relied on rhetorical tactics that would invite cynicism: personal attacks, guilt by association, and invidious comparisons of less-wealthy growers being somehow more needy than the masses of grape pickers who lived near or below the poverty level.[27]

It is surprising that these two highly charged letters elicited only one published response. In a letter to the editor, one of Chavez's followers contrasted the farmworkers' "quiet dedication" to the "sloganeering and smearing" that "the growers' anxious P.R. men" put into the Barr/Sanderson letter.[28]

Conclusion

To understand more fully the significance of Chavez's letter, we attempted to discover statements by those who had read the letter. In our search we looked at Chavez's own writings and the writings about Chavez. We found surprisingly few references to this letter. The "Letter from Delano" did strike a chord among sympathetic readers, for it was later anthologized in several collections of documents about the Chicano movement.[29] Yet these authors focused on Chavez's admirable qualities rather than the substance of his arguments, perhaps because by the late 1960s Chavez was seen as embodying so fully both the ideology he advocated and the union he led that he was indistinguishable from them. The editor of the *Christian Century* introduced the letter by announcing, "We are honored to present this moving testimonial by one whose cause we have supported."[30] In 1972 the editor of an anthology on Mexican Americans described the letter's author as "a Chicano who had been oppressed but not defeated, who is threatened but not afraid to speak. . . . Here is the Chicano of courage who is speaking and will be heard, who is acting and will be felt."[31]

Another set of responses emphasized the letter's similarity to a widely celebrated rhetorical document of the period, and one that Chavez had acknowledged as a model for his Good Friday statement: Martin Luther King's "Letter from Birmingham Jail." In an interview Chavez's speech writer, Marc Grossman, acknowledged that Chavez based his letter on Dr. King's.[32] Both leaders spoke for ethnic minorities who had suffered from long-standing discrimination and who languished on low rungs of the nation's economic, political, and social ladders; both men employed the same rhetorical form; and like King, Chavez wrote "as a Christian and as an American" who appealed to "not only those named in the salutation but also, a larger, more general group."[33]

To students of rhetoric, the Barr/Sanderson letter raises the question of whether the growers were capable of understanding Chavez's Good Friday letter. Whereas Chavez reached out to growers to find shared values and create mutual respect, the growers responded with personal attacks and avoided the substantive issues raised by Chavez. They found his letter to be puzzling, a solemnly stated and historically oriented document containing unfamiliar, odd, or inappropriate images, format, use of language, arguments, evidence, and themes. Although the two sides disagreed on many issues, constructive communication and common ground might be possible—but not until growers better comprehended the man and his message.

The responsibility for communicating with audiences rested with Chavez as well, of course, and he may have miscalculated or disregarded the need to send a clear message to the growers who formed part of his audience. It might also be possible that the growers were really not part of his audience. The letter may have been addressed to Barr, but given that it was a public letter, it was intended at least as much for readers who would support Chavez.

For his audiences of Mexican Americans the rhetorical profile of the letter translated into a message easily understood and filled with deep levels of meaning. Its author's persona and its intent, format, style, arguments, evidence, and themes satisfied expectations and understandings that were formed by the rhetorical history these audiences possessed. This history included a history of Chavez and of the invention and manner of discourse that constituted part of their broader rhetorical legacy as Mexican Americans. For the other vital segment of Chavez's audience in the two liberal religious journals that printed his letter, those predominantly Anglo political liberals who had continued to provide needed moral and financial assistance to his movement, he tapped into other powerful rhetorical dynamics and met audience expectations.

If Chavez and the growers each can be held partially responsible for their misunderstanding, apologists for both sides could find justifications for not contributing more to a communication of shared meaning that might lead to a more cooperative relationship in their intense conflict—Chavez because as a pragmatic rhetor he may have consciously discounted the growers in preference for sending a powerful message to his Mexican American and liberal supporters, the growers because they lacked the historical information to understand the Good Friday letter or the motivation and trust to seek common ground with its author. Professionals in the study of public address cannot so easily evade their obligation for thorough and insightful rhetorical analysis, however. In the case of Cesar Chavez's letter, such analysis rests upon extensive research into rhetorical history. An understanding of the meaning and symbols of the Good Friday letter requires the application of insights and principles derived from Chavez's rhetorical history, here seen to include his worldview and experience that led to his conception of rhetoric; his rhetorical profile as represented in his speaking, writing, and interviews over a lifetime; and the rhetorical legacy and cultural interpretations of his ethnic group that explain much about the form and symbols he used. Our study of the letters by Chavez and the growers indicates that rhetorical history is indispensable to our discipline's study of public communication and, if our discipline's scholarship is taken seriously, vital to the prospects for fruitful communication between different ethnic and cultural groups.

A Disciplinary History of Rhetorical History

Retrospect and Prospect

Ronald H. Carpenter

In 1954 I began my M.A. in Speech (as we called it then). Although you might call me the oldest author represented in this volume, I prefer "gerontologically challenged"; but either way, my vintage may allow autobiographical commentary. As a novitiate in a seminary of what was called historical-critical methodology, I elected for my M.A. program at Western Reserve University to take a two-semester sequence in American public address taught by Clair Henderlider, a 1946 Iowa Ph.D. and disciple of A. Craig Baird. Our Old and New Testaments were compiled by Baird and Lester Thonssen in *Speech Criticism*, which offered a comprehensive history of rhetorical theory as well as canons of criticism to employ in our studies of American orators.[1] Our hymnal comprised the studies of those speakers in *History and Criticism of American Public Address*, edited by William Norwood Brigance.[2] And we paid homage, as if at Stations of the Cross, to exemplars of discourse included in compendia such as Baird's *American Public Addresses 1740–1952* or Wayland Parrish and Marie Hochmuth [Nichols], *American Speeches*.[3] Each semester we wrote several long papers about those American orators and their speeches, for once baptized and confirmed in the historical-critical method, we were zealots.[4] But four decades later, I ask what happened to the "historical" in that historical-critical method? Mine is a rhetorical question in two ways. In form it requires no answer because you know the importance of "historical" declined in our disciplinary research base; in content I add my voice to that of the other authors in this volume who urge its reemphasis.

The Evolution of the Historical-Critical Method

In 1925 Herbert Wichelns published "The Literary Criticism of Oratory." Of course he was not advocating literary criticism but explaining how our scholarship differed from that by English department faculty, from whom we recently had split. Arguing for criticism whose "point of view is patently single," he proclaimed, "It is not concerned with permanence, nor with beauty. It is concerned with effect. It regards speech as a communication to a specific audience, and holds its business to be analysis and appreciation of the orator's method of imparting his [sic] ideas to his hearers."[5] Here was catechistic dogma for an emergent historical-critical method to explicate, in situational contexts, influential rhetorical elements operative in discourse. But an outlook once sufficiently unified to be hyphenated divided into disparate modes, which were epitomized for our discipline by Bruce Gronbeck as *"intrinsic,"* finding *"confirming materials inside a rhetorical artifact,"* or *"extrinsic,"* using substantial supporting evidence *"outside a rhetorical artifact"*; and whereas the former yields *"appreciation of structure"* or *"generation of norms"* that are *"not subject to tests of truthfulness or falsehood but to tests of consistency and insightfulness,"* the latter leads to *"appreciation," "explanation,"* or *"generation of theory"* that is *"subject to tests of truthfulness or falsehood"* (but Gronbeck's wording suggests he apparently favors "intrinsic" criticism that probes the "interesting" or "insightful" aspects of discourse).[6]

As a frame of reference for the following commentary, I paraphrase Gronbeck's dichotomy to indicate my view of differing conclusions reached by two methodological orientations in contradistinction to one another:

(1) When rhetorical analyses embody historiographical research to a significant extent, primary source correspondence, memorabilia, diaries, telephone conversation transcripts, or other documents "extrinsic" to the text help explain what happened as a prelude to discourse, choices during rhetors' creative processes, and demonstrable message effects for intended audiences.

(2) When rhetorical analyses have discourse itself as a primary if not exclusive focus of an "intrinsic" analysis, critics more likely interpret—in *their* informed if not atypical readings of those texts—what presumably "really" was said and therefore what terminology

222 / Ronald H. Carpenter

most appropriately designates presumed rhetorical precepts or paradigms embodied as functional therein.

One goal of this volume is to refocus rhetorical studies to embody more historiographical methodology and "extrinsic" materials to inform conclusions about discourse. Admittedly, essays included here use varying degrees of primary sources external to texts; indeed, several of those analyses remain, in large measure, intrinsic textual readings supplemented sparingly with evidence from extrinsic sources. But all of the authors are responding to the same felt need.

Even cursory examination suggests that what Gronbeck calls "intrinsic" readings of texts characterize the rhetorical analyses now predominating in our journals. Yes, rhetorical, literary, psychological, or any other critical constructs often inform insightful readings to describe the impress of discourse. Recall, for instance, "The Quest Story and Nixon's November 3, 1969 Address," in which Herman Stelzner uses "a literary genre in which the subjective experiences of life are central. The themes in such stories vary, but the genre is one of the oldest, hardiest, and most popular. Perhaps its persistent appeal is due to 'its validity as a symbolic description of our subjective personal experience of existence as historical.'" The "quest" paradigm entails "essential elements" of (1) a hero who attains (2) a precious object or goal after (3) a long, arduous journey and overcoming (4) guardians of that object with the aid of (5) helpers whose knowledge or special powers assist the endeavor.[7] Whether accounting for the import of Tara, Oz, or Nixon's goals for war in Vietnam, the paradigm can yield the *"consistency and insightfulness"* that Gronbeck extols. And Stelzner's essay remains relevant after Walter Fisher's "narrative paradigm," which views rhetoric as stories "competing with other stories . . . and as rational when they satisfy the demands of narrative probability and fidelity" acquired "culturally" by *"homo narrans"* through "universal faculty and experience."[8] Whatever their origins in rhetorical theory, literary studies, or other disciplines, some constructs unquestionably help us to account more meaningfully for how discourse achieves its ends.[9]

Furthermore, we know the scholarly value of close readings of texts per se in historical contexts. As James Jasinski reminds us in this volume, rhetorical discourse of the past, such as *The Federalist Papers*, can yield valuable clues to "what happens *to* ideas *in* practice." Thus, for some research, those texts themselves may constitute primary source evidence of "the ways specific discursive strategies and textual dynamics shape and reshape the contours of political concepts and ideas," such as how "an American community, and its constituent subcommunities, confronted threats to its existence (internal as well as external) and engaged in its own reconstruction." For example, "the colonists gradually lost the habit of using certain words and gradually acquired the habit of using others," and ascertaining those changes can reveal "how discourse functions to establish such conditions of possibility or how textual forms enable and constrain beliefs and practices." In many cases these research endeavors also may be included under the rubric of doing rhetorical history; for as Moya Ball reminds us in her essay herein, "as soon as we begin to consider the meaning of discourse within its historical context, we are playing the role of analyst."

But widespread reliance on "extrinsic" sources for "historical" research *did* disappear from our former historical-critical method, and I therefore am impelled to account for what Stephen Lucas calls the "schism in rhetorical scholarship" and a trend away from historiography undergirding criticism published in our journals and recommended in essays about methodology.[10] Moreover, regarding myself as a rhetorical critic whose analyses and conclusions are informed by historiographical research with primary source collections "extrinsic" to texts I study, my purpose herein is twofold: (1) in retrospect, to comment—albeit anecdotally—about that decline and its disadvantages for our discipline, and (2) in prospect, to argue for reemphasizing historiography as an advantageous facet of our disciplinary research base—both for individual scholarship and for programmatic adaptations in our doctoral departments.

About Time

Consider at the outset this truism: graduate education and subsequent scholarly publication in our discipline changed its time framework. Before the 1960s we often completed M.A. degrees and obtained positions in higher education (teaching basic courses or coaching forensics); many of our Ph.D. courses then were taken during summers; and we took several years to complete dissertations— without losing our jobs. Now, entry-level positions in higher education require doctorates "in hand" or dissertation progress so far along that major professor X can write to prospective chairperson Y that newly employed Z will have an oral defense before the end of the fall semester. Moreover, tenure must be attained in five years, founded upon publications (typically journal articles) from dissertations by the fourth year. We no longer follow the doctoral program time frame of, for example George Bohman, my chair at Wayne State University when I was a fresh Ph.D. out of the University of Wisconsin. The date of Bohman's M.A. was 1934, his Ph.D. 1947; and younger departmental "hotshots" chided him about slow academic progress. But examine footnotes in Bohman's piece on colonial oratory for the Brigance volumes.[11] Many summers after 1934 were spent at state historical societies and other manuscript repositories.

Few graduate students today could do that research travel or write grant proposals for funding in following years to find materials to write about still later. Historiographical research by graduate students became impractical, except where their university libraries held archival collections for immediate scrutiny. Thus, dissertations became, to an appreciable extent, projects accomplished ideally in not much more than one year of full-time effort. After all, as "speech" became "speech communication," more of our dissertations were empirical studies, whose qualitative or quantitative methodologies—assuming parsimonious design—typically yielded completion in approximately one year or only slightly longer. With rhetorical criticism as their methodological approach, candidates might complete their dissertations in comparable spans of time as empirical peers—if those studies were of the "intrinsic" type identified by Gronbeck; but for all practical purposes, scholarship using "extrinsic" materials found in primary source repositories located elsewhere became impractical, given expectations for the terminal degree now required for employment.

We also tended to misapply Thonssen and Baird. For too many dissertations and attempts to publish therefrom, *Speech Criticism* fostered what sometimes were labeled derisively as "cookie cutter" studies undermined by two factors. First, Thonssen and Baird seemingly recommended individual chapters or sections about rhetors' *logos*, *pathos*, and *ethos* as well as *dispositio*, *elocutio*, and *actio*. But Edwin Black demonstrated potential shortcomings of obsequious neo-Aristotelian (and neo-Ciceronian) criticism for a discipline striving to enhance its scholarly status in academia.[12] Second, "historical-critical" studies often suffered because of how they accomplished what Thonssen and Baird called "reconstructing" the social setting and determining "effects." Because of that factor of time (or, more accurately, the lack thereof), explicating effects and social settings often became exercises in summarizing *secondary* sources; for instead of finding primary source documentation to ascertain rhetors' roles within specific social contexts, some critics recounted historians' overviews of eras in which discourse functioned. Yes, for all his other notable scholarly efforts embodying primary source materials, Robert Newman nevertheless relied largely on secondary sources to write an exemplary essay tracing the origins and implications of "Lethal Rhetoric: The Selling of the China Myths."[13] Not only do we understand more fully how Douglas MacArthur's address to Congress in 1951 "raised to the highest level of consciousness the themes which were to dominate American China policy for two decades" but also the long-term rhetorical bases of the tragic military involvement of Americans in Asia since the end of World War II.[14] But Newman's exemplar is contrapuntal in quality to many uses of secondary sources fostered by *Speech Criticism.*

Similarly, for their obsequious efforts to accomplish what *Speech Criticism* required as describing rhetors' backgrounds, earlier critics typically turned to biographies and other secondary sources that rarely offered evidence that only our disciplinary eyes would notice in diaries, correspondence, scrapbooks, and other primary source memorabilia. Carol Jablonski's use of such primary materials in this volume, however, illustrates advantages of using those "extrinsic" sources, for her analysis of Dorothy Day's role as a social movement leader derives impetus from the letter Jablonski found among Day's collected papers, in a file labeled "honors declined" and with the notation at its top, "not sent." For the statement "not sent" to Father Theodore Hesburgh, president of the University of Notre Dame, was as revealing about rhetoric, if not more so, as any of Day's discourse actually read or heard by intended audiences.

What many earlier students of *Speech Criticism* did to account biographically for speakers' rhetorical choices was *not* historiography applied well, and that neglect of primary sources resembled the ilk of omission characterizing much of their reliance on secondary sources to make claims about effects of discourse. Thus, I understand why a distinguished member of the University of Wisconsin History Department, Howard K. Beale, said upon meeting me in one of my doctoral minor courses, "Are you doing another of those God damned rhetorical criticisms for a dissertation?" With the insignificance of summarizing secondary sources, particularly for people outside our discipline, describing discourse insightfully—*and creatively*— became increasingly important; and because terminology from traditional rhetorical theory often was deemed inadequate for those purposes (particularly by skeptical empiricists among us), humanistically inclined scholars sought guidance or new critical paradigms from someone other than Thonssen and Baird.

Historiography and Rhetorical Analysis

Our new messiah in the 1960s and early 1970s was Kenneth Burke. But Burke's writings were obscure, so Marie Hochmuth Nichols explained his paradigms and how we might use them in our critical efforts.[15] Dramatism prevailed as myriad studies found in discourse sources of identification and consubstantiality, strategies for creating guilt and achieving redemption, hierarchies and degrees of mystification, or pentadic scene-act ratios and the like. Years later we still argue in journals and at conventions about what Burke *really* offered as paradigms for our scholarship (at the 1997 Southern States Communication Association Convention, for instance, Burke's critical constructs were specified focal points of three programs involving a total of fourteen individual papers and two formal responses). In the latter 1970s we found another messiah in Ernest Bormann, whose "fantasy theme" paradigm spawned numerous studies finding "rhetorical visions."[16] Bormann's essay won the 1983 Woolbert Prize for impact on our scholarship (although another SCA award the same year went to Gerald Mohrmann for his questions about fantasy theme analyses).[17] Thus, for most dissertations with committee-approved paradigms for explicating rhetorical texts, libraries at hand offered published sources complementing those projects sufficiently to make them feasible. And if dissertations were predicated on some critical paradigm as yet not used within speech communication but found in some other discipline, so much the better, for those young scholars were "creative" in extending our disciplinary boundaries.

Burkes or Bormanns or Fishers may help us name what we ascertain by other means, but insightful conceptual terminology—in itself—does not warrant descriptions of discourse defensible until replaced by "better" paradigms from within—or without—the discipline. In "Discovering Rhetorical Imprints: La Follette, 'Iago,' and the Melodramatic Scenario," Carl Burgchardt demonstrates how Robert M. La Follette's political speeches incorporated rhetorical techniques from his contest oration as a Wisconsin undergraduate in 1879.[18] Burgchardt's essay once was reputable simply for itself, but it likely was unpublishable until he responded to a journal referee's "so what's new?" with a metaphor about rhetorical "imprints." Finding something new to call it became as important, if not more so, than ascertaining what happened and how it came about rhetorically. And Moya Ball's chapter herein attests to a contemporary disciplinary predisposition favoring the "new" over mere "historical recounting," which Roderick Hart epitomized as an endeavor wherein "theory construction is offered no ride at all."[19] Her experiences merit reiteration:

I detect a . . . state in the speech communication discipline in which scholars become so caught up with the excitement surrounding new methodological models that they are willing to suspend their contact with what may be the more enduring but, perhaps, more pedestrian methods of inquiry such as rhetorical history. . . . Those of us who practice rhetorical history may have shared [Martin J.] Medhurst's experience of having a paper returned to him by a reviewer with the comment that, although he had chosen to examine a politically and historically important speech, his work did not have a "shred of newsworthy theoretical commentary." Some of my work on Vietnam decision making received the reviewer's comment, "you are writing history, not rhetoric."

But historiography can complement rhetorical analysis. Consider "The Romance as Rhetorical Dissociation: The Purification of Imperialism in *King Solomon's Mines*," in which Jeff Bass finds that H. Rider Haggard's novel and other nineteenth-century British romances "figured prominently in the larger rhetorical effort 'to mold the popular attitude toward the glories of empire.' "[20] Adapted from his dissertation in 1977, Bass therefore could not utilize *The Private Diaries of Sir H. Rider Haggard 1914–1925,* published in 1980.[21] But he might have utilized the Haggard Collection that the Huntington Library acquired in 1953. Having examined those papers, I juxtapose "intrinsic" interpretations by Bass with "extrinsic" quotations from Haggard himself as well as his nineteenth-century readers.

Restricting himself largely to the text that is the subject of his investigation, Bass reads this rhetorical purpose out of—or into—*King Solomon's Mines:* "Haggard describes one of the most characteristic paradigms of imperial expansion—the overthrow of an indigenous ruler and the establishment of a rival claimant (one approved by the imperial nation) on the throne. By manipulating the conventional romantic structure, Haggard dissociates the paradigm's 'appearance' as unwarranted intervention in the affairs of a foreign culture from what he considers to be its essential 'reality'—the act of establishing order and justice in place of barbarism and the transformation of the identities of Briton and African that results from this act." Moreover, for "his conception of imperialism's true reality," Haggard "constructs the novel on the principle of rhetorical dissociation" and "creates an appearance-reality dichotomy that relegates his characters' desire for material wealth to a position of minimal importance." Other rhetorical intentionality is attributed to Haggard with assertions that the novelist must "diminish the importance of material wealth" and articulate the "true reward of imperialism" as "the ultimate means of self-realization." Here are Haggard's words in an address on July 14, 1905, to the Imperial South African Association:

By means of public credit . . . I think I am right in saying we could move tens of thousands of persons out of this country who are not wanted here, to the waste lands of the Empire, to be the strength to the Empire. . . . The cry now among a large section of people in this country is "Keep them at home." But I ask again, what is the use of keeping tens of thousands of people rotting in our cities when they might be building up an Empire, . . . many who could, with great advantage, be moved from these shores to South Africa, to Canada, and elsewhere in the dominion of Empire. . . . Now is the time to seize the opportunity, to seize the day, move your waste population here, or some of it, on to the waste lands of Rhodesia.[22]

Is Haggard's "true reality of imperialism" that of "establishing justice" and minimizing "the importance of material wealth," or does he fear strife from unemployed masses in England, a "waste population" whose economic lot could be improved in Africa or elsewhere?

As for assertions that Haggard "constructs," "dissociates," or "seeks to correct" by "manipulating the conventional romantic structure," the novelist himself said "I 'write my books first and make up the plot afterward'! at any rate to some extent."[23] Moreover, Edmund Gosse in 1887 compared another of Haggard's novels to *King Solomon's Mines* "before the impression the book has left upon my mind in any degree wears off":

Briefly, I think it places you in the very front rank of imaginative authors. I am aware that those are strong words, and I am not in the habit of flinging such things about. . . . In construction I think you have been successful to a very marvelous degree. The quality of the invention increases as you go on, and the latest chapters are the best. Indeed it does not appear to me that I have ever been thrilled and terrified by any literature as I have by pp. 271–306 of "She." . . . These are only a few of the really marvelous things that the book contains. I was a great admirer and, as you know, a warm welcomer of "King Solomon's Mines," but I confess that exceedingly picturesque and ingenious book did not prepare me for "She."[24]

And Haggard's publisher explained his "hankering" for more from the author: "Hunting, adventure, some of the peculiar vein of humor of those early years, romance—all of these I can do with but no mysticism if you please. Now you know just the sort of book I want and there are lots of other thick heads who want just the same thing."[25]

Haggard himself attested that his stories were "written quite easily, dictated straightaway and except for a few Zulu details not altered at all—also more or less invented as I went along. It was the same thing with 'She' which I did with my own hand in six weeks, beginning to write it with no idea in my head save that of a woman who had discovered the trick of long life."[26] Yes, rhetorical goals and some sense of their techniques may manifest themselves unconsciously in authors' efforts, but lacking clues in Haggard's diary or correspondence, the claim is moot for a novel that his contemporaries characterized as having "no mysticism" but plenty of "first class . . . romance" for "thick heads." Without complementary historiography with "extrinsic" sources, "intrinsic" criticism—however consistent with its interpretative paradigm—can differ substantially from essays in the first volume in the Michigan State University Press Rhetoric and Public Affairs Series, *Eisenhower's War of Words: Rhetoric and Leadership,* edited by Martin Medhurst.[27] Drawing amply upon archival materials to explain Eisenhower as rhetor, several chapters therein likely will stand tests of "insightfulness" *and* "truthfulness or falsehood."

Historiography and the Rhetorical Process

Another shortcoming—and a major one in my view—of earlier attempts to publish historical-critical research was the assumption that seemed to underlie efforts by many erstwhile authors: that single speeches—in and of themselves—were instrumental, and significantly so, in altering the course of events. Yes, one speech just might do so. Suppose Richard Nixon had not delivered in September 1952 the television address known as the "Checkers Speech." Without his persuasive explanation for the "secret" fund from campaign contributors in California, Nixon might have been removed as candidate for vice president on the Republican ticket with Dwight Eisenhower; he could have returned to a law practice in Whittier, California; and the course of history likely would have been different. I have described a similar impress of one speech when accounting for General Douglas MacArthur's persuasiveness in Tokyo on the evening of August 23, 1950. Opening weeks of the Korean War constituted a debacle for American troops as they retreated in disorder down the peninsula to a perimeter around the port city of Pusan (talk of another "Dunkirk" was rampant). To alleviate their dire situation, MacArthur planned an amphibious landing by the First Marine Division at Inchon, behind the North Korean Peoples Army. When the Joint Chiefs of Staff in Washington learned of his intentions, and of major shortcomings of that site, two of them flew to Tokyo to dissuade MacArthur. In a showdown conference, nine Navy and Marine officers delineated disadvantages of Inchon; the Joint Chiefs expressed immediate agreement with their recommended alternative site for the landing; MacArthur then spoke on behalf of Inchon. The Joint Chiefs of Staff changed their minds and endorsed Inchon to President Truman. The Marines landed; the North Korean Peoples Army retreated throughout Korea; and within ten weeks American forces were at the Yalu River border with Red China. The course of history was altered.[28] Surely such rhetorical efforts are exceptions rather than the rule, however.

As that self-characterized rhetorical critic whose conclusions about discourse are informed by historiographical research with materials extrinsic to texts, I am mindful of an admonition from Samuel Becker: attributing persuasive effect to any one particular statement is rash. After all, attitudes and actions most likely are molded by a matrix of messages, many of which are, in Becker's wise words, "unorganized" and "overlaid" to form a complex communication "mosaic" that "consists of an immense number of fragments or bits of information on an immense number of topics . . . scattered over time and space and modes of communication. Each individual must grasp from this mosaic those bits which serve his [sic] needs, must group them into message sets which are relevant for him at any given time . . . and close the gaps between them in order to arrive at a coherent picture of the world to which he can respond." Therefore, rhetorical scholars should heed Becker's corollary observation that attitudes or actions rarely result from "any one communication encounter, or even a series of encounters by a single speaker or writer."[29] Yes, our disciplinary impulse to explicate effectiveness, if not artistry, encourages examining those rhetorical texts that seem salient, qualitatively, among that "immense number of fragments or bits of information." Still, that scholarship derives authoritativeness, in my view, when the discourse examined is situated firmly amidst other likely "texts" constituting the communication "mosaic" conducing to persuasion.

Some essays in this volume exemplify how rhetorical history can help reconstruct communication mosaics surrounding particular texts we study, to situate that discourse more firmly in the *total process* of persuasion on particular issues. Steven Goldzwig, for instance, illustrates how archival materials offer "the best evidence of the individual motives, methods, beliefs, and values of political actors as they wrestle to shape public philosophy and implement public policy. The persuasive appeals launched by and directed at presidents, cabinet members, officers, advisors, friends, enemies, interest groups, and various other public and private constituencies provide an important nexus for the exploration of rhetorical history. It makes a difference who gives the advice, who takes the advice, who ignores it, and why." Thus, Goldzwig's case study of Truman's efforts to desegregate the armed forces utilizes personal letters to and from the president, ongoing correspondence between other major participants during the process, logs and memos "for the record" of telephone conversations between those participants, and transcripts of what was said in various meetings. And Timothy Jenkins achieves a similar account of rhetorical process with various primary source and archival materials from the communication "mosaic" of Missourians in the advent of the Civil War.

But Moya Ball's chapter herein reminds us of another advantage of

[margin annotation:] } history as holistic

this volume's scholarly orientation: "As we begin to make meaning out of discourses in historical contexts, we step closer also to the theoretical implications of rhetorical history." To analyze American escalation of the war in Vietnam, Ball was interested "not only in the public address of presidents and other spokespersons but also in the more private communication of policy-making groups"; and she therefore examined "internal constraints on the decision-making process, including the communication patterns, rhetorical strategies, and interpretations of events shared by the presidents and their advisors." Social psychologist Irving Janis had posited a widely accepted theory that highly cohesive groups, because of factors such as illusions of invulnerability, become victims of a "groupthink," which in turn typically leads to defective if not disastrous decisions (particularly about military courses of action).[30] For the war in Vietnam, however, Ball found American policy making to be characterized instead by a distinct lack of cohesiveness among the decision makers, and the important point here is her commentary about using declassified materials at the John F. Kennedy and Lyndon B. Johnson Libraries.

Archival collections . . . contain a wealth of resources for communication scholars who are willing to combine their perspectives with the meticulous data-gathering techniques of historical researchers. Indeed, it seems to me that when a communication researcher begins to depend on archival sources for his or her interpretations, the real business of analysis begins in that, instead of relying on the authority of secondary accounts, we are left with primary sources that demand our making statements of our own, that demand we become active rhetorical analysts.

Yes, the scholarly result is akin to case studies if not that "grounded theory" and "process by which researchers discover theory from the basic data collected." But Moya Ball's overall conclusion *is* valid: "doing rhetorical history has important theoretical implications." For just as rhetorical history can corroborate or clarify extant theory so too can its concluding implications amend that theory. So several methodological aspects of historiography merit further commentary.

Methodological Considerations

My interest for many years has been in historical writings as a subtle but pervasive mode of rhetoric. For example, Carl Becker's textbook, *Modern History*, was widely used in the United States from the 1930s into the 1950s (after Becker died, his publisher updated the volume every few years to continue its sales in the public schools).

An NEH fellowship facilitated my summer at Cornell University with Becker's papers, reading many letters *to* the historian and his publisher for reactions to his textbook with numerous topics, over 800 pages, and myriad sentences. Readers singled out his chapter about causes of World War I; their letters identified an attitude shaped by Becker's book as it applied to an impending World War II; and they quoted Becker's exact sentence epitomizing that sentiment. Moreover, letters *from* Becker explained his rhetorical objective while writing about World War I, when it was formed, why, and from whom he learned about specific sentence conformations for impress and where they should be placed in discourse.[31] At the 1976 Kansas Conference on Significant Form in Rhetorical Criticism, Edwin Black responded somewhat indignantly to my paper on Becker and other historians as Jeremiahs, suggesting my conclusions about persuasiveness of their specific sentences could have been reached without reading the texts themselves.[32] But would Black's marvelously perceptive critical eye discern my conclusions about suasory effects on intended audiences—and their sources in specific sentences—by reading *only* these historians' texts? Thus, the following reminder and advice are in order.

Historiographical research with archival materials is not the exclusive domain of scholars with graduate work in history. Lucas accurately perceives little difference between "historical method" and "critical method" when "it comes to the study of public address," for "the central task of each is making inferences about probabilities on the basis of limited data." Furthermore, he reminds us that historiography is founded not so much on methodology as on being "*methodical* in selecting, ordering, and criticizing evidence," and parallels between "method in history and prevailing ideas about method in rhetorical criticism should be so patent as to require little elaboration."[33] Having used collections at the Library of Congress, Huntington Library, Naval War College, Marine Corps Museum, Douglas MacArthur Archives, and special collections in various university libraries, I am categorical: *pertinence of some primary source material leaps off the page with its relevance for rhetorical critics willing to go beyond reading discourse alone.*

The rhetorical role of historians as opinion leaders, for instance, was revealed initially to me upon discovering a letter in the Allan Nevins Collection at the Huntington Library. My original research purpose was an examination of his longhand revisions in successive drafts of *The Ordeal of the Union,* for those emendations might delineate the parameters of stylistic prowess for which Nevins was acclaimed. When examining his correspondence for evidence of how readers reacted to his style or form, I found the clue to how historians' substance or content could function rhetorically. A woman had written to Nevins about her reading novelist Irving Stone's biographical account of Jessie Benton Fremont. Perceiving John C. Fremont's wife as someone to emulate, the woman looked at Stone's bibliography and saw its listing of Nevins's book, *Fremont, Pathfinder of the West*; and to corroborate what she had learned first from a source in popular culture, that woman thereupon read the historian's book as the more credible source for further information—and profusely thanked Nevins for his book that "ends too soon. Somehow you begin to feel you know these people personally and you don't want to lose them."[34] As Samuel Becker avers, "when people are exposed to information which they believe is important, they will generally turn to additional sources to verify or supplement what they got from the original source."[35] I corroborated this phenomenon with correspondence in Merle Curti's papers in the Wisconsin State Historical Society.[36] Reexamining my archival materials about still other historical writing, I redirected my analysis to identify historians' significant role with style and narrative as achieving persuasion in the form of opinion leadership that reinforces credibly what people learn from other sources. As Joseph Klapper concluded, people typically are "crucially influenced in many matters" by that "opinion leader" who is "characteristically more competent," with "access to wider sources of pertinent information," and therefore a "super representative" whose significant influence is on behalf of "constancy and reinforcement."[37] And for this volume, Timothy Jenkins also explicates how "the rhetorical discourse of opinion leaders assumes a distinctive character . . . as a means of preparing for the emergence of revolutionary activity," and that role in the advent of the Civil War is demonstrated not so much by texts of public statements by Southern governors but by their personal correspondence to one another, as found in various archives.

Primary Resources

Knowing where to find primary source materials is increasingly easy. Prior to visiting San Marino, California, to examine the Allan Nevins Collection, I had read the Bass essay about *King Solomon's Mines* (a book that intrigued me as a youngster); and in a few minutes in our library reference room, I learned that Huntington Library holdings included H. Rider Haggard's speech to the Imperial South African Association, ninety-four pieces of his correspondence from 1878 to 1925, and his "Notes for Discussion on Imagination—Its Advantages and Its Evils."[38] My trip to California allowed me to examine two collections. To develop my NEH proposal for research at Cornell University, I consulted the *National Union Catalog of Manuscript Collections*, which described seven shelf feet of Carl Becker's Papers there (MS 62-2359) as including "correspondence with former students and other historians concerning the study and writing of history." Now, in a university library having electronic interface with RLIN (Research Libraries Information Network), this description is obtained as a computer printout:

Becker, Carl Lotus, 1873–1945. Papers, 1898–1956. 21.1 cubic feet. Historian; professor of history, Cornell University. Summary: Includes correspondence with former students and other historians concerning the study and writing of history, especially Frederick Jackson Turner and Charles Homer Haskins; papers relating to Ezra Cornell and the early history of Cornell University; lectures; reviews; articles; notes on European and American history and for a bibliography of Becker's writings; six letters to Elias R. B. Willis, a Cornell librarian and friend, concerning the MANCHESTER GUARDIAN, the state and its role (1925), contrasts between Cornell University and the University of Chicago (1929), John Jay Chapman, his friend George Gemmill, and a poem satirizing academicians (1924); an undated letter to Laurence Bradford Packard; an autographed book; reprints; and biographical information including letters to and from Becker, photographs, and reminiscences about Becker by friends, relatives, and former students. Indexes: Unpublished guide. Described in REPORT OF THE CURATOR AND ARCHIVIST, 1950–1954, 1954–1958, 1958–1962.[39]

For some rhetorical studies RLIN provides information—literally in seconds or a few minutes at most—about locations of major primary source collections, and those printouts sometimes identify still other collections elsewhere in which pertinent materials also appear. Moreover, detailed guides or registers describing those collections are obtained easily from most repositories.

Today, scholars often can use primary source collections without expensive travel to, and lodging at, their repositories. I used Barbara Tuchman's collected correspondence to analyze her historical writing as rhetorical discourse and to describe her impress upon John Kennedy during the Cuban Missile Crisis, when he repeated to his advisors the moral learned from her account of the beginning of World War I, *The Guns Of August*. RLIN indicated the Tuchman Papers were at Yale University; by telephone I learned that a forty-two-page register described the collection and could be sent to me for $3.10. From that guide, I ascertained the precise boxes containing correspondence about (1) writing and revising her manuscript for *The Guns of August* as well as (2) reactions from readers after its publication. By mail I arranged for Yale Library to duplicate and send me those 508 items from Tuchman's papers—at a cost of $143.95. Research was completed without travel to New Haven; my department supported the research by paying the $143.95; the only cost to me was $3.10 for the collection guide.[40] Archival sources often can be used far more easily now to complement critical readings of discourse—with relatively minimal financial cost. Doing rhetorical history now is more feasible than before.

Problems and Prospects

Residual counterarguments still may regard "historical" as an anachronism from the days of Baird and Brigance. No! In his "Editor's Preface" for an issue of the *Quarterly Journal of Speech*, Robert Ivie urged "productive criticism" that is "deliberately creative." Seemingly eschewing the orientation that this volume espouses, Ivie as editor reflects the bifurcation in rhetorical scholarship when he advocates an endeavor that "invents social knowledge instead of discovering it. It originates insight as opposed to apprehending actuality. It manufactures practical wisdom rather than deriving conclusions from observed phenomena." Yet Ivie as scholar admits those "sparks of insight" must have "accountability to perceived realities," as well as "coherence and consistency with relevant facts."[41] And Ivie's reliance on "relevant facts" derived from archival sources is demonstrated in his chapter, "Eisenhower as Cold Warrior," in *Eisenhower's War of Words: Rhetoric and Leadership*, the volume edited by Martin J. Medhurst. Therein, Ivie goes beyond the manifest wording of Eisenhower's campaign discourse in October 1952 to ascertain its rhetorical goal of waging "psychological warfare" during the cold war, the rationale for so doing, and specific means by which those objectives might be attained. And conclusive evidence of Eisenhower's rhetorical goals and methods for "psychological warfare" that is "carefully concealed" was found not so much in the text of his discourse but rather in his confidential correspondence and, more significantly, documents in the papers of C. D. Jackson, appointed by Eisenhower specifically as his "advisor on psychological warfare," which are in the Dwight David Eisenhower Library (including the "Draft for NSC [National Security Council]: Proposed Plan for Psychological Warfare Offensive").[42]

The authors in this collection know that historiography supplies those "facts" and "realities" about which Ivie writes as editor (and incorporates as scholar). Yet the nature of historiographical research and the reporting of its results often pose problems for erstwhile publishers when they submit articles to various journals in communication studies. Although writing any history admittedly yields only incomplete reconfigurations of the past, scholars who use primary source collections typically have "hands on" experiences with relevant documents that cause their conclusions to be expressed with a certitude sometimes troublesome to our journal editors and their referees predisposed toward close readings of texts for analyses held to "tests of consistency and insightfulness" more so than "tests of truthfulness or falsehood." And therein resides another potential problem for scholars doing rhetorical history.

Historiography too often constrains creative speculation. In his opening chapter here, David Zarefsky urges "productive" criticism that answers the question, "How does this relate to the 'ongoing conversation' about what our discipline advances as knowledge about rhetoric and communication?" But here is the crux of the constraint: whereas "intrinsic"-oriented rhetorical critics characteristically start with texts of discourse and the concepts or paradigms to explicate them, historiographers using primary sources "extrinsic" to texts start with *collections!* Admittedly, historiographically oriented critics appreciate the importance of the rhetorical texts they study; perhaps they also have a prior sense of some paradigm as a possible focal point for their initial inquiry; but *in the scholarly outcome of historiographical research, any explanatory rhetorical paradigm more likely only grows out of what is found in primary source collections and other materials to which those collections lead.* Moreover, a "productive" yield of doing rhetorical history well may be one of "theory building," as Moya Ball's essay herein indicates, only by amending extant "knowledge about rhetoric and communication." So in prospect, whether in this more conservative mode of productive criticism or another one favoring more "newsworthy theoretical commentary," future scholars who do rhetorical history must be willing, if their primary sources permit, to exert intellectual boldness; and increased predilection for that endeavor may be derived from appreciating how our discipline stands in contradistinction to other disciplines.

Phillip Tompkins has argued that rhetorical criticism asks "functional questions; e.g., how do sender, message, and receiver interact in concrete, verifiable ways?" rather than "structural" inquiries of English department "Mandarins" who "teach us but to name our tools."[43] His observation is poignant for me because for the past twenty years at the University of Florida, I have been in the English Department (with several communication courses transferred there). I attest to an academic pecking order in which English is deemed more "scholarly" than communication, although that aura is likely from faculties whose dissertations tend to reach publication as books because the vast MLA membership assures markets for those books, and that larger discipline also means journal outlets for every specialty (e.g., the eighteenth century) as well as various orientations (e.g., psychoanalytic criticism). Yet for English departments, Jonathan Culler laments "the most important and insidious legacy of the New Criticism is the widespread and unquestioning acceptance of the notion that the critic's job is to interpret literary works."[44] And he deplores critics who "spend their time attempting to work out the meaning of particular works," for "there is more to the discipline of literary studies than the recording and exchange of such interpretive readings." But this trend is endemic "in the way American criticism has trivialized every interesting theoretical project that has come along, treating it as an 'approach' or a technique of interpretation"; and Culler names this culprit: "Our tenure system creates a need for theories and methods that generate numerous small projects which can be completed in less than six years and listed in curriculum vitaes. Since interpretation can generate an endless series of twenty-page articles, it suits our system better than theories whose projects would take years to complete. Even critics who are committed to these other projects find themselves pressed by our system of rewards to produce numerous short pieces for conferences, colloquia, journals, Festschriften, and the like."[45]

In some ways, when the goal is scholarly publication, our discipline is not that different from English. After all, when rhetorical critics read out of or into discourse what was said, as newly named or renamed precept, I suggest they often are akin to Culler's literary critics—and unlikely imitations of English "Mandarins" who publish books about literature as it may "transmit cultural values."[46] Although we also are interested in cultural values, our outlook toward discourse—derived in part from the pragmatic communication skills we teach undergraduates—is different. In most English departments that offer doctorates, teaching composition—described in print by my chair here as well as my dean as the "primary mission" of this department—is delegated to graduate assistants and nontenure-track faculty. Indeed, most published scholarship in English departments is irrelevant for teaching composition. At the University of Florida, for example, tenure-track faculty hired in English specifically to teach technical or "professional" writing were required to publish traditional literary criticism for tenure and promotion; and increasingly, composition courses are taught by our Ph.D. products who, as nontenure-track appointees here two or three years after completing their degrees, still cannot get jobs teaching elsewhere in their fields of literary interest (reflecting a trend in higher education generally).

In communication generally and its species called communication studies, however, courses in which students acquire prowess in a fundamental human activity reflect directly most of our research—whether about interpersonal communication or public address in its various forms or any modes of discourse in between. And that is a significant difference between our discipline and that of English. Therefore, the study of Senator Mansfield's ethos with respect to Vietnam is pertinent for reconsideration here. Disregard momentarily Olson's historiography on behalf of demonstrating that Mansfield "made himself an authority on the Far East by proclaiming himself one." Yes, the historiographical detective makes good use of fascinating tidbits: Mansfield's stay in China as a marine after World War I was limited to only twelve days; his time in Japan consisted of a one-day fueling stop; and when teaching Far Eastern history at the University of Montana, Mansfield's lecture notes were extensive about China and Japan but included only one and one-half pages of material about Indochina. But Olson also can be viewed as offering virtually a textbook primer delineating how people may create credibility for themselves in public life or other arenas. And that essential pragmatism undergirding our research with archival sources differentiates us from English department faculty whose conclusions about Chaucer, Wordsworth, or Melville have little direct bearing on what their graduate students as teaching assistants do in classrooms on behalf of expository and argumentative writing. But a final, more significant, factor mandates returning "historical" to the historical-critical method.

Looking Ahead: The Value of Rhetorical History

At the 1986 Speech Communication Association Convention Awards Banquet in Chicago, Carroll Arnold praised our increasing production of scholarly books. For as those tomes grew in number our discipline attained greater academic prestige so that we no longer were viewed as teaching or coaching voice and diction, forensics, and public speaking with hoary precepts articulated in antiquity. Yet more scholarly books will yield still higher status in academia. A trend is clear: *like English, history, and several other disciplines, the facet of our discipline known earlier as rhetoric and public address and now, in many departments, as communication studies also is becoming book-driven.* Even cursory looks at our scholarly books already published indicate that although some of them posit rhetorical theory generally, others examine specific discourse; and from their experiences, scholars in rhetorical history know that research consistently finding its way to publication as books relies, appreciably, on historiography with primary sources that complement interpretations of texts we analyze.[47] If more of our disciplinary dissertations were designed—from the outset—to utilize primary source collections and other archival materials, we would produce more scholarly books and do so sooner in our careers.

At the 1997 Southern States Communication Association Convention, two successive program time slots were devoted to a single panel of scholars' papers about "Rhetorical Studies in the 21st Century." In his formal response paper to those statements, Martin Medhurst emphasized the following disciplinary goal:

We need to continue and accelerate a trend that began in the middle 1980s, about fifteen years ago, and has matured in the 1990s. I refer to the trend toward publishing scholarly books. Not that long ago, one could count on two hands the number of scholarly books in print in rhetorical studies at any given time, and most of those bore the names of Kathleen Hall Jamieson or Roderick Hart. But then there was Ivie, and Turner, and Hogan, and before we knew it a whole new phenomenon had unfolded before our very eyes. We were no longer just an article-based field that focused on speech pedagogy. In the 1990s alone, scholars trained in the rhetorical tradition have already produced over 100 books, not counting textbooks. It is not by accident that as the number of books has increased, so too has the recognition of our field by other members of the academy. There is, I believe, a direct relationship between writing scholarly books and one's intellectual credibility on campus. This needs to continue.[48]

Rhetorical historians could nominate other authors for Medhurst's listing, and a significant number of their books have scholarly bases in historiography that informed rhetorical criticism therein.

Vintage again warrants final autobiographical musings. After using an "extrinsic" methodology for six *Communication Monographs* and *Quarterly Journal of Speech* essays as well as several book chapters and articles in our regional journals and elsewhere—and then using them as bases for two books—my retrospective view is that I should have written those books first; for I submit, albeit from hindsight, that with careful planning in early stages of ascertaining topics and locating materials, the time frame to produce a book from a historiographically based dissertation often may approximate that of writing "intrinsic" criticism, compressing it for a journal article or two, and then making rounds of successive journal editorships for publication.

My retrospection likely is shared by Greg Olson, whose chapter herein relies admirably on archival, primary source materials. The substantial part of his research with the Mansfield Papers was done for his doctoral dissertation at the University of Minnesota, finished in 1988, and his research trips to Montana were taken while he was still a graduate student. Like so many other prospective scholars in speech communication, however, Olson was oriented toward publishing journal articles from his dissertation, for that is how we were accustomed to earning tenure in our discipline. He accordingly made submissions to journals under various editors and referees. After being caught between changing editorships and differing sets of referees, Olson decided instead to flesh out materials from his doctoral dissertation and publish *Mansfield and Vietnam: A Study in Rhetorical Adaptation;* and although this book was reviewed in the *Quarterly Journal of Speech* as "an exemplar of this genre of scholarship," its publication in 1995 was too late for Olson to earn tenure at Marquette University.[49] Had he eschewed potential journal articles in favor of first writing his book, Olson's fate in academia might have been different.

But Olson's dilemma (and my hindsight) aside, still another advantage accrues from books that do rhetorical history. Medhurst's "response" to papers about "Rhetorical Studies in the 21st Century" also included his anaphoric observation:

The books we write need consistently to be reviewed—and reviewed positively—in both disciplinary and interdisciplinary outlets beyond the field of communication proper. I look forward to the day when members of our profession can have *The Journal of American History* say this of their work: "This study deserves the attention of all scholars and students of the Vietnam War." I look forward to the day that *Choice* describes one of our books as "a valuable aid in understanding the complex mix that produced America's Vietnam policy." I look forward to the day when *Books in Review* calls one of our products "well researched, clearly written, . . . one that adds considerably to our knowledge." I look forward to reading in the *Pacific Historical Review* that one of our own has written a "perceptive and balanced interpretation," resulting in "an excellent book" that is "informative and thoughtful." . . . All of those journals did say exactly those things about Gregory A. Olson's *Mansfield and Vietnam: A Study in Rhetorical Adaptation,* which was published in 1995 by Michigan State University Press. But Olson is the exception, not the rule. We need to reverse that.[50]

The authors represented in *Doing Rhetorical History* know that rhetorical history will help correct a course of "exception" and vector it instead toward that "rule." And remember: our journal articles most likely are read by people *within* our discipline; our books—as a result of publishers' promotion of them, how they are reviewed, and their appearances in various indexes now computer generated by title and subject—come to the attention of readers in *other* disciplines. The result is increased academic stature. Thus, whatever we perceived retrospectively as shortcomings of the "historical" in our earlier "historical-critical method" are more than counterbalanced advantageously by prospects of doing rhetorical history.

In the final analysis, however, most dissertations that rely extensively on primary source collections realistically may require longer periods of time to complete than purely "intrinsic" analyses of texts. Therefore, our discipline should reconsider anticipated time frames for completing dissertations. Although this change may pose problems in a discipline already bifurcated to some extent into empiricists and humanists (if you will), I submit that instead of emulating a schedule of approximately one year or slightly more for completion of empirical theses, rhetorical criticism dissertations—whether primarily "extrinsic" studies, "intrinsic" readings of texts, or some happy combination thereof—normatively will need at least two years full-time work for completion. But that time frame more closely approximates English and history dissertations that *do* tend to reach publications as books.

To conclude, my idiosyncratic observations, of course, are moot; this final assertion voiced on behalf of my colleagues conducting rhetorical history hopefully is incontrovertible: restoring historiography to more of our dissertations and doing more rhetorical history for our subsequent research will enhance what we read among ourselves and—through resultant scholarly books—our disciplinary credibility throughout academia. Nearly five centuries ago in 1509, Stephen Hawes extolled that "gylted goddesse of the hygh renowne," Dame Rethoryke.[51] For research leading to publication as scholarly books, rhetorical analysts know that now and in the new century, the most helpful handmaiden to that exalted being is Clio.

Notes

Introduction: Rhetorical History as Social Construction

1. William Norwood Brigance, ed., *A History and Criticism of American Public Address*, 2 vols. (New York: McGraw-Hill, 1943); Marie Kathryn Hochmuth, ed., *A History and Criticism of American Public Address*, vol. 3 (New York: Russell and Russell, 1955).

2. Sources of the first two instances shall remain nameless, both to protect the misinformed and because their name is legion; the editor mentioned prefaced these remarks by noting that "theory-oriented essays stand a better chance of acceptance than applications studies." The final quotation comes from Roderick P. Hart, "Doing Criticism My Way: A Reply to Darsey," *Western Journal of Communication* 58 (fall 1994): 309. Indeed, Hart goes on to suggest that those who cannot speak theory to him should "go write history books."

3. Barnet Baskerville, "Must We All Be 'Rhetorical Critics'?," *Quarterly Journal of Speech* 63 (April 1977): 107–16; Bruce E. Gronbeck, "Rhetorical History and Rhetorical Criticism: A Distinction," *Speech Teacher* 24 (November 1975): 309–20; and Donald Bryant, "Some Problems of Scope and Method in Rhetorical Scholarship," *Quarterly Journal of Speech* 23 (April 1937): 182–89. Gronbeck would likely suggest that his essay in this volume provides a more developed conception of rhetorical history than his earlier work, which he now characterizes as espousing an "objectivist" position.

4. Interestingly, "history" and "rhetoric" display similar ambiguities, referring to the objects of study as well as the process by which they are studied. Working independently on chapter two, Clark and McKerrow arrived at

a schema similar to that used here, referring to the former category as "rhetoric and history" and the second as "the rhetoric of history."

5. "Report of the Committee on the Scope of Rhetoric and the Place of Rhetorical Studies in Higher Education," *The Prospect of Rhetoric,* ed. Lloyd F. Bitzer and Edwin Black (Englewood Cliffs, N.J.: Prentice-Hall, 1971), 208.

6. "Report of the Committee on the Advancement and Refinement of Rhetorical Criticism," in *The Prospect of Rhetoric,* 220.

7. Gregory A. Olson, *Mansfield and Vietnam: A Study in Rhetorical Adaptation* (East Lansing: Michigan State University Press, 1995).

8. Moya Ann Ball, *Vietnam-on-the-Potomac* (New York: Praeger, 1992).

9. See Roderick P. Hart, "Contemporary Scholarship in Public Address: A Research Editorial," *Western Journal of Speech Communication* 50 (summer 1986): 284; and characterizations of common perceptions offered by Thomas W. Benson, "History, Criticism, and Theory in the Study of American Rhetoric," in *American Rhetoric: Context and Criticism,* ed. Thomas W. Benson (Carbondale: Southern Illinois University Press, 1989), 16.

10. Kathleen J. Turner, *Lyndon Johnson's Dual War: Vietnam and the Press* (Chicago: University of Chicago Press, 1985).

11. Baskerville, "Must We All Be 'Rhetorical Critics'?," 115, 116.

12. Jacques Barzun and Henry F. Graff, *The Modern Researcher,* 5th ed. (Boston: Houghton Mifflin, 1992), 44.

13. Donald C. Bryant, "Rhetoric: Its Function and Its Scope," *Quarterly Journal of Speech* 39 (December 1953), repr. in Douglas Ehninger, *Contemporary Rhetoric: A Reader's Coursebook* (Glenview, Ill.: Scott, Foresman, & Co., 1972), 28. Note that Bryant does not suggest that "fiction" means made of whole cloth; he thus uses the term in a different sense from Clark and McKerrow in their assessment of history and fiction in chapter two of this volume.

14. Karlyn Kohrs Campbell, *The Rhetorical Act* (Belmont, Calif.: Wadsworth Publ., 1982), 4.

15. Turner, *Lyndon Johnson's Dual War,* 184–85; Kathleen J. Turner, *Comic Creations of Women: A Century of Funnies Females,* chap. 1, in progress; also Turner, "Muting the Majority: Empowerment and Constraint in Depictions of Women in Comic Strips" (paper presented at the Southern States Communication Association Convention, Birmingham, Alabama, April 1990). See William B. Hesseltine, "Speech and History," *Central States Speech Journal* 12 (spring 1961): 178–79, for an early, albeit limited, articulation of this argument.

16. David M. Potter, "The Tasks of Research in American History," in *History and American Society: Essays of David M. Potter,* ed. Don E. Fehrenbacher (New York: Oxford University Press, 1973), 28–38. The characterizations of political and military history come from the revised edition of Barzun and Graff's *Modern Researcher* (New York: Harcourt, Brace, and World, 1970), 197; and from John Richard Green as quoted in Arthur Marwick, *The Nature of History,* 3d ed. (Chicago: Lyceum, 1989), 57.

17. Potter, "Tasks of Research," 33, 35.

18. This characterization of common perceptions comes from Benson, "History, Criticism, and Theory," 16.

19. Bruce E. Gronbeck, "The Rhetoric of Social-Institutional Change: Black Action at Michigan," in *Explorations of Rhetorical Criticism*, ed. G. P. Mohrmann, Charles J. Stewart, and Donovan J. Ochs (University Park: Pennsylvania State University Press, 1973), 98.

20. Robert G. Gunderson, "Reflections on History and Rhetorical Criticism," *The Speech Teacher* 35 (October 1986): 409.

21. Arthur Schlesinger Jr., "On the Writing of Contemporary History," *Atlantic Monthly*, March 1967, 74.

22. L. B. Meyer, *Music, the Arts, and Ideas: Patterns and Predictions in Twentieth-Century Culture* (Chicago: University of Chicago Press, 1967), 143; Charlotte Watkins Smith, *Carl Becker: On History and the Climate of Opinion* (Carbondale: Southern Illinois University Press, 1956), 47; Barzun and Graff, *Modern Researcher*, rev. ed., 8.

23. Ronald H. Carpenter assesses rhetorical dimensions of historical writing in the essays collected in *History as Rhetoric: Style, Narrative, and Persuasion* (Columbia: University of South Carolina Press, 1995). See especially his introductory chapter, "On Style and Narrative in History: A *Rhetorical* Perspective," 1–17.

24. Carr is quoted by Marwick, *Nature of History*, 21; see also 15–17, where Marwick articulates society's functional and poetic needs for history.

25. Jean-Paul Sartre, *L'Etre et Le Neant* (Paris: Gallimard, 1981), 49, as cited by Catharine Savage Brosman, *Reading Behind the Lines: The Interpretation of War*, Fall 1990 Mellon lecture (New Orleans: The Graduate School of Tulane University, 1991), 19.

26. Ronald H. Carpenter, "Frederick Jackson Turner and the Rhetorical Impact of the Frontier Thesis," *Quarterly Journal of Speech* 63 (April 1977): esp. 128; see also Ronald H. Carpenter, "America's Opinion Leader Historians on Behalf of Success," *Quarterly Journal of Speech* 69 (May 1983): 111–26.

27. John Berger, *Ways of Seeing* (New York: Penguin Books, 1972), 11.

28. Schlesinger, "On the Writing of Contemporary History," 74.

29. Pieter Geyl, *Napoleon: For and Against*, quoted by Arthur Schlesinger Jr. in "The Man of the Century," *American Heritage* 45 (May/June 1994), 84.

30. See, for example, discussions of the work of R. G. Collingwood in Barzun and Graff, *Modern Researcher*, 5th ed., 153, and Marwick, *Nature*, 291–94. Marwick argues that although Collingwood's ideas, including his contention that "every age must write history afresh," are provocative, they lend themselves to the implication that history is a "mere relativist fantasy" rather than "a cumulative body of knowledge" (290). For concise examples of the historical debate over Vietnam, see the three selections by Loren Baritz, Guenter Lewy, and Walter LeFeber on "Vietnam: Crisis in American Foreign Policy," in *Conflict and Consensus in Modern American History*, vol. 2, 7th ed., ed. Allen F. Davis and Harold D. Woodman (Lexington, Mass.: D. C. Heath, 1988), 465–509.

31. Warren, as cited by Brosman, *Reading Behind the Lines*, 9; George Orwell, *1984* (1949; New York: New American Library, 1961), 32.

32. Brosman argues that "the writers of history organize the events of

which they write according to, and out of, their own private necessities and the states of their own selves" (ibid., 8). Although individual predilections and prejudices clearly play a role in historical constructions, the significant role of society in generating, shaping, and fulfilling those predilections and prejudices cannot be denied.

33. W. H. Walsh, *Philosophy of History* (1951; repr., New York: Harper & Row, 1960), 24; see also David M. Potter, "Explicit Data and Implicit Assumptions in Historical Study," in *History and American Society*, esp. 20–22. The phrase "pictures in their heads" is borrowed from Walter Lippmann in *Public Opinion* (New York: Harcourt, Brace, 1922), chap. 1.

34. Marwick, *The Nature of History* (New York: Dell, 1970), 210. For some reason—perhaps his concern about perceptions of history as "mere relativist fantasy" cited in n. 30—Marwick deleted this delicious phrase from later editions of this work.

35. Stewart offers this paraphrase from H. M. and N. K. Chadwick's preface to *Growth of English Literature* in *The Last Enchantment* (New York: Fawcett-Crest, 1978), 480.

36. Gunderson, "Reflections," 410.

37. Kathleen J. Turner, "The Presidential Libraries as Research Facilities: An Analysis of Resources for Rhetorical Scholarship," *Communication Education* 35 (July 1986): 252.

38. Maurice Hungiville, "Footnotes for Journalists, Deadlines for Scholars," *Chronicle of Higher Education*, October 31, 1977, 32.

39. Carl L. Becker, "Everyman His Own Historian," *American Historical Review* 37 (January 1932), repr. in *The Historian as Detective: Essays on Evidence*, ed. Robin W. Winks (New York: Harper & Row, 1968), 19–20. Elsewhere Becker notes that historical facts are not "pebbles to be gathered in a cup"; see Smith, *Carl Becker*, 52.

40. Becker, "Everyman," 19.

41. Barzun and Graff, *Modern Researcher*, 5th ed., 134.

42. Robin G. Collingwood, *The Idea of History* (New York: Oxford University Press, 1956), repr. in Winks, *Historian as Detective*, 59.

43. Ray McKerrow, "Rhetoric as History: An Archeological Perspective," unpublished lecture, University of Alabama, Birmingham, Alabama, May 21, 1980, p. 2.

44. Susan J. Douglas, *Where the Girls Are: Growing Up Female with the Mass Media* (New York: Times Books/Random House, 1994), 9.

45. Warren I. Susman, *Culture as History: The Transformation of American Society in the Twentieth Century* (New York: Pantheon Books, 1973), xii.

46. Turner, *Comic Creations of Women*, chap. 1.

47. Potter, "Explicit Data," 22.

48. We know of some in the field who write fine rhetorical histories but who, unlike Professor Carpenter, would blanche at the label. Given the importance of symbols for creating our sense of reality, the reluctance to acknowledge the term is significant.

49. Anthony Brandt, "Morning on the Upper Delaware," *American Heritage* 45 (April 1994): 64.

1. Four Senses of Rhetorical History

1. Barnet Baskerville, "Must We All Be 'Rhetorical Critics'?" *Quarterly Journal of Speech* 63 (April 1977): 107–16.

2. William Norwood Brigance, ed., *A History and Criticism of American Public Address* (New York: McGraw-Hill, 1943), 2 vols.; Marie Kathryn Hochmuth, ed., *A History and Criticism of American Public Address*, vol. 3 (New York: Russell and Russell, 1955).

3. Kenneth Burke, "Language as Action: Terministic Screens," *On Symbols and Society*, ed. Joseph R. Gusfield (Chicago: University of Chicago Press, 1989), 115; repr. from *Language as Symbolic Action* (Berkeley and Los Angeles: University of California Press, 1966).

4. Baskerville, "Must We All?" 110.

5. Herbert A. Wichelns, "The Literary Criticism of Oratory," *Studies in Rhetoric and Public Speaking in Honor of James Albert Winans* (New York: Century, 1925), 181–216, esp. 209.

6. Compare Michael Leff, "Rhetorical Timing in Lincoln's 'House Divided' Speech," *The Van Zelst Lecture in Communication* (Evanston, Ill.: Northwestern University, 1983) with David Zarefsky, *Lincoln, Douglas, and Slavery: In the Crucible of Public Debate* (Chicago: University of Chicago Press, 1990), 43–46.

7. James Darsey, "Must We All Be Rhetorical Theorists? An Anti-Democratic Inquiry," *Western Journal of Communication* 58 (summer 1994): 164–81.

8. John Waite Bowers, "The Pre-Scientific Function of Rhetorical Criticism," *Essays on Rhetorical Criticism*, ed. Thomas R. Nilsen (New York: Random House, 1968), 126–45.

9. Kenneth Burke, *The Philosophy of Literary Form* (1941; repr., New York: Vintage, 1957), 94–96.

10. David Zarefsky, " 'Public Sentiment is Everything': Lincoln's View of Political Persuasion," *Journal of the Abraham Lincoln Association* 15 (summer 1994): 23–40.

11. Bruce E. Gronbeck, "Rhetorical History and Rhetorical Criticism—A Distinction," *Speech Teacher* 24 (November 1975): 310.

12. George C. Edwards III, "Presidential Rhetoric: What Difference Does It Make?" *Beyond the Rhetorical Presidency*, ed. Martin J. Medhurst (College Station: Texas A&M University Press, 1996), 199–217.

13. George Kennedy, *The Art of Persuasion in Greece* (Princeton: Princeton University Press, 1963); George Kennedy, *The Art of Rhetoric in the Roman World, 300 B.C.–A.D. 300* (Princeton: Princeton University Press, 1972); George Kennedy, *Classical Rhetoric and Its Christian and Secular Traditions from Ancient to Modern Times* (Chapel Hill: University of North Carolina Press, 1980); George Kennedy, *Greek Rhetoric Under Christian Emperors* (Princeton: Princeton University Press, 1983); George Kennedy, *A New History of Classical Rhetoric* (Princeton: Princeton University Press, 1994); Wilbur Samuel Howell, *Logic and Rhetoric in England, 1500–1700* (Princeton: Princeton University Press, 1956); Wilbur Samuel Howell,

Eighteenth-Century British Logic and Rhetoric (Princeton: Princeton University Press, 1971).

14. Edward Schiappa, *Protagoras and Logic: A Study in Greek Philosophy and Rhetoric* (Columbia: University of South Carolina Press, 1991).

15. For Poulakos's major book on the subject, see *Sophistical Rhetoric in Classical Greece* (Columbia: University of South Carolina Press, 1995).

16. See especially Michael Leff, *Decorum and Rhetorical Interpretation: The Later Humanistic Tradition and Contemporary Critical Theory* (Naples, Italy: Estratto da Vichiana, 1990).

17. Allan Megill and Donald N. McCloskey, "The Rhetoric of History," *The Rhetoric of the Human Sciences: Language and Argument in Scholarship and Public Affairs,* ed. John S. Nelson, Allan Megill, and Donald N. McCloskey (Madison: University of Wisconsin Press, 1987), 221–38.

18. David Zarefsky, "Causal Argument among Historians: The Case of the American Civil War," *Southern Speech Communication Journal* 45 (winter 1980): 187–205.

19. J. H. Hexter, "The Rhetoric of History," *Doing History* (Bloomington: Indiana University Press, 1971), 15–76; Hayden White, *Metahistory: The Historical Imagination in Nineteenth-Century Europe* (Baltimore: Johns Hopkins University Press, 1973); Hans Kellner, *Language and Historical Representation: Getting the Story Crooked* (Madison: University of Wisconsin Press, 1989); Nancy S. Struever, "Historical Discourse," *Handbook of Discourse Analysis,* vol. 1, *Disciplines of Discourse,* ed. Teun A. van Dijk (London: Academic Press, 1985), 249–71.

20. Stephen P. Depoe, *Arthur M. Schlesinger, Jr., and the Ideological History of American Liberalism* (Tuscaloosa: University of Alabama Press, 1994).

21. Richard E. Neustadt and Ernest R. May, *Thinking in Time: The Uses of History for Decision Makers* (New York: The Free Press, 1986).

22. The concept of cultural memory is examined in J. Robert Cox, "Cultural Memory and Public Moral Argument," *The Van Zelst Lecture in Communication* (Evanston, Ill.: Northwestern University, 1987).

23. Ernest J. Wrage, "Public Address: A Study in Social and Intellectual History," *Quarterly Journal of Speech* 33 (December 1947): 451–57.

24. Celeste Michelle Condit and John Louis Lucaites, *Crafting Equality: America's Anglo-African Word* (Chicago: University of Chicago Press, 1993).

25. David Zarefsky, "Subordinating the Civil Rights Issue: Lyndon Johnson in 1964," *Southern Speech Communication Journal* 48 (winter 1983): 103–18; letter from Joseph Medill to Abraham Lincoln, August 26 (?), 1858, Robert Todd Lincoln Collection of the Papers of Abraham Lincoln, reel 3, frames 1333–36, Library of Congress.

26. Leland M. Griffin, "When Dreams Collide: Rhetorical Trajectories in the Assassination of President Kennedy," *Quarterly Journal of Speech* 70 (May 1984): 111–31. For examples of the argument that escalation in Vietnam followed a predictable rhetorical trajectory, see Richard A. Cherwitz, "Lyndon Johnson and the 'Crisis' of Tonkin Gulf: A President's Justification of War," *Western Journal of Speech Communication* 42 (spring 1978):

93–104; F. M. Kail, *What Washington Said: Administration Rhetoric and the Vietnam War, 1949–1969* (New York: Harper & Row, 1973).

27. Hans Meyerhoff, *The Philosophy of History in Our Time* (Garden City, N.Y.: Doubleday, 1959), 10.

28. J. Michael Hogan, *The Nuclear Freeze Campaign: Rhetoric and Foreign Policy in the Telepolitical Age* (East Lansing: Michigan State University Press, 1994).

29. Theodore O. Windt Jr., *Presidents and Protesters: Political Rhetoric in the 1960s* (Tuscaloosa: University of Alabama Press, 1990).

30. David Zarefsky, *President Johnson's War on Poverty: Rhetoric and History* (Tuscaloosa: University of Alabama Press, 1986).

31. David Zarefsky, "Rhetorical Interpretations of the American Civil War," *Quarterly Journal of Speech* 81 (February 1995): 108–20.

32. Edward Connery Lathem, ed., *Bernard Bailyn on the Teaching and Writing of History* (Hanover, N.H.: University Press of New England, 1994), 12.

2. The Rhetorical Construction of History

1. The initial quotation is cited in Steven Weber, "The Myth Maker," *New York Times Magazine*, October 25, 1985, 76. The second quotation is from Michel-Rolph Trouillot, *Silencing the Past: Power and the Production of History* (Boston: Beacon Press, 1995), 5.

2. Carl Becker, *Everyman His Own Historian* (Croft, 1935), 235.

3. Hayden White, *Metahistory: The Historical Imagination in Nineteenth-Century Europe* (Baltimore: Johns Hopkins University Press, 1973).

4. Michael Calvin McGee, "In Search of the 'People': A Rhetorical Alternative," *Quarterly Journal of Speech* 61 (October 1975): 235–49 (emphasis in original).

5. Erik H. Erickson, *Life History and the Historical Moment* (New York: Norton, 1975), 114.

6. For a different account, from which part of this essay has been adapted, see Raymie McKerrow, "Perspectives on History and Argument," in *Proceedings of the Second International Conference on Argumentation*, ed. Frans H. van Eemeren, Rob Grootendorst, J. Anthony Blair, and Charles A. Willard (Amsterdam, The Netherlands: International Society of the Study of Argumentation, 1991), 5–12.

7. Hayden White, "The Politics of Historical Interpretation: Discipline and De-sublimation," in *The Politics of Interpretation*, ed. W. J. T. Mitchell (Chicago: University of Chicago Press, 1983): 128 (emphasis in original).

8. White, "Politics of Historical Interpretation," 128.

9. Nancy Struever, "Topics in History," *History and Theory*, Beiheft 19 (1980): 67.

10. Allen Megill and Donald McCloskey, "The Rhetoric of History," in *The Rhetoric of the Human Sciences*, ed. John S. Nelson, Allen Megill, and Donald McCloskey (Madison: University of Wisconsin Press, 1987), 221.

11. Kenneth Burke, *Language as Symbolic Action* (Berkeley: University of California Press, 1966), 45; see Raymie E. McKerrow, "Critical Rhetoric: Theory and Praxis," *Communication Monographs* 56 (June 1989): 102.

12. Raymie E. McKerrow, "Critical Rhetoric," 102. See Michael Calvin McGee, "A Materialist's Conception of Rhetoric," in *Explorations in Rhetoric*, ed. R. E. McKerrow (Glenview, IL: Scott, Foresman, & Co., 1982), 23–48.

13. Trouillot, *Silencing the Past*, 8.

14. Portions of this essay are adapted from E. Culpepper Clark, "Argument and Historical Analysis," in *Advances in Argumentation Theory and Research*, ed. J. Robert Cox and Charles A. Willard (Carbondale: Southern Illinois University Press, 1982), 298–317.

15. Jean E. Howard, "Towards a Postmodern, Politically Committed, Historical Practice," in *Uses of History: Marxism, Postmodernism and the Renaissance*, ed. Francis Baker, Peter Hulme, and Margaret Iverson (Manchester, England: Manchester University Press, 1991), 108–9.

16. Claude Lévi-Strauss, *The Savage Mind* (Chicago: University of Chicago Press, 1966), 257–58.

17. See Fred Weinstein, *History and Theory after the Fall: An Essay on Interpretation* (Chicago: University of Chicago Press, 1990).

18. Trouillot, *Silencing the Past*, 8.

19. White, "Politics of Historical Interpretation," 128.

20. See Michael Calvin McGee, "In Search of the 'People'" and Raymie E. McKerrow, "Critical Rhetoric."

21. Bernard Bailyn, "Commentary on Papers Presented at the Smithsonian Institution's Sixth International Symposium," in *Kin and Communities: Families in America*, ed. A. J. Lichtman and J. R. Challinor (Washington, D.C.: Smithsonian, 1979), 28.

22. Gigliola Rossini, "The Criticism of Rhetorical Historiography and the Ideal of Scientific Method: History, Nature and Science in the Political Language of Thomas Hobbes," in *The Language of Political Theory in Early-Modern Europe*, ed. Anthony Pagden (Cambridge: Cambridge University Press, 1987), 312–13.

23. Jörn Rüsen, "Rhetoric and Aesthetics of History: Leopold von Ranke," *History and Theory* 29 (1990): 192.

24. Stuart Clark, "The *Annales* Historians," in *The Return of Grand Theory in the Human Sciences*, ed. Quentin Skinner (Cambridge: Cambridge University Press, 1985), 189–90.

25. Emmanuel Le Roy Ladurie, *The Mind and Method of the Historian*, trans. Sian Reynolds and Ben Reynolds (Chicago: University of Chicago Press, 1981), 8.

26. Ladurie, *The Mind and Method of the Historian*, 9.

27. John H. Plumb, "How Freedom took Root in Slavery," *New York Review of Books* 22 (1975): 3.

28. Robert W. Fogel and Stanley L. Engerman, *Time on the Cross* (Boston: Little, Brown, & Co., 1974), 5.

29. Thomas Farrell, "Knowledge in Time: Toward an Extension of Rhetorical Form," in *Advances in Argumentation Theory and Research*, ed.

J. Robert Cox and Charles A. Willard (Carbondale: Southern Illinois University Press, 1982), 123.

30. See Chaim Perelman and Lucie Olbrechts-Tyteca, *The New Rhetoric: A Treatise on Argumentation*, trans. John W. Wilkinson and Purcell W. Weaver (Notre Dame, Ind.: University of Notre Dame Press, 1969); Charles A. Willard, *Argumentation and the Social Grounds of Knowledge* (University, Ala.: University of Alabama Press, 1983). The quotation is from Edward C. Reilly, "Richard M. Weaver versus the Neo-Conservatives: A Comparative Study in Ideological Argument" (master's thesis, University of Maine, 1990), 144.

31. Bruce Gronbeck, "The Argumentative Structures of Selected Eighteenth-Century British Political Histories," in *Argument and Critical Practices: Proceedings of the Fifth SCA/AFA Conference on Argumentation*, ed. Joseph W. Wenzel (Annandale, Va.: Speech Communication Association, 1987): 574.

32. Hayden White, "Rhetoric and History," in *Theories of History: Papers Read at a Clark Library Seminar*, ed. Hayden White and Frank E. Manuel (Los Angeles: University of California, 1978), 15.

33. Rex Martin, *Historical Explanation: Re-enactment and Practical Inference* (Ithaca, N.Y.: Cornell University Press, 1977), 44.

34. Jacques Barzun, "History: The Muse and Her Doctors," *American Historical Review* 77 (1972): 46.

35. Trouillot, *Silencing the Past*, 25.

36. Barzun, "History," 64.

37. Christopher Lloyd, *The Structure of History* (Oxford, England: Blackwell, 1993), 25.

38. See Dominick Lacapra, *Rethinking Intellectual History: Texts, Contexts, Language* (Ithaca, N.Y.: Cornell University Press, 1983); Lacapra, *History and Criticism* (Ithaca, N.Y.: Cornell University Press, 1985); Lacapra, "A Review of a Review," *Journal of the History of Ideas* 49 (1988): 677–87; Anthony Pagden, "The Linguistic Turn in Intellectual History," *Journal of the History of Ideas* 49 (1988): 519–29; Bryan D. Palmer, *Descent into Discourse: The Reification of Language and the Writing of Social History* (Philadelphia: Temple University Press, 1990).

39. Lacapra, *Rethinking Intellectual History*, 35.

40. Carole Blair and Mary Kahl, "Introduction: Revising the History of Rhetorical Theory," *Western Journal of Speech Communication* 54 (1990): 148.

41. For a sampling of recent work in conceptual history, see Terence Ball, *Transforming Political Discourse: Political Theory and Critical Conceptual History* (New York: Blackwell, 1988); Terence Ball, T. James Farr, and Russell L. Hanson, eds., *Political Innovation and Conceptual Change* (Cambridge: Cambridge University Press, 1989); Terence Ball and John G. A. Pocock, eds., *Conceptual Change and the Constitution* (Lawrence: University Press of Kansas, 1988); John G. A. Pocock, *Politics, Language, and Time: Essays on Political Thought and History* (New York: Atheneum, 1971); Pocock, "The Concept of a Language and the *Metier d'historien*: Some Considerations on

Practice," in *The Language of Political Theory in Early-Modern Europe,* ed. Anthony Pagden (Cambridge: Cambridge University Press, 1987): 19–38; Quentin Skinner, *The Return of Grand Theory in the Human Sciences* (Cambridge: Cambridge University Press, 1985).

42. Quentin Skinner, "The Idea of Negative Liberty: Philosophical and Historical Perspectives," in *Philosophy in History,* ed. Richard Rorty, J. B. Schneewind, and Quentin Skinner (Cambridge: Cambridge University Press, 1984), 201.

43. Richard Rorty, "The Historiography of Philosophy: Four Genres," in *Philosophy in History,* ed. Richard Rorty, J. B. Schneewind, and Quentin Skinner (Cambridge: Cambridge University Press, 1984): 50–53.

44. Ball, *Transforming Political Discourse,* 14.

45. Takis Poulakos, "Historiographies of the History of Rhetoric: A Brief History of Classical Funeral Orations," *Western Journal of Speech Communication* 54 (1990): 174.

3. The Rhetorics of the Past: History, Argument, and Collective Memory

1. Adam Smith, *Lectures on Rhetoric and Belles Lettres,* ed. John M. Lothian (1972; repr., London: Thomas Nelson and Sons, 1963); Joseph B. Priestley, *A Course of Lectures on Oratory and Criticism,* ed. Vincent L. Bevilacqua and Richard Murphy (1777; repr., Carbondale: Southern Illinois University Press, 1965); and Hugh Blair, *Lectures on Rhetoric and Belles Lettres,* ed. Harold F. Harding, 2 vols. (1783; repr., Carbondale: Southern Illinois University Press, 1963).

2. Smith, *Lectures,* 102.

3. Blair, *Lectures,* 2:260.

4. See especially Hayden White, *Metahistory: The Historical Imagination in Nineteenth-Century Europe* (Baltimore: Johns Hopkins University Press, 1973). The "rhetoric of history" also can be understood as the study of "historical discourse," the label given to this arena of study by Nancy Struever in her "Historical Discourse," in *Handbook of Discourse Analysis,* vol. 1, *Disciplines of Discourse,* ed. Teun A. van Dijk (New York: Academic Press, 1985), 249–71.

5. By scientific history I mean the work on the philosophy of history coming out of the 1950s that attempted to characterize epistemologically the nature of historical explanation as well as those who attempted to demonstrate that the past could be reconstructed on scientific principles. For summaries of the issues, see Fritz Stern, ed., *The Varieties of History: From Voltaire to the Present* (Cleveland: Meridian Books, 1956); Karl R. Popper, *The Poverty of Historicism* (New York: Harper & Row, 1957); George H. Nadel, ed., *Studies in the Philosophy of History* (New York: Harper & Row, 1965); William H. Dray, ed., *Philosophical Analysis and History* (New York: Harper & Row, 1966); Lee Benson, *Toward the Scientific Study of History: Se-*

lected Essays (Philadelphia: J. B. Lippincott Co., 1972); and Bruce E. Gronbeck, "Historical Explanation and Rhetorical Criticism" (paper presented to the Speech Communication Association convention, 1977). At the center of multiple controversies that have swirled around ideas of historical fact, historical explanation, and scientific history is the matter of objectivity; see Peter Novick, *That Noble Dream: The "Objectivity Question" and the American Historical Profession* (Cambridge: Cambridge University Press, 1988). Then, for good measure, with the coming of the young Marxist historians especially in England (see, e.g., nn. 23–25 below) and the blossoming of the so-called *Annales* ("total history") historians in the Sixth Section of the Ecole Pratique des Hautes Etudes in Paris, social and cultural history writing came to challenge almost all of the dominant schools of or approaches to history flowing from the pre–World War II era. See Lynn Hunt, ed., *The New Cultural History* (Berkeley: University of California Press, 1989), esp. her introduction, 1–22.

6. This argument is developed in Robert F. Berkhofer Jr., "The Challenge of Poetics to (Normal) Historical Practice," in *The Rhetoric of Interpretation and the Interpretation of Rhetoric,* ed. Paul Hernadi (Durham, N.C.: Duke University Press, 1989), 183–200. This essay is the foundation of chapter two of his book, *Beyond the Great Story: History as Text and Discourse* (Cambridge, Mass.: Belknap Press of Harvard University Press, 1995), 26–44. He calls the separation of the past from history writing about that past "dereferentialism" (see esp. 12–16). Nancy Struever argues that there are, rather, three sorts of discursive constructions of the past: history as narrative, history as rhetorically styled (the tropological project of Hayden White), and history as argument (see n. 4 above).

7. I develop the argument more fully in Bruce E. Gronbeck, "The Rhetoric of History: Eighteenth-Century British Political Histories" (Giles Wilkeson Gray lecture, Louisiana State University, 1987).

8. Michael J. Janas, "Rhetoric, History, and the Collective Memory: The Civil War in Contemporary America" (Ph.D. diss., University of Iowa, 1994); cf. John C. Nerone, "Professional History and Social Memory," *Communication* 11 (1989): 89–104.

9. See Allan Megill, "Disciplinary History and Other Kinds," in *Argument and Critical Practices: Proceedings of the Fifth SCA/AFA Conference on Argumentation,* ed. Joseph W. Wenzel (Annandale, Va.: Speech Communication Association, 1987), 557–64.

10. Its multiple utilities—and indeed even its multiple academic uses—have been the source of much anguish among scholars of history. The rise of the "new historicism," with its radical focus on discursive constructions as both data and method of composition within unabashedly poetic and political understandings of language, blew open metahistory; talk about history and history writing grew loud in the 1980s. Most of the resulting issues are discussed in H. Aram Veeser, ed., *The New Historicism* (New York: Routledge, 1989). This is not to say that the poets and politicians own history writing. Robert P. Newman, for example, excoriates the so-called Hiroshima cult for letting their politics ruin their ability to understand Truman's deci-

sion to drop the atomic bomb on August 6, 1945. See Newman's *Truman and the Hiroshima Cult*, Rhetoric and Public Affairs Series (East Lansing: Michigan State University Press, 1995).

11. The complex relationships between past and present negotiated via the concept of "tradition" are explored brilliantly in Edward Shils, *Tradition* (Chicago: University of Chicago Press, 1981). On the Confederate battle flag controversy, see Janas (n. 8 above).

12. Donald C. Bryant, *Rhetorical Dimensions in Criticism* (Baton Rouge: Louisiana State University Press, 1973), 14.

13. See John H. Hexter, *Reappraisals in History: New Views on History and Society in Early Modern Europe* (New York: Academy Library, Harper Torchbooks, 1961). For a useful discourse on three different ways of understanding the phrase "the rhetoric of history," see Struever (n. 4 above).

14. White, *Metahistory*, 17–18; quoted in Berkhofer, "Challenge," 186–87.

15. Kellner calls this creating a passage, a way to move between loci one has selected as beginnings and endings. See chapter three of Hans Kellner, *Language and Historical Representation: Getting the Story Crooked* (Madison: University of Wisconsin Press, 1989), 55–77.

16. William E. H. Lecky, *A History of England in the Eighteenth Century*, 8 vols. (New York: Longmans, Green, and Co., 1925).

17. William E. H. Lecky, *Democracy and Liberty*, 2 vols. (New York: Longmans, Green, and Co., 1886), 1:21.

18. Ibid., 1:21–22.

19. My understanding of the relationships between contexts and events is influenced by Michel Foucault's discussion of *episteme* in *The Order of Things: An Archaeology of the Human Sciences* (New York: Pantheon Books, 1971).

20. Jack P. Greene built an anthology that assembled economic, intellectual, political, moral-psychological, popular, and philosophical accounts of the American Revolution. See his *The Reinterpretation of the American Revolution, 1763–1789* (New York: Harper & Row, 1968).

21. Richard L. Bushman, *From Puritan to Yankee: Character and the Social Order in Connecticut, 1690–1765* (Cambridge, Mass.: Harvard University Press, 1967).

22. Kellner, *Language and Historical Representation*, 55.

23. E. P. Thompson, "Eighteenth-Century English Society: Class Struggle without Class?" *Social History* 3 (1978): 150. Notice that Thompson here is attempting a reconstruction of consciousness in the broadest possible way, characterizing a whole society in a manner reminiscent of some *Annales* historians (see n. 5 above); in his book on the English working class, however, he works at the other extreme—on the consciousness of individuals upon whom he finds inscribed the social evils of the age. Both the British Marxist and French *Annales* historians work within varied understandings of historical research.

24. E. P. Thompson, *The Making of the English Working Class* (New York: Pantheon Books, 1963), 12–13.

25. As well, Thompson's attacks not simply on institutionally closed his-

torians but especially on fellow Marxists who ignore history in their commitment to "theory" are legendary; see Gregor McLennan, "E. P. Thompson and the Discipline of Historical Context," in Richard Johnson, Gregor McLennan, Bill Schwarz, and D. C. Sutton, eds., *Making Histories: Studies in History-Writing and Politics* (London: Centre for Contemporary Cultural Studies, 1982), 96–130. McLennan's full version of various Marxist theories of history can be found in his *Marxism and the Methodologies of History* (London: NLB, 1981), chap. 10, 206–32.

26. Lecky, *History of England*, 5:261.

27. See, e.g., Bruce E. Gronbeck, "The Argumentative Structures of Selected Eighteenth-Century British Political Histories," in *Argument and Critical Practices*, 569–77. Cf. Janas (see n. 8 above).

28. See, e.g., Bill Schwarz, " 'The People' in History: The Communist Party Historians' Group, 1946–56," in Johnson et al., *Making Histories*, 44–95.

29. Interestingly, when discussing differences between broad and narrow histories, Maurice Mandelbaum goes to a map analogy; see *The Anatomy of Historical Knowledge* (Baltimore: Johns Hopkins University Press, 1977), 15–16. So, Lecky's examination of 1688–89 to 1832 in the name of offering a history of eighteenth-century England and Namier's intense examination of 1760 as a pivotal year in understanding the structure of eighteenth-century British politics would be, to Mandelbaum, simply maps offered on different scales. To be sure, Namier's study would have far more details about a particular year but presumably would fit cleanly inside the larger frame provided by Lecky. Mandelbaum recognized no differences in contexts when discussing the "anatomy" of history per se. See Lewis Namier, *The Structure of Politics at the Accession of George III*, 2d ed. (New York: St. Martin's Press, 1961).

30. William L. Shirer, *The Rise and Fall of the Third Reich: A History of Nazi Germany* (New York: Fawcett Publications, 1960); David G. McCullough, *Truman* (New York: Simon & Schuster, 1992).

31. For an interesting introduction to psychoanalytic history, see Barbara DeConcini, *Narrative Remembering* (Lanham, Md.: University Press of America, 1990).

32. See C. Behan McCullagh, *Justifying Historical Descriptions* (Cambridge: Cambridge University Press, 1984), for a technical reading of history writing and truth testing of and from the past.

33. Bruce E. Gronbeck, "Argument from History[1] and Argument from History[2]: Uses of the Past in Public Deliberation," in *Argument in Controversy: Proceedings of the Seventh SCA/AFA Conference on Argumentation*, ed. Donn W. Parson (Annandale, Va.: Speech Communication Association, 1991), 96–99.

34. Martin Luther King Jr., *I Have a Dream* (San Francisco: Harper San Francisco, 1993).

35. James B. Hanson, "Karl Marx and Fredrich Engels Defend the Communist Society: Refutation in *The Communist Manifesto*," in *Argument in Controversy*, 886–88.

36. Mandelbaum, *Anatomy of Historical Knowledge*, 66.

37. G. R. Boynton, "Talking a Good Story: Models of Argument; Models of Understanding in the Senate Agriculture Committee," in *Argument and Critical Practices*, 429–38.

38. Douglas Ehninger and Wayne Brockriede, *Decision by Debate* (New York: Dodd, Mead, & Co., 1963).

39. Chaim Perelman and Lucie Olbrechts-Tyteca, *The New Rhetoric: A Treatise on Argumentation*, trans. J. Wilkinson and P. Weaver (Notre Dame, Ind.: University of Notre Dame Press, 1969).

40. David Zarefsky, "Echoes of the Slavery Controversy in the Current Abortion Debate," in *Argument in Controversy*, 889–95.

41. The past also can be used to "re-member" the present, to reassemble for us now what has been left out of today's discussions. This view has been identified and explored in Marcuse's writings by J. Robert Cox in "Memory, Critical Theory, and the Argument from History," *Argumentation and Advocacy* 27 (1990): 1–13.

42. A. L. Rowse, *The Use of History*, new rev. ed. (New York: Collier, 1963), 20.

43. See Aristotle's *Memoria et Reminiscentia*, in *The Basic Works of Aristotle*, ed. Richard McKeon (New York: Random House, 1941), 607–17.

44. Claude Lévi-Strauss, "The Structural Study of Myth," in *Structural Anthropology*, trans. C. Jacobson and B. G. Schoepf (New York: Basic Books, 1963), 1:206–32.

45. Quoted in Barry Schwartz, Yael Zerubavel, and Bernice Barnett, "The Recovery of Masada: A Study in Collective Memory," *Sociological Quarterly* 27 (1986): 149.

46. Ibid.

47. Ibid., 140.

48. Quoted in Michael Kammen, *Mystic Chords of Memory: The Transformation of Tradition in American Culture* (New York: Alfred A. Knopf, 1991), 11.

49. Ibid., 13.

50. Quoted in Schwartz, Zerubavel, and Barnett, "Recovery of Masada," 155, 157.

51. Frances Yates, *The Art of Memory* (Chicago: University of Chicago Press, 1966), 1.

52. J. Frederick Reynolds, ed., *Rhetorical Memory and Delivery: Classical Concepts for Contemporary Composition and Communication* (Hillsdale, N.J.: Lawrence Erlbaum Associates, 1993).

53. See note 8 above.

54. See notes 8 and 41 above, as well as Michael Billig, "Collective Memory, Ideology, and the British Royal Family," in *Collective Remembering*, ed. David Middleton and Derek Edwards (London: Sage, 1990), 54–78; and John Nerone, "Professional History and Social Memory," *Communication* 11 (1989): 89–104.

55. Popular Memory Group, "Popular Memory: Theory, Politics, Method," in Johnson et al., *Making Histories*, 207.

56. Kammen, *Mystic Chords*, 704.

4. Theoretical Implications of Doing Rhetorical History: Groupthink, Foreign Policy Making, and Vietnam

1. E. B. White, "Farewell, My Lovely," *Essays of E. B. White* (New York: Harper & Row, 1977), 164.

2. Bruce E. Gronbeck, "Rhetorical History and Rhetorical Criticism: A Distinction," *Speech Teacher* 24 (1975): 310.

3. Roderick P. Hart, "Contemporary Scholarship in Public Address: A Research Editorial," *Western Journal of Speech Communication* 50, no. 3 (summer 1986): 283–95.

4. Martin J. Medhurst, "Public Address and Significant Scholarship: Four Challenges to the Rhetorical Renaissance," *Texts in Context,* ed. Michael C. Leff and Fred J. Kauffeld (Davis, Calif.: Hermagoras Press, 1989), 36.

5. Isocrates, "Antidosis," *Readings from Classical Rhetoric,* ed. Patricia P. Matsen, Philip Rollinson, Marion Sousa (Carbondale: Southern Illinois University Press, 1990), 249.

6. Marie Hochmuth Nichols, *Rhetoric and Criticism* (Baton Rouge: Louisiana State University Press, 1963), 20.

7. Hannah Arendt, *Between Past and Future* (New York: Viking, 1961), 45.

8. Aristotle, *Aristotle's Theory of Poetry and Fine Arts,* trans. S. H. Butcher (New York: Dover, 1951), 1447. Also, Paul Ricoeur has an interesting dicussion of mimesis in *Reflection and Imagination,* ed. Mario J. Valdes (Toronto: University of Toronto Press, 1991), 137–55.

9. A. Robert Caponigri, *Time and Idea: The Theory of History in Giambattista Vico* (Notre Dame, Ind.: University of Notre Dame Press, 1968), x.

10. Ibid., 55–56.

11. Kathleen J. Turner succinctly expresses this point of view in her paper, "Rhetorical History as Social Construction," presented at the Southern Speech Communication Association Convention in Tampa, Florida, April 1991.

12. Turner, "Rhetorical History."

13. Thomas W. Benson, "History, Criticism, and Theory in the Study of American Rhetoric," in *American Rhetoric: Context and Criticism,* ed. Thomas W. Benson (Carbondale: Southern Illinois University Press, 1989), 8.

14. John Nerone, "Theory and History," *Communication Theory* 3, no. 2 (May 1993): 148–57.

15. See, for instance, Ernest G. Bormann, *The Force of Fantasy* (Carbondale: Southern Illinois University Press, 1985); Karlyn K. Campbell, *Man Cannot Speak for Her* (New York: Praeger, 1989); Robert T. Oliver, *The Influence of Rhetoric in the Shaping of Great Britain* (Newark: University of Delaware Press, 1986); Kathleen J. Turner, *Lyndon Johnson's Dual War: Vietnam and the Press* (Chicago: University of Chicago Press, 1985); and David Zarefsky, *President Johnson's War on Poverty: Rhetoric and History* (Tuscaloosa: University of Alabama Press, 1986). These authors represent a small fraction of communication scholars doing rhetorical history research.

16. A short list of such works includes Peter Braestrup, *Vietnam as History* (Washington, D.C.: University Press of America, 1984); Frances Fitzgerald, *Fire in the Lake* (New York: Vintage Books, 1973); William Conrad Gibbons, *The U.S. Government and the Vietnam War, Part II* (New Jersey: Princeton University Press, 1986); R. B. Smith, *An International History of the Vietnam War* (New York: St. Martin's Press, 1985).

17. As far back as 1955 Edwin Black suggested using the language of rhetoric to look at "group discussion." See Edwin Benjamin Black, "A Consideration of the Rhetorical Causes of Breakdown in Discussion," *Speech Monographs* 22, no. 1 (March 1955): 15–19. Also, in the 1970s, Ernest G. Bormann and his students developed a distinctive rhetorical language for examining small group communication. See Ernest G. Bormann, "Fantasy and Rhetorical Vision: Ten Years Later," *Quarterly Journal of Speech* 68 (August 1982): 288–305.

18. Moya A. Ball, "Revisiting the Gulf of Tonkin crisis: an analysis of the private communication of President Johnson and his advisers," *Discourse and Society* 2, no. 3, (1991): 281–96.

19. Irving L. Janis, *Victims of Groupthink* (Boston: Houghton Mifflin, 1972).

20. Ibid., 13.

21. Irving L. Janis, *Groupthink: Psychological Studies of Policy Decisions and Fiascoes* (Boston: Houghton Mifflin, 1982).

22. Moya A. Ball, *Vietnam-on-the-Potomac* (New York: Praeger, 1992).

23. Group fantasy sharing is the process by which people experience symbolic convergence. Bormann (1982) writes that "[the term] symbolic suggests that we are dealing with signs and objects to which are attached meaning," and "convergence" indicates that the communication brings together two or more private worlds into a common view. Groups of people will thus share fantasy themes composed of imaginative communication that is couched in figurative language and story lines. When these themes are repeated, they can be classified into taxonomies or stock narratives, which Bormann labels "fantasy types."

24. Oral History Interview of Roswell Gilpatric by Dennis J. O'Brien, August 12, 1970, John F. Kennedy Library.

25. Oral History Interview of Robert F. Kennedy by John Martin, March 1, 1964, John F. Kennedy Library.

26. Oral History Interview of Gilpatric, August 12, 1970.

27. Transcript, telephone conversation between Forrestal and Hilsman, June 7, 1962, box 2, Hilsman Papers, John F. Kennedy Library.

28. Oral History Interview of Robert F. Kennedy by John B. Martin, February 28, 1964, John F. Kennedy Library.

29. For instance, some of those modifications included changes from the language of the New Frontier to a language that was reminiscent of the Old Frontier. President Johnson, in a committee meeting, said he wanted to make the South Vietnamese "good rangers" and that, if there were any security leaks, he would "shoot at sunrise." See handwritten notes of Executive Committee Meeting in Cabinet Room, December 1, 1964, box 1, Meeting Notes File, Papers of Lyndon B. Johnson, Lyndon Baines Johnson Library.

30. See talk by Bundy to Overseas Press Writers, February 26, 1964, attached to memorandum, Bundy to the President, March 10, 1964. Box 1, Aides File—Bundy, National Security Files, Lyndon Baines Johnson Library.

31. See memorandum, Klein to Bundy, April 2, 1965, boxes 11 and 12, Agency File, NSF, Lyndon Baines Johnson Library.

32. For example, a study by Courtright attempts to replicate Janis's groupthink in a laboratory setting, defining "cohesiveness" as "interpersonal attraction." John A. Courtright, "A Laboratory Investigation of Groupthink," *Communication Monographs* 45 (August 1978): 229–46. More recent works that seem to accept Janis's premise about groupthink and cohesiveness include Michael W. Mansfield, "Political Communication in Decision-Making Groups," *New Directions in Political Communication*, ed. David L. Swanson and Dan Nimmo (Newbury Park, Calif.: Sage, 1990): 255–304; and Rebecca J. Welch Cline, "Groupthink and the Watergate Cover-Up: An Illusion of Unanimity," *Group Communication in Context*, ed. Lawrence R. Frey (Hillsdale, N.J.: Lawrence Erlbaum Associates, 1994): 199–223. Cline recognizes that there is a group dynamic such as an illusion of unanimity; however, she does not appear to use her findings to question the nature of the relationship between cohesiveness and groupthink.

33. Graham T. Allison, *Essence of Decision: Explaining the Cuban Missile Crisis* (Boston: Little, Brown, & Company, 1971).

34. Robert P. Newman, "Foreign Policy: Decision and Argument," *Advances in Argumentation Theory and Research*, ed. J. Robert Cox and Charles Arthur Willard (Carbondale: Southern Illinois University Press, 1982).

35. For example, see memorandum, Rostow to President, April 21, 1961, box 64A, Staff Memoranda, President's Office Files, John F. Kennedy Library.

36. For an in-depth discussion of the cold war rhetorical vision, see John F. Cragan, "The Cold War Rhetorical Vision, 1946–1972" (Ph.D. diss., University of Minnesota, 1972).

37. In some respects President Kennedy triggered this aspect of the New Frontier's rhetorical vision when, in his inaugural address, he alluded to the passing of a torch to a "new generation of Americans born in this century." Gary Wills suggests that the Kennedy campaign had carefully crafted a non-Eisenhower persona; see *The Kennedy Imprisonment* (Boston: Little, Brown, & Company, 1981): 149.

38. Rusk used to refer to the North Vietnamese as "bandits"; see Memorandum for the Record, September 20, 1964, box 2, M. Bundy Memos, Aides file, NSF, Lyndon Baines Johnson Library. Other advisors labeled the North Vietnamese society "primitive," "yellowland," and a "bunch of bullies." See Sigma I-64 Critique, April 6–9, 1964, box 30–33, Agency File, NSF, Lyndon Baines Johnson Library.

39. This process was very similar to John Dewey's reflective thinking model in which a problem is defined, a situation analyzed, alternative solutions proposed, and a final solution chosen. I argue in *Vietnam-on-the-Potomac*, 168, that this classical model was used to justify a solution that had already emerged.

40. Terministic screens are discussed by Kenneth Burke in "Language as

Action: Terministic Screens," *On Symbols and Society*, ed. Joseph R. Gusfield (Chicago: University of Chicago Press, 1989): 114–22.

41. Thomas S. Kuhn, *The Essential Tension* (Chicago: The University of Chicago Press, 1977).

42. Author's conversations with archivists at the Kennedy and Johnson Presidential Libraries.

43. Larry Berman, *Planning a Tragedy* (New York: Norton, 1982); see also, for example, Pierre Salinger, *With Kennedy* (New York: Doubleday, 1966); Theodore C. Sorensen, *The Kennedy Legacy* (New York: Macmillan, 1969); and Michael Maclear, *The Ten Thousand Day War* (New York: Avon Books, 1981).

44. In June 1964 Walt Rostow complained about the president's stalling. Memorandum to William Bundy (brother of McGeorge Bundy), June 11, 1964, DSDOF, Lyndon Baines Johnson Library. See Ball, *Vietnam-on-the-Potomac;* and Kenneth Burke, *A Rhetoric of Motives* (New York: Prentice-Hall, 1950).

45. John M. Newman, *JFK and Vietnam* (New York: Warner Books, 1992).

46. In the Conference on Vietnam held at the Johnson Presidential Library in Austin, Texas, October 15–17, 1993, other scholars, such as William C. Gibbons, seemed to be reaching a similar conclusion.

47. Moya A. Ball, "A Case Study of the Kennedy Administration's Decision-making Concerning the Diem Coup of November, 1963," *Western Journal of Speech Communication* 54 (fall 1990): 557–74.

48. Summary record of National Security Council Meeting, October 2, 1963, 6:00 P.M., box 314, Meetings File, NSF, John F. Kennedy Library.

49. Memorandum, Walt Rostow to President Kennedy, July 1961, box 23-231, Regional Security Southeast Asia, NSF, John F. Kennedy Library. Also, a letter from Theodore H. White to President Kennedy in October 1961 expressed the possibility of allowing younger military officers to "knock off" Diem in a coup. See letter, 10/11/61, box 128, Vietnam 1960–61, President's Office Files, John F. Kennedy Library.

50. Memorandum, Ray S. Cline to Bundy, September 26, 1963, box 200-201, Countries File—Vietnam, NSF, John F. Kennedy Library.

51. Message, Bundy to Lodge and Harkins, October 24, 1963, box 200-201, Countries File—Vietnam, NSF, John F. Kennedy Library.

52. This paper reflects only a small portion of the knowledge generated. Perhaps one of the most controversial insights generated was that John F. Kennedy may have become the leader in death that he had not been in life. I do not doubt that President Kennedy was a socioemotional leader in his administration; I have doubts about his task leadership.

53. R. G. Collingwood, *The Idea of History*, rev. ed. (Oxford: Clarendon Press, 1993), 247–48.

54. Conference on Vietnam, Lyndon Baines Johnson Library, Austin, Texas, October 15–17, 1993.

55. Roland Barthes, quoted by D. P. Gaonkar, "Rhetoric and Its Double: Reflections on the Rhetorical Turn in the Human Sciences," *The Rhetorical Turn*, ed. Herbert W. Simon (Chicago: University of Chicago Press, 1990), 341.

56. Barney G. Glaser and Anselm Strauss, *The Discovery of Grounded Theory* (New York: Aldine Publishing Company, 1967).

57. Leonard C. Hawes, "Alternative Theoretical Bases: Toward a Presuppositional Critique," *Communication Quarterly* 25, no. 1 (winter 1977): 63–68.

58. Allan Janik and Stephen Toulmin, *Wittgenstein's Vienna* (New York: Simon & Schuster, 1973): 27.

5. A Constitutive Framework for Rhetorical Historiography: Toward an Understanding of the Discursive (Re)constitution of "Constitution"

1. See Ernest J. Wrage, "Public Address: A Study in Social and Intellectual History," *Quarterly Journal of Speech* 33 (1947): 451–57; Michael Calvin McGee, "The 'Ideograph': A Link Between Rhetoric and Ideology," *Quarterly Journal of Speech* 66 (1980): 1–16; Dilip Parameshwar Gaonkar, "The Oratorical Text: The Enigma of Arrival," *Texts in Context*, ed. Michael C. Leff and Fred J. Kauffeld (Davis, Calif.: Hermagoras Press, 1989), 255–75. My debt to Gaonkar's essay will become apparent in the course of this essay.

2. Gaonkar, "Oratorical Text," 273. Gaonkar elaborates on his analysis of the instrumentalist tradition in "The Idea of Rhetoric in the Rhetoric of Science," *Southern Communication Journal* 58 (1993): 258–95. I extend and qualify Gaonkar's analysis in "Instrumentalism, Contextualism, and Interpretation in Rhetorical Criticism," in William Keith and Alan G. Gross, eds., *Rhetorical Hermeneutics* (Albany: SUNY Press, 1997), 195–224. Some of the issues Gaonkar and I raise with respect to the instrumental tradition, in particular the way it tends to link critic to advocate and both to the immediate rhetorical situation, were anticipated by Thomas Nilsen. See Nilsen, "Criticism and Social Consequences," *Quarterly Journal of Speech* 42 (1956): 173–78.

3. Gaonkar, "Oratorical Text," 272. My project is a response to Stephen E. Lucas's call for a "thorough rethinking" of "the nature of rhetorical influence" in "The Schism in Rhetorical Scholarship," *Quarterly Journal of Speech* 67 (1981): 9.

4. Gaonkar, "Oratorical Text," 268; see also 275.

5. Ronald Beiner, *Political Judgment* (Chicago: University of Chicago Press, 1983), esp. 95–96.

6. Michael Leff, "Things Made by Words: Reflections on Textual Criticism," *Quarterly Journal of Speech* 78 (1992): 223–31.

7. Ernesto Laclau and Chantel Mouffe speak to the seeming paradox of the constitutive position: "The fact that every object is constituted as an object of discourse has nothing to do with whether there is a world external to thought, or with the realism/idealism opposition. An earthquake or the falling of a brick is an event that certainly exists, in the sense that it oc-

curs here and now, independently of my will. But whether their specificity as objects is constructed in terms of 'natural phenomena' or 'expressions of the wrath of God' depends upon the structuring of a discursive field. What is denied is not that objects exist externally to thought, but the rather different assertion that they could constitute themselves as objects outside any discursive condition of emergence." See *Hegemony and Socialist Strategy: Toward a Radical Democratic Politics* (London: Verso, 1985), 108.

8. Louis A. Montrose, "Professing the Renaissance: The Poetics and Politics of Culture," in H. Aram Veeser, ed., *The New Historicism* (New York: Routledge, 1989), 16.

9. My thinking on this distinction is indebted to a number of sources. On the intentional invitations of a text, see James Boyd White, *When Words Lose Their Meaning: Constitutions and Reconstitutions of Language, Character, and Community* (Chicago: University of Chicago Press, 1984), and Wayne Booth, *The Company We Keep: An Ethics of Fiction* (Berkeley: University of California Press, 1988). On the extensional release of potential energy, see Stephen Greenblatt, *Shakespearean Negotiations: The Circulation of Social Energy in Renaissance England* (Berkeley: University of California Press, 1988), esp. 1–20.

10. Booth, *Company We Keep*, 265. Booth's position on this issue is, I believe, essentially the same as Foucault's; both underscore the ubiquity of discursive forces that shape human existence. For example, see Michel Foucault, "The Subject and Power," in Hubert L. Dreyfus and Paul Rabinow, *Michel Foucault: Beyond Structuralism and Hermeneutics*, 2d ed. (Chicago: University of Chicago Press, 1983), 208–26.

11. On this point see James Farr, "Conceptual Change and Constitutional Innovation," in Terence Ball and J. G. A. Pocock, eds., *Conceptual Change and Constitution* (Lawrence: University Press of Kansas, 1988), 19.

12. Explicitly, see Maurice Charland, "Constitutive Rhetoric: The Case of the *Peuple Québécois*," *Quarterly Journal of Speech* 73 (1987): 133–50; less explicitly, see Michael Calvin McGee, "In Search of 'The People': A Rhetorical Alternative," *Quarterly Journal of Speech* 61 (1975): 235–49.

13. For example, in my study of discursive reconstitution in early American rhetoric, I focus on the interrelationship between alterations in thinking about liberty and virtue and the norms of the political culture. See James Jasinski, "The Feminization of Liberty, Domesticated Virtue, and the Reconstitution of Power and Authority in Early American Political Discourse," *Quarterly Journal of Speech* 79 (1993): 146–64.

14. Anthony Giddens, *Central Problems in Social Theory: Action, Structure and Contradiction in Social Analysis* (Berkeley: University of California Press, 1979), 43–44. Giddens claims that "the pressing task facing social theory today," and, I think it fair to interpolate, rhetorical theory, "is not to further the conceptual elimination of the subject, but on the contrary to promote *a recovery of the subject* without lapsing into subjectivism" or a commitment to a kind of existential autonomy (44; emphasis in original). See also Giddens, *Modernity and Self-Identity: Self and Society in the Late Modern Age* (Stanford: Stanford University Press, 1991). For an indi-

rect extension of Giddens's perspective in discourse analysis, see George Kamberalis and Karla Scott, "Other People's Voices: The Co-Articulation of Texts and Subjectivities," *Linguistics and Education* 4 (1992): 354–403.

15. See Stephen Greenblatt, *Renaissance Self-Fashioning: From More to Shakespeare* (Chicago: University of Chicago Press, 1980). For a somewhat more radical approach to the process of self-constitution, see the essays collected in Deborah Battaglia, ed., *Rhetorics of Self-Making* (Berkeley: University of California Press, 1995).

16. Carroll Smith-Rosenberg, "Dis-Covering the Subject of the 'Great National Discussion,' 1786–1789," *Journal of American History* 79 (1992): 841–73. Smith-Rosenberg's essay should be of particular interest to rhetorical historians given her contention that "we must move . . . from the history of political ideas to the history of political *rhetoric*" (845; emphasis in original).

17. My thinking on this subject has been influenced by Giddens, 198–233, and Stephen Kern, *The Culture of Time and Space, 1880–1918* (Cambridge: Harvard University Press, 1983). I have begun to explore this dimension in "Civic Revitalization and the Time/Space Dynamics of Antebellum Public Address" (paper presented at the Speech Communication Association Convention, San Francisco, Calif., 1989). I draw from that paper in my discussion.

18. J. Robert Cox, "The Fulfillment of Time: King's 'I Have a Dream' Speech (August 28, 1963)," and Robert Hariman, "Time and the Reconstitution of Gradualism in King's Address: A Response to Cox," in *Texts in Context*, 181–204, 205–17.

19. See the discussion of "presence" in Chaim Perelman and Lucie Olbrechts-Tyteca, *The New Rhetoric: A Treatise on Argumentation*, trans. J. Wilkinson and P. Weaver (Notre Dame, Ind.: University of Notre Dame Press, 1969), 115–20, 142–79.

20. Kern, *Culture*, 153.

21. Bruce James Smith, *Politics and Remembrance: Republican Themes in Machiavelli, Burke, and Tocqueville* (Princeton: Princeton University Press, 1985), xi.

22. J. G. A. Pocock, *The Machiavellian Moment: Florentine Political Thought and the Atlantic Republican Tradition* (Princeton: Princeton University Press, 1975).

23. David Carr, *Time, Narrative, and History* (Bloomington: Indiana University Press, 1986), esp. 163–68.

24. Communal reconstitution is a key theme in White's *When Words Lose Their Meaning* and in his essay "Heracles' Bow: Persuasion and Community in Sophocles' *Philoctetes*," in *Heracles' Bow: Essays on the Rhetoric and Poetics of the Law* (Madison: University of Wisconsin Press, 1985). I explore an element of communal reconstitution, the issue of norms or bonds of affiliation, in James Jasinski, "(Re)constituting Community through Narrative Argument: *Eros* and *Philia* in *The Big Chill*," *Quarterly Journal of Speech* 79 (1993): 467–86. Communal reconstitution is, I would argue, an aspect of many epideictic performances, although rhetorical critics have not developed this relationship as well as they might. One example that does

bring this issue to the surface to at least some degree is Celeste Michelle Condit, "The Function of Epideictic: The Boston Massacre Oration as Exemplar," *Communication Quarterly* 33 (1985): 284–98.

25. Murray Edelman, *Constructing the Political Spectacle* (Chicago: University of Chicago Press, 1988), 103.

26. Giddens, *Central Problems*, 220.

27. In rhetorical studies, see Stephen E. Lucas's discussion of how Paine's *Common Sense* helped reconstitute American political discourse in *Portents of Rebellion: Rhetoric and Revolution in Philadelphia, 1765–76* (Philadelphia: Temple University Press, 1976), esp. 254–62. See also Celeste Michelle Condit and John Louis Lucaites's study of the reconstitution of "equality" in *Crafting Equality: America's Anglo-African Word* (Chicago: University of Chicago Press, 1993). For similar projects not grounded in contemporary rhetorical studies, see David Green, *Shaping Political Consciousness: The Language of Politics in America from McKinley to Reagan* (Ithaca, N.Y.: Cornell University Press, 1987), and Daniel T. Rodgers, *Contested Truths: Keywords in American Politics since Independence* (New York: Basic Books, 1987).

28. Giddens, *Central Problems*, 218 (emphasis in original in first passage, emphasis added in the second passage).

29. This approach to intentions and textual production can be found in Kenneth Burke, *A Grammar of Motives* (Berkeley: University of California Press, 1969), and Mikhail Bakhtin, *The Dialogic Imagination*, ed. M. Holquist, trans. C. Emerson and M. Holquist (Austin: University of Texas Press, 1981). With respect to Burke, Robert Wess argues that his "new rhetoric decenters the rhetor in introducing a level of motivation beyond its deliberate control." See Robert Wess, *Kenneth Burke: Rhetoric, Subjectivity, Postmodernism* (Cambridge: Cambridge University Press, 1996), 189.

30. On the problem of intentions in rhetorical history, see Condit and Lucaites, *Crafting Equality*, 255.

31. Richard Rorty, *Contingency, Irony, and Solidarity* (Cambridge: Cambridge University Press, 1989), 6, 16.

32. Bernard Bailyn, *The Ideological Origins of the American Revolution* (Cambridge: Harvard University Press, 1967), 204–5.

33. I would argue that Bailyn inversely mirrors Rorty in terms of how they would explain conceptual change. Rorty privileges metaphor, whereas Bailyn understands language, or at least the language practices of the American colonists, as fundamentally "expository and explanatory: didactic, systematic, and direct, rather than imaginative and metaphoric" (19). I agree with Rorty that it is difficult to invent a new language, or describe how others invented a new language, without recourse to metaphor. But I also think Rorty goes too far in valorizing metaphor.

34. See Farr, "Conceptual Change and Constitutional Innovation," and James Farr, "Understanding Conceptual Change Politically," *Political Innovation and Conceptual Change*, ed. Terence Ball, James Farr, and Russell Hanson (Cambridge: Cambridge University Press, 1989), 24–49. The conceptual histories in *Political Innovation* illustrate the conceptual history project.

35. Farr, "Conceptual Change," 16; Farr, "Understanding," 32.

36. Farr, "Understanding," 33–34 (emphasis in original).

37. Farr, "Conceptual Change," 23–26 (emphasis in original); see also "Understanding," 35–36.

38. Farr, "Understanding," 38–39 (emphasis in original).

39. My point is similar to the critique of the conceptual history tradition developed by McKerrow, who notes that "even though they clearly understand a 'structurational' perspective on language, they lack a vocabulary for expressing it as part of their argument." Raymie E. McKerrow, "Perspectives on Historiography and Argument," *Proceedings of the Second International Conference on Argumentation*, ed. Frans H. van Eemeren et al. (Amsterdam: SICSAT, 1991), 9.

40. Perelman and Olbrechts-Tyteca, *New Rhetoric*, 201–5; Charles Madigan, *Chicago Tribune*, August 15, 1993, sec. 4, p. 7.

41. I explore the constitutive potential of the oxymoron in James Jasinski, "Antithesis and Oxymoron: Ronald Reagan's Figurative Rhetorical Structure," *Reagan and Public Discourse in America*, ed. Michael Weiler and W. Barnett Pearce (Tuscaloosa: University of Alabama Press, 1992), 121–34. See also Robert G. Gunderson, "The Oxymoron Strain in American Rhetoric," *Central States Speech Journal* 28 (1977): 92–95.

42. Farr, "Conceptual Change," 23.

43. Among the many studies, Charles H. McIlwain's *Constitutionalism: Ancient and Modern* (1940; repr., Ithaca, N.Y.: Cornell University Press, 1947) is a (frequently contested) classic, as is J. W. Gough, *Fundamental Law in English Constitutional History* (London: Oxford University Press, 1955). For recent studies I found useful, see Herman Belz, "Constitutionalism and the American Founding," in Leonard W. Levy and D. J. Mahoney, eds., *The Framing and Ratification of the Constitution* (New York: Macmillan, 1987), 333–54; Stanley N. Katz, "The American Constitution: A Revolutionary Interpretation," in Richard Beeman, Stephen Botein, and Edward C. Carter II, eds., *Beyond Confederation: Origins of the Constitution and American National Identity* (Chapel Hill: University of North Carolina Press, 1987), 23–37; Graham Maddox, "Constitution," in *Political Innovation*, 50–67; and Gerald Stourzh, "Constitution: Changing Meanings of the Term from the Early Seventeenth to the Late Eighteenth Century," in *Conceptual Change*, 35–54.

44. McIlwain, *Constitutionalism*, 72–73.

45. Thomas Hobbes, *Leviathan* (London: Everyman, 1994), 122.

46. Gough, *Fundamental Law*, 117–20; 170–71; see also Bailyn, *Ideological Origins*, 198–201.

47. Maddox, "Constitution," 63.

48. Gordon Wood, *The Creation of the American Republic, 1776–1787* (New York: Norton, 1972), 292.

49. *The Federalist Papers*, ed. C. Rossiter (New York: New American Library, 1961), 331. Subsequent references will be made parenthetically in the text. I say "with a touch of hyperbole" because one of the problems of the Confederation period noted by advocates for constitutional reform was

the inability of state constitutions to prevent state legislatures from becoming a "vortex" of power, thereby violating their constitution and the "rules of justice." See Wood, *Creation*, 403–9.

50. On the importance of textuality and "printedness" in resolving the paradox of sovereignty, see Michael Warner, "Textuality and Legitimacy in the Printed Constitution," in *The Letters of the Republic: Publication and the Public Sphere in Eighteenth-Century America* (Cambridge: Harvard University Press, 1990), 97–117. My analysis in this section focuses on one part, the reconstruction of the idea of limitation, of a very complex conceptual development. A central issue that I cannot consider fully in the context of this essay is the reconstitution of sovereignty, specifically how the "radical" seventeenth-century concept of the "popular sovereignty" becomes appropriated by "conservative" constitutional reformers in the late 1780s and is used to explain and justify the new American system. Important work on this topic includes Edmund S. Morgan, *Inventing the People: The Rise of Popular Sovereignty in England and America* (New York: Norton, 1988); Jack P. Greene, *Peripheries and Center: Constitutional Development in the Extended Polities of the British Empire and the United States, 1607–1788* (Athens: University of Georgia Press, 1986), esp. 200–207; and Peter S. Onuf, *The Origins of the Federal Republic: Jurisdictional Controversies in the United States, 1775–1787* (Philadelphia: University of Pennsylvania Press, 1983), esp. 198–207.

51. On the Jeffersonian tradition, see Garry Wills, *Explaining America: The Federalist* (New York: Penguin Books, 1981), 47–48.

52. On this issue, see David F. Epstein, *The Political Theory of The Federalist* (Chicago: University of Chicago Press, 1984), 40–50.

53. Wills, *Explaining America*, 47.

54. Epstein, *Political Theory*, 42.

55. My understanding of distinctions and their relationship to dissociative structures has been informed by David Goodwin, "Distinction, Argumentation, and the Rhetorical Construction of the Real," *Argumentation and Advocacy*, 27 (1991): 141–58; and Goodwin, "The Dialectic of Second-Order Distinctions: The Structure of Arguments about Fallacies," *Informal Logic* 14 (1992): 11–22. I want to thank Joe Wenzel for calling my attention to Goodwin's work.

56. Greene (in *Peripheries*) discusses how the Federalists in 1787 responded to the traditional "imperium in imperio objection" brought by some Antifederalists (203). Although insightful, Greene does avoid discussing the way Federalists also appropriated the objection. In #15 Hamilton attacks the opposition for "aim[ing] at things repugnant and irreconcilable; at an augmentation of federal authority without a diminution of State authority; at sovereignty in the Union and complete independence in the members. They still, in fine, seem to cherish with blind devotion the political monster of an *imperium in imperio*" (108).

57. In McIlwain's terms, the sovereign is limited to the realm of *gubernaculum* and considered supreme within it, thereby securing the realm of *jurisdictio*. McIlwain terms this the "prime principle of medieval constitutionalism" (77–79). An important question in both pre- and early modern

debates, which I cannot go into here, is whether absolute sovereign power could be arbitrary.

58. See sources cited in note 50 above.

59. On the divisibility of sovereignty, see Epstein, *Political Theory*, 45–50; Green, *Peripheries*, 203–7; Onuf, *Origins*, 198–207.

60. Skepticism regarding "parchment" barriers can be detected in the political pamphlets of seventeenth-century England. In *Leviathan* Hobbes noted "that Covenants being but words, and breath, have no force to oblige, contain, constrain, or protect any man," and the anonymous author of the pamphlet *Touching the Fundamental Laws, or Politique Constitution of this Kingdom* contrasted a Constitution "written in the very heart of the Republique" with the inferior sort produced by "pen and paper" (quoted in Gough, 100).

61. On the linguistic anxiety of the founding period, see Thomas Gustafson, *Representative Words: Politics, Literature, and the American Language, 1776–1865* (Cambridge: Cambridge University Press, 1992), esp. 195–298.

62. Wood, *Creation*, 266.

63. Epstein, *Political Theory*, 45, 47 (emphasis in original).

64. See Katz, "The American Constitution," 23–37.

6. Oaths Registered in Heaven: Rhetorical and Historical Legitimacy in the Inaugural Addresses of Jefferson Davis and Abraham Lincoln

1. John Morley, *The Life of William Ewart Gladstone*, 2 vols. (New York: Macmillan, 1911), 1:78–79. Gladstone's enunciation of this belief was generally regarded as a *faux pas;* he himself admitted that it was a gross indiscretion. Sources discussing the debate over British recognition of the Confederacy are numerous. See, e.g., Philip Magnus, *Gladstone* (New York: E. P. Dutton, 1964), 153–54; Donaldson Jordan and Edwin J. Pratt, *Europe and the American Civil War* (Boston: Houghton Mifflin, 1931), 113–19; D. P. Crook, *The North, the South, and the Powers, 1861–1865* (New York, 1964), 227–29; Howard Jones, *Union in Peril: The Crisis over British Intervention in the Civil War* (Chapel Hill: University of North Carolina Press, 1992), 182–86. A rhetorical perspective on the speech is found in Walter R. Fisher, "Gladstone's Speech at Newcastle-on-Tyne," *Speech Monographs* 26 (November 1959): 255–62.

2. Channing, quoted in Drew Gilpin Faust, *The Creation of Confederate Nationalism: Ideology and Identity in the Civil War South* (Baton Rouge: Louisiana State University Press, 1988), 2; Faust, 6.

3. Faust, *Creation*, 6; for a critical review of historical research related to the questions of why the South lost the war, see James M. McPherson, "American Victory, American Defeat," in *Why the Confederacy Lost*, ed. Gabor S. Boritt (New York: Oxford University Press, 1992), 17–42. Of special relevance is McPherson's discussion of permutations of the "internal conflict" thesis.

4. Carl Degler, "One Among Many: The United States and National Unification," in *Lincoln, the War President*, ed. Gabor S. Boritt (New York: Oxford University Press, 1992), 97–98.

5. David Zarefsky and Victoria J. Gallagher, "From 'Conflict' to 'Constitutional Question': Transformations in Early American Public Discourse," *Quarterly Journal of Speech* 76 (August 1990): 247–61.

6. Faust, *Creation*, 6.

7. William Tecumseh Sherman, *Memoirs of General W. T. Sherman* (New York: Library of America, 1990), 180–81; Grady McWhiney, *Braxton Bragg and Confederate Defeat* (Tuscaloosa: University of Alabama Press, 1991), 154.

8. Lynda Lasswell Crist and Mary Seaton Dix, eds., *The Papers of Jefferson Davis*, 8 vols. (Baton Rouge: Louisiana State University Press, 1971–1994), 7:36–37.

9. *Papers of Jefferson Davis*, 7:40–45; William C. Davis, *Jefferson Davis: The Man and His Hour* (New York: HarperCollins, 1991), 303–6.

10. Eric H. Walther, *The Fire-Eaters* (Baton Rouge: Louisiana State University Press, 1992), 151–52; William Kauffman Scarborough, ed., *The Diary of Edmund Ruffin*, vol. 1, *Toward Independence October 1856–April 1861* (Baton Rouge: Louisiana State University Press, 1972), 483.

11. Brooks D. Simpson, *Let Us Have Peace: Ulysses S. Grant and the Politics of War and Reconstruction, 1861–1868* (Chapel Hill: University of North Carolina Press, 1991), 9.

12. E. Merton Coulter, *The Confederate States of America 1861–1865* (Baton Rouge: Louisiana State University Press, 1950), 14–15; N. B. Beck, "The Secession Debate in Georgia, November 1860–January 1861," *Antislavery and Disunion: Studies in the Rhetoric of Compromise and Conflict*, ed. J. Jeffery Auer (New York: Harper & Row, 1963), 353; William B. Hesseltine and Larry Gara, "New Governors Speak for War, January 1861," *Antislavery and Disunion*, 368–69, 372; Robert G. Gunderson, *The Old Gentlemen's Convention: The Washington Peace Conference of 1861* (Madison: University of Wisconsin Press, 1961), 9–10.

13. *Macon Daily Telegraph*, April 23, 1861; Duane E. Tucker, "Carl Schurz's Republican Jubilation Speech, November 16, 1860," in *Antislavery and Disunion*, 286–87; Ulysses S. Grant, *Personal Memoirs of U. S. Grant*, 2 vols. (New York, 1885), 1:218.

14. *The Diary of Edmund Ruffin*, 1:492–93, 588.

15. *Congressional Globe*, 36th Cong., 2d sess., 1440; Wendell Phillips, *Speeches, Lectures, and Letters* (Boston, 1863), 294–313; Gunderson, *Old Gentlemen's Convention*, 5.

16. Lincoln, *Speeches and Writings, 1859–1965*, 190, 194.

17. Lincoln, *Speeches and Writings, 1859–1965*, 202, 210; Robert G. Gunderson, "Lincoln and the Policy of Eloquent Silence: November 1860 to March 1861," *Quarterly Journal of Speech* 47 (February 1961): 1–9.

18. Lincoln, *Speeches and Writings, 1859–1865*, 200, 201; *Cleveland Plain Dealer*, February 12, 1861, *Lexington Kentucky Statesman*, February 19, 1861, cited in Gunderson, "Eloquent Silence," 4–5.

19. Lincoln, *Speeches and Writings, 1859–1865*, 207, 209.

20. Lincoln, *Speeches and Writings, 1859–1865,* 214, 211, 205, 206, 211, 207.

21. Sherman, *Memoirs,* 184.

22. John Quincy Adams, "Inaugural Address," March 4, 1825, *Inaugural Addresses,* 47; Martin Van Buren, "Inaugural Address," March 4, 1837, *Inaugural Addresses,* 67.

23. The debate over the Foot Resolution, of which Webster's and Hayne's speeches—and Thomas Hart Benton's speeches—were an important part, took place in January 1839 and can be found in *Register of Debates,* 21st Cong., 1st sess. Thomas Hart Benton offers his view of the famous debate in *Thirty Years' View,* 2 vols. (New York, 1856), 1:130–43. For a description of the debate and Madison's reaction see Maurice Baxter's definitive biography of Webster, *One and Inseparable: Daniel Webster and the Union* (Cambridge, Mass.: Belknap Press, 1984), 179–91.

24. Lincoln, "Address at Cooper Institute, New York," February 27, 1860, *Speeches and Writings, 1859–1865,* 111–17. For an excellent rhetorical assessment of the address see Michael C. Leff and G. P. Mohrmann, "Lincoln at Cooper Union: A Rhetorical Analysis of the Text," *Quarterly Journal of Speech* 40 (October 1974): 346–58.

25. "James Wilson's Summation and Final Rebuttal," December 11, 1787, in *The Debate on the Constitution: Federalist and Antifederalist Speeches, Articles, and Letters during the Struggle over Ratification, Part One: September 1787 to February 1788* (New York: The Library of America, 1993), 836–37.

26. "Patrick Henry's Opening Speech: A Wrong Step Now and the Republic Will Be Lost Forever," *The Debate on the Constitution, Part Two: January to August, 1788,* 596–97.

27. All quotations from Davis's Inaugural Address are taken from *Papers of Jefferson Davis,* 7:46–50; specific page numbers of quotations are indicated in the text. Quotations from the various presidential inaugurals are taken from *Inaugural Addresses,* as are quotations from Lincoln's First Inaugural, 119–26; page numbers of quotations are indicated in the text.

28. In none of these states had a popular referendum on secession been held. Texas did hold an election to ratify the session ordinance on February 23 (34,000 plus were for secession, whereas 11,000 were opposed), but this, of course, took place after the state government had already committed itself to the Confederacy. Virginia and Tennessee were the only other states of the Confederacy to seek ratification of secession through a popular referendum.

29. *Webster and Hayne's Speeches in the United States Senate on Mr. Foot's Resolution of January, 1830. Also, Daniel Webster's Speech in the United States Senate, March 7, 1850, on the Slavery Compromise* (Philadelphia: T. B. Peterson & Brothers, n.d.), 69–70.

30. *New York Evening Post,* February 18, 1861, in *Northern Editorials on Secession,* 2 vols., Howard Cecil Perkins, ed. (New York & London: D. Appleton-Century, 1942), 607.

31. Strong quoted in Allan Nevins, *The Ordeal of the Union,* 6 vols. (New York & London: Charles Scribners' Sons, 1950), 4:458.

32. See William C. Davis, *A Government of Our Own*, 165; Louis T. Wigfall to Jefferson Davis, February 18, 1861, *Papers of Jefferson Davis*, 7:51.

33. Cited in John Niven, *John C. Calhoun and the Price of Union* (Baton Rouge: Louisiana State University Press, 1988), 173.

34. For a discussion of the debate in England over the recognition of the Confederacy, see James R. Andrews, "The Rhetorical Shaping of National Interest: Morality and Contextual Potency in John Bright's Parliamentary Speech against Recognition of the Confederacy," *Quarterly Journal of Speech* 79 (February 1993): 40–60.

35. Cited in Dorothy Stirling, *Ahead of Her Time: Abby Kelley and the Politics of Antislavery* (New York: Norton, 1991), 315.

7. Borderland Denouement: Missourians and the Rhetorical Inauguration of the "Unholy Crusade," Spring 1861

1. William S. Stewart [to Samuel and Margaret Stewart], March 17, 1861, in the "William S. Stewart Letters, January 13, 1861, to December 4, 1862," ed. Harvey L. Carter and Norma L. Peterson, *Missouri Historical Review* 61, no. 2 (January 1967): 203–4; *Liberty (Mo.) Weekly Tribune*, March 22, 1861, p. 2, col. 3.

2. Thomas L. Snead, *The Fight for Missouri, From the Election of Lincoln to the Death of Lyon* (New York: Charles Scribner's Sons, 1886), 93–94; *Columbia Missouri Statesman*, April 5, 1861, p. 2, col. 1.

3. This essay is drawn from a much larger project that examined the first year of the Civil War in Missouri from a social movement perspective. A fundamental premise of this project was that events such as the war—taken as an attempted political "revolution"—do not happen suddenly but rather unfold over time. To trace the development and radicalization of public argument leading toward revolutionary activity, the project viewed this process as occurring in six stages. This essay, focusing on what I have called "rhetorical estrangement," explores the fourth stage of the revolutionary process.

4. "Journal of the State Convention," in *Journal and Proceedings of the Missouri State Convention, Held at Jefferson City and St. Louis, March 1861* (St. Louis: George Knapp & Company, Printers and Binders, 1861), 36.

5. *Liberty (Mo.) Weekly Tribune*, March 29, 1861, p. 2, col. 1; *St. Joseph (Mo.) Free Democrat*, March 30, 1861, p. 2, col. 1; *St. Louis (Mo.) Herald*, n.d., in the *Weekly California (Mo.) News*, March 30, 1861, p. 2, col. 5; *Bolivar (Mo.) Weekly Courier*, March 16, 1861, p. 2, col. 1.

6. *St. Louis (Mo.) Herald*, n.d., in the *Weekly California (Mo.) News*, April 13, 1861, p. 1, col. 5; William S. Stewart [to Samuel and Margaret Stewart], April 7, 1861, in the "William S. Stewart Letters," 205.

7. *Liberty (Mo.) Tribune*, April 12, 1861, p. 2, col. 1; *Richmond, Mo., North-West Conservator*, April 12, 1861, p. 2, col. 1.

8. Two especially helpful accounts of the Fort Sumter affair are Abner

Doubleday, "From Moultrie to Sumter," in *Battles and Leaders of the Civil War, Being for the Most Part Contributions by Union and Confederate Officers*, ed. Robert Underwood Johnson and Clarence Clough Buel (New York: The Century Company, 1887–1888), 1:40–49; and Stephen D. Lee, "The First Step in the War," in *Battles and Leaders of the Civil War*, 1:74–81.

9. *Liberty (Mo.) Tribune*, April 12, 1861, p. 2, col. 1; *St. Louis Daily Missouri Republican*, April 14, 1861, p. 2, col. 1.

10. Abraham Lincoln, "By the President of the United States: A Proclamation," April 15, 1861; Simon Cameron [to C. F. Jackson], April 15, 1861; both in *The War of the Rebellion: A Compilation of the Official Records of the Union and Confederate Armies* (Washington: Government Printing Office, 1881–1901), series 3, vol. 1, 67–68, 68–69 [hereafter cited as *O.R.*].

11. *Liberty (Mo.) Tribune*, April 19, 1861, p. 2, col. 5; *St. Louis Daily Missouri Republican*, April 16, 1861, p. 2, col. 1; *Huntsville (Mo.) Randolph Citizen*, April 16, 1861, p. 2, col. 1.

12. B[eriah] Magoffin to Simon Cameron, April 15, 1861, in *O.R.*, series 3, vol. 1, 70; John W. Ellis to Simon Cameron, April 15, 1861, in *O.R.*, series 3, vol. 1, 72; John Letcher to Simon Cameron, April 16, 1861, in *O.R.*, series 3, vol. 1, 76.

13. C[laiborne] F. Jackson to Simon Cameron, April 17, 1861, in *O.R.*, series 3, vol. 1, 82–83.

14. C[laiborne] F. Jackson to Simon Cameron, April 17, 1861, draft correspondence reproduced in the *Missouri Historical Review* 55, no. 3 (April 1961), verso back cover. Representative dispatches from Northern states seeking permission to exceed their requisition of militia troops may be seen in the replies of the governors of Massachusetts, Ohio, Indiana, and Illinois. See O[liver] P. Morton to Abraham Lincoln, April 15, 1861, in *O.R.*, series 3, vol. 1, 70; John A. Andrew to S[imon] Cameron, April 15, 1861, in *O.R.*, series 3, vol. 1, 71–72; W[illiam] Dennison to Abraham Lincoln, April 15, 1861, in *O.R.*, series 3, vol. 1, 73; O[liver] P. Morton to Simon Cameron, April 17, 1861, in *O.R.*, series 3, vol. 1, 80; Richard Yates, Lyman Trumball, et al. to Abraham Lincoln, April 17, 1861, in *O.R.*, series 3, vol. 1, 80–81.

15. Thomas Hicks to The President of the United States [Abraham Lincoln], April 17, 1861, in *O.R.*, series 3, vol. 1, 79–80.

16. Isham G. Harris to Simon Cameron, April 17, 1861, in *O.R.*, series 3, vol. 1, 81; Isham G. Harris to Simon Cameron, April 20, 1861, in *O.R.*, series 3, vol. 1, 91–92.

17. *Richmond (Mo.) North-West Conservator*, May 3, 1861, p. 4, col. 1; H. M. Rector to Simon Cameron, April 22, 1861, in *O.R.*, series 3, vol. 1, 99; William Burton to Simon Cameron, April 25, 1861, in *O.R.*, series 3, vol. 1, 114. See also R. Patterson to Simon Cameron, April 25, 1861, in *O.R.*, series 3, vol. 1, 110.

18. *Richmond (Mo.) North-West Conservator*, April 19, 1861, p. 2, col. 3; *Liberty (Mo.) Weekly Tribune*, April 19, 1861, p. 2, col. 1; *Fulton (Mo.) Missouri Telegraph*, April 19, 1861, p. 2, col. 2.

19. *Columbia Missouri Statesman*, April 19, 1861, p. 2, cols. 2–3; *Weekly California (Mo.) News*, April 20, 1861, p. 2, col. 1.

20. *Richmond (Mo.) North-West Conservator*, May 3, 1861, p. 1, col. 3; *Huntsville (Mo.) Randolph Citizen*, April 25, 1861, p. 2, col. 4. The rapid growth in Governor Jackson's popularity has also been noticed by at least one historian; see Arthur Roy Kirkpatrick, "Missouri in the Early Months of the Civil War," *Missouri Historical Review* 55, no. 3 (April 1961): 236.

21. *Weekly California (Mo.) News*, April 27, 1861, p. 2, col. 4; *Liberty (Mo.) Weekly Tribune*, April 26, 1861, p. 2, col. 6.

22. *Richmond (Mo.) North-West Conservator*, April 19, 1861, p. 2, col. 3; *Huntsville (Mo.) Randolph Citizen*, April 25, 1861, p. 2, col. 3; *Columbia Missouri Statesman*, [April 26, 1861], in the *Bolivar (Mo.) Weekly Courier*, May 4, 1861, p. 2, col. 4.

23. *Bethany (Mo.) Star*, April 25, 1861, p. 3, col. 1; Bob [Gardiner] to Dear Bro[ther], April 24, 1861, in the Ann Henshaw Gardiner Papers, Special Collections Department, William R. Perkins Library, Duke University, Durham, North Carolina.

24. Snead, *Fight for Missouri*, 147; *Anzeiger des Westens*, editorial for April 16, 1861, republished April 19, 1861, in *Germans for a Free Missouri: Translations from the St. Louis Radical Press, 1857–1862*, ed. and trans. Steven Rowan (Columbia, Mo.: University of Missouri Press, 1983), 178–79; Basil Duke, *Reminiscences of General Basil Duke, C.S.A.* (Garden City, N.Y.: Doubleday, Page & Company, 1911), 43.

25. [Colton Greene], ["Reminiscences"], 14, unpublished memoir, Thomas L. Snead Papers, Missouri Historical Society, St. Louis, Missouri; Snead, *Fight for Missouri*, 147; Duke, *Reminiscences*, 43.

26. D. M. Frost to C. F. Jackson, April 15, 1861, in *The Rebellion Record: A Diary of American Events, With Documents, Narratives, Illustrative Incidents, Poetry, Etc.*, ed. Frank Moore (New York: G. P. Putnam, 1862), vol. 2, 494; Snead, *Fight for Missouri*, 148.

27. D. M. Frost to C. F. Jackson, April 15, 1861, in *The Rebellion Record*, vol. 2, 494.

28. [Colton Greene], ["Reminiscences"], 14–16, unpublished memoir, Thomas L. Snead Papers, Missouri Historical Society, St. Louis, Missouri; Duke, *Reminiscences*, 43–44.

29. Duke, *Reminiscences*, 44; C. F. Jackson to Jefferson Davis, April 17, 1861, in the Jefferson Davis Papers, 1861–1862, Special Collections Department, William R. Perkins Library, Duke University, Durham, North Carolina; [Colton Greene], ["Reminiscences"], 16, unpublished memoir, Thomas L. Snead Papers, Missouri Historical Society, St. Louis, Missouri. While Captains Duke and Greene were on their way to the provisional Confederate capital, the Jackson administration fixed its attention on comparatively local supplies of arms and munitions. For accounts of the schemes to attain these supplies, see D. M. Frost to C. F. Jackson, April 15, 1861, in *The Rebellion Record*, vol. 2, 494; R. I. Holcombe to Thomas L. Snead, October 27, 1885, Thomas L. Snead Papers, Missouri Historical Society, St. Louis, Missouri; S[eth] Williams to W. Steele, April 22, 1861, in *O.R.*, series 1, vol. 1, 670; Floyd C. Shoemaker, "Missouri's Proslavery Fight for Kansas, 1854–1855," *Missouri Historical Review* 49 (October 1954–July 1955): 50–51; Nathaniel

Grant to H. K. Craig, April 21, 1861, in *O.R.*, series 1, vol. 1, 649; Benjamin Ferrar to Simon Cameron, April 21, 1861, in *O.R.*, series 1, vol. 1, 649–50.

30. C. F. Jackson to David Walker, April 19, 1861, in the *Columbia Missouri Statesman*, August 2, 1861, p. 4, col. 1. Jackson's private correspondence with Walker was apparently printed in the summer of 1861 as part of the "Journal" of the Arkansas State Convention, hence its appearance as an item of interest in an August issue of a Missouri newspaper.

31. Duke, *Reminiscences*, 44; [Colton Greene], ["Reminiscences"], 17–19, unpublished memoir, Thomas L. Snead Papers, Missouri Historical Society, St. Louis, Missouri. In working out the details of the arms transfer, Greene and Duke were struck by the mixture of personalities and attitudes in the Davis cabinet. Whereas Secretary Walker was clearly averse to helping the Missourians generally, "others were inclined to entertain a roseate view of the situation, not only in our region, but everywhere else," Basil Duke recalled, noting that "only Mr. Benjamin . . . seemed to consider the matter serious or at all difficult." "Davis & Benjamin were the only men of the cabinet who comprehended the gravity of the situation then," Colton Greene agreed, "but they only faintly realized that a great war was impending. . . . Toombs, who was warmly the friend of Missouri & took a great interest in us personally, seemed to be out of place," Greene continued. "He deplored the want of preparations for war" and spoke frankly with the Missourians concerning the grave military situation of the South.

32. William C. Davis, *Jefferson Davis, The Man and His Hour: A Biography* (New York: HarperCollins, 1991), 40–56; [Colton Greene], ["Reminiscences"], 18, unpublished memoir, Thomas L. Snead Papers, Missouri Historical Society, St. Louis, Missouri.

33. [Colton Greene], ["Reminiscences"], 17–18, unpublished memoir, Thomas L. Snead Papers, Missouri Historical Society, St. Louis, Missouri.

34. Snead, *Fight for Missouri*, 67; C. F. Jackson, "[Proclamation] Calling a Special Session of the General Assembly," in *The Messages and Proclamations of the Governors of the State of Missouri*, ed. Buel Leopard and Floyd C. Shoemaker (Columbia, Mo.: The State Historical Society of Missouri, 1922), 3:384.

35. C. F. Jackson to J. W. Tucker, April 28, 1861, James O. Broadhead Papers, Missouri Historical Society, St. Louis, Missouri.

36. *St. Louis Daily Missouri Republican*, April 27, 1861, p. 2, col. 1.

37. C. F. Jackson to J. W. Tucker, April 28, 1861, James O. Broadhead Papers, Missouri Historical Society, St. Louis, Missouri.

38. Ibid. (emphasis in original).

39. C. F. Jackson, "Special Session Message, May 3, 1861," in *The Messages and Proclamations of the Governors of the State of Missouri*, 3:343–44.

40. Ibid., 344–45.

41. Ibid., 345–47.

42. Ibid., 347–48.

43. For accounts of the journey of Greene and Duke and of their reception in the South, see [Colton Greene], ["Reminiscences"], 19–21, and Duke, *Reminiscences*, 44–50.

44. Duke, *Reminiscences*, 50–51; Jefferson Davis to C. F. Jackson, April 23, 1861, in *O.R.*, series 1, vol. 1, 688.

8. Civil Rights and the Cold War: A Rhetorical History of the Truman Administration's Desegregation of the United States Army

1. Martin J. Medhurst, Robert L. Ivie, Philip Wander, and Robert L. Scott, *Cold War Rhetoric: Strategy, Metaphor, and Ideology* (Westport, Conn.: Greenwood Press, 1990), 8.

2. William C. Berman, *The Politics of Civil Rights in the Truman Administration* (Ohio State University Press, 1970), 34.

3. Richard Dalfiume, *Desegregation of the United States Armed Forces: Fighting on Two Fronts, 1939–1953* (Columbia: University of Missouri Press, 1969), 138–39.

4. Ibid., 139.

5. Berman, *Politics of Civil Rights*, 12.

6. Ibid.

7. Ibid., 53–54.

8. Ibid., 57.

9. *Public Papers of the Presidents of the United States: Harry S. Truman, 1947* (Washington, D.C.: U.S. Government Printing Office, 1963), 9 (hereafter cited as *Public Papers, 1947*).

10. Ibid., 11.

11. Ibid., 311–12.

12. Ibid., 312.

13. *Public Papers of the Presidents of the United States: Harry S. Truman, 1948* (Washington, D.C.: U.S. Government Printing Office, 1964), 122 (hereafter cited as *Public Papers, 1948*).

14. Ibid., 126.

15. Berman, *Politics of Civil Rights*, 85.

16. Ibid., 117.

17. Ibid., 117; 117 n. 130.

18. Dalfiume, *Desegregation*, 173.

19. David McCullough, *Truman* (New York: Touchstone/Simon & Schuster, 1992), 651.

20. Robert H. Ferrell, *Harry S. Truman: A Life* (Columbia: University of Missouri Press, 1994), 297.

21. "Executive Order 9981 Establishing the President's Committee on Equality of Treatment and Opportunity in the Armed Services," 7-26-48, PSF, box 145, Harry S. Truman Library (hereafter referred to as HSTL).

22. Dalfiume, *Desegregation*, 176. Fahy Committee members included Judge Charles Fahy, chair, former solicitor general of the United States; Lester Granger, executive secretary, Urban League; John H. Sengstacke, editor of the *Chicago Defender*, a black newspaper; Dwight Palmer and Charles Luckman, both industrialists; William Stevenson, educator; and Alphonsus

J. Donohue, a Catholic layperson. Presuming Truman would be elected, the committee prepared for formal operations in January 1949. See Berman, *Politics of Civil Rights*, 123.

23. Memo, Royall to Clifford, 8-26-48, Segregation in the Armed Forces (1947–1949), Clifford Papers, box 16, HSTL.

24. Memo, Nash to Clifford, 9-2-48, Segregation in the Armed Forces (1947–1949), Clifford Papers, box 16, HSTL. The army issued "The Negro in the Army" in late April of 1949. See "The Negro in the Army," 4-28-49, Army—Government Printed Material, Fahy Committee, box 7, HSTL.

25. Memo, Clifford to Royall, 9-2-48, Segregation in the Armed Forces (1947–1949), Clifford Papers, box 16, HSTL.

26. Memo, Dawson to HST, 9-9-48, OF 1285-0 (1948–April 1950), box 1651, HSTL.

27. Royall to HST, 9-17-48, Agencies-Military (Fahy Committee), PSF, box 145, HSTL.

28. Memo, Forrestal to Secretaries of the Army, Navy, and Air Force, 10-21-48, Meeting with the President, 1-12-49, President's Committee on Equality of Treatment and Opportunity in the Armed Forces (hereafter referred to as Fahy Committee), box 2, HSTL.

29. Memo, Royall to Forrestal, 12-2-48, Army—The Royall Plan, Fahy Committee, box 6, HSTL.

30. Memo, Symington to Forrestal, 12-22-48, Armed Services—Experimental Units, Fahy Committee, box 13, HSTL.

31. Memo, Brown to Secretaries of Defense, Army and Air Force, 12-28-48, Armed Services Experimental Units, Fahy Committee, box 13, HSTL.

32. Service secretary liaisons to the Fahy Committee had all been appointed by the end of December. See memo, Marx Leva to Secretaries of the Army, Navy, and Air Force, 12-30-48, Military Liaison, Fahy Committee, box 1, HSTL.

33. Draft to Committee, 1-12-49, Fahy Committee, PSF, box 145, HSTL.

34. "Meeting of the President and the Four Service Secretaries with the President's Committee on Equality of Treatment and Opportunity in the Armed Services," Transcript, 1-12-49, Meeting with the President, 1-12-49, Fahy Committee, box 2, HSTL.

35. Kenworthy to Wechsler, 1-18-49, Committee Members and Staff—E. W. Kenworthy, Fahy Committee, box 1, HSTL.

36. Memo, Kenworthy to Sengstacke, "Questions Submitted by Mr. Fahy—March 28," John H. Sengstacke, Fahy Committee, box 1, HSTL.

37. Memo, Royall to Clifford, 3-29-49, "Statement of Honorable Kenneth C. Royall, Secretary of the Army, Before the President's Committee on Equality of Treatment and Opportunity in the Armed Services, March 28, 1949," Segregation in the Armed Forces (1947–1949), Clifford Papers, box 16, HSTL.

38. See, e.g., McCullough, *Truman*, 736–39.

39. Memo, Johnson to Secretaries of the Army, Navy, Air Force, and Chair of Personnel Policy Board, 4-6-49, Charles Fahy (1), Fahy Committee, box 1, HSTL; letter, Johnson to Fahy, 4-18-49, Charles Fahy (1), Fahy Committee, box 1, HSTL.

40. Memo for Mr. Fahy, "Interim Report," 4-27-49, Charles Fahy (1), Fahy Committee, box 1, HSTL.

41. Memo to Mr. Fahy, 5-12-49, "The Yeast . . . ," Charles Fahy (1), Fahy Committee, box 1, HSTL.

42. "Initial Recommendations," 5-24-49, Fahy Committee, box 5, HSTL. The Gillem Board report is found in "Utilization of Negro Manpower in the Postwar Army Policy," Circular No. 124, 4-27-46, Army—Gillem Board Report, Fahy Committee, box 6, HSTL.

43. Memo, Gray to Secretary of Defense, 5-26-49, PC IX, Armed Services—Second Replies, Fahy Committee, box 5, HSTL.

44. "A Progress Report to the President," 6-7-49, Fahy Committee, PSF, box 145, HSTL.

45. Letter, Kenworthy to Fahy, 6-23-49, Committee Members and Staff—E. W. Kenworthy, Fahy Committee, box 1, HSTL.

46. See, e.g., Truman's "Special Message to Congress on Reorganization of the National Military Establishment, March 5, 1949," *Public Papers of the Presidents of the United States: Harry S. Truman, 1949* (Washington, D.C.: U.S. Government Printing Office, 1964), 163–66.

47. Memo, Fahy Committee to Secretary of the Army, 7-14-49, Army Outline Plan of July 6, 1949, For Utilization of Negro Manpower to Provide Further Equality of Opportunity, Fahy Committee, box 8, HSTL.

48. Letter, Fahy to HST, 8-27-49, OF 1285-0 (1948–April 1950), box 1651, HSTL.

49. Letter, Kenworthy to Fahy, 8-8-49, McCloy Committee, Fahy Committee, box 13, HSTL.

50. Letter, Kenworthy to General Edwards, 8-30-49, General Correspondence—E, Fahy Committee, box 4, HSTL.

51. Memo, Fahy to HST, 9-26-49, Correspondence—President's Committee on Equality of Treatment and Opportunity in the Armed Services, Nash Files, box 28, HSTL; Memo, Gray to Secretary of Defense, 9-30-49, Secretary of the Army Gordon Gray, Fahy Committee, box 4, HSTL; record of telephone conversation of Charles Fahy to White House, 10-3-49, Nash Files, box 28, HSTL.

52. Memo, Niles to HST, 10-5-49, Correspondence—President's Committee on Equality of Treatment and Opportunity in the Armed Services, Nash Files, box 28, HSTL.

53. Memo, Fahy to HST 10-6-49, White House—Further Interim Report, Fahy Committee, box 2, HSTL.

54. "Further Interim Report to the President," 10-6-49, White House—Further Interim Report, Fahy Committee, box 2, HSTL.

55. Memo, Kenworthy to Fahy Committee, 10-29-49, Committee Members and Staff—E. W. Kenworthy, Fahy Committee, box 1, HSTL.

56. Memo, Gray to Fahy, 11-17-49, Gordon Gray—Secretary of the Army, Fahy Committee, box 4, HSTL.

57. Memo, Kenworthy to Fahy Committee, 11-18-49, Committee Members and Staff—E. W. Kenworthy, Fahy Committee, box 1, HSTL.

58. Memo, Kenworthy to Fahy, 11-26-49, Committee Members and Staff—E. W. Kenworthy, Fahy Committee, box 1, HSTL.

59. Memo For the Record by Kenworthy, "Telephone Conversation with Mr. Fahy 27 November," 11-28-49, Committee Members and Staff—E. W. Kenworthy, Fahy Committee, box 1, HSTL.

60. Letter, Palmer to Kenworthy, 11-28-49, Committee Members and Staff—E. W. Kenworthy, Fahy Committee, box 1, HSTL.

61. Memo for the Record by E. W. Kenworthy, "Telephone Conversation with Mr. Philleo Nash 9 December 1949," 12-9-49, Committee Members and Staff—E. W. Kenworthy, Fahy Committee, box 1, HSTL. At the request of the White House, the Army withheld revised Circular 124. See memo, Fahy to HST, 12-14-49, White House—Memoranda to White House, Fahy Committee, box 2, HSTL.

62. Letter, Flanders to HST, 12-13-49, Letters and Memos for the President, Fahy Committee, box 2, HSTL; letter, HST to Flanders, 12-17-49, OF 93-B (July–December 1949), box 443, HSTL.

63. Transcript, Meet the Press, NBC Television Broadcast, undated, Gordon Gray—Secretary of the Army, Fahy Committee, box 4, HSTL.

64. Press Release, 1-12-50, Representative Jacob Javits, Fahy Committee, box 11, HSTL.

65. Memo, Fahy to HST, 1-16-50, Letters and Memos for the President, Fahy Committee, box 2, HSTL.

66. Press release, 1-16-50, "Army Revises Policy Governing Utilization of Negro Manpower," Special Regulations No. 600-629-1—Utilization of Negro Manpower in the Army, Attachment to Pace to Niles, 2-21-51, OF 93-B (1951–1953), box 443, HSTL; memo, Clifford to HST, undated (estimated at January 16, 1950), Correspondence—President's Committee on Equality of Treatment and Opportunity in the Armed Services, Nash Files, box 28, HSTL.

67. Niles to HST, 2-7-50, Civil Rights and Minorities: Civil Rights—Negro Affairs (1949–1952), Niles Papers, box 27, HSTL.

68. Letter, Gray to HST, 3-1-50, Civil Rights and Minorities: Civil Rights—Negro Affairs, (1949–1952), Niles Papers, box 27, HSTL; and see OF 1285, HSTL.

69. Letter, Kenworthy to Severeid, 2-24-50, Committee Members and Staff—E. W. Kenworthy, Fahy Committee, box 1, HSTL.

70. Memo, Fahy to Niles, 3-13-50, Civil Rights and Minorities: Civil Rights—Negro Affairs (1949–1952), Niles Papers, box 27, HSTL.

71. Berman, Politics of Civil Rights, 175.

72. Dalfiume, Desegregation, 200.

73. Public Papers of the Presidents of the United States: Harry S. Truman, 1950 (Washington, D.C.: U.S. Government Printing Office, 1965), 431.

74. William E. Pemberton, Harry S. Truman: Fair Dealer and Cold Warrior (Boston: Twayne Publishers, 1989), 147.

75. Dalfiume, Desegregation, 220.

76. Berman, Politics of Civil Rights, 239.

77. Ibid., 118. For the original discussion see Milton Konvitz, Expanding Liberties: Freedom's Gains in Postwar America (New York: Viking, 1966), 260.

78. See, e.g., Philip Wander, "The Rhetoric of American Foreign Policy," Quarterly Journal of Speech 70 (November 1984): 339–61.

79. This is one key thesis in my book-length project (in progress) on civil rights and the contemporary presidency.

9. "The Deciding Factor": The Rhetorical Construction of Mansfield's Credibility and the Eisenhower Administration's Policy on Diem

1. Memo, George Christian to Merriman Smith, May 17, 1968, Office Files of Mike Manatos, box 73, Lyndon Baines Johnson Library, Austin, Texas.

2. Kenneth P. O'Donnell, David F. Powers, and Joe McCarthy, "*Johnny, We Hardly Knew Ye*" (Boston: Little, Brown, & Co., 1972), 15–16. See also "Twisted History," *Newsweek*, Dec. 23, 1991, 48; Robert Sam Anson, "The Shooting of JFK," *Esquire*, Nov. 1991, 174–76; and Richard Corliss, "Who Killed J.F.K.?," *Time*, Dec. 23, 1991, 70.

3. Finney, "Retiring Senate Leader," editorial, *New York Times*, Mar. 5, 1976, 12. See also Stanley Karnow, *Vietnam* (New York: Penguin, 1984), 594; and Stephen Ambrose, *Nixon*, vol. 3 (New York: Simon & Schuster, 1991), 41, 234.

4. See, for example, Doug Lowenstein, "'The system works,' says Mansfield," *Great Falls Tribune*, Mar. 12, 1976, Mansfield scrapbooks, #280.

5. John Newman, *JFK and Vietnam* (New York: Warner Books, 1992), 25.

6. See Aristotle, *Rhetoric*, bk. 1, chap. 2, in *The Basic Works of Aristotle*, ed. Richard McKeon (New York: Random House, 1941), 1329–30.

7. Charles E. Hood Jr., "'China Mike' Mansfield: The Making of a Congressional Authority on the Far East" (Ph.D. diss., Washington State University, 1980), 353. See also Mansfield, "Lecture notes on Indo-China," n.d., Mansfield papers, series 4, container 6; and Gregory A. Olson, *Mansfield and Vietnam: A Study in Rhetorical Adaptation* (East Lansing: Michigan State University Press, 1995), 7–9.

8. Mansfield to Harry S. Truman, Jan. 17, 1947, Mansfield papers, series 22, container 113, #10. See also Hood, "'China Mike,'" 349–52.

9. Hood, "'China Mike,'" 349; "Biographical Sketch," *New York Times*, Jan. 5, 1958, sec. 4, p. 5; Eugene J. Kraszewski, "Senator Mike Mansfield and the Origins of American Involvement in the Second Indochina War," Seminar Paper, Cornell University, 1974, 3, 6, Mansfield papers; Vaughn Davis Bornet, *The Presidency of Lyndon B. Johnson* (Lawrence: University Press of Kansas, 1983), 67; and Richard Reeves, *President Kennedy: Profile of Power* (New York: Simon & Schuster, 1993), 442.

10. Hood, "'China Mike,'" 211–12.

11. Valeo, letter to author, Sept. 12, 1990. See also Valeo, oral history interviews, Senate Historical Office, Washington, D.C., 1985–86, 146, 333, 346–47. For evidence that Mansfield courted the press in 1953–54, see Mansfield papers, series 13, container 6.

12. Hood, "'China Mike,'" 34, 211–12.

13. As quoted in William Conrad Gibbons, *The U.S. Government and the Vietnam War*, pt. 1 (Princeton: Princeton University Press, 1986), 52, 264, 313.

14. Olson, *Mansfield and Vietnam*, 13–16; and Valeo, oral history interviews, 161, 231.

15. John P. Glennon, ed., *Foreign Relations of the United States 1952–1954, Indochina*, vol. 13, pt. 1 (Washington: USGPO, 1982), 553–54 (hereafter cited as *FRUS*). See also Douglas, interview with John F. Stewart, Washington, Nov. 9, 1967, John F. Kennedy Oral History Project, 15, John F. Kennedy Library, Boston, Mass.

16. Valeo, interview with the author, Washington, D.C., May 17, 1991.

17. Ellen Hammer, *A Death in November* (New York: E. P. Dutton, 1987), 47, 49.

18. Gibbons, *U.S. Government*, pt. 1, 93, 135. See also Cecil B. Currey, *Edward Lansdale: The Unquiet American* (Boston: Houghton Mifflin, 1988), 150; Thomas D. Boettcher, *Vietnam: The Valor and the Sorrow* (Boston: Little, Brown, & Co., 1985), 107–9; Karnow, *Vietnam*, 217; Townsend Hoopes, *The Devil and John Foster Dulles* (Boston: Atlantic, Little, Brown, & Co., 1973), 251; and Chester L. Cooper, *The Lost Crusade* (New York: Dodd, Mead, & Co., 1970), 125.

19. Valeo, oral history interviews, 66, 95.

20. William White, "Mansfield to Make Indo-China Inquiry," *New York Times*, Sept. 16, 1953, 1.

21. Mansfield, *Indochina: Report on a Study Mission to the Associated States of Indochina, Vietnam, Cambodia, Laos*, 83d Cong., 1st sess., Oct. 27, 1953, S. Rept. (Washington, D.C.: USGPO), III, 1–8. See also *Executive Sessions of the Senate Foreign Relations Committee*, vol. 6, 1953 (Washington: USGPO, 1977), 46–53 (hereafter cited as *ESSFRC*); and Valeo, oral history interviews, 92, 95.

22. Mansfield to Hurd, Dec. 4, 1953; Mansfield to de Borchgrave, Dec. 8, 1953; Hurd to Mansfield, Dec. 1, 1953; de Borchgrave to Mansfield, Dec. 4, 22, 1953; copy of cable from de Borchgrave to *Newsweek*, Dec. 4, 1953, Mansfield papers, series 13, container 6.

23. MacArthur to Mansfield, Nov. 2, 1953; Merchant to Mansfield, Nov. 17, 1953; and Nolting to Mansfield, Nov. 25, 1953, Mansfield papers, series 13, containers 6 and 7, #5. See also Valeo, oral history interviews, 91, 116–17, 204 for Mansfield's influence on Dulles and the lack of interest on the SFRC.

24. Rebecca Holder (Secretary to Edward R. Murrow), telegram to Mansfield, Feb. 18, 1954, Mansfield papers, series 13, container 7, #5.

25. Mansfield, "Indo-China Crisis," Feb. 8, 1954, Mansfield papers, series 13, container 37, #18.

26. Hurd to Mansfield, Feb. 21, 25, 1954, Mar. 2, 29, 1954; Mansfield to Hurd, Mar. 17, 1954, Mansfield papers, series 13, container 6.

27. Mansfield to William Ellis, Feb. 19, 1954, Mansfield papers, series 13, container 6.

28. Vanden Heuvel to Mansfield, Mar. 8, June 17, 1954; Mansfield to van-

den Heuvel, Mar. 23, 1954, Mansfield papers, series 13, container 6. See also Mansfield, memo, Indo-China, Mar. 18, 1954, and Mansfield, "Geneva and Indo-China," Mar. 22, 1954, Mansfield papers, series 13, container 7, #5.

29. Jack Dowling to Mansfield, Apr. 1, 1954; de Borchgrave to Mansfield, Apr. 2, 1954; David Schoenbrun to Mansfield, Apr. 2, 1954; Mansfield to Schoenbrun, Apr. 14, 16, 1954; Larry Allen to Mansfield, Mar. 23, 31, 1954, May 5, 26, 1954, Jan. 25, 1955; and Mansfield to Allen, May 14, 1954, Mansfield papers, series 13, container 6.

30. Mansfield to de Borchgrave, Apr. 14, 1954; Mansfield to vanden Heuvel, Apr. 15, 1954; Mansfield to Hurd, Apr. 14, 1954. See also Bowles to Mansfield, n.d.; Hurd to Mansfield, Apr. 22, 1954; and vanden Heuvel to Mansfield, Apr. 21, 1954, Mansfield papers, series 13, container 6.

31. Hurd to Mansfield, Apr. 18, May 12, 1954; Mansfield to Hurd, Apr. 23, 1954; Mansfield, "Indochina Massacre," Apr. 23, 1954; Nong Kimny to Mansfield, Apr. 29, 1954; and Tran Van Kha to Mansfield, May 3, 1954, Mansfield papers, series 13, containers 6 and 7.

32. William Knowland and Mansfield, "Our Policy in the Far East: A Debate," *New York Times Magazine*, May 16, 1954, 12. See also Herbert Elliston to Mansfield, May 18, 1954; and Mansfield to Elliston, May 19, 1954, Mansfield papers, series 13, container 6, #2.

33. John Foster Dulles Papers (hereafter cited as JFDP), Telephone Call Series, Aug. 13–20, 1954, box 2, folder 1, Dwight David Eisenhower Library (hereafter cited as DDE Library), Abilene, Kansas.

34. John Foster Dulles to Mansfield, Apr. 4, 1952, Mansfield papers, series 14, container 15, #28. See also Anna Kasten Nelson, "John Foster Dulles and the Bipartisan Congress," *Political Science Quarterly* 102 (1987): 43, 49; Eleanor Lansing Dulles, *John Foster Dulles: The Last Year* (New York: Harcourt, Brace, & World, 1963), 192; Ernest Lindley, "Bipartisan Progress," *Newsweek*, Oct. 18, 1954, 36; and Pat Holt, oral history interview, Senate Historical Office, Washington, D.C., 1980, 80–81.

35. See, for example, Mansfield and Knowland, "The Leading Question," CBS Radio Division, May 16, 1954, 2–5, 12; and Mansfield, "Geneva: Failure of a Policy," July 8, 1954, 30–31, Mansfield papers, series 13, container 7 and container 37, #39. See also Dulles to George, Aug. 13, 1954, JFDP, Telephone Call Series, box 2, folder 1, DDE Library and Valeo, interview with the author.

36. Marvin Kalb and Elie Abel, *Roots of Involvement* (New York: Norton, 1971), 92–93. See also "Dulles Taking Mansfield as Advisor," *Great Falls Tribune*, Aug 21, 1954, Mansfield scrapbooks, #12; Mansfield, interview with Richard D. Challener, Washington, D.C., May 10, 1966, John Foster Dulles Oral History Project, 2, Princeton University Library; Gibbons, *U.S. Government*, pt. 1, 273; and Lindley, "Bipartisan Progress," 36.

37. Valeo, interview with author.

38. Dulles, memorandum of conference with the president, Oct. 18, 1954, and memorandum of conversation, Oct. 30, 1954, JFDP, White House Memoranda, box 1, folder 1, DDE Library.

39. Lindley, "Bipartisan Progress," 36.

40. Mansfield, Summary of meeting with Guy La Chambre, Aug. 27, 1954, Mansfield papers, series 22, container 95, #2.

41. Assistant Secretary of State Robertson, "Rough Draft" of a message to Senator Mansfield, n.d. (1954), Mansfield papers, series 22, container 95, #2.

42. As quoted in Robert Shaplen, *The Lost Revolution*, rev. (New York: Harper & Row, 1966), 118.

43. Mansfield, message sent September 24, 1954, Mansfield papers, series 22, container 95, #2.

44. Collins papers, box 24, #6, DDE Library. See also Summary of Meetings, Sept. 25, Oct. 19, 1954, *FRUS*, 1952–1954, pt. 2, 2069, 2144; Gibbons, *U.S. Government*, pt. 1, 283; and John D. Montgomery, *The Politics of Foreign Aid* (New York: Praeger, 1962), 222.

45. Mansfield, *Report On Indochina*, 83d Cong., 2d sess., Oct. 15, 1954, S. Rept. (Washington, D.C.: USGPO), 1–12, 14.

46. "So We Built a Bomber Base for Communists in Indo-China," editorial, *Milwaukee Journal*, Oct. 19, 1954, Mansfield papers, series 13, container 6; and Hammer, *A Death in November*, 69–70.

47. David L. Anderson, *Trapped by Success: The Eisenhower Administration and Vietnam, 1953–1961* (New York: Columbia University Press, 1991), 83; Cooper, *The Lost Crusade*, 134.

48. Hoover, telegram to Dulles and Heath, Oct. 22, 1954, *FRUS*, 1952–1954, pt. 2, 2159–60. See also Victor Bator, *Vietnam: A Diplomatic Tragedy* (Dobbs Ferry, N.Y.: Oceana, 1965), 181–83; Valeo, letter to author, Feb. 20, 1990; Dulles to embassies, Aug. 18, 1954, Collins papers, box 24, folder 3, DDE Library; Hoopes, *The Devil and John Foster Dulles*, 253; Boettcher, *Vietnam*, 107–9; and Gibbons, *U.S. Government*, pt. 1, 285–87. The *New York Times* also believed that Eisenhower's letter was released as a result of Mansfield's report; see "Eisenhower Asks Vietnam Reform," *New York Times*, Oct. 25, 1954, 1.

49. Bator, *Vietnam*, 183–84.

50. Memorandum of conversation, Oct. 25, 1954; Dillon, telegram to State, Oct. 23, 1954; Dulles, telegram to Dillon, Nov. 5, 1954, *FRUS*, 1952–1954, pt. 2, 2165, 2182, 2214.

51. Dulles to Mansfield, August 23, 1954, JFDP, Subject Series, box 9, DDE Library. See also memorandum of conversation, Dulles, Mendes-France, et. al., Nov. 17, 1954, *FRUS*, 1952–54, pt. 2, 2266; and *ESSFRC*, vol. 6, 1954, 711–15.

52. Michael Gravel, ed., *Pentagon Papers*, vol. 1 (Boston: Beacon Press, 1971), 222–23. See also *FRUS*, 1952–1954, pt. 2, 2379, 2141–42, 2145; and Gibbons, *U.S. Government*, pt. 1, 284.

53. Memorandum of Conference, Oct. 31, 1954, *FRUS*, 1952–1954, pt. 2, 2198–99. See also J. Lawton Collins, *Lightning Joe* (Baton Rouge: Louisiana State University Press, 1979), 411; and James R. Arnold, *The First Domino: Eisenhower, the Military, and America's Intervention in Vietnam* (New York: William Morrow & Co., 1991), 249.

54. Collins, telegram to Dulles, Dec. 6, 1954, 3–4, Collins papers, box 25, #3, DDE Library; and memorandum of conversation, Mansfield, Robertson,

Morton, and Young, Dec. 7, 1954, *United States–Vietnam Relations, 1945–1967*, bk. 10 (Washington, D.C.: USGPO, 1971), 806–8. See also Collins, *Lightning Joe*, 378–95.

55. Anderson, *Trapped by Success*, 83.

56. *FRUS*, 1952–1954, pt. 2, 2378–79, 2398. See also *FRUS: 1955–1957*, vol. 1 (Washington, D.C.: USGPO, 1985), 2; and Anderson, *Trapped by Success*, 83.

57. *FRUS*, 1952–1954, pt. 2, 2393–94. See also Collins, telegram to Paris, Dec. 16, 1954, Collins papers, box 25, #3, DDE Library.

58. Gibbons, *U.S. Government*, pt. 1, 285.

59. Mansfield, John Foster Dulles Oral History Project, 1–2, 4–5, 9–11, 15–17.

60. *FRUS*, 1952–1954, pt. 2, 2400–2403 and *United States–Vietnam Relations*, bk. 10, 853–55.

61. *ESSFRC*, vol. 7, 1955 (1978), 400–402, 413.

62. Edward G. Lansdale, *In the Midst of Wars* (New York: Harper & Row, 1972), 150, 171, 239. See also Bernard B. Fall, "The Political-Religious Sects of Vietnam," *Pacific Affairs*, September 1955, 235; Anderson, *Trapped by Success*, 48–49; Graham Greene, "Last Act in Indo-China," *New Republic*, May 9, 1955, 9–10; Currey, *Edward Lansdale*, 152; and Arnold, *The First Domino*, 233.

63. This account of Diem's battle with the sects draws from the following sources: Collins papers, box 25, folders 1 & 3, box 26, folders 1–6, May (1)–(2), DDE Library; Fall, "The Political-Religious Sects of Vietnam," 235–53; Collins, *Lightning Joe*, 397–407; Lansdale, *In the Midst of Wars*, 244–312; Gibbons, *U.S. Government*, pt. 1, 293–99; Anderson, *Trapped by Success*, 97–119; Arnold, *The First Domino*, 264–81; Hammer, *A Death in November*, 71–74; Buttinger, *Vietnam: A Dragon Embattled*, vol. 2 (New York: Praeger, 1967), 865–85; Cooper, *The Lost Crusade*, 139–43; Shaplen, *The Lost Revolution*, 119–28; and Karnow, *Vietnam*, 222–23.

64. JFDP, Telephone Calls Series, box 3, telephone conv-General, Mar. 7, 1955–Apr. 29, 1955 (3); and box 10, telephone conv-White House, Mar. 7, 1955–Aug. 29, 1955 (3), DDE Library.

65. Mansfield, memo, Apr. 1, 1955, Mansfield papers, series 22, container 107, #11.

66. Telegram from Dulles to Collins, Apr. 4, 1955, *FRUS*, 1955–1957, vol. 1, 196–97. See also Collins to Dulles, Mar. 31, 1955, box 25; and Dulles to Collins, Apr. 8, 1955, box 26, Collins papers, DDE Library.

67. Telegram from Collins to Dulles, Apr. 7, 1955, and memorandum of conversation between Young and Mansfield, Apr. 8, 1955, *FRUS*, 1955–1957, vol. 1, 219, 221–22.

68. Telegram from Dulles to Collins, Apr. 9, 1955, and telegram from Collins to Dulles, Apr. 10, 1955, *FRUS*, 1955–1957, vol. 1, 230, 234–35. See also Collins and Kidder, telegrams to Dulles, Apr. 9, 1955, *United States–Vietnam Relations*, bk. 10, 894–906.

69. Dulles to Collins, Apr. 20, 1955, JFDP, Subject Series, box 9, container 1, DDE Library. See also memorandum of conversation, Dulles and French Ambassador, Apr. 11, 1955; telegrams from Dulles to Collins, Apr. 11, 1955;

Dulles to Collins, Apr. 20, 1955, *FRUS, 1955–1957*, vol. 1, 236–41, 271; Gibbons, *U.S. Government*, pt. 1, 295; and Elie Abel, "General Collins in Washington for Talk on Vietnam Crisis," *New York Times*, Apr. 22, 1955, 1–2.

70. Mansfield, mémo, Apr. 21, 1955, Mansfield papers, series 22, container 107, #11.

71. As quoted in Shaplen, *Lost Revolution*, 122.

72. Gibbons, *U.S. Government*, pt. 1, 295–96. See also Anderson, *Trapped by Success*, 109; memorandum from Sebald to Dulles, Apr. 23, 1955; memorandum from Davis to Hensel, Apr. 25, 1955, *FRUS, 1955–1957*, vol. 1, 280–87.

73. Mansfield, Summary of Remarks of General Lawton Collins, Apr. 27, 1955, Mansfield papers, series 22, container 107, #11; and Valeo, interview with author.

74. Mansfield, letter to author, June 2, 1993. See also Shaplen, *Lost Revolution*, 122; Gibbons, *U.S. Government*, pt. 1, 295–96; Anderson, *Trapped by Success*, 109–10; telegrams from Dulles to Embassy in France, Apr. 27, 1955, *FRUS, 1955–1957*, vol. 1, 294–98; Currey, *Edward Lansdale*, 175–77; and Gravel, *Pentagon Papers*, vol. 1, 233–34.

75. Editorial note; telegram from Dulles to Embassy in France, Apr. 27, 1955; and Memorandum of Discussion at the National Security Council, Apr. 28, 1955, *FRUS, 1955–1957*, vol. 1, 299–301, 307–11.

76. Mansfield, untitled speech, Apr. 29, 1955, Mansfield papers, series 13, container 37, #56. See also *Cong. Rec.*, May 2, 1955, 5288–91; "U.S. Reiterates Vietnam Backing," *New York Times*, Apr. 30, 1955, 1–2; and Buttinger, *Vietnam*, 2:1111.

77. Memorandum from Young to Robertson, Apr. 30, 1955, *FRUS, 1955–1957*, vol. 1, 337–38.

78. Telegrams from Dulles to Paris Embassy, Apr. 30, 1955, and Dulles to Collins, May 1, 1955, *FRUS, 1955–1957*, vol. 1, 340, 344–45.

79. William II. Stringer, "U.S. Backs Saigon Premier; France Acts to Jettison Him," *Christian Science Monitor*, Apr. 30, 1955, 1; Abel, "Gen. Collins in Washington," 1; and Abel, "U.S. Reiterates Vietnam Backing," *New York Times*, Apr. 30, 1955, 1.

80. *ESSFRC*, 495–97, 510; and Mansfield, Dulles Oral History Project, 8.

81. Diem to Mansfield, May 4, 1955, Mansfield papers, series 22, container 95, #5.

82. Alsop, interview with Richard D. Challener, Washington, D.C., Mar. 4, 1966, John Foster Dulles Oral History Project, 10–11; Boettcher, *Vietnam*, 107; and Hoopes, *The Devil and John Foster Dulles*, 253–57. For Mansfield's nickname "Godfather," see Hilaire du Berrier, "Report from Saigon," *American Mercury*, September 1958, 49; and Bernard B. Fall, *VietNam Witness* (New York: Praeger, 1960), 286.

83. "Personal and Otherwise," *Harper's Magazine*, Jan. 1956, 24.

84. Montgomery, *The Politics of Foreign Aid*, 223.

85. Robert S. McNamara, with Brian VanDeMark, *In Retrospect: The Tragedy and Lessons of Vietnam* (New York: Times Books, 1995), 32–33, 322.

86. U. Alexis Johnson with Jef Olivarius McAllister, *The Right Hand of Power* (Englewood Cliffs, N.J.: Prentice-Hall, 1984), 202, 441.

87. See Valeo, oral history interviews, 67.

88. Unsigned note, Official File series of the White House Central Files, folder title "OF 181-C Indo-China," DDE Library. See also Thomas W. Branigar, archivist DDE Library, letter to author, June 12, 1991; and Mansfield, letter to author, postmarked June 6, 1991.

89. Robertson to Hoover, Nov. 22, 1955, *FRUS*, 1955–1957, vol. 1, 585–86.

90. Montgomery, *Politics of Foreign Aid*, 221.

10. Declining Honors: Dorothy Day's Rhetorical Resistance to the Culture of Heroic Ascent

1. Karlyn Kohrs Campbell, ed., *Twentieth Century Women Orators: A Bio-Critical Dictionary* (Westport, Conn.: Greenwood Press, 1994).

2. Historical narratives tell how Roman Catholic immigrants attempted to negotiate their identities as American citizens. In the twentieth century Catholic immigrants were compelled to assert their patriotism as Americans in the face of Protestant discrimination and fears of communism. See, for example, James Hennesey, S.J., *American Catholics: A History of the Roman Catholic Community in the United States* (New York: Oxford University Press, 1981); Jay Dolan, *The American Catholic Experience: A History from Colonial Times to the Present* (Garden City, N.Y.: Image, 1985); James S. Olson, *Catholic Immigrants in America* (Chicago: Nelson Hall, 1987). Essays that examine tensions in immigrant Catholic communities are included in *Urban American Catholicism: The Culture and Identity of the American Catholic People*, ed. Timothy J. Meagher (New York: Garland Publishing, 1988). Andrew Greeley was the first to report the economic ascendence of Catholic Americans. For a discussion of his original study and its reception, see Andrew Greeley, *The Catholic Myth: The Behavior and Beliefs of American Catholics* (New York: Macmillan, 1990), 68–76. The original study is *Religion and Career* (New York: Sheed and Ward, 1963). Follow-up studies include *The American Catholic: A Social Portrait* (New York: Basic Books, 1977), and *American Catholics since the Council: An Unauthorized Report* (Chicago: The Thomas More Press, 1985).

3. "Convention Nomination Acceptance Speeches," *Congressional Digest* 67 (1988): 232–40.

4. Norman Lifton, "Saintliness and Deviance: The Catholic Worker Movement" (Ph.D. diss., University of Connecticut, 1981). Lifton also describes the problems Day's social labeling as a "saint" created for the movement, as members dealt with the "burden of having to live up to . . . exceptional value" (558).

5. Dorothy Day, *The Long Loneliness* (New York: Harper & Row, 1952), 26. Future references to this book will be in the text as *LL*.

6. William Miller, *Dorothy Day: A Biography* (San Francisco: Harper & Row, 1982). See also Mel Piehl, *Breaking Bread: The Catholic Worker and the Origin of Catholic Radicalism in America* (Philadelphia: Temple University Press, 1982).

7. For a summary of Catholic social thought and action in the late 1920s see David J. O'Brien, *American Catholics and Social Reform: The New Deal Years* (New York: Oxford University Press, 1968), 46.

8. "The success of the Catholic Worker–inspired civil defense campaign confirmed Dorothy Day's status as second only to the venerable A. J. Muste among the leaders of American pacifism" (Piehl, *Breaking Bread*, 215–16). See also Nancy Roberts, *Dorothy Day and the Catholic Worker* (Albany: SUNY Press, 1984), 152–54.

9. Piehl, *Breaking Bread*, 198.

10. Anne Klejment and Alice Klejment, *Dorothy Day and the Catholic Worker: A Bibliography and Index* (New York, Garland, 1986).

11. Dorothy Day, *Eleventh Virgin* (New York: Albert and Charles Boni, 1924).

12. Dorothy Day, *From Union Square to Rome* (1938; repr., New York: Arno Press, 1978).

13. Dorothy Day, *On Pilgrimage* (New York: Catholic Worker Books, 1948); Dorothy Day, *On Pilgrimage: The Sixties* (New York: Curtis Books, 1972).

14. Dorothy Day, *House of Hospitality*, 1939.

15. Day, *LL.*

16. Dorothy Day, *Thérèse* (Notre Dame, Ind.: Fides, 1960).

17. Dorothy Day, *Loaves and Fishes* (New York: Harper & Row, 1963).

18. Peter Maurin, *Easy Essays* (London: Sheed and Ward, 1938). A slightly different edition, published under the same title, is available from Chicago: Franciscan Herald Press, 1977.

19. Ammon Hennacy, *The Book of Ammon* (New York: Catholic Worker Books, 1975); James H. Forest, *Love Is the Measure: A Biography of Dorothy Day* (New York: Paulist Press, 1986).

20. Piehl, *Breaking Bread*; Roberts, *Dorothy Day*; William Miller, *A Harsh and Dreadful Love: Dorothy Day and the Catholic Worker Movement* (New York: Liveright, 1973); Robert Coles, *A Spectacle unto the World: The Catholic Worker Movement* (New York: Viking, 1973); Patricia F. McNeal, *The American Catholic Peace Movement, 1928–1972* (New York: Arno, 1978); Michele Teresa Aronica, R.S.M., *Beyond Charismatic Leadership: The New York Catholic Worker Movement* (New Brunswick: Transaction Books, 1987); Patrick G. Coy, ed., *A Revolution of the Heart: Essays on The Catholic Worker* (Philadelphia: Temple University Press, 1988).

21. Miller, *Dorothy Day*; Robert Coles, *Dorothy Day: A Radical Devotion* (Reading, Mass.: Addison-Wesley, 1987); Roberts, *Dorothy Day*; June O'Connor, *The Moral Vision of Dorothy Day: A Feminist Perspective* (New York: Crossroad, 1991); Ruth Diana Anderson, "The Character and Communication of a Modern-Day Prophet: A Rhetorical Analysis of Dorothy Day and the Catholic Worker Movement" (Ph.D. diss., University of Oregon, 1979).

22. William Miller, *All Is Grace: The Spirituality of Dorothy Day* (New York: Doubleday, 1987).

23. Dorothy Day–Catholic Worker Collection, series D-8, box 4. In an editorial in the September 1983 issue of *Salt*, Fr. Henry Fehren called for Day's

canonization. *Salt* acted as a clearinghouse for eyewitness accounts of her influence. Bruce Buursma, "Catholic Magazine Sets Drive for Sainthood for Dorothy Day," *Chicago Tribune*, August 23, 1983, 2, 5; Bart Pollack, "Effort Begun to Declare Catholic Worker Founder a Saint," *Syracuse Herald Journal*, Sept. 3, 1983, A4. See also Kenneth L. Woodward, *Making Saints: How the Catholic Church Determines Who Becomes a Saint, Who Doesn't, and Why* (New York: Simon & Schuster, 1990), 29–36.

24. Lifton, "Saintliness and Deviance," 350; see also *Time*, December 29, 1975, 47–49, 55–56; *Newsweek*, December 27, 1976, 61.

25. Day told this to an interviewer; it is frequently mentioned in stories about her. See, for example, Forest, *Love Is the Measure*, 113, 206; Robert Ellsberg, "Remarks on the Death of Dorothy Day at Memorial Service at Haley House," Boston, Mass., December 17, 1980, Dorothy Day–Catholic Worker Collection, series D-8, box 4.

26. One of the major arguments against her canonization, in fact, comes from followers who believe that canonization would "gussy her up" and take her away from ordinary people. See Daniel Berrigan, Introduction, *LL*. Jim Forest offers another point of view on this in "We Are Called to Be Saints," *Pax Christi* 10 (1985): 18.

27. See, for example, Fr. Henry Fehren, "I Was Going to Write a Letter," *U.S. Catholic* 53 (1988): 38–40; Msgr. George Higgins, "Dorothy Day Qualifies for Sainthood as 'Gift of God,'" *Catholic Herald*, Sept. 15, 1983; Joan Chittister, O.S.B., "Viewpoint Woman: Do Call Her a Saint," *Pax Christi USA* 13 (1988): 16.

28. Norman K. Denzin, *Interpretive Biography* (Newbury Park, Calif.: Sage, 1989), 83.

29. Ibid., 26.

30. Day had a strong impulse to indoctrinate. In February 1940, for example, she wrote in the *CW*: "we must reiterate again and again what are our aims and purposes," not only for new readers and those whom the movement served, but also "for ourselves. Together with the Works of Mercy, feeding, clothing and sheltering our brothers, we must indoctrinate. Otherwise we are scattered members of the Body of Christ. . . . Otherwise our religion is an opiate, for ourselves alone, for our comfort or for our individual safety or indifferent custom. . . . If we do not keep indoctrinating, we lose the vision, we become merely philanthropists, doling out palliatives" ("Our Aims and Purposes," repr. in *A Penny a Copy*, ed. Thomas C. Cornell and James H. Forest [New York: Macmillan, 1968], 43–45). Day's anarchism strongly informed her attitudes toward persuasion. In diary notes she wrote, "The true anarchist loves his brother according to the new law [of the New Testament], ready to die rather than compel his brother to go his totalitarian way, no matter how convinced he may be that his way is the only way" (Miller, *All Is Grace*, 141).

31. Maurin's rhetorical habits are referenced in Day's autobiography. "Peter often gave the impression of being a dangerous and unbalanced radical when he began 'indoctrinating' someone who was unprepared. . . . Peter was the most persistent soul in the world and he was looking for apostles to share his work" (*LL*, 172). Ade Bethune, a close associate of Day's from the begin-

ning of the movement, told Nancy L. Roberts in an oral history interview that "Peter Maurin could think of nothing he liked better than to stand in the middle of Union Square and harangue people" (Dorothy Day–Catholic Worker Collection, series W-9; see also Miller, *Harsh and Dreadful Love*, 20).

32. One way she sought to establish common ground was to acknowledge that she and the members of the Catholic Worker movement did not hold themselves above or apart from the rest of American culture but partook of it as did others. See Carol J. Jablonski, "Dorothy Day (1897–1980), Co-founder, Catholic Worker movement," in Campbell, *Women Orators*, 170.

33. Day may have been displaying deference to Roman Catholic institutions. In a correspondence to the city of New York in July 1960 (later published in the *Catholic Worker*), Day wrote that "we are not judging individuals, but are trying to make a judgment on the system under which we live and with which we admit that we ourselves compromise daily in many small ways, but which we try and wish to withdraw from as much as possible." See "This Money Is Not Ours," in *A Penny A Copy*, 204–5. Piehl also describes Day's unwavering commitment to the Church (*Breaking Bread*, 90–94).

34. Roderick P. Hart, "The Rhetoric of the True Believer," *Speech Monographs* 38 (1971): 249–61; Karlyn Kohrs Campbell, *Man Cannot Speak for Her*, vol. 1 (Westport, Conn.: Greenwood Press), 13.

35. My understanding of Day's search for community has been informed by James Terrance Fisher, *The Catholic Counterculture in America 1933–1962* (Chapel Hill: North Carolina University Press, 1989). Piehl also describes Day's mystical leanings (*Breaking Bread*, 84).

36. Dorothy Day–Catholic Worker Collection, Marquette University Archives, series D-5, box 4.

37. Letter to Georgetown University, 1973, torn up and not sent.

38. The colleges and universities from which Day accepted honors and awards include Assumption University, Windsor, Ontario (Christian Culture Award, March 1, 1970); City College of New York (Newman Alumni Award, October 6, 1972); DePaul University (St. Vincent DePaul Medal, May 8, 1974); King's College (Civitas Dei Award, 1974); Manhattan College (Saint La Salle Medal, May 19, 1975); College of St. Benedict (President's Medal, May 4, 1976); College of Steubenville (Poverello Medal, May 8, 1977); College of St. Catherine (Alexandrine Medal, May 21, 1976). Day was also honored in celebrations at Boston College (Dorothy Day Week, April 11–14, 1972) and Marquette University (November 8–9, 1977).

39. Dorothy Day–Catholic Worker Collection, series D-5, box 4.

40. Letter catalogued with Father Theodore Hesburgh–Dorothy Day Correspondence, Hesburgh Papers, University of Notre Dame Archives.

41. Dorothy Day–Catholic Worker Archives, series D-5, box 4. The letter has many cross-outs and inserted words. For the purposes of readability I have left out these marks in the original text.

42. Hesburgh's telegram, dated March 10, reads: "I am delighted to inform you that Notre Dame has named you Laetare Medalist for 1972. We take pride in welcoming you to the select circle of extraordinary Catholic women and men who, by achievement and personal example, have brought glory to the Church and our beloved country. The announcement will not be made

in the press until Sunday, but I am delighted to extend my personal congratulations and good wishes in advance. I know that many others will rejoice in seeing this honor conferred upon you" (Archives of the University of Notre Dame, UPHS 57).

43. Day's status as a convert to Catholicism and her identification with female saints help explain her frequent self-deprecation (Fisher, *Catholic Counterculture*, 1–24; Piehl, *Breaking Bread*, 89–90). Day also used self-deprecation strategically; see Roberts, *Dorothy Day*, 93. For a critical reading of Day's self-deprecation, see Mary Mason, "Dorothy Day and Women's Spiritual Autobiography," in *American Women's Autobiography*, ed. Margo Culley (Madison: University of Wisconsin Press, 1992), 185–217.

44. Day was eventually cleared of all tax liabilities in the case.

45. Letter catalogued with Father Theodore Hesburgh–Dorothy Day Correspondence, Hesburgh Papers, University of Notre Dame Archives, UPHS 57.

46. Although Day responded affirmatively to Hesburgh's suggestion in early April that she attend the ceremonies, her illness continued to be a problem. On May 13, Day wrote to say it was "no use"; she could not attend. Her "last minute" decision to attend the ceremonies came in time for press releases and commencement programs to record the event (University of Notre Dame Archives UPHS, 57; UDIS 55/1; PNDP 1300-1972).

47. Lifton, "Saintliness and Deviance," 516–18; Piehl, *Breaking Bread*, 90–94.

48. Yet even a letter from Day's former editor at *Commonweal*, George Shuster, who was then assistant president of Notre Dame, could not persuade Day to accept an honorary degree from Stonehill College in 1973 (Dorothy Day–Catholic Worker Collection, series D-5, box 4).

49. University of Notre Dame Archives, UPHS 57.

50. Letter dated April 6 from Day to Hesburgh, University of Notre Dame Archives, UPHS 57.

51. Manuscript of postscript for Italian edition of *A Harsh and Dreadful Love*, 1981, p. 3 (Marquette University Archives UNIV C-17, series 2-WDM).

52. Forest, *Love Is the Measure*, 181.

53. Robert J. Branham and W. Barnett Pearce, "Between Text and Context: Toward a Rhetoric of Contextual Reconstruction," *Quarterly Journal of Speech* 71 (1985): 23.

54. Branham and Pearce, 24.

11. History and Culture as Rhetorical Constraints: Cesar Chavez's Letter from Delano

1. John C. Hammerback and Richard J. Jensen, "'A Revolution of Heart and Mind': Cesar Chavez's Rhetorical Crusade," *Journal of the West* 27 (April 1988): 70.

2. Tony Castro, *Chicano Power: The Emergence of Mexican America* (New York: Saturday Review Press, 1974), 96.

3. Winthrop Yinger, *Cesar Chavez: The Rhetoric of Nonviolence* (Hicksville, N.Y.: Exposition Press, 1975), 58. Yinger printed texts of several other letters in his book and additional letters may be found in the UFW's newspaper, *El Malcriado*. Other letters may be found in Julian Nava, ed., *Viva La Raza!* (New York: D. Van Nostrand Co., 1973), 148; *Los Angeles Times*, Jan. 2, 1991, sec. B, p. 5; and Thomas E. Hachey and Ralph E. Weber, eds., *American Dissent from Thomas Jefferson to Cesar Chavez: The Rhetoric of Reform and Revolution* (Huntington, N.Y.: Robert E. Krieger Publishing Company, 1981), 155–70.

4. Haig Bosmajian, "The Letter from Birmingham Jail," in Arthur L. Smith, ed., *Language, Communication and Rhetoric in Black America* (New York: Harper & Row, 1972), 195.

5. For a discussion of Chavez's career and his public discourse, see John C. Hammerback, Richard J. Jensen, and Jose Angel Gutierrez, *A War of Words: Chicano Protest in the 1960s and 1970s* (Westport, Conn.: Greenwood Press, 1985), 33–52; and John C. Hammerback and Richard J. Jensen, "Ethnic Heritage as Rhetorical Legacy: The Plan of Delano," *Quarterly Journal of Speech* 80 (1994): 53–70.

6. In 1985 Chavez was described as "one of the last representatives of a dying breed—the charismatic 1960s hero." See Evan Barr, "Sour Grapes: Cesar Chavez 20 Years Later," *The New Republic*, Nov. 25, 1985, 20. Histories of Chavez and his union include Ronald B. Taylor, *Chavez and the Farm Workers* (Boston: Beacon Press, 1975); Yinger, *Cesar Chavez*; Peter Matthiessen, *Sal Si Puedes* (New York: Dell, 1973); Eugene Nelson, *Huelga!* (Delano: Farm Workers Press, 1966); John Gregory Dunne, *Delano* (New York: Farrar, Straus, & Giroux, 1967); Mark Day, *Forty Acres: Cesar Chavez and the Farm Workers* (New York: Praeger, 1971); Jacques E. Levy, *Cesar Chavez: Autobiography of La Causa* (New York: Norton, 1977); Richard Griswold del Castillo and Richard Garcia, *Cesar Chavez: A Triumph of Spirit* (Norman: University of Oklahoma Press, 1995).

7. Cesar Chavez, "Letter from Delano," *Christian Century*, April 23, 1969, 539. The letter appeared in the *National Catholic Reporter*, April 23, 1969, 4. The letter is also printed in Yinger, *Cesar Chavez*, 112–15.

8. R. K. Sanderson and E. L. Barr, "Why Grape Growers Do Not 'Render unto Cesar,'" *Christian Century*, June 11, 1969, 810–11.

9. For a discussion of studies of written documents and their findings in relation to Mexican American discourse, see Hammerback and Jensen, "Ethnic Heritage as Rhetorical Legacy," 53–70.

10. Alberto Gonzalez, "Mexican 'Otherness' in the Rhetoric of Mexican Americans," *Southern Communication Journal* 55 (spring 1990): 280–82.

11. Ibid., 287–88.

12. Kathleen M. Hall Jamieson, "Generic Constraints and the Rhetorical Situation," *Philosophy and Rhetoric* 6 (summer 1973): 169.

13. Hammerback and Jensen, "Ethnic Heritage as Rhetorical Legacy," 65.

14. "Introduction," in Carlota Cardenas de Dwyer, ed., *Chicano Voices* (Boston: Houghton Mifflin, 1975), vii.

15. Ramon Saldivar, "Introduction," Ramon Saldivar, ed., *Chicano Nar-*

rative: The Dialectics of Difference (Madison: University of Wisconsin Press, 1990), 5.

16. Hammerback and Jensen, "Ethnic Heritage as Rhetorical Legacy," 54.

17. For a discussion of the plan as rhetoric as well as earlier plans, see Hammerback and Jensen, "Ethnic Heritage as Rhetorical Legacy," 53–70. For a discussion of the Mexican plan, see Thomas Davis and Amado Virulegio, *The Political Plans of Mexico* (Lanham, Md.: University Press of America, 1987). The book has a lengthy discussion of the history of the Mexican plan as well as English translations of more than two hundred plans.

18. For discussions of Chavez's view of the world, his conception of public discourse, and the rhetorical profile that characterized his discourse, see John C. Hammerback and Richard J. Jensen, "The Rhetorical Worlds of Cesar Chavez and Reies Tijerina," *Western Journal of Speech Communication* 44 (1980): 166–76; Hammerback and Jensen, "'A Revolution of Heart and Mind,'" 69–74; John C. Hammerback and Richard J. Jensen, "Teaching the 'Truth': The Righteous Rhetoric of Cesar Chavez"; Hammerback, Jensen, and Gutierrez, *War of Words*, 33–52; John C. Hammerback and Richard J. Jensen, *The Rhetorical Career of Cesar Chavez* (College State: Texas A&M University Press, 1998).

19. Fernando Pedro Delgado, "Los Planes del Movimiento Chicano: The Function of a Rhetorical Genre and Constitutive Rhetoric" (paper presented at the Western States Communication Association Convention, San Jose, Feb. 27, 1994). Delgado furthers his discussion of plans in "Chicano Movement Rhetoric: An Ideographic Interpretation," *Communication Quarterly* 43 (fall 1995): 446–54.

20. Hammerback and Jensen, "Ethnic Heritage as Rhetorical Legacy," 55–56.

21. This and subsequent citations from the letter are taken from Chavez, "Letter from Delano," 539–40.

22. Sanderson and Barr, "Why Grape Growers," 810–11.

23. Ibid., 810; Chavez, "Letter from Delano," 540.

24. Andrew King, *Power and Communication* (Prospect Heights, Ill.: Waveland Press, 1987), 57.

25. John W. Bowers, Donovan J. Ochs, and Richard J. Jensen, *The Rhetoric of Agitation and Control*, 2d ed. (Prospect Heights, Ill.: Waveland Press, 1993), 10.

26. Sanderson and Barr, "Why Grape Growers," 810–11.

27. Ibid.

28. Winthrop Yinger, "Viva La Causa," *Christian Century*, April 27, 1969, 116.

29. The letter has been anthologized in Edward Simmer, ed., *Pain and Promise: The Chicano Today* (New York: Mentor, 1972), 29–32; Yinger, *Cesar Chavez*, 112–15.

30. Chavez, "Letter from Delano," 539. In 1969 the circulation for the *National Catholic Reporter* was 95,195.

31. Simmer, "Prologue," in *Pain and Promise: The Chicano Today*, 18.

32. Marc Grossman, personal interview, October 14, 1995.

33. Bosmajian, "Letter from Birmingham Jail," 196; Malinda Snow,

"Martin Luther King's 'Letter from Birmingham Jail' as Pauline Epistle," *Quarterly Journal of Speech* 71 (1985): 319.

Postscript: A Disciplinary History of Rhetorical History: Retrospect and Prospect

1. Lester Thonssen and A. Craig Baird, *Speech Criticism* (New York: Ronald Press, 1948).

2. William Norwood Brigance, ed., *A History and Criticism of American Public Address*, 2 vols. (New York: McGraw-Hill, 1943). The third volume in the series, edited by Marie Hochmuth [Nichols], did not appear until 1955.

3. A. Craig Baird, *American Public Addresses 1740–1952* (New York: McGraw-Hill, 1956); Wayland Parrish and Marie Hochmuth, *American Speeches* (New York: Longmans, Green and Company, 1954). In my subsequent doctoral program at Wisconsin, that study of public address was supplemented by essays and speeches in Chauncey Goodrich, *Select British Eloquence: Embracing the Best Speeches Entire of the Most Eminent Orators of Great Britain for the Last Two Centuries; with Sketches of Their Lives, an Estimate of Their Genius, and Notes, Critical and Explanatory*, repr. ed. (Indianapolis: Bobbs-Merrill Company, 1963).

4. My zeal on behalf of one of those efforts, a term paper, led to a manuscript sufficiently long that when found in my files years later it could be the basis for a book to appear in the Greenwood Press Series on American Orators.

5. Herbert A. Wichelns, "The Literary Criticism of Oratory," in *Studies in Rhetoric and Public Speaking in Honor of James Albert Winans* (New York: Russell and Russell, 1962), 181–216; see in particular 209 and 213.

6. Bruce Gronbeck, "Rhetorical History and Rhetorical Criticism: A Distinction," *Speech Teacher* 24 (November 1975): 309–20 (emphases in original).

7. Herman Stelzner, "The Quest Story and Nixon's November 3, 1969 Address," *Quarterly Journal of Speech* 57 (April 1971): 163–72 (see in particular 163–64).

8. Walter R. Fisher, "Narration as a Human Communication Paradigm: The Case of Public Moral Argument," *Communication Monographs* 51 (1984): 2, 6–8, 14–15.

9. For example, to explain in part the impress of Barbara Tuchman's book *The Guns of August* on President John Kennedy during the Cuban Missile Crisis, I used Hayden White's paradigm of the emplotment metaphors of metonymy and synecdoche as they can undergird historical writing and therefore the responses of readers to that discourse. See my *History as Rhetoric: Style, Narrative, and Persuasion* (Columbia: University of South Carolina Press, 1995): 222–60.

10. Stephen Lucas, "The Schism in Rhetorical Scholarship," *Quarterly Journal of Speech* 67 (February 1981): 1–20.

11. George V. Bohman, "The Colonial Period," in *History and Criticism of American Public Address*, 1:3–54.

12. Edwin Black, *Rhetorical Criticism: A Study in Method* (New York: Macmillan, 1965): see in particular pp. 91–131. Black's book was reprinted by the University of Wisconsin Press in 1978.

13. Robert P. Newman, "Lethal Rhetoric: The Selling of the China Myths," *Quarterly Journal of Speech* 61 (April 1975): 113–28.

14. Ibid., 124.

15. Marie Hochmuth, "Kenneth Burke and the 'New Rhetoric,'" *Quarterly Journal of Speech* 38 (April 1952): 133–44. See also Marie Hochmuth Nichols, *Rhetoric and Criticism* (Baton Rouge: Louisiana State University Press, 1963): 79–92.

16. Ernest Bormann, "Fantasy and Rhetorical Vision: The Rhetorical Criticism of Social Reality," *Quarterly Journal of Speech* 58 (December 1972): 396–407.

17. Gerald Mohrmann, "An Essay on Fantasy Theme Criticism," *Quarterly Journal of Speech* 68 (May 1982): 109–32.

18. Carl R. Burgchardt, "Discovering Rhetorical Imprints: La Follette, 'Iago,' and the Melodramatic Scenario," *Quarterly Journal of Speech* 71 (November 1985): 441–56.

19. See Roderick P. Hart, "Contemporary Scholarship in Public Address: A Research Editorial," *Western Journal of Speech Communication* 50 (summer 1986): 283–95.

20. Jeff D. Bass, "The Romance as Rhetorical Dissociation: The Purification of Imperialism in *King Solomon's Mines*," *Quarterly Journal of Speech* 67 (August 1981): 259–69.

21. *The Private Diaries of Sir H. Rider Haggard 1914–1925*, ed. D. S. Higgins (New York: Stein and Day Publishers, 1980).

22. Haggard to a meeting of the Imperial South African Association, July 14, 1905, Haggard Papers, Huntington Library (hereafter cited as HM).

23. Haggard to A. P. Watt, November 14, 1906, HM 43587.

24. Edmund W. Gosse to Haggard, January 8, 1887, HM 43488.

25. Charles James Longman to Haggard, January 6, 1907, HM 43641.

26. Haggard to Rudyard Kipling, November 10, 1912, HM 43536.

27. Martin Medhurst, ed., *Eisenhower's War of Words: Rhetoric and Leadership* (Lansing: Michigan State University Press, 1994).

28. See my "General Douglas MacArthur's Oratory on Behalf of Inchon: Discourse That Altered the Course of History," *Southern Communication Journal* 58 (fall 1992): 1–12; and "On Rhetoric in Martial Decision Making," in *Rhetoric in Community: Case Studies in Unity and Fragmentation*, ed. J. Michael Hogan (Columbia: University of South Carolina Press, 1998).

29. Samuel Becker, "Rhetorical Studies for the Contemporary World," in *The Prospect of Rhetoric*, ed. Lloyd Bitzer and Edwin Black (Englewood Cliffs, N.J.: Prentice-Hall, 1971), 22–25, 33.

30. I too had relied to some extent on the Janis concept of "groupthink" when accounting for the rhetorical influence of Alfred Thayer Mahan's historical writings on Japanese naval planners in their decision making for the Pearl Harbor attack, but I found the pertinent contribution of Irving Janis to

be that of the role of "bolstering," from someone with additional pertinent information, that often occurs at pivotal moments when group cohesiveness seems to waver. See my "Admiral Mahan, 'Narrative Fidelity,' and the Japanese Attack on Pearl Harbor," *Quarterly Journal of Speech* 72 (1986): 290–305; or chapter five in Carpenter, *History as Rhetoric*.

31. Ronald H. Carpenter, "Carl Becker and the Epigrammatic Force of Style in History," *Communication Monographs* 48 (December 1981): 318–39; or chapter three in Carpenter, *History as Rhetoric*. Similarly, several historians of World War II proclaimed that Japanese naval strategy and tactics were influenced by Alfred Thayer Mahan's writings, but what the Japanese applied from Mahan, specifically, is not easily ascertainable from only reading his works. Thus, my rhetorical criticism of Mahan's influence also relied on translations of Admiral Yamamoto's correspondence while planning the attack, translations of battle orders, and memoirs of Commander Fuchida, who led the aircraft over Pearl Harbor and argued with Admiral Nagumo on the bridge of the *Akagi* about what to do after the first strike had been completed. See citations in note 30 above.

32. See my "The Historical Jeremiad as Rhetorical Genre," in *Form and Genre: Shaping Rhetorical Action*, ed. Karlyn Kohrs Campbell and Kathleen Hall Jamieson (Falls Church, Va.: Speech Communication Association, 1977): 103–17.

33. Lucas, "Schism," 15–16 (emphasis in original).

34. See Carpenter, *History as Rhetoric*, 10–11; or my "America's Opinion Leader Historians on Behalf of Success," *Quarterly Journal of Speech* 69 (May 1983): 111–26.

35. Samuel Becker, "Rhetorical Studies," 35.

36. Carpenter, *History as Rhetoric*, 9–10.

37. Joseph T. Klapper, *The Effects of Mass Communication* (New York: Free Press, 1960), 34–36, 51; or Carpenter, *History as Rhetoric*, 7–8 and 16 for other pertinent sources on this aspect of persuasion.

38. *Guide to Literary Manuscripts in the Huntington Library* (San Marino: Huntington Library, 1979), 207.

39. The "Unpublished Guide" to the Becker papers was thirty-eight pages, listing every item (by name and date) in the collection. For a description of RLIN (if your library does not have access), write to Program Coordination Division (Archives and Manuscripts), The Research Libraries Group, Inc., Jordan Quadrangle, Stanford CA 94305.

40. That research led initially to a paper that I presented at the 1987 Speech Communication Association Convention in Boston, "Barbara Tuchman, John F. Kennedy, and Why the 'Missiles of October' Did Not Become the Guns of August: The Rhetoric of Narrative in History" and, subsequently, to that aforementioned chapter in Carpenter, *History as Rhetoric*.

41. Robert L. Ivie, "Productive Criticism," *Quarterly Journal of Speech* 81 (February 1995): editor's preface.

42. Robert L. Ivie, "Eisenhower as Cold Warrior," in Medhurst, *Eisenhower's War of Words*, 7–25.

43. Phillip K. Tompkins, "The Rhetorical Criticism of Non-Oratorical Works," *Quarterly Journal of Speech* 55 (1969): 430–39.

44. Jonathan Culler, "Beyond Interpretation," *Comparative Literature* 28 (1976): 246.

45. The Society for Critical Exchange devoted an entire issue to commentary about Culler's "Beyond Interpretation," including the rejoinder from which this quotation is taken: Jonathan Culler, "The Critical Assumption," *SCE Reports* 6 (fall 1976): 77–85.

46. Culler, "Critical Assumption," 83.

47. Under the rubric of Rhetoric and Public Address or Communication Studies, some stellar books that have generated theory include Joshua Meyrowitz, *No Sense of Place: The Impact of Electronic Media on Social Behavior* (New York: Oxford University Press, 1985), and Walter R. Fisher, *Human Communication and Narration: Toward a Philosophy of Reason, Value, and Action* (Columbia: University of South Carolina Press, 1987).

48. Martin J. Medhurst, "Response" to the panel of papers on "Rhetorical Studies in the 21st Century: Theory, Practice, Pedagogy," Southern States Communication Association Convention, Savannah, 1997.

49. *Mansfield and Vietnam* (Lansing: Michigan State University Press, 1995); see the review by Peter Ehrenhaus, *Quarterly Journal of Speech* 83 (February 1997): 119–20.

50. Medhurst, "Response."

51. Stephen Hawes, *The Pastime of Pleasure.* Introduction by William Edward Mead (London: Oxford University Press, 1928), 31 (line 668).

Contributors

James R. Andrews is Professor of Speech Communication, Adjunct Professor of American Studies, and Adjunct Professor of Victorian Studies at Indiana University. He is the author of numerous critical studies that have appeared in such scholarly journals as the *Quarterly Journal of Speech* and *Communication Monographs;* he is a past editor of *Communication Studies,* has served on numerous editorial boards, and is the author, coauthor, or editor of seven books, including *The American Ideology* (with Kurt W. Ritter; SCA, 1978), *The Practice of Rhetorical Criticism* (Longman, 1983, 1990), and *American Voices* (with David Zarefsky; Longman, 1989). He received the Winans-Wichelns Award for Distinguished Scholarship in Rhetoric and Public Address and twice won the American Forensic Association's Award for Outstanding Research. In 1993 he received the Speech Communication Association's Douglas Ehninger Distinguished Rhetorical Scholar Award.

Moya Ann Ball is Associate Professor of Speech Communication at Trinity University, San Antonio, where she teaches courses in rhetorical theory and criticism, political communication, and small group communication. Her teaching and her research both rely on extensive use of archival resources. She has published several essays on presidential decision making and the Vietnam War, as well as the book *Vietnam-on-the-Potomac* (Praeger, 1992).

Ronald H. Carpenter is Professor of English and Communication Studies at the University of Florida. His publications include *Douglas MacArthur, Warrior as Wordsmith* (with Bernard Duffy; Greenwood Press, 1997); *History as Rhetoric: Style, Narrative, and Persuasion* (University of South Carolina Press, 1995); *The Eloquence of Frederick Jackson Turner* (Huntington Library, 1983); and numerous book chapters and essays in such outlets as *Communication Monographs, Quarterly Journal of Speech, Style, Language and Style,* and *Presidential Studies Quarterly.* He is also a communication consultant for corporate executives, bar associations, public relations professionals, the U.S. Naval War College, and other groups.

E. Culpepper Clark is Dean of the College of Communication and Professor of History at the University of Alabama. His latest book, *The Schoolhouse Door: Segregation's Last Stand at the University of Alabama* (Oxford, 1993), was listed among the notable books of 1993 by the *New York Times Book Review.* His writings on historical method and rhetoric have appeared in the *Quarterly Journal of Speech, International Journal of Oral History, Communication Education,* and three published collections.

Steven R. Goldzwig is Associate Professor in the Department of Communication Studies at Marquette University. He is the coauthor of *In a Perilous Hour: The Public Address of John F. Kennedy* (Greenwood Press, 1995). He has published a number of essays on political and legal communication. He is currently writing a book-length study on the contemporary presidency and civil rights.

Bruce E. Gronbeck is the A. Craig Baird Distinguished Professor of Public Address, Department of Communication Studies, at the University of Iowa. His doctoral training was centered in eighteenth-century British historical and political studies, out of which the essay for this volume grows. His primary areas of teaching and writing include political discourse, rhetorical and media criticism, and cultural studies. He has coedited *Media, Consciousness, and Culture: Explorations of Walter Ong's Thought* (with Thomas J. Farrell and Paul A. Soukup; Sage, 1991); *Presidential Campaigns and American Self-Images* (with Arthur H. Miller; Westview, 1994); and *Critical Approaches to Television* (with Leah A. Vande Berg and Lawrence A. Wenner; Houghton Mifflin, 1998).

John C. Hammerback is Professor of Communication and Chair of the Department at North Carolina State University. He teaches and writes about public communication, rhetorical theory, and rhetorical criticism and has won awards for teaching and service at California State University, Hayward. His scholarly contributions include authoring or coauthoring thirty essays in journals, books, and a CD-ROM; many convention papers; and appointments on numerous editorial boards. His coauthored article, "The Plan of Delano: Ethnic Heritage as Rhetorical Legacy," was honored by the Intercultural/International Division of the Speech Communication Association as the best essay published in 1994. He is coauthor of *A War of Words: Chicano Protest in the 1960s and 1970s* (with Richard J. Jensen and Jose Angel Gutierrez; Greenwood Press, 1985); coauthor of *The Rhetorical Career of Cesar Chavez* (with Richard J. Jensen; Texas A&M, 1998); and coeditor of *In Search of Justice* (with Richard J. Jensen; Rodopi, 1987).

Carol J. Jablonski is Associate Professor of Communication at the University of South Florida. Her work focuses on the rhetoric of social and institutional change and includes the study of contemporary movements for change within the Roman Catholic Church. Her essays on the movement for women's ordination and the reforms of Vatican II have appeared in the *Quarterly Journal of Speech.*

James Jasinski is Assistant Professor of Communication and Theatre Arts at the University of Puget Sound. He is an associate editor of the *Quarterly Journal of Speech* and serves on the editorial board of *Communication Studies* and the Sage Publications series in Rhetoric and Society. His work on the history of American public discourse has appeared in the *Quarterly Journal of Speech, Rhetoric Society Quarterly*, and a number of essay collections. He is currently completing *Key Concepts in Contemporary Rhetorical Studies*, to be published by Sage.

Timothy C. Jenkins is Instructor of Communication at Alice Lloyd College, Pippa Passes, Kentucky, and a Ph.D. candidate at Indiana University in Bloomington, where he is continuing his research into the border states during the first year of the Civil War. This essay is adapted from his master's thesis, "Children of Compromise, Brothers at War: The Rhetoric of Revolution in Missouri, 1861," directed by Dr. James R. Andrews.

Richard J. Jensen is Professor and Director of Graduate Studies in the Greenspun School of Communication at the University of Nevada, Las Vegas. His research has focused on rhetoric in minority movements, labor unions, and religious settings. He has made more than forty presentations at professional conferences and published more than thirty articles and seven books, including *A War of Words: Chicano Protest in the 1960s and 1970s* (with John C. Hammerback and Jose Angel Gutierrez; Greenwood Press, 1985); *In Search of Justice* (coedited with John C. Hammerback; Rodopi, 1987); *Clarence Darrow: The Creation of an American Myth* (Greenwood, 1992); *The Rhetoric of Agitation and Control,* 2d ed. (with John Waite Bowers and Donovan J. Ochs); and *The Rhetorical Career of Cesar Chavez* (with John C. Hammerback; Texas A&M, 1998).

Raymie E. McKerrow is Professor in the School of Interpersonal Communication at Ohio University. He is an associate editor of *Communication Monographs* and serves on the editorial boards for *Communication Studies, Communication Quarterly,* and *Argumentation and Advocacy.* His current research centers on reconceptualizing rhetoric to better meet the needs of a multicultural world. His work has appeared in *Communication Monographs, Quarterly Journal of Speech, Rhetorica, Philosophy and Rhetoric,* and in national and international argumentation conference proceedings.

Gregory Allen Olson is Instructor at the University of Wisconsin-Oshkosh. He is interested in congressional rhetoric and has published *Mansfield and Vietnam: A Study in Rhetorical Adaptation* (Michigan State, 1995), as well as essays in the area.

Kathleen J. Turner is Associate Professor of Communication at Tulane University. Her research and teaching center on communication as a process of social influence, particularly in the areas of media, politics, and popular culture. Author of *Lyndon Johnson's Dual War: Vietnam and the Press,* the first book in communication to be published by the University of Chicago Press (1985), she is completing the rhetorical history *Comic Creations of Women: A Century of Funnies Females.*

David Zarefsky is Dean of the School of Speech and Professor of Communication Studies at Northwestern University. He is the author of *President Johnson's War on Poverty: Rhetoric and History* (University of Alabama Press, 1986) and *Lincoln, Douglas, and Slavery: In the Crucible of Public Debate* (University of Chicago Press, 1990), both of which received the Speech Communication Association's Winans-Wichelns Award for Distinguished Scholarship in Rhetoric and Public Address. He is a former President of SCA and one of its Distinguished Scholars.

Index

Ball, Moya, 3–4, 15, 224, 227–28, 231–32, 237
Ball, Terence, 45
Banks, Nathaniel, 100
Bao Dai, 183, 186, 187
Barnett, Bernice, 58
Barr, E. L., Jr., 208, 213, 214, 216–18, 219
Barthes, Roland, 70
Barzun, Jacques, 5, 9, 12, 43, 44
Baskerville, Barnet, 2, 4, 20, 21, 22
Bass, Jeff, 228–29, 234
Bator, Victor, 180
Batterham, Forster, 195
Bay of Pigs, 64–65
Beale, Howard K., 226
Becker, Carl, 9, 11, 34, 232–34; papers of, 235
Becker, Samuel, 231, 234
Beiner, Ronald, 74
Bendetsen, Karl, 161, 162
Benjamin, Judah P., 134
Benson, Thomas W., 63
Bentham, Jeremy, 82
Benton, Thomas Hart, 269 (n. 23)
Berman, Larry, 68–69, 70
Berman, William C., 145, 147, 148, 167
Berrigan, Daniel, 196
Berrigan, Philip, 196
Bethany (Mo.) Star, 130
Billig, Michael, 59
Binh Xuyen, 183–84, 186, 187
Bitzer, Lloyd, 73
Black, Edwin, 225, 233
Blair, Carole, 45
Blair, Hugh, 47
Boettcher, Thomas, 187
Bohman, George, 224–25
Bolivar (Mo.) Courier, 120
Bolstering, 292–93 (n. 30)
Books, publication of, 30, 239–42
Booth, Wayne, 75
Bormann, Ernest, 67, 227, 258 (n. 23)
Bowers, John Waite, 22
Bowles, Chester, 176
Bracketing, 51, 59
Bragg, Braxton, 98
Bragg, Mrs. Braxton, 98
Branham, Robert J., 206
Braudel, Fernand, 40
Brett, Robert Barnwell, 100, 113
Brigance, William Norwood, 20, 221, 225, 236

Brown, John Nicholas, 151
Brown v. Board of Education, 168
Bryant, Donald C., 2, 5, 50
Buchanan, James, 100
Buddhism, 183
Bundy, McGeorge, 66
Burgchardt, Carl, 227
Burke, Kenneth, 20, 24, 36, 69, 195, 226–27
Burton, William, 126
Bush, George, 60

Caesar, Julius, 48
Calhoun, John C., 105, 106, 115, 125, 142
California Grape and Tree Fruit League, 15, 208, 216; response to Chavez's Letter from Delano, 208, 210, 211–12, 216–18, 219
California (Mo.) News, 128
"Call" to public office, 107–108
Cambodia, 171, 176. *See also* Indochina
Cameron, Simon, 125
Campbell, Karlyn Kohrs, 5, 200
Canon, rhetorical, 23
Cao Dai, 183, 187
Carolina doctrine, 110
Carpenter, Ronald H., 9, 15
Carr, David, 77
Carr, E. H., 9
Catholic University, 200
Catholic Worker, 195, 196, 202, 287 (n. 33)
Catholic Worker movement, 7–8, 191, 192, 193, 195, 196, 197, 199, 200, 201, 202, 204, 205, 206, 287 (n. 32)
Catholics, Roman, 15, 173, 183, 193, 195, 196, 197, 203
Charleston (S.C.) Mercury, 99
Charmed communication system, 206
Chavez, Cesar, 8, 15, 207–20; as public speaker, 206; public letters of, 206–207; leadership of the United Farm Workers, 206, 208, 219, 289 (n. 6); Letter from Delano, 208, 210, 211, 212–16; grape growers' response to, 208, 210, 211–12, 216–18, 219; persuasive style and philosophy of, 211–13, 214–15, 219
Checkers speech, 230
Chestnut, James, Jr., 100
Chicago Press and Tribune, 29

(History, *continued*)
20, 28, 36–37; as narrative, 12, 34, 35, 36, 38, 43–44, 46, 49, 50, 52, 53, 253 (n. 6); rhetoric of, 27–29, 34, 36–44, 46, 50–54, 59, 60, 254 (n. 13); of public address, 29; and fiction, 33, 35–39, 40; expressed, 34; ontological nature of, 33, 35, 37, 44, 46; three relationships between rhetoric and, 34–35, 245 (n. 30), 253 (n. 6); as argument, 35, 38, 39–44, 45, 49, 50, 52, 53, 253 (n. 6); as orations, 36; as partial and interested, 37–38, 46; as social construction, 38, 40; six characteristics of rhetoric and, 48–50; three senses of rhetoric and, 50; two rhetorical techniques of, 51–52, 59; root term of, 63; scientific, 252 (n. 5). *See also* Memory; Rhetorical history

History of public address, 29. *See also* Historical-critical method; Rhetorical history; Speeches

Hitler, Adolf, 60
Ho Chi Minh, 67, 175, 176
Hoa Hao, 183, 187
Hobbes, Thomas, 39–40, 84
Hochmuth, Marie (later Marie Hochmuth Nichols), 62, 221, 226–27
Hogan, Michael, 30, 240
Hood, Charles E., 171
Hoover, Herbert, Jr., 180, 189
Hoopes, Townsend, 188
Howard, Jean, 37
Howell, Wilbur Samuel, 27
Huerta, Dolores, 216
Humphrey, Hubert, 186
Huntington Library, 228–29, 233, 234–35
Hurd, Volney, 174–75, 176, 187

Idea of History, The, 43
Ideas, 72, 73, 96, 223
Ideographs, 35, 72
Immigrant narrative, 57, 191–93, 284 (n. 2)
Inaugural addresses, 107–109, 111; of Abraham Lincoln, 6, 23, 98, 103, 104, 107, 108–109, 110–16; of Jefferson Davis, 6, 104, 107–108, 109–110, 112–16; of Franklin D. Roosevelt, 29, 111
Inclusion, 209
Indiana, 106

Indochina, 3, 171–81, 185, 188–89, 239. *See also* Cambodia; Laos; Southeast Asia; Thailand; Vietnam
Instrumentalist analysis, 15, 73, 74, 78–79, 80, 91
Integration, 7, 15, 153, 157, 167; arguments based on national security, 145–47, 152; arguments based on military preparedness, 146, 154, 157, 168; Army statements on, 149–50, 153–55; arguments based on economy, 152
Intellectual history, 30, 45, 72, 79
Intelligence tests, 157, 165
Intentional persuasion, 74, 78
Intentionality, 228
Interdisciplinary connections, 31, 70–71, 227, 237–39, 241
Interposition, 110
Intrinsic analysis, 222–24, 225, 228–30, 237, 242
Isocrates, 62
Ivie, Robert, 236, 240

Jablonski, Carol, 7–8, 15, 226
Jackson, Andrew, 107, 115, 139, 140
Jackson, C. D., 236
Jackson, Claiborne Fox, 7, 15, 119, 130–41; response to Lincoln's call for militia, 122, 124–25, 126, 128, 138–40; on military reinforcement, 130–33, 134–35, 139–41; call for special session of state legislature, 132, 135; response to Arkansas convention, 133–34; exchange with Sterling Price and ensuing publicity, 135–37; message to state legislature, 138–40
James, William, 43
Jamieson, Kathleen Hall, 209, 246
Janas, Michael, 49, 59
Janik, Allan, 71
Janis, Irving, 4, 64–65, 66, 68, 232, 292–93 (n. 30)
Japan, 171, 177, 239
Jasinski, James, 6, 15, 223
Javits, Jacob, 164
Jefferson, Thomas, 107, 122, 125
Jeffersonian tradition, 84, 85, 86, 139, 142
Jenkins, Timothy C., 6–7, 15, 231, 234
Jensen, Richard, 8, 15
Jesuits, 199
Jewish history, 58

Molloy, Monk, 1
Monroe, James, 107
Montana, 171
Montgomery, John D., 188
Montrose, Louis, 74
Morse, Wayne, 69
Morton, Thruston B., 181
Mott, Lynda, 102
Mournier, Emmanuel, 203
Munich, 28
Murrow, Edward R., 174
Mystic Chords of Memory, 57

NAACP, 145, 146
Narrative, 67, 144; in history, 12, 34, 35, 36, 38, 43–44, 46, 49, 50, 52, 53, 253 (n. 6); immigrant, 57, 191–93, 284 (n. 2)
Narrative paradigm, 223
Nash, Philleo, 149, 163
National Catholic Reporter, 208
National character, concepts of, 6, 27, 30, 54–55, 57, 76, 95–98, 107, 116–17
National defense, 145–47, 152, 164, 166–68
National History Standards, 29
National Security Council, 186
Navy, 149, 150, 151, 157, 230
Nerone, John, 59, 63
Neustadt, Richard, 28
Nevins, Allan, 233–34
New Criticism, 238
New Frontier, 67, 258 (n. 29), 259 (n. 37)
New Jersey, 103, 114
New York Call, 194
New York Evening Post, 110
New York Times, 172, 173, 177, 187
Newman, John M., 69
Newman, Robert, 66, 68, 225–26
Newsweek, 174, 178
Ngo Dinh Diem, 3, 69–70, 171, 173, 175, 178–88, 189
Nichols, Marie Hochmuth, 62, 221, 226–27
Niles, David K., 160, 164, 165
Nitze, Paul, 65
Nixon, Richard, 28, 60, 170, 223, 230
Nolting, Frederick, Jr., 174
Nong Kimny, 176
North Carolina, 123, 137
North Vietnam, 67. *See also* Vietnam
Nullification, 105, 106

Objectivity, 8, 44
O'Donnell, Kenneth, 170
Olbrechts-Tyteca, Lucie, 82, 83
Olson, Gregory Allen, 3, 4, 15, 239, 240–41
Opinion leaders, 119, 120, 130, 234. *See also* Leadership; Media
Ontology, 33, 35, 37, 44, 46
Orwell, George, 10
Oswald, Lee Harvey, 29
"Other," the, 76
Oxymoron, 83

Pacifism, 7, 195–96, 201
Palmer, Dwight R. G., 162–63
Paradox, radical's, 206
Parrish, Wayland, 221
Paschal, Nathaniel, 136–37
Paz, Octavio, 209
Pearce, W. Barnett, 206
Pearson, Drew, 172
Pemberton, William, 167
Pennsylvania, 106
Pentagon Papers, 181
"People," the, 9, 88–89, 91, 106, 107, 108, 110, 112, 113, 115, 116, 138
Perelman, Chaim, 82, 83
Pericles, 62
Personalist Manifesto, 203
Personalist philosophy, 195, 203
Philippines, the, 171
Phillips, Wendell, 102
Piehl, Mel, 196
Pierce, Franklin, 107
Plan: as Mexican rhetorical tradition, 8, 210–11, 212, 215–16; rhetorical characteristics of, 212–13
Plan of Delano, 211
Plato, 27
Plimpton, George, 216
Plumb, J. H., 41
Pocock, J. G. A., 77, 80
Policy making, 66, 232. *See also* Decision making
Political genealogy, 104–106, 113, 116. *See also* Legitimacy
Political history, 5, 9, 30, 49, 51–52, 84
Polk, James K., 107–108
Pool of conventional wisdom, 6
Popular memory, 60
Potter, David, 5–6, 13
Poulakos, John, 27
Pragmatic orientation, 239

Presidential libraries, 11; Harry S. Truman, 7; John F. Kennedy, 64, 68, 232; Lyndon B. Johnson, 64, 68, 232; Dwight D. Eisenhower, 189, 236
Price, Sterling, 119, 135–37
Priestly, Joseph, 47
Primary resources. *See* Archival resources
Problem solving. *See* Decision making
Process versus product, 2, 4, 15, 72–73, 231
Psychoanalytical history, 54
Publication, 23, 24–25, 30; of books, 239–42
Publicity, 136–37, 152–53, 155–56, 160, 162, 165, 215
"Publish or perish," 14, 224–26, 236–37, 238, 240–41
"Publius," 85, 86–90

Quarterly Journal of Speech, 1, 24, 30, 236, 240, 241
Quest story, 223
Quotas, 156–57, 158, 159, 160–61, 163, 164, 165

Radical's paradox, 206
Randolph (Mo.) Citizen, 123, 129
Ranke, Leopold von, 27, 40
Reagan, Ronald, 60
Rector, Henry M., 126
Reflective thinking, 259 (n. 39)
Republicanism, 108
Republicans, 102, 111, 120, 123, 128, 129, 134, 136, 142, 178, 189, 190
Research Libraries Information Network, 235
Revolution, American, 51–52, 79, 105, 110
Reynolds, Fred, 59
Rhetoric, 21, 50, 70, 96, 97–98; as process versus product, 2, 4, 15, 72–73, 231; history of, 8–13, 26, 27–29, 34, 36–44, 46, 50–59; of history, 27–29, 34, 36–44, 46, 50–54, 59, 60; as history, 34, 35, 62; as force in history, 34, 45–46
Rhetorical analysis, 14, 68, 224
Rhetorical criticism, 236, 238; definitions of, 2–3, 61, 222–23; relationship to rhetorical history, 20–22, 222, 224, 230–31; neo-Aristotelian, 225

Rhetorical estrangement, 6–7, 119, 130, 141–42, 270 (n. 3)
Rhetorical history: status of, 1–2, 13–15, 19–20, 61–62, 223–24, 227–28, 236; definitions of, 2–3, 25–26, 30, 52, 61, 222; as social construction, 2–15; contributions of, 2, 3–8, 15, 25, 27, 28–29, 30–32, 44–46, 62–63, 64, 68–69, 70–71, 73–74, 143–44, 194, 209–10, 220, 229–30, 231–32, 236, 237, 239–42; relationship to rhetorical theory, 2, 3–4, 15, 22, 23–25, 30, 62, 63, 73, 226, 227–28, 232, 237, 239; relationship to rhetorical criticism, 2–3, 15, 20–22, 25, 30, 62, 63, 233; four senses of, 26–31. *See also* Historical-critical method; History; Rhetoric
Rhetorical perspective, 4–5, 30, 62, 63, 69
Rhetorical studies of historical events, 26, 30–32. *See also* Rhetorical history
Rhetorical theory, 2, 3–4, 15, 22, 23–25, 30, 62, 63, 73, 226, 227–28, 232, 237, 239
Rhetorical use of the past, 10, 28, 35, 37, 44, 48, 49, 53, 54–56, 59, 60, 97, 256 (n. 41)
Rhett, Robert Barnwell, 100, 113
Richards, James P., 182
Richmond (Mo.) North-West Conservator, 121, 127, 129
Rise and Fall of the Third Reich, The, 54
RLIN, 235
Roach, James, 98
Robertson, Walter, 181–82, 184, 185, 189
Roe v. Wade, 56
Roosevelt, Franklin D., 28, 29, 111
Roots, 33
Rorty, Richard, 45, 79, 264 (n. 33)
Rossini, Giglioli, 39
Rostow, Walt W., 260 (n. 44)
ROTC, 159, 199, 201, 203
Rowse, A. L., 56
Royall, Kenneth C., 149–51, 153–55, 157; and Royall Plan, 150–51
Ruffin, Edmund, 100, 101–102
Rusen, Jorn, 40
Rusk, Dean, 65, 66, 259 (n. 38)

St. Joseph (Mo.) Gazette, 121
St. Louis Arsenal, 131
St. Louis (Mo.) Herald, 120–21
St. Louis Missouri Republican, 122–23, 136–37

About the Series

STUDIES IN RHETORIC AND COMMUNICATION
Series Editors:
E. Culpepper Clark, Raymie E. McKerrow, and David Zarefsky

The University of Alabama Press has established this series to publish major new works in the general area of rhetoric and communication, including books treating the symbolic manifestations of political discourse, argument as social knowledge, the impact of machine technology on patterns of communication behavior, and other topics related to the nature or impact of symbolic communication. We actively solicit studies involving historical, critical, or theoretical analyses of human discourse.